Secret Power

"Stefania Maurizi's book on the persecution of Julian Assange is the definitive text on this tragedy. To read it is to resist, it is a must-read. Free Assange."
—Roger Waters, co-founder of Pink Floyd

"A rigorous, compelling, and highly readable reconstruction of the Julian Assange and WikiLeaks case by an investigative journalist who has worked for over a decade on the WikiLeaks secret documents and has fought for the last seven years to unearth the key documentation exposing the persecution of Julian Assange and WikiLeaks. I highly recommend this work. No one conveys better the urgency of averting the extradition and prosecution of Assange, which would demolish First Amendment protection of freedom of the press in America."
—Daniel Ellsberg, US whistleblower who leaked the Pentagon Papers

"The vindictive hounding of Julian Assange by the US government deserves as wide an audience as possible. There is no journalist better placed to tell the story than Stefania Maurizi, who has been following the story closely for more than a decade and personally knows most of those involved. But what stands out is her sheer perseverance. Many journalists would have given up after her multiple requests under the Freedom of Information Act were largely rebuffed. But she proved dogged, engaging in what she describes as 'trench warfare', taking them to court, the legal costs often paid for by her personally. Through this persistence, she uncovered lots of new information, making it a must-read for all journalists. If Assange can be persecuted on the flimsy grounds exposed by Maurizi, then all journalists anywhere in the world who challenge the US are at risk."
—Ewen MacAskill, Pulitzer Prize winner for Public Service

"Stefania Maurizi's book is the best possible tribute to Julian Assange's sacrifice on behalf of Western citizens whose governments have been committing, in their name, crimes against humanity. She has herself sacrificed much to write this book and has researched it in a manner that should be at the heart of journalism textbooks the world over. A book to read, behold and promote to anyone who cares about the truth and the dangers involved in telling it."
—Yanis Varoufakis, Professor of Economics,
University of Athens, and co-founder of DiEM25

"Stefania Maurizi's revelation of the role of the UK Crown Prosecution Service, then run by Keir Starmer, in the persecution of Julian Assange was a journalistic landmark. Her book is a lesson to all who expose the malign secrets of state power."
—John Pilger, journalist and documentary filmmaker

"A gripping first-hand account of the Assange affair."
—Gavin Jones, senior Reuters correspondent in Rome

"Heroic freedom-fighter or maverick controversialist—Assange is a polarising character. But we can all agree that the hundreds of thousands of downloaded classified documents he published revealed much of the heinous barbarity of the post-9/11 US-led wars in Afghanistan, Iraq, and Guantanamo Bay. This book is a passionate plea in Julian's defence. To extradite would send the message that no journalist or publisher is safe anywhere in the world; a truth recognised by Obama's administration which determined that to prosecute Assange for publishing documents would gravely imperil press freedom. Assange was recently diagnosed with autism. People on the spectrum are the garlic in life's salad and how dull life would be without them – a case of the bland leading the bland. This book proves that Assange has the courage of his convictions; and the criminality of convicting him for his courage."
—Kathy Lette, bestselling author

"Everything you think you know about this story is not what you think. Maurizi brilliantly tells the real story of what happened with WikiLeaks and the powers that went out to destroy it."
—John Goetz, Editor of Investigations at German State Broadcaster NDR

"An exceptional book by an exceptional journalist. Written like a political thriller, Stefania Maurizi's Secret Power is not only one of the best accounts of the WikiLeaks revolution and the man behind it – Julian Assange. It's also a deeply disturbing investigation into the military-intelligence complex and secret power determined to dismantle the last strongholds of democracy, namely freedom of the press."
—Srecko Horvat, philosopher and author of *Poetry from the Future*

"The story of the aftermath of the biggest story in journalism in generations brilliantly laid out by Maurizi. This book is equally as important as it is sad it had to be written. A must read for everyone interested in finding out how democratic and free, the "free and democratic west" indeed is, when push comes to shove."
—Helgi Seljan, investigative journalist at Stundin, Iceland

"Maurizi's relentless, rigorous and courageous work has produced compelling evidence for the flagrant and deliberate illegality of Julian Assange's persecution. She has decisively contributed to my official investigation into the case as the United Nations Special Rapporteur on Torture."
—Professor Nils Melzer, United Nations Special Rapporteur on Torture (2016–2022)

Secret Power

WikiLeaks and Its Enemies

Stefania Maurizi

Foreword by Ken Loach
Translated by Lesli Cavanaugh-Bardelli

PLUTO  PRESS

First published 2022 by Pluto Press
New Wing, Somerset House, Strand, London WC2R 1LA
and Pluto Press Inc.
1930 Village Center Circle, Ste. 3-384, Las Vegas, NV 89134

www.plutobooks.com

British Library Cataloguing in Publication Data
A catalogue record for this book is available from the British Library

ISBN 978 0 7453 4762 2   Hardback
ISBN 978 0 7453 4761 5   Paperback
ISBN 978 0 7453 4764 6   PDF
ISBN 978 0 7453 4763 9   EPUB

This book is printed on paper suitable for recycling and made from fully managed and sustained forest sources. Logging, pulping and manufacturing processes are expected to conform to the environmental standards of the country of origin.

Typeset by Stanford DTP Services, Northampton, England

Simultaneously printed in the United Kingdom and United States of America

To my mother, with love and gratitude

To those who have the moral courage to risk life, freedom and economic security to bring out the truth

Contents

Foreword

Ken Loach

This is a book that should make you very angry. It is the story of a journalist imprisoned and treated with unbearable cruelty for exposing war crimes, of the determination by British and American politicians to destroy him, and of the quiet connivance of the media in this monstrous injustice.

Julian Assange is now well known. WikiLeaks, in which Assange played a leading role, exposed the dirty secrets of the Iraq war, as well as much else. Thanks to Assange and the team, we saw horrific war crimes such as those depicted in the Collateral Murder video or those committed by the US contractors as happened in Nisour Square in Baghdad, where fourteen civilians were shot dead. Two children were killed and seventeen people wounded. Trump, in his final days as President, pardoned the killers. But he ensured that Assange remain in prison.

The work of WikiLeaks has been extensive. Its fundamental principles should inform all democratic societies. The people must know all that is being done in their name. When politicians hide shameful secrets, journalists have a responsibility to expose them. And it is politicians who should pay the price, with punishment by law where there is illegality. None of this has happened in the case of Julian Assange and the crimes and corruption WikiLeaks has exposed have gone unpunished.

Stefania Maurizi has followed the case from the beginning. She has unearthed documents using Freedom of Information laws that expose the attacks on Julian Assange. She has followed in detail these extraordinary events over the last decade. At the heart of this story is the terrible price paid by one man, treated with extreme cruelty, because he laid bare the reality of unaccountable power hidden by an appearance of democracy.

As I write, the challenge is for the British judicial system. Britain boasts that its courts are independent, that it respects the rule of law and that its lawyers are incorruptible. Well, we shall see. Julian Assange is a journalist whose crime was to tell the truth. For that he has lost his freedom, and spent the last two years in solitary confinement in a high security prison with the predictable devastating consequences for his mental health.

If extradited to the USA, he will be incarcerated for the rest of his life. Will a British court collude with such a horrific injustice?

In Britain there are other matters to concern us: the great expense and resources used to keep Assange isolated in the Ecuadorian Embassy; the abject cowardice of the press and broadcasters in their failure to defend journalistic freedom; and the allegation that the Crown Prosecution Service, led at the time by Keir Starmer, trapped Assange in a legal and diplomatic nightmare.

If we think we live in a democracy, we should read this book. If we care about truth and honest politics, we should read this book. And if we believe that the law should protect the innocent, we should not only read the book but demand that Julian Assange should be a free man.

For how much longer can we accept that the mechanism of the secret state, responsible for the most egregious crimes, continues to make a mockery of our attempts to live in a democracy?

(Spring 2021)

Introduction: The Man Who Stood Up to Secret Power

For over a decade now, one man has been the target of the most powerful institutions on earth. Some have planned to kill him, or to kidnap him. They have stolen the best years of his life. These institutions include the Pentagon, the CIA and the National Security Agency (NSA). They embody the heart of what President Dwight Eisenhower, one of the principal architects of the victory over the Nazis in Europe, called the United States "military-industrial complex," the same complex that Eisenhower himself, though formerly a great military leader, warned his country against. The power and influence exerted by these institutions are felt in every corner of the globe; they plan wars, coup d'états, assassinations. They sway governments and elections.

That man is Julian Assange. He is the founder of WikiLeaks, an organization that has radically transformed journalism, exploiting the potential of the internet and systematically breaching state secrecy when that secrecy is used not to protect the safety and security of citizens, but to conceal state crimes, to ensure impunity for the officials in the institutions that commit those crimes, and to keep the public from discovering the truth and holding them to account.

Julian Assange and the WikiLeaks journalists have published hundreds of thousands of secret Pentagon, CIA and NSA files exposing civilian massacres, torture, political scandals and political pressure on foreign governments. These revelations have unleashed the fury of the U.S. authorities, but in reality there is not a single government in the world that has warm feelings for Assange and WikiLeaks. Even those less buffeted by their publications to date regard them with a wary eye, conscious that, sooner or later, the WikiLeaks method may also take root in their own countries and expose their own dirty secrets. And it is not just governments, armies and secret services that hate them and see them as enemies; they are equally feared by powerful economic-financial institutions, often in league with diplomats and intelligence agencies, as the most profitable financial operations thrive in secrecy.

As I write, Julian Assange risks 175 years in a maximum-security prison in the United States. His physical and mental health have been devastated. Other WikiLeaks journalists presumably live in apprehension of meeting the same fate.

But this case goes far beyond Julian Assange and WikiLeaks. It is the battle for a journalism that sheds light on the highest level of power, where secret services, armies and diplomats operate. A level that the ordinary citizen in our democracies—especially European democracies—usually does not even perceive as relevant to everyday life, seldom the focus of newscasts and talk shows. The ordinary citizen looks at the power that is visible: the politics that determine one's chances of finding a job, healthcare, a pension. And yet that invisible power, shielded behind state secrecy, conditions our lives immensely. It decides, for example, if one's country will spend twenty years waging war in Afghanistan while lacking the resources for schools and hospitals, as in the case of Italy. Or if a German citizen can be suddenly kidnapped, tortured, raped and handed over to the CIA because he is mistaken for a dangerous terrorist. Or if a man can disappear from the heart of Milan at mid-day, kidnapped by the CIA and Italian secret services.

The ordinary citizen has no control over this secret power, because she has no access to the restricted information on how it operates. But, for the first time in history, WikiLeaks has ripped a gaping hole in this secret power, giving billions of people systematic and unrestricted access to enormous archives of classified documents revealing how our governments behave when, completely shielded from public and media scrutiny, they prepare wars or commit atrocities.

It is solely because of this activity that Julian Assange risks being entombed in prison forever. And he is not the only one at serious risk: secret power does not want to destroy Julian Assange alone.

It wants to destroy him, the WikiLeaks journalists and ultimately to kill a revolution. Yet, if there is any journalism worth practicing, it is precisely the journalism that unveils abuse at the highest levels of power. And there is no freedom of the press if journalists are not free to uncover and report state criminality without ending up dead or imprisoned for life. Under authoritarian regimes it is not possible to do so without facing severe consequences. But in a truly non-authoritarian society, this must be permitted.

That is why this case will decide the future of journalism in our democracies, and to some degree in dictatorships as well, as all governments will feel even more empowered to stifle freedom of information if the "free Western world" can forever imprison a journalist who revealed the killing of thousands of innocent civilians, a journalist who exposed torture and gross violations of human rights.

Julian Assange and his organization burst into my professional life eleven years ago. The intrigue and disruption they have brought to my journalism has never abated. From 2009 to the present day we have worked together, they for WikiLeaks, I for my newspaper—first *L'Espresso* and *la Repubblica*, now *il Fatto Quotidiano*—on the publication of millions of classified documents. I have traveled around the world with CIA and NSA secrets. Assange and his journalists have taught me to use cryptography to protect my sources. I was with him in Berlin when his computers disappeared into thin air. I was in the Ecuadorian embassy in London when he, his staff, his partner and their child, his lawyers and his visitors were covertly filmed and recorded, and my phone was secretly unscrewed, opened in two.

In the course of these years, there have been various attempts to intimidate me. I have been brazenly followed. I was once robbed in Rome, where important documents I was carrying were stolen from me and never seen again. But no one has ever locked me up in prison, or even threatened or interrogated me. I have never had to pay the terrible price Julian Assange has paid. After he published secret U.S. government files in 2010, he was deprived of his freedom. For over a decade, he has been unable to walk as a free man. What I have witnessed since 2010, the treatment he has endured, the grave decline in his health, the smear campaign against him, the legal persecution of WikiLeaks and of its sources—first and foremost that exemplar of tremendous moral courage, Chelsea Manning—have filled me with a profound disquiet. This disquiet has grown in parallel with my discovery of the state cruelty and criminality laid bare by the secret files disclosed by WikiLeaks.

This book is a journey into those files, and into the story of Julian Assange and the WikiLeaks journalists, through what I have experienced and discovered in over ten years of working alongside them. For the very reason that I have not paid the terrible price Assange has paid, I feel compelled to tell this story, to help defend the freedom of journalists to shine light into the darkest corners of our governments, and the public's right to know about them.

1
The WikiLeaks Revolution

MY SOURCE AT RISK

It all started in 2008, when one of my sources stopped talking to me because she became convinced she was being illegally wiretapped.

When a person contacts one of us journalists to confide sensitive information—information that someone with power would want to keep hidden—they do so only if they trust they will not be found out and face dire consequences, like dismissal from their job, crushing lawsuits or, in extreme cases, prison or even death. My source had had the courage to seek me out, but after our first few meetings, her fears had prevailed.

I waited a long time for her to show up for what would have been our last meeting. In the end I realized she was not going to show, and that there would be no further meetings. I had no way of knowing for sure if she really was being illegally wiretapped or if she was just being paranoid, but fortunately I took her fears very seriously.

Throughout the years I had spoken with dozens of journalistic sources. Some had given me snippets of useful information, while others had only wasted my time, and yet others had made it possible for me to bring off remarkable scoops. But none had ever had so profound an impact on my life and my profession as she did. That source, who had not wanted to reveal a single word of what she knew, changed my work forever.

In fact it was at that moment that I realized I needed to find a much more secure way of communicating with sources. The old techniques, unfortunately still used in all newsrooms today, were and are completely outdated; they are wholly inadequate for a world where police forces, spies in the employ of big companies, and secret services can listen in on journalists and everyone who talks to us with astonishing ease.

If I had studied law, I would have looked to the laws for protection. But I had studied mathematics, so it was natural for me to look to encryption and passwords for a possible solution. I had learned a bit about cryptography at university. My knowledge was only theoretical, but the art of protecting communication between two people, so that it is not indiscriminately accessible to everyone, had intrigued me.

As Philip Zimmermann, inventor of the PGP (Pretty Good Privacy) program for encrypting emails and documents, had written:[1] "You may be planning a political campaign, discussing your taxes, or having an illicit affair. Or you may be communicating with a political dissident in a repressive country. Whatever it is, you don't want your private electronic mail (email) or confidential documents read by anyone else. There's nothing wrong with asserting your privacy."

Not only is there nothing wrong with it, but it is a basic right of journalists and our sources; if we cannot guarantee that those who give us confidential information will be protected, no one will give us information any more.

In the old analog world before the digital era, the apparatuses of the state, from police forces to secret services, could steam open letters to read a private citizen's correspondence, or eavesdrop on telephone conversations and transcribe them one by one, but these methods took time, and could not be used systematically on entire populations. But with digital communications, everything changed. Monitoring the email correspondence of millions has become mere child's play.

It was precisely this transformation that had prompted Philip Zimmermann, a U.S. computer software engineer and pacifist, to create his PGP program. Right from the start, he had caught sight of a looming risk for democracy.

1. Philip Zimmermann, "Why I wrote PGP," June 1991: www.philzimmermann. com/EN/essays/WhyIWrotePGP.html

His concerns can be summed up in this testimony he gave before a U.S. Senate committee in 1996:[2] "The Clinton Administration seems to be attempting to deploy and entrench a communications infrastructure that would deny the citizenry the ability to protect its privacy. This is unsettling because in a democracy, it is possible for bad people to occasionally get elected—sometimes very bad people. Normally, a well-functioning democracy has ways to remove these people from power. But the wrong technology infrastructure could allow such a future government to watch every move anyone makes to oppose it. It could very well be the last government we ever elect."

Zimmermann was not a radical. He was a pacifist who believed in political dissent and had in fact been arrested for his peaceful protests against nuclear weapons. Foreseeing the threat posed by digital communication for democracy, he engaged in an act of civil disobedience: just as the U.S. Senate was seeking to pass Senate Bill 266—a bill allowing the government to access anyone's communications—he created PGP, a software program for encrypting emails. He then distributed it completely free of charge, to make it as widespread as possible before the government could make encryption illegal.

It was a revolutionary move. As Zimmerman himself explained it,[3] prior to PGP it was not possible for an ordinary citizen to communicate with someone over long distances in a secure manner, without the risk of being intercepted. That power was solely and firmly in the hands of the state. But that monopoly ended with PGP. It was 1991.

The U.S. government did not just stand by and watch, however: it placed Zimmermann under investigation. But ultimately the investigation was closed in 1996 without any indictment. With

---

2. Testimony of Philip R. Zimmermann to the Subcommittee on Science, Technology, and Space of the U.S. Senate Committee on Commerce, Science, and Transportation, June 26, 1996: https://philzimmermann.com/EN/testimony/index.html
3. Philip Zimmermann, Creator of PGP, Phil Zimmermann talks at Bitcoin Wednesday, July 30, 2018: www.youtube.com/watch?v=M8zoNx8svC4&ab_channel=BitcoinWednesday

users ranging from Amnesty International to political activists in Latin America and the ex-Soviet Union, PGP began to spread throughout the world, generating crucial debate on civil liberties and surveillance and inspiring the creation of other kinds of software for communications encryption.

The day my source didn't show up for our appointment marked a turning point for me. If codes and passwords could protect activists, then they could protect us journalists and the people who talk to us too.

It was one of my sources in the encryption world who first put Julian Assange and WikiLeaks on my radar, in 2008. They had yet to publish the great news scoops that would make them famous the world over, so very few people knew of them. *"You should take a look at that bunch of lunatics,"* my expert friend told me. The "lunatics" he was referring to were Assange and his team at WikiLeaks. My cryptographer friend's tone was joking, but his respect for them was evident. If someone with his expertise and dedication to human rights was taking an interest in them, I felt, they must be doing something worthy of attention.

I began to look at the work done by WikiLeaks methodically. Created just two years before, in 2006, the group was truly in its infancy. The idea was revolutionary: to harness the power of the internet and of encryption to obtain and then "leak"—hence the name "WikiLeaks"—classified documents of significant public interest. Just as traditional media receive information from unknown persons, who send letters or packets of documents to newsrooms, so Assange and his organization received sensitive files, sent in electronic form by anonymous sources to their online platform. The identity of those sharing sensitive documents was protected by advanced technological solutions like encryption, along with other ingenious techniques.

In 2006, when WikiLeaks was founded, there was not a single major newspaper in the world systematically offering encryption-based protection to its sources; it took years for the most influential daily in the world, the *New York Times*, and other major media to decide to adopt it, inspired by the intuition of WikiLeaks.

Julian Assange and his organization were without doubt pioneers. They were especially interested in "whistleblowers," people who, in the course of their work in a government or private company, become aware of abuses, gross corruption or even war crimes or torture committed by their superiors or their colleagues, and decide to expose them in the public interest, providing journalists with factual information. A whistleblower is an individual who acts in accordance with his or her conscience. They do not look away, pretending not to see. They blow the whistle knowing that the consequences they will face may be harsh, in some cases even lethal. Those who unveil crimes committed by secret services are literally putting their lives on the line, and often can count on only two forms of protection: hiding behind anonymity, or doing the exact opposite, coming out into the open and hoping for the support of public opinion.

By leveraging the power of the internet and encryption, WikiLeaks offered advanced technical solutions to protect whistleblowers. They not only provided a shield to those blowing the whistle in the public interest, they also attracted sources with particular talents and professional experiences, potentially sources with access to important information. Because, after all, who back then could really appreciate a tool as complex and unusual as encryption? Those who had studied it, or who worked in the field of computer science or intelligence. The technologically advanced structure of WikiLeaks appealed to an entire community familiar with the language of science and technology.

The results were soon forthcoming, and when I began observing them attentively from the outside, during that far-off year of 2008, I was deeply impressed.

SAYING NO TO THE PENTAGON

It was one of the most impenetrable places in the world. The Guantanamo detention camp, created by the George W. Bush administration on January 11, 2002, exactly four months after the attack on the Twin Towers, had fast become a symbol of the inhumanity of Bush's war on terror. According to then-defense secretary Donald Rumsfeld, only the world's most dangerous terrorists were confined there: *the worst of the worst*. In reality, no one knew exactly who all the prisoners were and what went on inside the camp. It was run by a military task force, the JTF-Gtmo (Joint Task Force Guantanamo), but no one had any factual information on its operations. Only the International Committee of the Red Cross was allowed access to the detention camp and, in a classified report in November 2004, the committee claimed that the prisoners were physically and psychologically tortured.[4]

A few months earlier, in April of 2004, the great U.S. investigative journalist Seymour Hersh had unveiled[5] that torture was rampant in the prison of Abu Ghraib in Iraq, and the photos of the atrocities committed by the U.S. troops who had invaded the country and toppled Saddam Hussein's regime just one year earlier had made their way around the world. Still today, the images are jaw-dropping in their cruelty: they would later be immortalized in the cycle of paintings entitled *Abu Ghraib* by Colombian artist Fernando Botero, who captured the ferocity of the war dogs set upon the defenseless prisoners, terrified they might be ripped to shreds at any moment.

Many suspected that the International Committee of the Red Cross did not have access to all the detainees in Guantanamo, and one of the leading U.S. organizations for civil and human rights, the American Civil Liberties Union (ACLU), had sought in vain to obtain the task force's operations manual. The ACLU had attempted to request a copy of the manual from the U.S. authorities under the Freedom of Information Act, the tool that allows citizens to access government records of public interest. No dice; the Bush administration rejected the request. WikiLeaks were the ones to divulge the manual, in November 2007.[6]

---

4.   Neil A. Lewis, "Red Cross finds detainee abuse in Guantánamo," *New York Times*, November 30, 2004.
5.   Seymour Hersh, "Torture at Abu Ghraib," *New Yorker*, April 30, 2004.
6.   The document revealed by WikiLeaks is entitled: *Camp Delta Standard Operating Procedures* (*SOP*) and is available at: https://wikileaks.org/wiki/Camp_Delta_Standard_Operating_Procedure (accessed May 19, 2022).

The document was a file from the U.S. Department of Defense, the Pentagon, and was dated March 2003, just one year after the detention camp was opened. It was signed by General Geoffrey D. Miller who, according to press accounts cited by the American magazine *Wired*,[7] had visited Abu Ghraib in 2003, shortly before the appalling episodes of torture on its inmates, documented by Hersh, came to light. The manual confirmed what many had suspected: the U.S. authorities had lied; some prisoners were kept beyond the reach of the International Committee of the Red Cross, leaving the committee unable to monitor their treatment: "No access, No contact of any kind with the ICRC. This includes the delivery of ICRC mail," read the manual.

No physical torture was described in the file, but forms of psychological torture were detailed: solitary confinement and techniques to psychologically subjugate detainees were there in all their harshness. The document explained how to use dogs in the detention camp, how to handle questions and relations with journalists, especially the guidelines on conversations with the press, focused on progress in the international fight against terrorism.

When this file came to my attention, I was amazed not only that WikiLeaks had managed to obtain it, but that Julian Assange's organization had defied the Pentagon's demand to remove it from their website insofar as, the U.S. Department of Defense had written to WikiLeaks, its "publication has not been approved."[8] Standing up to a demand from the Pentagon, whose power and influence hold sway throughout the world, takes independence and courage. Assange and WikiLeaks were not just pioneers in the use of technology to protect individuals revealing secrets in the public interest, they were brave as well. And for me, that bravery was a glimmer of hope in the darkness surrounding journalism in those years.

---

7. Ryan Sigel, "Sensitive Guantánamo Bay manual leaked through Wiki site," *Wired*, November 14, 2007.
8. The email from the Pentagon to WikiLeaks is available on the WikiLeaks website: https://wikileaks.org/wiki/Camp_Delta_Standard_Operating_Procedure (accessed May 19, 2022).

The war on terror had exposed the brutality of the Bush administration, but also the considerable responsibility of the mainstream media, which had so often shown no skepticism towards the machinations of their government. Like in the months preceding the invasion of Iraq, the *New York Times* had published unsubstantiated articles on Saddam Hussein's attempts to procure weapons of mass destruction. The *Times* contributed to a media campaign that rendered acceptable—even to a public opinion politically at odds with the Bush administration—the invasion of Iraq and the devastating war that followed, a bloodbath that cost at least 600,000 lives.[9]

And that was not the only time mainstream American media had become a tool of their government rather than a means of constraining it. For years the *New York Times* chose not to use the word "torture" for the atrocious interrogation techniques employed in prisons in Iraq, Afghanistan, Guantanamo and various countries around the world where the CIA operated its so-called "black sites" in complete secrecy in the name of the fight against terrorism. Techniques like waterboarding, in which a human being is tied to a slanted board, a cloth placed over his eyes and water poured over his face to trigger the sensation of drowning. Rather than calling these practices "torture," up until 2014 the *New York Times* regularly referred to them as "enhanced interrogations,"[10] a cryptic term that kept public opinion from perceiving the inhumanity of operations like a detainee being left to die of cold, as Gul Rahman did in Afghanistan.[11]

Things did not go any better with the *Washington Post*. In 2005 it had agreed not to publish the names of the Eastern European countries where the CIA's secret prisons were located: Poland, Lithuania and Romania. Here too, the request not to name names

---

9.   Philip Bump, "15 years after the Iraq war began, the death toll is still murky," *Washington Post*, March 20, 2018. The death toll will be discussed in chapter 5.

10.   Only in August 2014 did the *New York Times* acknowledge that those interrogation techniques were torture, as admitted by the executive editor, Dean Baquet, in this article: "The executive editor on the word 'torture'," *New York Times*, August 7, 2014.

11.   Larry Siems, "Inside the CIA's black site torture room," *Guardian*, October 9, 2017.

had come from the Bush administration, and the newspaper had complied.[12]

In such a landscape a new journalism, aggressive and courageous, not intimidated by the Pentagon and not willing to publish or hide information based on government manipulation, was as necessary as air. That was what WikiLeaks promised. But that was not all. The organization had also impressed me for another reason.

PUBLISHING WHAT NO ONE DARED TO PUBLISH

In 2008 a major Swiss bank, Julius Baer, had come into the sights of Julian Assange's organization. It was the very same bank that would surface two years later in an Italian criminal investigation on Angelo Balducci, former chair of Italy's Board of Public Works, ultimately involved in a corruption scandal that cost him his appointment as "Gentleman of His Holiness," the highest honor the Holy See could bestow at the time on a Catholic layman.

Thanks to a Swiss whistleblower, Rudolf Elmer,[13] who had found the courage to leak a series of internal documents from Julius Baer's branch in the Cayman Islands, WikiLeaks had exposed the bank's alleged involvement in crimes ranging from tax evasion to money laundering, and immediately found the bank on its back. It demanded that the file be removed and took legal action. But what looked to be a classic battle, with a foregone conclusion, developed into a fully fledged fiasco.

WikiLeaks had been designed to make censoring the files it published difficult; its servers were located in unknown sites, the identities of those working for the organization were not public, apart from those of Julian Assange and the German spokesman for WikiLeaks at the time, Daniel Schmitt,[14] and tracing an address for Assange and his staff was problematic, to say the least. But Julius Baer enlisted an aggressive law firm specializing in celeb-

12. Dana Priest, "CIA holds terror suspects in secret prisons," *Washington Post*, November 2, 2005.
13. Tax Gap Reporting Team, "Isles of plenty," *Guardian*, February 13, 2009.
14. Daniel Schmitt was actually a pseudonym for Daniel Domscheit-Berg.

rity lawsuits, Lavely & Singer of Los Angeles, who, in their efforts to track down those responsible for the publications, targeted WikiLeaks as an "entity of unknown form" along with Dynadot LLC, WikiLeaks' domain name registrar, a company with headquarters in California. The bank's lawyers requested and obtained from the judge an order that the files be removed. It seemed like a done deal. Only it wasn't.

WikiLeaks set about creating "mirrors," sites with identical content to the one banned by the judge, which began to bounce around the world. At that point, Julius Baer's lawyers requested the complete shutdown of WikiLeaks and a ban on transfer of the forbidden content to other sites. This move boomeranged, however, as the request for complete shutdown prompted the leading U.S. organizations for the defense of digital and civil rights to enter the fray. From the Electronic Frontier Foundation (EFF), headquartered in San Francisco, to the American Civil Liberties Union (ACLU), some of the most influential American civil rights institutions backed WikiLeaks in federal court, invoking the First Amendment, the fundamental principle of the U.S. Constitution that provides powerful protection of the press and freedom of expression. In March 2008 the judge overturned the order, rejecting the bank's demand that the WikiLeaks site be shut down completely and ruling that publication of the files enjoyed constitutional protection under the First Amendment.

This staunch resistance from Assange's organization and the legal battle that had ensued, backed by influential organizations like the EFF and the American Civil Liberties Union, had brought the name of Julius Baer to the pages of the world's leading newspapers, from the *New York Times*[15] to the *Guardian*, obtaining the exact opposite effect to that desired by the powerful bank. The documents Julius Baer had wished to see discreetly removed were now an affair of international interest. As if that were not enough, WikiLeaks also published its correspondence with the

15. Adam Liptak and Brad Stone, "Judge orders WikiLeaks web site shut," *New York Times*, February 19, 2008.

bank's lawyers, to whom it had responded, unfazed: "keep your tone civil."[16]

I was amazed at this display of backbone. I did not yet know Julian Assange personally, but I was studying him and his organization from afar, through their work. They were showing the courage to publish extremely sensitive files, putting themselves at risk while defying institutions which, from both the legal and extra-legal standpoint, intimidated even the editorial staffs of news media with the most lavish budgets and important connections. I was impressed by their strategic approach as well. If they had played the Julius Baer match as a traditional news outlet would have done, they would very likely have taken a considerable beating. Italian or British or Swiss newspapers, for example, must operate within the limits established by the laws of the country in which they are registered; their publications would have little chance of enjoying the press protection afforded by the American Constitution. But by playing the game on the global level, exploiting the resources of the internet and international alliances with civil and digital rights advocates, availing themselves of the powerful shield offered by the First Amendment and the bullhorn of the traditional media, WikiLeaks had inflicted a resounding defeat on a very wealthy bank.

For an investigative journalist forced to contend with the intimidating power of the rich and the powerful and their lawsuits every day, and the resulting severe constraints on press freedom, watching that fiasco unfold was a spectacular sight. With all the power of their money and their lawyers, Julius Baer had slunk back home with their tail between their legs, while WikiLeaks had succeeded in publishing what many newspapers would have considered unpublishable, because too risky from the legal standpoint.

The Julius Baer case, like that of the Guantanamo manual, was proof that the battle against secrecy could be won. And I abso-

---

16. The correspondence is available on the WikiLeaks website: www.wikileaks.com/wiki/Full_correspondence_between_Wikileaks_and_Bank_Julius_Baer (accessed May 19, 2022).

lutely had to track Assange down because, as a journalist, that battle was also my own.

A PHONE CALL IN THE NIGHT

Elusive and mysterious, who were Julian Assange and WikiLeaks? It took some time before I was able to establish a connection with them. To find out more, I contacted activists, experts in state secrets and encryption, every contact and every scrap of information that might help me understand who they were. Initially, WikiLeaks was organized like a wiki: they accepted documents, analyzed them and then published them, asking everyone to help examine the files and advance a debate on what they revealed. They did not routinely work with journalists; they had some media partners, but not large teams of partners as they did in later years. But one night, they asked for my help.

It was the summer of 2009. When the phone rang, it was the dead of night. I was having a hard time waking, but my phone kept ringing relentlessly and I finally dragged myself up. "This is WikiLeaks," I heard someone say. I could barely understand what was going on, but in the end I grasped that the person on the phone was Daniel Schmitt. He was relaying a message: I had one hour to download a file from the internet, after which it would be removed so it could not be accessed by others. He told me they were running some checks on the file's authenticity and what it revealed. "Can you give us a hand?" he asked.

I immediately downloaded the file and began to examine it. It was a recording dating back to July 2008. You could hear Walter Ganapini, at that time the councilor for the environment of Italy's Campania region, talking about the infamous garbage crisis that had brought images of Naples drowning in trash to newspapers and televisions across the world.

The strongman in the game was not Ganapini, however, but the special commissioner for the waste emergency, Gianni De Gennaro, who would go on to join the Department of Information Security (DIS), the coordinating body of Italian intelligence.

At the time of the emergency, when Ganapini was meeting with citizens' committees and associations, someone had recorded one of the conversations and forwarded it to WikiLeaks. In the long audio file lasting over three hours, the councilor analyzed why the garbage crisis had got to the point it had, even though—in his own words—a landfill like Parco Saurino was available and could have accommodated Campania's garbage for six months, thereby preventing the disaster.

"As far as Parco Saurino is concerned," Ganapini said, "one day I haggled over it with the current head of intelligence—it's no small thing to be the head of intelligence." The councilor went on: "that site is definitely a national mystery." The recording offered a glimpse into the possible role of Italy's secret services in the garbage crisis in Campania, and specifically into what Ganapini defined as a "national mystery": Parco Saurino, in the Caserta area of Santa Maria La Fossa, is in the heart of the realm of the Casalesi, the mafia clan which has built its huge fortunes on illegal waste trafficking. The councilor was alluding to intervention on the part of intelligence services and possibly to state–mafia deals on the garbage crisis. "I know that state-against-state negotiations exist in this country," he added.

Particularly disturbing, then, was a segment in which Ganapini described how he had been the target of an attempted assault in Gesù Square, in the heart of Naples, by four people in full-face helmets. "I did get some warnings, let's say, that I had seen something I shouldn't have," he explained.

Besides sharing the file with me that night, WikiLeaks had put me in touch with a person familiar with some of the facts mentioned in the recording and asked me to do all the journalistic checks I deemed necessary. In the days that followed, I contacted a number of people, first of all Ganapini himself, referencing an excerpt of a few minutes that had ended up on YouTube a short time before and had been picked up by the Italian daily *la Repubblica*. The councilor had dismissed it at the time as a fabricated editing job, but the recording of over three hours that I had listened to contained all the elements mentioned on YouTube. In the face of my pointed and detailed questions, Ganapini put up a wall, confirming only the threats and the disquieting encounter in Gesù Square. After a series of checks, on August 6, 2009, I published an article with the more significant excerpts in *L'Espresso*,[17] the renowned Italian news magazine I was working for at the time, which had already conducted important investigations into the garbage crisis, while WikiLeaks published the audio file on its site.[18]

With that document, Julian Assange and his organization had gone from the secrets of Guantanamo to the mysteries of the Italian Republic. But after publishing that file, all my attempts to contact WikiLeaks met with failure.

LIKE A BAND OF REBELS

I tried to track them down again, but to no avail. I realized that, logistically, that was how they operated. Like a band of rebels that conducts a raid and then vanishes, they would strike and then disappear. They changed contacts and were keenly aware of the surveillance which police forces, armies, secret services and big corporations use against the journalists they perceive as a threat. After all, that was exactly what had sparked my interest in WikiLeaks, when my source had stopped speaking with me. For the time being, they had vanished into thin air, but I knew that sooner or later they would surface again. In the meantime, I kept up with their work from afar.

In London, in September 2009, two news giants, the BBC and the *Guardian* newspaper, reported that a ship had dumped toxic waste which belonged to the Trafigura oil trading multinational into the waters off the Ivory Coast. According to official estimates later cited by the United Nations, 15 people died as a result, 69 were

---

17.   Stefania Maurizi, "Dai rifiuti spunta lo 007," *L'Espresso*, August 6, 2009: https://espresso.repubblica.it/palazzo/2009/08/06/ news/dai-rifiuti-spunta-lo-007-1.15163 and in the WikiLeaks website: https://wikileaks.org/wiki/Dai_rifiuti_spunta_lo_007
18.   The file is available on the WikiLeaks website: https://wikileaks.org/wiki/Ganapini_servizi_segreti_presidenza_della_repubblica,_1-4_Jul_2008 (accessed May 19, 2022).

hospitalized and over 108,000 required medical treatment.[19] Trafigura denied this devastation, however, and to quash the scandal enlisted one of London's most combative law firms specializing in lawsuits against the media: Carter-Ruck. While the BBC began to withdraw its reports on the case, the *Guardian* had in hand a dossier, the Minton Report, confirming the dangerous nature of the waste: "the compounds listed above," read the file, "are capable of causing severe human health effects through inhalation and ingestion. These include headaches, breathing difficulties, nausea, eye irritation, skin ulceration, unconsciousness and death."

The research underpinning the Minton Report had been commissioned by consultants of the multinational itself, so they were aware of it.[20] Someone had forwarded a copy of the report to the London newspaper. But Trafigura appealed to the judge and put the *Guardian* over the barrel with a "super-injunction," a court order that not only barred the newspaper from publishing the file but also mandated that it not disclose to readers that it was gagged by court order. It was WikiLeaks and some foreign newspapers that ended up publishing the report.[21] Blogs and social networks, especially Twitter, did the rest, as millions began searching for it on the internet. It was a spectacular defeat for the oil trading giant.

As with the Julius Baer bank, WikiLeaks had bypassed censorship in the Trafigura case because it had been designed to do so. Just as multinationals use loopholes in the various jurisdictions to evade laws and taxes, Assange's creation used its global structure as a news organization born from the internet to attempt to expand the mesh of press freedom.

Scarcely two months had passed after the Trafigura case when WikiLeaks scored another sensational scoop: in November 2009 they divulged over half a million messages from U.S. citizens

19. This estimate was also reported by the UN: "Ten years on, the survivors of illegal toxic waste dumping in Côte d'Ivoire remain in the dark," August 19, 2016: www.ohchr.org/en/press-releases/2016/08/ten-years-survivors-illegal-toxic-waste-dumping-cote-divoire-remain-dark. Accessed August 18, 2022.

20. David Leigh, "Minton Report: Carter-Ruck give up bid to keep Trafigura study secret," *Guardian*, October 16, 2009.

21. The Minton Report is available on the WikiLeaks website: https://wikileaks.org/wiki/Minton_report:_Trafigura_toxic_dumping_along_the_Ivory_Coast_broke_EU_regulations,_14_Sep_2006 (accessed May 19, 2022).

recorded on September 11, 2001, in a span of time ranging from five hours before the attack to twenty-four hours after it.[22]

The messages had been exchanged through a technology very popular at the time in the U.S. and beyond: pagers. These devices, later completely supplanted by cell phones, were also employed by officials of government agencies like the FBI, the Pentagon and the New York Police Department. The intercepted communications contained not only messages from ordinary citizens but also information from the field revealing how certain federal authorities had responded to the emergency, such as by giving instructions to ensure the operability of institutions at such a critical time.

"Who could have intercepted these communications?" computer security guru Bruce Schneier had immediately wondered, commenting on the revelations from WikiLeaks. Someone must have come into possession of them and sent them to Assange's organization. "It's disturbing to realize that someone, possibly not even a government, was routinely intercepting most (all?) of the pager data in lower Manhattan as far back as 2001. Who was doing it? For what purpose? That, we don't know," Schneier concluded.[23]

After that major scoop, a little more than three months went by and WikiLeaks materialized in my life again.

DESTROY WIKILEAKS

This time it was Julian Assange himself who came forward. It was March of 2010, and he wanted to direct my attention to a secret Bush administration file that his organization had just published.

The file had to do with WikiLeaks itself and was an analysis conducted by the U.S. Army Counterintelligence Center (ACIC), the military counter-espionage unit specialized in identifying entities that might pose a threat to American troops, facilities and information. The document described Assange's organization as follows: "Wikileaks.org was founded by Chinese dissidents, jour-

---

22. The messages are available on the WikiLeaks website: https://911.wikileaks. org/files/index.html

23. Bruce Schneier, "Leaked 9/11 text messages," November 26, 2009: www. schneier.com/blog/archives/2009/11/leaked_911_text.html

nalists, mathematicians, and technologists from the United States, China, Taiwan, Europe, Australia, and South Africa. Its Web site became operational in early 2007. The advisory board for Wikileaks.org includes journalists, cryptographers, a 'former US intelligence analyst' and expatriates from Chinese, Russian, and Tibetan refugee communities."[24]

The characterization of WikiLeaks as an organization founded by dissidents, journalists, mathematicians and expatriates corresponded to the description on WikiLeaks' own site, and American counterintelligence neither contested nor evinced any skepticism as to the truthfulness of the information referencing a collective effort behind its creation.

As for Assange, the file defined him as follows: "Julian Assange is a former computer hacker convicted[25] by the Australian government for hacking into US government and DoD [Department of Defense] computer networks in 1997. He is widely known for his support for open government initiatives, leftist ideology, anti-US views, and opposition to the Global War on Terrorism."

The file proceeded to argue that since anyone could upload a file to WikiLeaks, with "no editorial review or oversight to verify the accuracy of any information posted," the site "could be used to post fabricated information; to post misinformation, disinformation, and propaganda."

Had it been true that Assange's organization did not verify the authenticity of files before publishing them, that risk would have been a real one, but my personal experience belied that claim. Although I had had little contact with WikiLeaks up to that time, from our few interactions I had gathered that files were in fact subject to verification, partly because, as I had noted from the very

---

24. The file is available on the WikiLeaks website: https://file.wikileaks.org/file/us-intel-wikileaks.pdf (accessed May 19, 2022).
25. What the U.S. Army Counterintelligence Center (ACIC) reports on Julian Assange is not correct: it is true that when a teenager, Julian Assange was a hacker, but in December 1996 he was not convicted for hacking the U.S. government's networks as the ACIC document reports, but rather the hacking charges related to RMIT, Northern Telecom, the Australian Telecommunications Corporation and the Australian National University. Victoria County Court Press Office, communication to author, March 14, 2022.

start, there was a considerable level of paranoia in the organization. And to destroy the credibility of a news organization, what could be easier than sending it fake files, waiting for them to be published and then crying fake?

The U.S. counterintelligence analysis did indeed fully capture the aim of Assange's creation, however: "The goal of Wikileaks. org is to ensure that leaked information is distributed across many jurisdictions, organizations, and individual users because once a leaked document is placed on the Internet it is extremely difficult to remove the document entirely." That was exactly what Assange and his staff had done to bypass censorship in the cases of Julius Baer and Trafigura, thus overcoming the limitations and legal barriers faced by traditional media.

The secret file listed some of the tools used by WikiLeaks to protect sources sending them files, such as PGP and Tor, the software that protects a user surfing the internet by making it hard for those monitoring him to discover which sites he is visiting and what activities he is conducting. In acknowledging that the WikiLeaks' "developers and technical personnel appear to demonstrate a high level of sophistication in their efforts to provide a secure operating environment for whistleblowers desiring to post information to the Web site," U.S. counterintelligence did not rule out that "The purchase of more secure equipment, transmission means, and encryption protocols is possible if additional financial resources are made available to the organization." Despite that, according to the document, an adversary with the capacity and the means could "obtain access to Wikileaks.org's Web site, information systems, or networks that may assist in identifying those persons supplying the data and the means by which they transmitted the data."

Going by that analysis, a number of nations, "including China, Israel, North Korea, Russia, Vietnam, and Zimbabwe have denounced or blocked access to the Wikileaks.org Web site to prevent citizens or adversaries from accessing sensitive information, embarrassing information, or alleged propaganda." The U.S. government, on the other hand, had not censored it thus far, though the file spelt out U.S. counterintelligence's view clearly: "Wikileaks.org, a publicly accessible Internet Web site, represents a potential force protection, counterintelligence, operational security (OPSEC), and information security (INFOSEC) threat to the US Army," because the possibility of a U.S. government employee providing sensitive or secret information to the site "cannot be ruled out."

Having concluded that WikiLeaks constituted a threat, it needed to be destroyed. How? Through more presentable methods than those used by regimes like China, or countries like Israel which, according to the document, solved the problem at the root through authoritarian tools like complete censorship. But although the intentions of the U.S. were more presentable, they were no less alarming: "Wikileaks.org uses trust as a center of gravity by assuring insiders, leakers, and whistleblowers who pass information to Wikileaks.org personnel or who post information to the Web site that they will remain anonymous," the file read, "The identification, exposure, or termination of employment of or legal actions against current or former insiders, leakers, or whistleblowers could damage or destroy this center of gravity."

I was blown away when I read that document. The file bore the date of March 2008. WikiLeaks had been founded on October 4, 2006; it was slightly over one year old when the counterintelligence of a superpower, the United States, had decided it had to be destroyed. By going after its sources: singling out, firing and imprisoning those who sent WikiLeaks files that should not be made public, like those on the Guantanamo prison camp. Taking out an aggressive organization like Assange's, which had had the courage to say no to the Pentagon, would leave the information megaphone largely in the hands of the old media, which in so many cases—though not all—had proven submissive to the demands of a government like that of the U.S., whose influence is felt in every corner of the globe. WikiLeaks needed to be neutralized precisely because it was not part of that club and did not play by its rules.

The situation appeared troubling on every front. According to the document, regimes like China nipped WikiLeaks in the bud, censoring it, while democracies like the United States plotted to destroy it through techniques that were more presentable but still incompatible with freedom of the press, like assault on its journalistic sources and the whistleblowers exposing abuses. What did the future have in store for Julian Assange and WikiLeaks?

2

The Exceptional Courage of
Chelsea Manning

COLLATERAL MURDER

Not even a month after Julian Assange contacted me to flag the U.S. counterintelligence report, WikiLeaks became an international sensation. On April 5, 2010, they published *Collateral Murder*, a classified video in which an American Apache helicopter is seen gunning down defenseless civilians in Baghdad while the crew laughs.[1] Within twenty-four hours, the images had been seen on YouTube by 2 million people, without counting viewers of the TV channels relaying the video throughout the world.

The footage dated back to July 12, 2007 and was a Pentagon file. It had been shot in real time by one of two Apache helicopters flying over the city that day on the lookout for insurgents, and the carnage was shown without filters or censorship. Around a dozen civilians—including an esteemed war photographer aged 22, Namir Noor-Eldeen, and his 40-year-old assistant and driver, Saeed Chmagh, both employed by the Reuters international press agency—were blown to pieces by the Apache helicopter's 30mm cannon fire, while two Iraqi children were severely injured. Their father, Saleh Matasher Tomal, driving by in a van, had stopped to try to help the Reuters photographer's driver as he lay wounded on the ground, but the helicopter riddled him with bullets as well and finished off the survivor. Only the two children seated inside the vehicle, aged 5 and 10 years old, miraculously survived, though with serious injuries. Going by the conversations captured in the

---

1.   *Collateral Murder* is accessible on the WikiLeaks website: https://collateralmurder. wikileaks.org/ (accessed May 19, 2022).

video, for the crew the entire spectacle was a source of satisfaction. "All right, hahaha," says one of them laughing, "I hit 'em." And then "Look at those dead bastards." When American troops in a Bradley fighting vehicle reach the scene of the slaughter a few minutes later, the Apache crew seems to enjoy themselves anew: "I think they just drove over a body," says one of them, observing the Bradley as it advances. "Really?!" asks another. "Yeah!" answers his crewmate, laughing.

U.S. authorities had initially claimed that those killed were insurgents, and later that the attack had occurred in the context of combat operations against hostile forces. The video belied those official statements: no combat was in progress.[2] The Reuters international press agency, which tried to piece the facts together afterward, was led to believe the official version, to the point that Dean Yates—head of Reuters' correspondence office in Baghdad at the time of the attack—would later accuse the U.S. authorities of deliberately deceiving him, using very harsh words in recounting the back story to the *Guardian*.

After the death of his two colleagues, Yates met with two U.S. generals who had overseen the investigation into the massacre. In the course of the meeting, they showed him a few minutes of the footage. Yates was led to believe that the helicopter opened fire against his colleagues because the crew had seen armed men acting suspiciously: the photographer was wandering around, and the American soldiers had mistaken his camera with telephoto lens for an RPG, a rocket-propelled grenade launcher. Reuters tried in all manner of ways to obtain the complete footage to verify the facts on their own, even requesting a copy under the Freedom of Information Act (FOIA), but all their attempts had been futile; not even a powerful news organization like Reuters with all its resources could obtain the footage. It was only after WikiLeaks published *Collateral Murder* that Yates was able to understand how

---

2. Paul Daley, "'All lies': how the US military covered up gunning down two journalists in Iraq," *Guardian*, June 14, 2020; Paul Daley, "Julian Assange indictment fails to mention WikiLeaks video that exposed US 'war crimes' in Iraq," *Guardian*, June 14, 2020.

events had really unfolded. "They fucked us," he told the *Guardian* years later,[3] referring to the U.S. military authorities, "they just fucked us. They lied to us. It was all lies." In the years following the deaths of his colleagues, Yates slid into a mental hell, suffering from a post-traumatic stress syndrome that brought him to the brink of suicide.

Two weeks after WikiLeaks released *Collateral Murder*, Ethan McCord, one of the U.S. soldiers who had rushed to the scene of the carnage a few minutes later, described the traumatic incident to the American magazine *Wired*[4] as follows: "It was pretty much a shock when we got there to see what had happened, the carnage and everything else." To the *Wired* journalist who objected: "But you had been in combat before. It shouldn't have surprised you what you saw," McCord replied: "I have never seen anybody being shot by a 30-millimetre round before. It didn't seem real, in the sense that it didn't look like human beings."

According to Ethan McCord, there were weapons at the scene of the slaughter; some of the people killed had been carrying them. In any event, the video showed no threatening action at all from the Iraqis targeted by the helicopter, nor any combat operation. If the initial shots fired by the Apache were indeed triggered by the presence of those weapons, and in particular by having mistaken a camera with telephoto lens for a rocket launcher, the hail of munitions against the van, which decimated entirely unarmed civilians trying to aid the wounded Reuters photographer's assistant as he crawled along the ground, seemed hard to justify.

McCord would later go back over that day in detail. Upon reaching the site of the slaughter, he ran towards the van spurred on by the children's cries, while a fellow soldier could not bear the scene and began to vomit before running away. The horrific wounds on the two children, their lacerated father, the blood everywhere, the bits of glass in the little girl's body, him racing with the

---

3. Daley, "'All lies': how the US military covered up gunning down two journalists in Iraq."
4. Kim Zetter, "US soldier on 2007 Apache attack: what I saw," *Wired*, April 20, 2010.

little ones in his arms to try to save them, with his platoon leader shouting at him to stop worrying about "those fucking kids." "It happens daily in Iraq," McCord said. "[T]this is the end, we need to bring the soldiers home now," he added, explaining that in 2007 the rules of engagement, the internal directives that delineate how soldiers should conduct themselves in the war theater and in which situations shooting is legitimate, were "a joke."[5] According to those rules, U.S. troops could kill anyone they perceived as a threat, and "many soldiers got threatened just by the fact that you were looking at them, so they fired their weapons at anybody who was looking at them."

It is one thing to kill civilians without meaning to do so in the course of combat; taking deliberate aim at them is another. In the first case, we speak of collateral damage, in the second, of war crimes. The video documented how the Apache helicopter exterminated civilians, especially the seriously injured Reuters photographer's assistant and the two men trying to rescue him, who did not pose any threat whatsoever to the American forces. *Collateral Murder* could pave the way to an investigation into war crimes committed by U.S. soldiers.

To allow the public to determine whether the attack was in compliance with the rules of engagement (RoE) or not, WikiLeaks published not only the video, but also four classified RoE files for the years 2006 and 2007.[6] Those four reports are among the documents for which Julian Assange risks spending the rest of his life in a U.S. maximum-security prison.

It was only after *Collateral Murder* was published that Dean Yates realized how the official statements and few minutes of footage shown to him by the U.S. military during their meeting had misled him completely. "I came to blame Namir [the Reuters' photographer killed by the Apache helicopter] for that attack, thinking that the helicopter fired because he made himself look suspicious and

---

5. These quotes come from a public speech Ethan McCord gave in 2010, after WikiLeaks revealed Collateral Murder. The speech is available at: www.youtube.com/watch?v=8tgzygMxZZc (accessed May 19, 2022).
6. The US Rules of Engagement for Iraq are available on the WikiLeaks website: https://collateralmurder.wikileaks.org/en/resources.html (accessed May 19, 2022).

it just erased from my memory the fact that the order to open fire had already been given," he would later tell the *Guardian*,[7] adding: "The one person who picked this up was Assange. On the day that he released the tape [April 5, 2010] he said that helicopter opened fire because it sought permission and was given permission. And he said something like, 'If that's based on the rules of engagement then the rules of engagement are wrong.'"[8]

Were it not for the courage of the source who forwarded the classified video to WikiLeaks, and that of Julian Assange's organization which published it, it is very likely that those images would never have surfaced, notwithstanding Reuters' efforts to uncover the truth. And WikiLeaks did not simply receive the materials and disseminate them indiscriminately on the internet; they carried out all the necessary journalistic checks first. They also endeavored to bring the story of the victims to light, collaborating with Icelandic investigative journalist Kristinn Hrafnsson, then working for RUV, the Icelandic national broadcasting service, and now editor-in-chief of WikiLeaks, who flew to Baghdad to track down the two Iraqi children and their mother.

After revealing *Collateral Murder*, WikiLeaks went from being an organization known only to a niche public to an international phenomenon. But something happened right afterwards whose outcome would prove tragic. The strategy devised by U.S. counter-intelligence was starting to fall into place.

A LESSON

On June 6, 2010, exactly two months after the *Collateral Murder* video was published, the American magazine *Wired* reported that a young American, just 22 years of age, had been arrested in Iraq after revealing in a chat that he had been the one to forward the *Collateral Murder* video to WikiLeaks, along with hundreds of thousands of other classified U.S. government files.

---

7. Daley, "'All lies': how the US military covered up gunning down two journalists in Iraq."
8. Ibid.

The news was a remarkable scoop: the revelations of a rather specialist magazine like *Wired*, normally read by digital technology enthusiasts, were taken up by media around the world. The 22-year-old was Chelsea (then Bradley) Manning, an intelligence analyst with the U.S. army deployed to Baghdad.

Analysts like Manning collect and examine information on enemy forces and potential threats. They routinely handle files that are classified, that is to say designated as officially secret, which they access through protected computer networks and only after being deemed fit to do so based on an authorization procedure known as "security clearance." To achieve this clearance, they must be vetted by government authorities, who perform background checks on the analyst's personality, psychological profile, and economic, social and family situation.

What immediately struck me and others observing WikiLeaks very closely at the time—chief among them an American constitutional lawyer and columnist later renowned for his outstanding journalism, Glenn Greenwald—was how the U.S. authorities had got to Manning. News of Manning's arrest had been broken by two *Wired* reporters, Kim Zetter and Kevin Poulsen.[9]

Before becoming a journalist, Poulsen had a history in the world of hacking and had carried out a number of cyber-attacks, particularly on telephone networks. Julian Assange had also been a hacker when he was in his teens and early twenties, but it was only much later on, in December 1996—when he was 25 years old—that he was sentenced for those hacking activities by Australian judge Leslie Ross of the Victoria County Court. Acknowledging that his actions had been driven solely and exclusively by "intellectual inquisitiveness," with no view to personal gain, the sentence handed down by the judge was very lenient: a 2,100 Australian dollars fine.[10]

---

9. Kim Zetter and Kevin Poulsen, "US intelligence analyst arrested in Wikileaks video probe," *Wired*, June 6, 2010.
10. The ruling was issued by the Australian judge Leslie Ross, December 5, 1996, County Court of Victoria, Melbourne, *The Queen v. Julian Paul Assange.*

In the case of Kevin Poulsen, on the other hand, it seems that the motivations behind his hacking had not always been so noble: on at least one occasion, it was to win a Porsche and a hefty cash prize. Sentenced to slightly more than five years, after paying his debt to American justice Poulsen began working as a journalist specializing in cybercrime. Two weeks before Manning's arrest, Poulsen had published an article on a well-known and controversial American hacker by the name of Adrian Lamo, who had also been found guilty of computer intrusions. The *Wired* journalist related how Lamo had been diagnosed with Asperger's syndrome, a form of autism spectrum disorder common among mathematicians, scientists, hackers and computer wizards. The *Wired* article described Lamo's struggles, amidst psychiatric issues and social hardships.

Barely 15 days later, Kevin Poulsen and fellow journalist Kim Zetter revealed in *Wired* that Manning had been arrested. Apparently right after the article on Adrian Lamo came out, Manning had contacted Lamo and, despite never having met him before, neither personally nor on the web, openly confessed during a chat to being the one who had sent the *Collateral Murder* video to WikiLeaks as well as other important classified U.S. government files, including about 260,000 diplomatic files. Revealing classified files means risking a formidable criminal conviction and sentence; in the case of the United States, even life in prison or death. Why, after revealing such files, had Manning contacted a stranger, already a focus of U.S. justice for hacking, and confessed it all? One thing is certain: immediately after collecting Manning's confidences, Lamo alerted the U.S. authorities, who immediately arrested the young intelligence analyst in Iraq, while Kevin Poulsen and *Wired* published the news, securing a scoop that hit headlines all around the world.

Was it really a coincidence, or were Kevin Poulsen and Adrian Lamo part of a conspiracy against Manning? Glenn Greenwald[11] publicly advanced doubts about the scoop in *Wired* and pointed out that not only had Kevin Poulsen and Adrian Lamo known

11.   Glenn Greenwald, "The strange and consequential case of Bradley Manning, Adrian Lamo and WikiLeaks," *Salon*, June 18, 2010.

each other for some time, but some of the people connected to the arrest, including Lamo himself, were part of a shadowy project called "Project Vigilant."[12]

Headed by a private company, Project Vigilant apparently monitored internet users' activities like a sort of "internet sheriff," forwarding information on suspicious cases to U.S. authorities. Since 2010, however, no proof of a conspiracy between Poulsen and Lamo has ever emerged. As of today, the truth is that U.S. authorities arrested Manning precisely for what was admitted in the chat to a perfect stranger in a moment of psychological fragility. And looking back, that arrest still serves as a lesson for journalists and their sources: you can protect a source with all the encryption and advanced solutions techniques that WikiLeaks had provided, but sometimes no technology can protect a source from their own human frailty.

In relaying the news of Manning's arrest, *Wired* had only published some excerpts of the conversation between the two, and those shreds of information made it impossible to get a complete picture of what had happened, but the young analyst in the chat came across as a highly intelligent and troubled 22-year-old. Manning would later come out as transgender and take the name Chelsea after an almost five-year struggle against the Pentagon to recognize her identity.

When *Wired* published the full conversation[13] one year after her arrest, Chelsea Manning's tale of moral integrity shone through in full force.

SHE COULD HAVE LOOKED THE OTHER WAY

"I was born in Central Oklahoma, grew up in a small town called Crescent,"[14] Manning told the stranger, recalling the place where she had lived as a child, a small town with a population of barely

---

12. Glenn Greenwald, "The worsening journalistic disgrace at Wired," *Salon*, December 27, 2010.
13. Evan Hansen, "Manning-Lamo chat logs revealed," *Wired*, July 13, 2011.
14. Ibid.

1,200 in the American state of Oklahoma. "I was short (still am), very intelligent (could read at 3 and multiply/divide by 4), very effeminate, and glued to a computer screen at these young ages [...] an easy target by kindergarten ... grew up in a highly evangelical town with more church pews than people so, I got pretty messed up at school ... 'girly boy' 'teacher pet,' etc. Home was the same, alcoholic father and mother ... mother was very nice, but very needy emotionally ... father was very wealthy (lots of nice toys/computer stuff), but abusive."[15]

The further Manning ventured into her tale, the more troubling her family situation appeared. "I lived in the middle of nowhere, so I had no neighbors to hang out with ... and my dad would never take me anyway, because after work he'd hit the bottle," she continued, describing how, during middle school, she was thrown out of the house: "My father in a drunken stupor got angry with me because I was doing some noisy homework while he was watching TV ... he went into his bedroom, pulled out a shotgun, and chased me out of the house ... the door was deadbolted, so I couldn't get out before he caught up with me ... so my mother (also wasted) threw a lamp over his head ... and I proceeded to fight him, breaking his nose, and made it out of the house ... my father let off one or two shots, causing damage, but injuring nobody, except for the belt lashing I got for 'making him shoot up the house'."[16]

After that violent incident, her parents separated. Later on her mother attempted suicide, after which she fell seriously ill and suffered a stroke. It was primarily Manning's desire to obtain benefits to support her college expenses that led her to enlist in the United States Army, not to fight in the battleground, but to employ her intellectual gifts as an intelligence analyst. A disaster waiting to happen; not only did she lack the violent disposition of many of her fellow soldiers, she was also a critical and independent spirit, entirely ill-suited to the role of a soldier obeying a superior's orders without question. Despite having been raised Catholic in a very small town characterized by strong evangelical faith—putting

15. Ibid.
16. Ibid.

her under significant social pressure—no one had ever been able to
make her conform. She told Lamo she was the only non-believer
in Crescent.

Once in Iraq, her situation had fast become critical. "I am very
isolated at the moment," she told Adrian Lamo in the chat, "lost
all of my emotional support channels ... family, boyfriend, trusting
colleagues ... I am a mess. I am in the desert, with a bunch of
hyper-masculine trigger happy ignorant rednecks as neighbors
... and the only safe place I seem to have is this satellite internet
connection."[17] Shortly after enlisting, she realized the mistake she
had made in choosing the army: "I think the thing that got me
the most ... that made me rethink the world more than anything
was watching 15 detainees taken by the Iraqi Federal Police ...
for printing 'anti-Iraqi literature'."[18] Continuing her explanation to
Lamo: "The Iraqi federal police wouldn't cooperate with US forces,
so I was instructed to investigate the matter, find out who the 'bad
guys' were, and how significant this was for the Federal Police ... it
turned out, they had printed a scholarly critique against [the Iraqi
Prime Minister] PM Maliki ... I had an interpreter read it for me
... and when I found out that it was a benign political critique
titled '*Where did the money go?*' and following the corruption trail
within the PM's cabinet ... I immediately took that information
and *ran* to the officer to explain what was going on ... he didn't
want to hear any of it ... he told me to shut up and explain how
we could assist the Federal Police in finding *MORE* detainees
... everything started slipping after that ... I saw things differently.
I had always questioned the [*sic*] things worked, and investigated
to find the truth ... but that was a point where I was a *part* of
something ... I was actively involved in something that I was completely against.[19]

Those were years in which torture and abuse were rampant in
Iraqi prisons, and a person with a conscience like Manning could

17. Ibid.
18. Ibid.
19. Ibid.

never have been complicit in a chain of command that tolerated and even encouraged war crimes and torture.

In Iraq, and in the networks where the U.S. government stored classified documents, Manning had seen many things, as she described to Lamo: "if you had free reign [*sic*] over classified networks for long periods of time … say, 8–9 months … and you saw incredible things, awful things … things that belonged in the public domain, and not on some server store in a dark room in Washington DC … what would you do?"[20]

Manning began to list some of them: "[Documents on] Guantanamo, Bagram [Air Base in Afghanistan]," she explained, "things that would have an impact on 6.7 billion people. Say … a database of half a million events during the Iraq war … from 2004 to 2009 … with reports, date time groups, latitude–longitude locations, casualty figures …? or 260,000 state department cables from embassies and consulates all over the world, explaining how the first world exploits the third, in detail, from an internal perspective?"[21]

Then her confession: "in other words … I've made a huge mess :- (I'm sorry … I'm just emotionally fractured. I'm a total mess."[22]

Chelsea Manning was clearly afraid of the possible consequences of what she had done, but the choice she made had been the right one. She had come upon appalling violations of human rights, like those in the *Collateral Murder* video showing civilians blown apart by the Apache helicopter; she had learned details about the torture practiced in Guantanamo, about scandals and abuses relayed in U.S. diplomatic correspondence. She could have looked the other way and played dumb, because the personal risk in exposing those files was too great. She could have forgotten what she had discovered and just left it behind her, mindful like the rest of us that we only have one life to live: why risk spending it in prison or on death row by leaking those secret files and being found out? But no: Chelsea had not looked the other way, she had made the hardest

20.   Ibid.
21.   Ibid.
22.   Ibid.

choice. She forwarded the files to Julian Assange's organization, including the *Collateral Murder* video, published barely a month before her chat with Adrian Lamo. Her attention had been drawn to WikiLeaks, she explained, by the pager messages recorded on September 11. "I immediately recognized that they were from an NSA database."[23]

The U.S. National Security Agency (NSA) is the most powerful, technologically advanced intelligence agency in the world, able to intercept the telephone and internet conversations of the entire planet. According to Chelsea Manning, then, the over half a million messages sent by Americans on September 11, 2001 and published by WikiLeaks in November 2009 came from an NSA database: someone with access to it had copied them and sent them to Julian Assange's organization, and their publication had been noticed by Manning—in fact, by the entire world.

In choosing not to look the other way, Manning had shown uncommon courage, and her exceptional moral caliber shone through in that chat.

"I WANT PEOPLE TO SEE THE TRUTH"

Adrian Lamo tried repeatedly to find out what kind of files Chelsea Manning had sent to WikiLeaks, besides the *Collateral Murder* video. Among those Manning described to him were about 260,000 secret U.S. diplomatic files. She told Lamo that the immense database contained "the non-PR-versions of world events and crises ... uhm ... all kinds of stuff like everything from the buildup to the Iraq War during [Colin] Powell, to what the actual content of 'aid packages' is."[24] Such as the aid to Pakistan: "PR that the US is sending aid to Pakistan includes funding for water/food/clothing ..." Manning explained. "[T]hat much is true, it includes that, but the other 85% of it is for F-16 fighters and munitions to aid in the Afghanistan effort, so the US can call in

---

23. Ibid.
24. Ibid.

Pakistanis to do aerial bombing instead of Americans potentially killing civilians and creating a PR crisis."[25]

After confessing to having forwarded secret files of this significance to WikiLeaks, Manning did not hide her apprehension: "God knows what happens now, hopefully worldwide discussion, debates, and reforms. If not ... then we're doomed as a species. I will officially give up on the society we have if nothing happens."[26]

The reaction sparked by WikiLeaks' publication of the *Collateral Murder* video only a few weeks earlier had given her hope: "Twitter exploded," she told Lamo, "People who saw, knew there was something wrong." Then came her explanation of why she had not turned the other way, had instead chosen to leak the classified files: "I want people to see the truth," she continued, "because without information, you cannot make informed decisions as a public." For that matter, if she had been motivated by self-interest she would have made different choices, as she candidly told Lamo: "if i were someone more malicious, I could've sold to russia or china and made bank?"[27] "Why didn't you?" he immediately asked. "Because it's public data," she answered, without hesitation. "Information should be free, it belongs in the public domain, because another state would just take advantage of the information."[28]

Thus Manning maintained that the motive behind her actions was a very honorable one: to expose war crimes and reveal the truth about important facts of public interest, in order to spark a debate around those glaring violations of human rights. She was not a spy who had sold information to a foreign power, which could use knowledge of such scandals to apply pressure and blackmail in international negotiations. She was a whistleblower, who after learning of egregious incidents, had leaked those documents in order to trigger public discussion, so that those responsible for possible war crimes like the ones in the *Collateral Murder* video could be identified and punished.

---

25. Ibid.
26. Ibid.
27. Ibid.
28. Ibid.

Ten years on, this truth is engraved in stone: Manning acted out of conscience, and not even the U.S. government ever tried to accuse her of handing over information to foreign powers, of playing in that bleak world of spies where selling secrets can bring big money.

Although she was just 22 years old, the chat showed Chelsea Manning to be not only an individual of profound integrity but one capable of intelligent political analyses as well. "I don't believe in good guys versus bad guys anymore … only a plethora of states acting in self-interest … with varying ethics and moral standards of course, but self-interest nonetheless," she told Lamo, adding, "I mean, we're better in some respects … we're much more subtle … use a lot more words and legal techniques to legitimise everything, it's better than disappearing in the middle of the night, but just because something is more subtle, doesn't make it right."[29]

Chelsea Manning bared her soul to that contact she had never met before, and although concerned about what might happen, she also told Lamo she considered it unlikely the U.S. authorities would track her down as the source of the WikiLeaks revelations. According to her, the security of the U.S. Army infrastructures and computer networks where secret files were stored was full of holes, to the point that her co-workers loaded forbidden files such as movies, music and games onto the same computers they used for working on classified materials. And when Lamo asked her how she was able to get out the files sent to WikiLeaks, she answered hypothetically: "Perhaps I would come in with music on a CD-RW [a compact disc which can be written, read, erased] labelled with something like 'Lady Gaga' … erase the music … then write a compressed split file. No-one suspected a thing."[30]

The spectacular failure on the part of the Pentagon's network security caused U.S. authorities enormous embarrassment when it emerged after Manning's arrest.

For his part, Adrian Lamo had assured her that their conversation would remain strictly confidential: "I'm a journalist and a

29. Ibid.
30. Ibid.

minister. You can pick either, and treat this as a confession or an interview (never to be published)."[31] Instead he had immediately run to report her. Arrested in Iraq in May 2010, Chelsea was first transferred to Kuwait and then imprisoned in Marine Corps Base Quantico in Virginia.

I looked on in dismay at Manning's arrest, both in view of the consequences she faced, and because it confirmed U.S. counter-intelligence's strategy: destroy Julian Assange's organization by going after the sources who leaked files to WikiLeaks to expose abuses and atrocities. And even as I feared the treatment the U.S. authorities had in store for Chelsea Manning, I wondered: how much longer could WikiLeaks go on?

---

31. Ibid.

3
Afghanistan: The Faraway War

FOREVER WAR

After the arrest of Chelsea Manning, it was clear the United States was not going to stand by and watch as Julian Assange and his staff published hundreds of thousands of secret U.S. government files.

Fifteen days after *Wired* published its international scoop, I flew to Brussels. I knew Assange had been invited to hold a seminar on freedom of expression at the European Parliament. The publication of the *Collateral Murder* video and arrest of Chelsea Manning had made WikiLeaks an international sensation, and the Brussels press office was literally besieged by journalists trying to hunt him down. The mystery surrounding WikiLeaks' founder and its entire staff, about whom very little was known, was pulling the media like a magnet.

I knew it was Assange who would be arriving in Brussels, not the German spokesman for WikiLeaks at the time, Daniel Schmitt, and I was able to talk to him in person and alone. He moved like a hunted man. It was obvious the U.S. authorities wanted to get their hands on him and his team, and the secret files in their possession, but it was equally obvious that they would never dare touch him while he was holding a seminar at the European Parliament. In fact the seminar concluded without incident.

One month later, however, all hell broke loose. On July 25, 2010, WikiLeaks published the Afghan War Logs, and the Pentagon was furious.[1]

The files consisted of 76,910 confidential reports on the war in Afghanistan, written by American troops on the ground between

---

1. The 76,910 secret Afghan War Logs are available on the WikiLeaks website: https://wardiaries.wikileaks.org/ (accessed January 10, 2022).

January 2004 and December 2009. They offered an unprecedented glimpse into that far-off, neglected war. Western media spoke of it very little,[2] even though the coalition troops fighting in Afghanistan—including Italian troops—had been there since 2001.

The conflict, which ended after twenty years with the withdrawal of U.S. and Western troops in August 2021, is a symbol of what American newspapers call the "Forever Wars," the perpetual wars against terrorism whereby the United States has destroyed the lives of thousands of young U.S. soldiers, annihilated thousands of innocent Afghani civilians, and spent over 2 trillion dollars.[3] And to what end?

This extremely poor country is also a prime example of the short-sightedness typical of American foreign policy: in order to fight communism, the United States supported and financed radical fundamentalists like Gulbuddin Hekmatyar, whose men would throw acid in women's faces, opening the Pandora's box of Islamic fanaticism which ultimately led to the attacks of September 11 and still finds the world in flames today.

To understand the revelations by WikiLeaks, it is helpful to quickly run through the series of events that led to this conflict in the first place.

Afghanistan's history is one of wars, invasions and civil warfare. Its strategic position placed it at the center of the ambitions of the British Empire and of the Soviet Union, and most recently of the U.S. war on terror. For a variety of reasons, none of these three powers has ever been able to defeat this infinitely more backward

---

2. According to the Tyndall Report, which monitors the U.S. broadcast television networks, in 2020, the year before the war ended, American national evening newscasts on CBS, ABC, and NBC devoted only 5 minutes to covering the conflict, and between 2015 and 2019, the war in Afghanistan failed to average even an hour of annual coverage on all three newscasts combined: 58 minutes total. See: Brendan Morrow, "Afghanistan got just 5 minutes of coverage on the network newscasts last year, analysis says," *The Week*, August 27, 2021.
3. The fact that the United States spent 2.313 trillion dollars for its 20-year war in Afghanistan has been assessed by the Costs of War project, founded by the Watson Institute for International and Public Affairs of Brown University: https://watson. brown.edu/costsofwar/figures/2021/human-and-budgetary-costs-date-us-war-afghanistan-2001-2022 (accessed May 19, 2022).

and poorer country; indeed, it is also sometimes called "the grave-yard of empires."

In 1979, Afghanistan was invaded by the Soviet Union and plunged into a war against the invader, fought on Afghanistan's side by the *mujahideen*, Islamic fundamentalists armed and financed by the CIA in an anti-communist capacity, through Pakistan. The supporters of the mujahideen included Osama bin Laden, born to a wealthy family of building constructors in Saudi Arabia, who had gone to fight the holy war in Afghanistan. The conflict between Soviets and mujahideen killed and uprooted millions. According to United Nations estimates, between 1979 and 1990 at least 6.2 million Afghanis fled into Pakistan and Iran.[4] Mired in the insurgency, a guerrilla war that left them battered and bruised, in 1989 the Soviets withdrew from the country.

At that point, Afghanistan collapsed into a civil war between the different mujahideen factions. That of Gulbuddin Hekmatyar was one of the most violent.

In 1994, a new military and political force emerged: the Taliban, Islamic fundamentalists trained in religious schools in Pakistan, who in the 1990s gained almost complete control over Afghanistan. The Taliban essentially established an apartheid regime, but unlike the race-based segregation in South Africa, the apartheid in Afghanistan was based on gender and targeted women: shut out of education, obliged to cover themselves from head to foot, no longer allowed to work outside the home and thus reduced to extreme poverty, no longer able to go outdoors without a male chaperone, not even to hospital. In a country where the capital alone counted 30,000 widows,[5] the consequences of not being able to leave one's home without a man even for health purposes could be truly dire. The Taliban announced a rigid gender segregation policy even

---

4. Rupert Colville, "Refugees Magazine Issue 108 (Afghanistan: the unending crisis)—The biggest caseload in the world," *Refugees* Magazine 108 (June 1, 1997): www.unhcr.org/uk/publications/refugeemag/3b680fbfc/refugees-magazine-issue-108-afghanistan-unending-crisis-biggest-caseload.html

5. *Final report on the situation of human rights in Afghanistan*, submitted by Mr Choong Hyun Paik, Special Rapporteur, in accordance with Commission on Human Rights resolution 1995/74, UN, E/CN.4/1996/64, February 27, 1996.

among hospital patients. The upshot was that in 1997, in Kabul, half a million women risked being forced to obtain healthcare in a single hospital, the Rabia Balkhi,[6] which had thirty-five beds and lacked the most rudimentary sanitary facilities. It was only after negotiations between the International Committee of the Red Cross and the Taliban that the risk of a major health catastrophe sparked by the Taliban directive was averted.

Immediately after September 11, the Taliban were accused of giving refuge to Osama bin Laden and his terrorist group, al-Qaeda, who were considered responsible for the attack. Citing this motivation, on October 7, 2001, an international coalition headed by the United States invaded Afghanistan. The tragedy of the Taliban's treatment of women immediately became a tool in U.S. and Western military propaganda to engender support for the military offensive. Thus the U.S. and its allies on the one hand used the plight of women under the Taliban to justify their attack on Afghanistan, while on the other hand critics of the United States offensive went so far as to tolerate the medieval Taliban's policies, arguing that it was the cultural norm for the country. In reality it was not the norm, as has been documented by reliable organizations like Physicians for Human Rights.[7]

After the start of the conflict in October 2001, it was only a matter of weeks before the Taliban were militarily defeated. But the U.S. troops, the International Security Assistance Force (ISAF) coalition troops[8] and the Afghan army and police forces fighting

---

6. In 2003, as a journalist I had learned about the impact of the Taliban's policies thanks to the work of the U.S. non-governmental organization (NGO), Physicians for Human Rights (PHR), a recipient of the 1997 Nobel Prize for Peace. PHR had documented the dire consequences of the Taliban's policies on the Afghani women's physical and mental health, using its medical expertise which, in recent decades has enabled the documentation of extremely grave violations of human rights, from the brutal regime of Pinochet's Chile to CIA torture during the war on terror. PHR has investigated the abuses perpetrated by both the Taliban and by U.S. troops in Afghanistan. See PHR reports: Vincent Iacopino, *The Taliban's war on women*, August 1998; PHR, *Women's health and human rights in Afghanistan: A population-based assessment*, 2001; Also: Caitriona Palmer, "The Taliban's war on women," *Lancet* 352, August 29, 1998.

7. See PHR reports in note 6.

8. ISAF fought the war in Afghanistan under NATO's lead until 2014. According to NATO figures, at its peak ISAF included 130,000 foreign troops from 51 countries

alongside the U.S. soon found themselves facing a Taliban insurgency that continued for twenty years, right up until the end of the war. Just as the Soviet Union had its Vietnam in Afghanistan, now it was the turn of the United States and its allies. This is the war which the Afghan War Logs, released by WikiLeaks in July 2010, allow their readers to piece together almost day by day.

A few months before releasing the files, WikiLeaks had published a confidential CIA memorandum[9] dated March 11, 2010. The memo had not made much of a splash, but it was important because it explained which strategies should be employed to head off the risk of French and German public opinion turning against the war and demanding the withdrawal of their troops. France and Germany had the largest contingents in Afghanistan at the time, after those of the United States and the UK: for the Pentagon, the withdrawal of their troops would have posed a problem, to say the least. One of the factors the CIA apparently most relied on was the indifference to the war in Western public opinion: it was very seldom discussed in newspapers and even less on television, so the related massacres and horrors sparked little, if any, reaction among the Western public. "The Afghanistan mission's low public salience," wrote the CIA in the file revealed by WikiLeaks, "has allowed French and German leaders to disregard popular opposition and steadily increase their troop contributions to the International Security Assistance Force (ISAF)."[10]

The file recommended not banking on apathy alone, however, but preparing possible persuasion strategies as well, in case the public mood shifted. The arguments to employ when addressing French citizens were the Taliban's possible return to power and the effects that this would have on the lives of Afghan women: "The prospect of the Taliban rolling back hard-won progress on girls'

(United States, United Kingdom, Germany, Italy, France, etc.). In 2015, a new mission was established, Resolute Support, which continued until the end of the war in Afghanistan in August 2021.

9.   As with all its revelations, WikiLeaks made the documents publicly available: https://wikileaks.org/wiki/CIA_report_into_shoring_up_Afghan_war_support_in_Western_Europe,_11_Mar_2010 (accessed January 10, 2022).

10.   Ibid.

education could provoke French indignation, become a rallying point for France's largely secular public."

The card to play with the Germans, on the other hand, was that of refugees: "messages that illustrate how a defeat in Afghanistan could heighten Germany's exposure to terrorism, opium, and refugees might help to make the war more salient to skeptics."

Despite its importance, the document had not made much of an impact. But when WikiLeaks released the Afghan War Logs on July 25, 2010, the files made headlines all around the world and the Pentagon's reaction was irate in the extreme.

AN EXTRAORDINARY WINDOW ON THE WAR

The 76,910 secret files detailed the war in a way never before possible. They were short reports written up by U.S. soldiers fighting on the ground. They contained factual information, including latitude and longitude of the sites where clashes, attacks and slaughters of civilians had taken place, all described with the exact time and date, in terse military jargon.

The files recorded significant events (SigActs, significant activities) in real time from January 2004 to December 2009, the period beginning with George W. Bush's second presidential term up to the first year of Barack Obama's administration. Each unit and outpost in the theatre of war produced extremely concise reports on attacks sustained, clashes, dead, wounded, kidnapped, prisoners, friendly fire, warning messages as well as details on incidents involving improvised explosive devices (IEDs), the makeshift, remotely operated devices placed along the roads that wreaked havoc on both soldiers and civilians.

Each report was like a snapshot capturing the conflict in Afghanistan at a specific time and in a specific place. By putting all the snapshots together, troops and intelligence could obtain a comprehensive overview of the war as it unfolded on the ground, action after action, so as to make operational plans and perform intelligence analyses. The reports were drafted by soldiers in the U.S. Army, their own account of the conflict. They did not contain information on *top-secret* events, because the files were classified only as *secret*.

The files brought to light hundreds of civilian victims never counted before. Based on the files, the *Guardian* counted at least 195 dead and 174 wounded, though stressing that the numbers were no doubt an underestimate. The files also offered a glimpse into the secret war being fought with special units never heard of before, like Task Force 373, and with drones, the unmanned aircraft which, controlled by U.S. soldiers at a base in Nevada, killed in far-off places like Afghanistan.

Task Force 373 was an elite unit that took its orders directly from the Pentagon and whose mission was to capture or kill high-level al-Qaeda and Taliban combatants. The decision as to who to capture and who to kill extra-judicially, with no legal due process, was apparently entrusted entirely to the task force.[11]

The value of the Afghan War Logs revealed by WikiLeaks lay precisely in their revelation of facts that the Pentagon propaganda machine had kept hidden. The secret operations of Task Force 373 were a prime example. The brutality of the night-time raids undertaken by these special forces had resulted in killings of allied Afghan forces, women and children. These kinds of attacks contributed to the strong resentment against American and coalition forces among the local populations.

The name "Task Force 373" never appeared in the military's official statements, however, and, as reported by the *Guardian*,[12] information was hidden to cover up errors and slaughters of innocents. During one of their operations, for example, the soldiers of Task Force 373 had killed seven children. News of their deaths was given in a coalition press release, but with no explanation of the context in which they had occurred. No one reported how those special forces often had literally no idea who they were killing: in that particular case, they had fired five missiles at a religious school,

---

11. WikiLeaks press release on Afghan War Logs, accessed May 19, 2022: https://wikileaks.org/afg/; Nick Davies, "Afghanistan War Logs: Task Force 373—special forces hunting top Taliban," *Guardian*, July 25, 2010.
12. Ibid.

a *madrasa*, convinced they were striking a leader of al-Qaeda, Abu Laith al-Libi. In another instance, they slaughtered seven Afghan policemen and wounded four, convinced that they were firing on men under a Taliban commander.

But the files not only unveiled carnage committed by U.S. troops, they also uncovered carnage committed by Taliban forces, especially their horrific attacks with IEDs. According to the *Guardian*, the Afghan War Logs database chronicled that between 2004 and 2009, IEDs had caused over 2,000 civilian deaths, and that 2009 had been an especially terrible year, with 100 attacks in just three days.[13] The London newspaper highlighted how IEDs were the Taliban's weapon of choice, the one they used to try to offset the Western troops' overwhelming technological superiority.

A ramping up of attacks against the U.S. and international coalition troops was notable in the files from the end of 2005 onwards. Digging through the database, the German weekly *Der Spiegel* determined that this escalation stemmed in part from the fact that the Taliban, and warlords like the notorious Gulbuddin Hekmatyar, were threatening local insurgents in order to make them undertake actions against the troops, or even paying them considerable sums, up to 10,000 U.S. dollars,[14] to do so.

The files also revealed other important information that had never emerged before: according to research into the database by the *New York Times*, the Taliban had obtained surface-to-air heat-seeking missiles entirely analogous to the Stingers the CIA had provided to the mujahideen twenty-five years earlier. Thus the same kind of weapons the Afghan insurgents had used to inflict devastating losses on the Soviets, ultimately forcing them to retreat, had ended up in the hands of the enemies of the U.S. in Afghanistan.[15]

---

13. Nick Davies and David Leigh, "Afghanistan War Logs: massive leaks of secret files exposes the truth of occupation," *Guardian*, July 25, 2010; Declan Walsh, Paul Simon and Paul Scruton, "WikiLeaks Afghanistan files: every IED attack with co-ordinates," *Guardian*, July 26, 2010.
14. Spiegel Staff, "Explosive leaks provide image of war from those fighting it," *Der Spiegel*, July 25, 2010.
15. C.J. Chivers, C. Gall, A.W. Lehren, M. Mazzetti, J. Perlez, E. Schmitt et al., "View is bleaker than official portrayal of war in Afghanistan," *New York Times*, July 25, 2010.

As for drones, often portrayed as infallible, zero-risk weapons—piloted from afar by soldiers operating in the complete safety of a U.S. military base, as if in a videogame—apparently they were not always so infallible. The files documented episodes, pieced together by *Der Spiegel*, of troops forced to undertake dangerous recovery operations after such unmanned aircraft crashed into the ground and the secret data in their computers risked ending up in enemy hands. In fact it was not always possible to erase the classified information contained in the drone's IT systems remotely, and when an operation failed, soldiers on the ground in Afghanistan were forced to embark on dangerous missions to recover the equipment.

As of today, the Afghan War Logs remain the only public source that can be used to reconstruct the attacks, deaths and extrajudicial killings that took place in Afghanistan between 2004 and 2009, given the secrecy of those military operations. They are also one of the very few sources we have to try to determine the number of civilians killed before 2007, for which no one seems to have reliable data, not even the United Nations mission in Afghanistan, UNAMA, which compiles these statistics.[16]

After twenty years, in August 2021 the seemingly interminable war came to an end. United States and coalition forces left Afghanistan in a dramatic withdrawal, a fiasco in which they could not even save the Afghani nationals who had aided their troops. Defeated and humiliated, the United States had lost the war. As I write, the Taliban are back in power, while ISIS has already gained ground in the country. As U.S. sanctions cut off the Taliban's access to any funding, Afghanistan draws close to an economic collapse that is already producing mass starvation, and the future of women in particular appears grim.

No one knows Afghanistan's future; the only thing we know for sure is that the United States' longest war resulted in complete failure, a failure that was already evident in the Afghan War Logs. There is no reliable data on how many civilians were killed between

16.   Liam McDowall, Director of Strategic Communications of UNAMA, email to author, November 18, 2020.

October 2001 and 2006, but we do know that between 2009 and 2019 alone, at least 35,518 civilians were killed and 66,546 wounded. This amounts to more than 3,000 civilian deaths every year: it is as if from January 2009 to December 2019 there had been a September 11 every year[17] in Afghanistan. Yet this war has always been off the radar of Western public opinion. And without the courage of Chelsea Manning and WikiLeaks, the war propaganda machine and state secrecy would never have allowed us to acquire the factual information we have drawn from the Afghan War Logs. The director of the *New York Times* at the time, Bill Keller, called the documents "an extraordinary window on that war."[18]

Right after their publication, the German weekly *Der Spiegel* interviewed Julian Assange,[19] asking: "You could have started a company in Silicon Valley and lived in a home in Palo Alto with a swimming pool. Why did you decide to do the WikiLeaks project instead?"

Assange replied: "We all only live once. So we are obligated to make good use of the time that we have and to do something that is meaningful and satisfying. This is something that I find meaningful and satisfying. That is my temperament. I enjoy creating systems on a grand scale, and I enjoy helping people who are vulnerable. And I enjoy crushing bastards. So it is enjoyable work."

The Pentagon saw it differently. At the revelation of the Afghan War Logs, they flew into a rage. Then Secretary of Defense Robert Gates immediately promised "an aggressive investigation," while Admiral Mike Mullen declared: "Mr. Assange can say whatever he likes about the greater good he thinks he and his source are doing. But the truth is they might already have on their hands the blood of some young soldier or that of an Afghan family."[20]

---

17. "Afghanistan protection of civilian in armed conflicts 2019," UNAMA, February 2020.
18. "The War Logs articles," *New York Times*, July 25, 2010.
19. John Goetz and Marcel Rosenbach, "I enjoy crushing bastards," *Der Spiegel*, July 26, 2010.
20. Philip Stewart and Adam Entous, "WikiLeaks may have blood on its hands, U.S. says," Reuters, July 30, 2010.

This was an accusation that the media would uncritically repeat for over a decade, gravely undermining WikiLeaks' reputation. But was it true?

THE PENTAGON'S POISON

The efforts of the U.S. Department of Defense to inject fear into the public debate around the WikiLeaks publication did not take long to bear fruit. A few days after the secret files on the war in Afghanistan were published, the notion that Julian Assange and his organization were dangerously irresponsible began to circulate in international newsrooms. Admiral Mike Mullen's words about "blood on their hands" referred to the fact that, according to the U.S. Department of Defense, the release of the 76,910 secret files had exposed U.S. troops, international coalition troops and their Afghan collaborators, who were providing them with information and assistance on the ground, to the risk of Taliban attacks, since some of the files contained identifying names or details.

It was self-evident that the Pentagon had a vested interest in discrediting WikiLeaks after it published those files, not to mention others before them like the *Collateral Murder* video. The Afghan War Logs constituted a veritable goldmine of information: the press and the public could compare the statements by the various military leaders and governments that had sent troops to Afghanistan with the data contained in the files and uncover the official lies, omissions and distortions. For the first time, the files made it possible to clear away the fog of war while a conflict was still under way, not twenty or thirty years later when the facts could be of interest only to professional historians.

Not since 1971, when Daniel Ellsberg had leaked the Pentagon Papers—7,000 top-secret files on the Vietnam conflict—had the public been able to access thousands of pages of confidential information on a war while it was still in progress. Admiral Mike Mullen's accusation called for a heavy dose of skepticism, since it was obvious that the Pentagon was furious with Assange. Yet those words immediately struck a chord in the media.

WikiLeaks had not published the revelations on Afghanistan on their own; they had done so in partnership with three major international newspapers: the *New York Times*, British daily the *Guardian* and German weekly *Der Spiegel*. As they had done with me in the case of the audio file on the garbage crisis in Naples, Assange and his staff chose to partner with reporters from those three leading newsrooms and work with them for several weeks, during which time the journalists had exclusive access to the secret files, to verify their authenticity and research the more significant revelations.

Once that work was done, the *New York Times*, the *Guardian* and *Der Spiegel* published their investigations based on the Afghan War Logs, as WikiLeaks made the 76,910 files available on their website. That way, after a period of exclusive access guaranteed to those three news outlets alone, the files could be read and analyzed by anyone.

Assange and his staff called that kind of cooperation a *media partnership*, and the strategy had served its purpose: the entire world had followed those revelations, which had had considerable international impact and been picked up by newspapers, television networks and media in every corner of the globe. By now WikiLeaks was a worldwide phenomenon.

Two things especially struck me about this organization. First of all, its choice to democratize access to knowledge and information by publishing the files for everyone, so that any citizen, any journalist, any researcher, any politician or activist in the world could read about the war in Afghanistan entirely on their own, and could do specific research into it and examine it without relying solely on what the newspapers had written. I found this choice revolutionary, because it meant any reader could access the original sources of the information the media published, any reader could look for the facts of greatest interest to him, could use the files to seek justice in court or even crosscheck the information reported by journalists in their articles: had they written about it accurately, or had they distorted it, exaggerated it, censored it? This democratization process gave power to ordinary readers: no longer passive recipients of whatever the newspapers, televisions or radios reported, for the first time they had direct access to the original sources, greatly diminishing the asymmetry between those who enjoy that privilege, like reporters, and those who do not.

Besides this democratization of information, I was once again amazed by the courage of Julian Assange and WikiLeaks. The U.S. Department of Defense had not only accused WikiLeaks of having put lives at risk, they had also ordered them to completely remove the Afghan War Logs from their website and to return the 15,000 files they had not released yet. "The only acceptable course is for WikiLeaks to take steps to immediately return all versions of all of those documents to the US government and permanently delete them from its website, computers and records," the Pentagon's spokesman, Geoff Morrell, publicly declared. He then added: "If doing the right thing is not good enough for them then we will figure out what alternatives we have to compel them to do the right thing."[21]

This sort of intimidation was not to be taken lightly. With the war on terror, the United States had shown they would stop at nothing, that they would use any means, legal and otherwise, from torture to drone assassinations, against whomever they perceived as a security threat. At the same time, their use of such brazenly brutal methods to neutralize Assange and WikiLeaks was unlikely; WikiLeaks was a Western media organization and by then very much in the public eye. A 2008 file from the Army Counterintelligence Center (ACIC), revealed by WikiLeaks itself, had made clear that the U.S. authorities aimed to crush WikiLeaks by targeting the sources that were sending it secret files, rather than striking WikiLeaks directly.

At any rate, they were threats to be taken very seriously. They sounded grotesque to anyone with even the vaguest notion of the lopsidedness between the Pentagon's power and resources and those of a small organization like WikiLeaks. At any time, the United States Department of Defense could have squashed them

---

21. Sue Pleming, "Pentagon tells WikiLeaks: 'Do right thing'," Reuters, August 5, 2010.

like a fly. But Assange and his staff did not bow down to that kind of intimidation. And they would pay a very high price for it.

THE FOG OF WAR

Two weeks had passed since the Afghan War Logs were published, and the Pentagon's accusations that Julian Assange and WikiLeaks might have put lives at risk were still major news in leading media around the world. Press secretary Geoff Morrell confirmed to the press that he had identified 15,000 files on the Afghanistan war that WikiLeaks had not yet published and which he considered to be extremely sensitive. Morrell also reported that a Pentagon task force made up of 100 intelligence experts[22] was working around the clock to sift through the almost 92,000 files—the 76,910 already published and 15,000 not yet made public—in search of sensitive names, to determine who was at risk. "We have yet to see any harm come to anyone in Afghanistan," Morrell admitted.[23]

Concerned about the publication of those 15,000 reports, a few days later international organizations including Amnesty International and Reporters Sans Frontières stepped in as well and condemned WikiLeaks for having "indiscriminately" published the others. In reality, the Afghan War Logs had not been released indiscriminately. Assange and his organization had worked on them with three leading newspapers. The *Guardian* itself had written:[24] "Most of the material, though classified 'secret' at the time, is no longer militarily sensitive. A small amount of information has been withheld from publication because it might endanger local informants or give away genuine military secrets."

And yet the Pentagon's accusations of "blood on their hands" spread, and the media were quick to suggest that existing divisions inside WikiLeaks were exacerbated by these allegations and that some individuals had left the organization.[25]

---

22. Ellen Nakashima, "Pentagon: undisclosed WikiLeaks documents 'potentially more explosive'," *Washington Post*, August 11, 2010.
23. Ibid.
24. Davies and Leigh, "Afghanistan War Logs: massive leak of secret files exposes truth of occupation."
25. Assange suspended the German spokesman, Daniel Domscheit-Berg.

The files had only been published a few days before, but the media's perceptions had already changed to the point that I found myself, along with U.S. journalist Glenn Greenwald, on Qatar's television network Al Jazeera, forced to address the scathing critiques levied against WikiLeaks. The Pentagon's accusations had so taken hold by then that they were treated as established fact, and virtually all public debate was focused on the actions of Julian Assange and his organization rather than those of the U.S. troops and the Taliban, who actually had killed thousands of innocent civilians.

The secret files had undoubtedly helped clear the fog of war, but not the fog of the Pentagon's propaganda. And in the months to come, that fog would descend over the public debate around WikiLeaks ever more thickly, making it harder and harder to distinguish the facts, in part because something happened that would change Assange's fate forever.

MEETING CONFIRMED

After publishing the Afghan War Logs, WikiLeaks kept a very low profile. They seemed to have disappeared. Then all of a sudden the silence was shattered by news that swept around the world like wildfire: the founder of WikiLeaks was under investigation in Sweden for rape and sexual molestation, and the magistrates had ordered his arrest, after two Swedish women had gone to the police.

The investigation was opened August 20, 2010, not even four weeks after the Afghanistan files were published. The Swedish press reported that after the revelations, Julian Assange had been traveling in the Scandinavian country for a conference on the files and had had sexual intercourse with two women there, of whom only the initials SW and AA were made public, though their full names soon began circulating.

There was not even time to understand what had happened before the arrest warrant was revoked. On August 21, the chief prosecutor of Stockholm, Eva Finné, officially communicated on the website of the judicial authority, the Swedish Prosecution Authority, that the arrest warrant issued the day before had been recalled. "I don't think there is reason to suspect that he has committed rape," the prosecutor wrote, giving no further details, as reported by the BBC.[26]

Four days later, on August 25, she closed the rape investigation entirely, stating that the accused's conduct towards SW did not constitute a crime. However, she did leave open the investigation into the alleged sexual molestation of the other woman, AA. On August 30, 2010, Julian Assange was questioned by the Swedish police about this allegation, and apparently the case was now limited to the crime of sexual molestation. But no: two days later, on September 1, 2010, a different prosecutor, Marianne Ny, re-opened the preliminary investigation into rape, sexual molestation and coercion after Claes Borgström, the legal counsel for the two women, requested a review of the decision to close it.

It was very hard to make sense of the news coming out of Stockholm. The flurry of openings and closings did not help either. But apart from the chaotic succession of news stories emerging from Sweden, there were two other key complications. First, the investigation was in a preliminary stage, so the exact facts were not known because protected by confidentiality, even though the news of the arrest warrant for rape had been leaked to the press in full violation of the privacy of the two women and Assange. Second, this Scandinavian country renowned for its culture of respect for women has a broad definition of what constitutes a sexual offence, so what is considered "rape" in Sweden does not necessarily correspond to the legal definition used in other parts of the world.

I looked on in dismay as the news came out of Stockholm. Despite all my appreciation for Julian Assange's work, rape is an abhorrent crime, if indeed that was what he had done.

I had arranged an appointment with WikiLeaks in Berlin for September 27, 2010, because I was interested in working on the secret files on the war in Afghanistan. I would have tried to use

26. "Swedish rape warrant for WikiLeaks' Assange cancelled," *BBC News*, August 21, 2010.

that occasion to learn more about the Swedish case. But the fact that Assange and his staff did not reply to my repeated messages led me to presume it had all fallen through. One evening, however, they finally materialized: the appointment was confirmed. That was all they said.

ALEXANDERPLATZ

I flew to Berlin and waited all day in a hotel. When it had grown so late I was certain the appointment was off, the telephone rang: it was a call from the reception desk. "It's Julian, can you come down?" I heard. It was night-time, around 11:00 p.m., and the rain and fog outside made leaving the hotel unenticing.

"Look, this is all they gave me at the airport," he told me as soon as I entered the lobby, holding up a small transparent plastic bag containing a white T-shirt, a toothbrush and a few little bottles of soap. He had no other luggage with him, apart from a shoulder bag he was clasping tightly, as if it might be snatched away from him at any moment. I had a hard time recognizing Julian Assange: he had dyed his very white hair a chestnut blond, and it was all plastered to his head by the rain. He looked tired and much thinner than when I had met with him in Brussels only three months before. We sat down in a secluded corner of the lobby, where the lights were rather dim. A boiling mug of tea brought a bit of warmth into that cold hall, where we sat far away from the big glass entrance doors to avoid being easily seen from outside.

He sipped his tea, lost in thought. "To get here I took a direct flight from Stockholm" he told me, "and yet my luggage got lost. Strange." He pulled his computer out of his shoulder bag.

"But what about that?" I asked. "Why would the suitcase with Julian Assange's socks get lost, but not the bag with his computer?" I pressed him skeptically, to dispel some of his paranoia.

"This is with *me* all the time," he replied without hesitation, pointing to his computer. "It can't disappear." The episode of his luggage going missing on a direct flight from Sweden was worrying him, and he feared some "incriminating" material might surface, like images of child pornography. Quite the contrary; despite numerous attempts by Assange and his contacts to recover it, his luggage was never found. Gone for good. There were a number of encrypted computers in his luggage: the encryption had probably protected the information. As he puzzled over what had happened, I began piecing the facts together in my mind too.

He had spent a few weeks in Sweden, then left that country on September 27, flying directly to Berlin to meet with me and other journalists. I had scheduled our appointment one month earlier, on August 25. WikiLeaks had published the 76,910 secret files on Afghanistan four weeks before and the Swedish case had exploded just five days earlier. To organize our meeting, I had used an unencrypted email. It would have been easy for an intelligence service to intercept the content of my message, with plenty of time to prepare a luggage theft. Airports are dangerous places for a journalist traveling with sensitive files. It is extremely easy for intelligence and police forces to make a computer disappear during security checks or after baggage check-in, simulating an ordinary loss. This method of operation is called *plausible deniability*, and is simply the way secret services operate. It enables them to carry out operations and then deny any role in their occurrence, which is attributed to altogether accidental or perfectly plausible causes. What could be more ordinary than an item of luggage getting lost in an airport? It got lost in the confusion, it happens. Is that really what had happened? It was impossible to say, but I used that meeting to agree with Julian Assange on how to protect our communication in the future, because that episode had once again impressed on me the urgent need for encryption.

We had only been talking a short time when the WikiLeaks spokesperson,[27] Kristinn Hrafnsson, arrived. Hrafnsson was an Icelandic investigative journalist who had previously worked for Iceland's public television and who had flown to Baghdad to track down the two Iraqi children wounded by the Apache helicopter. Hrafnsson and Assange embraced each other warmly. Once they

---

27. The German spokesman, Daniel Domscheit-Berg, had been suspended by Julian Assange.

were seated in front of me, I was looking at WikiLeaks' only two public faces, since the names of the other journalists had not been divulged.

It was late by then, and the dimly lit lobby with its soft glow invited a relaxation I could not afford: I needed to stay alert to catch every detail. Assange pulled out a flash drive from underneath his jumper. "I always have this with me too," he said, showing me the thick cord to which it was attached around his neck. He then pulled a small suitcase from his shoulder bag that looked like a child's toy. It contained a multitude of tiny slips of paper, rolled up like *pizzini*, the hand-written instructions used by Sicilian mafia bosses to communicate confidentially without using phones. They were passwords. We began discussing them. My only knowledge of encryption up to that point was theoretical: to earn my degree in mathematics, I had had to study a bit of cryptography too. But it had been precisely my desire to use encryption to protect files and sources that had led me to WikiLeaks, the only news organization in the world at that time that had been founded on the systematic use of encryption.

"How many 'Ns' did you notice?" Assange asked me at one point, as I contemplated a password made up of a very long string of words, letters and special characters. I had only seen one. "Look closer," he told me, with a slightly disappointed air. Actually, there were two "Ns": whoever had created the password had doubled the letter "N" in a word normally spelt with just one, to counter what experts call a "dictionary attack." He then explained that passwords must never be made public, not even after they are obsolete, because it becomes much easier for those trying to break them if they know the criteria used to create them. Talking with Assange was very interesting; we spoke of cryptography and of Afghanistan well into the night. In our conversations, Assange came across as an extremely intelligent person.

The next morning, Hrafnsson, Assange and I set out on foot from the hotel toward Alexanderplatz, where we settled down in a large café. Dingy and practically empty, the premises offered us a secluded room where we could work almost alone, aided by a plentiful supply of coffee and pastries. The founder of WikiLeaks laid two or three mobile phones on the counter which he had kept unassembled until then. He assembled one, which rang immediately. "They want to question me?" he said into the phone in English. "I was in Sweden for six weeks, couldn't they question me before?" After ending the call, he told me the person on the phone was his Swedish lawyer, Björn Hurtig.[28] He spoke to me of the Swedish case without concern, denying the allegations, and I found it hard to ask him specific, critical questions, since there was as yet no factual information on the investigation available with which to challenge his claims.

We focused our attention on the Afghanistan war files. Assange outlined the security conditions for working on the files: from that moment on, I would have to use encryption. I was not allowed to talk on the telephone about the secret files nor write about them in emails. The files must never be sent by electronic mail. For communication with WikiLeaks in regard to the files or any other sensitive matters, I could only use a specific encrypted chat. The files had to remain encrypted, and to work on them I could only use *air-gapped* computers, that is to say computers never connected to the internet, which he told me never to leave unattended, for any reason.

It was the first time I had ever had to comply with such strict work rules. I was not aware of a single journalist, Italian or not, who worked under those kinds of conditions, not even my associates dealing routinely with the mafia or terrorism, and not even, as I later discovered, journalists in the world's leading newsrooms, who were in fact annoyed by WikiLeaks' requirements.

The three of us discussed at length the work to be done on the files and the work already accomplished by the *Guardian*, the *New York Times* and *Der Spiegel*. Hrafnsson drew on his considerable experience as an investigative reporter. A man of few words, he seemed detached and hard to read at first, but in our lengthy con-

---

28. I reported about this phone call in my article: "L'eversore," published in the news magazine I was working for at the time (*L'Espresso*, December 9, 2010), and I also reported it in an affidavit for Julian Assange's defense dated May 5, 2011.

versation he impressed me as a very intelligent man, never arrogant, and with a pleasant manner. We signed a "media partners" agreement: I for *L'Espresso*, they as journalists with WikiLeaks. The objective of our agreement was an in-depth analysis of the Afghan War Logs, which would join those of the *Guardian*, the *New York Times* and *Der Spiegel*, since the war in Afghanistan was not of interest to the U.S., British and German public alone: Italy had almost 4,000 troops mired in that conflict, about which little was known and even less ever reported by the media or discussed in the public sphere.

It was only after the agreements were signed that WikiLeaks gave me access to the 91,910 Afghan War Logs.

I headed for the airport with the encrypted flash drive holding the secret files tucked inside my shoulder bag. As I left Berlin, I gripped it tightly. The light drizzle that was falling lent a bit of melancholy to that adrenaline-filled autumn day. I left the founder of WikiLeaks and its spokesman in that café in Alexanderplatz on September 28, 2010. It was the last time I ever met with Assange as a free man.

"OUR BOYS"

Baggage carts, suitcases, students, servicemen with their rucksacks, children with their plush toys and mini trolleys. The airport echoed with the usual bustle of travelers rushing about. I looked around warily, as watchful as a drug smuggler. I had just left Julian Assange and Kristinn Hrafnsson in Alexanderplatz and was now standing in the queue for international departures at the Berlin airport, en route to Rome. There were 91,910 files in my shoulder bag. I was in a NATO country, a foreign journalist with secret U.S. files which the Pentagon had ordered WikiLeaks to return to them.

I was working at that time for one of the most important Italian media outlets, the weekly *L'Espresso*, and it was unlikely the German authorities would arrest me, but it was not inconceivable that they would stop me and ask me questions, and I didn't want my shoulder bag to end up like Julian Assange's computers. The database was encrypted. Thanks to WikiLeaks, for the first time in my professional life, I and other international journalists were traveling with our materials protected, not immediately accessible to everyone. But if those files got lost or stolen in the airport it would be a very serious matter, which the U.S. authorities would undoubtedly use against all of us. I went through the security checks very carefully, not allowing myself a moment's distraction as I passed my suitcase and shoulder bag through the X-ray scanner, removed my shoes and went through the metal detectors. As I went through the queue, it was as if I had a hundred eyes and ears, so concentrated was I on detecting any abnormal movement around me. Finally, I landed in Rome. I had made it.

At long last, I could decrypt the database and dig for factual information on my country's role in that war, hitherto fought in general indifference and apathy.

Ever since November of 2001, when Italy had arrived in Afghanistan right after September 11, the Italian government's official version had never varied: our troops—"our boys" in the national rhetoric—are there to help the local population and protect them from the Taliban. But the files told another story: that of the real war, the one Italian troops had fought every day from 2004 to 2009, with hundreds of insurgents killed, air raids, IEDs, ambushes, kamikazes, dozens of wounded soldiers, some seriously, some less so, of which nothing had ever been reported in Italy. Mysterious episodes surfaced in the files that were hard to decipher, like an episode involving one of our officials firing against an agent of Kabul's secret services who had somehow blocked one of our missions on the ground.

Another hazy episode involved the transfer to our government of a prisoner who had been in Bagram, an American airbase in Afghanistan notorious for the torture of its prisoners. Thousands of suspected terrorists were detained in that military facility in horrific conditions, with no possibility of anyone obtaining information as to who they were or why they had been captured and imprisoned there. Some had been confined in that hell for years with no right to a lawyer and no chance of journalists investigating and reporting about them, because what happened in the base was shrouded in the utmost secrecy.

Put on board a C130 Hercules aircraft on December 20, 2009 in Bagram airport, the prisoner was described only as ISN 1455, with ISN standing for "Internment Serial Number," the number by which inmates in the custody of the U.S. Department of Defense are identified.[29]

The files did not contain information that might raise concerns of grave violence or abuse on the part of our troops against the local populations. Had there never been any such violence, or was the classification level of those reports not high enough to include them? The files were classified as *secret*, so events may have occurred that had not been recorded in the Afghan War Logs because they could only be recorded in *top-secret* reports.

In any case, one thing did emerge very clearly: how very little the Western troops had achieved in Afghanistan after so many years of war. The documents confirmed, for example, that even after almost a decade the Americans had no trust in the local forces at all, who in many cases had been trained by Italian soldiers.

The reports characterized the great majority of the Afghan police forces in the Herat region, under the control of the Italian troops, as not to be trusted. Many of them left to join the Taliban because they were not paid their salaries, and it was unclear where their salaries had gone. The Afghan policemen supplemented their wages through kidnappings, and reports suggested that the kidnappers and high-level Afghan police officers were complicit.

Another big mystery regarded development funds donated to Afghan authorities by Western governments: where did that money go? The files documented the lack of transparency surrounding the

---

29. Thanks to one of the most important American organizations for human and civil rights, ACLU, which had obtained a list of 645 detainees at Bagram in September 2009, I was able to discover that ISN 001455 corresponded to the name of Moez Bin Abdul Qadir Fezzani, and thanks to the American diplomacy cables revealed by WikiLeaks, I was able to verify that the mysterious prisoner was indeed the Tunisian in question. The list obtained by ACLU is available at the link: www.aclu.org/press-releases/aclu-obtains-list-bagram-detainees. The cable that confirms the detainee's identity is: 09STATE130318_a , dated December 22, 2009.

management of those resources. Among them, for example, were the minutes[30] of a meeting between the finance minister of the Afghan government during Hamid Karzai's presidency and a representative of the NATO mission, ISAF. The meeting had been called to discuss the construction of a road linking the district under Italian control, Herat, with Dowshi, a thoroughfare that would have run through Chaghcharan, a city in the province of Ghor, "the poorest area of Afghanistan." During the meeting, however, an argument had arisen: only 60 per cent of the funds delivered the year before had been spent; what had happened to the rest? The Americans concluded that they would "relook how money is being spent on roads and to insure [*sic*] the roads that are being constructed are in the right areas."[31] Much like what occurs with the local political cliques in Italy, in Afghanistan roads were built not on the basis of real needs, but at the discretion of the local potentates, and public monies disappeared without any real oversight.

I dug into the Afghan War Logs database for days with the help of my editor at *L'Espresso* at the time, Gianluca Di Feo. We ultimately achieved a detailed reconstruction of Italy's participation in the war during the years documented by the files, with a description of the combat operations that had never emerged in Italy before, except in the rare cases when one or more Italian soldiers were killed. It was only on those rare occasions that Afghanistan would appear in the newspapers and televisions for a few days, sparking some fleeting political reaction, only to be engulfed once more in silence.

My editor and I published our investigation in the weekly *L'Espresso*,[32] hoping to finally spark a real public debate, parliamentary inquiries, articles and investigations by Italian media, in part because, just one year before, on September 17, 2009, six "Folgore" paratroopers had been blown to bits in Kabul[33] by

---

30. The original file is available on the WikiLeaks website: https://wardiaries.wikileaks.org/id/84C205D3-D277-4AC9-A3A4-B0A757CF5C19/

31. Ibid.

32. Gianluca Di Feo and Stefania Maurizi, "Afghanistan, ecco la verità," *L'Espresso*, October 15, 2010.

33. "Afghanistan, attacco ai militari italiani: uccisi sei parà della Folgore, quattro feriti," *la Repubblica*, September 17, 2009.

a car bomb loaded with 150 kilograms of explosive, which had also killed around fifteen Afghani civilians, besides wounding four Italian soldiers and around sixty Afghan civilians.

With the Afghan War Logs, we had provided factual data and information to Italian policy makers, media and the public, finally giving them the chance to analyze and discuss that conflict beyond the fog of war and the propaganda of "our boys" going off to do good deeds. But no debate ensued. The silence of politicians and the inability or unwillingness of Italian media to team up, to help exert pressure on the institutions, were truly pathetic. With a country like that, the CIA had no cause for concern: it would never have to scramble to find the propaganda points it had prepared to influence the French and the Germans, in case the politicians, media and public opinion began to question their participation in the war.

I did not let the silence and apathy discourage me, however. A young soldier, Chelsea Manning, had risked everything to get those files out. A small news organization, that of Julian Assange, had shown exceptional courage in publishing them, despite the threats from the Pentagon. I wanted to do my part as well, with my investigative work. I had the opportunity to do research in databases unveiling the darkest corners of our governments, where abuse and atrocities protected by state secrecy take place which journalists are seldom able to prove. I had the chance to let the public know about them, because that was the only way citizens could make informed decisions and exert control over their institutions. I could not let this opportunity slip away from me. I would carry on.

4

The Cypherpunk

A HIGHLY INTELLIGENT INDIVIDUAL

I was impressed by Julian Assange and his organization. I had been trying to learn more about them for a long time, and not only did I scrutinize every interaction I had with them, I also spoke with anyone who had the expertise to comprehend a phenomenon like WikiLeaks. One of the people who helped me make sense of them was the American cryptography expert Bruce Schneier,[1] dubbed by *The Economist* "a security guru."

A few weeks after the Afghan War Logs were published, I asked Schneier how the then-alleged WikiLeaks source Chelsea Manning could have downloaded that deluge of secret files without anyone noticing anything out of the ordinary. Schneier's reply: "Every day, hundreds of thousands of classified documents are consulted and downloaded from the Pentagon networks by the military. Why should anyone notice anything unusual?"[2] He explained to me that following the September 11 attacks, access to secret files had been extended to a very high number of intelligence analysts, troops and contractors, namely individuals in the employ of private companies working for the U.S. government. "One of the factors that led to the tragedy of the Twin Towers," he told me, "was the inability of the various agencies to exchange information to prevent the attack: the CIA didn't talk to the NSA, which in turn did not communicate with the FBI, and so on. After the catastrophe, the decision was made to broaden access and the sharing of confidential files."[3]

---

1. Bruce Schneier's work can be accessed on his website: www.schneier.com/
2. Stefania Maurizi, *Dossier WikiLeaks: Segreti Italiani* (Milano: BUR Rizzoli, 2011).
3. Ibid.

Clearly, expanding the range of individuals who could consult confidential files meant increasing the likelihood of files being leaked. "How can you stop a system like that?" asked Schneier.[4]

As for Julian Assange himself, I gradually obtained scraps of information about him.

I knew he had studied physics and mathematics for a few years at the University of Melbourne, in Australia. That did not surprise me; he definitely showed traits I had often seen in individuals I had known during my years in the faculties of Mathematics and Physics: logical intelligence and an inquisitive mind, unusual behavior that can strike an outsider as bizarre, intense focus on an objective, to the point of forgetting mundane, practical needs— like getting a ticket to catch a train—difficulty in social relations, interest in intellectual work, pursued with an almost obsessive intensity, to the point of neglecting human interaction.

It was not until later that I learned more about his past.

Assange's adolescence had been an unconventional one. Born on July 3, 1971 in Townsville, on the north-eastern coast of Australia, to Christine Hawkins and John Shipton, who were separated, he grew up with his mother, taking the surname of her new husband, Brett Assange, a theatre director. Theatre and art were his mother's primary interests, and she raised him as they moved from one city to another. Their nomadic lifestyle led him to attend dozens of different schools, some even for just one day. The need to travel would stay with him, as would his sense of being a child of the web, with no geolocation: someone who looked at the world globally. It was not by chance that he had created a stateless news organization like WikiLeaks.

You can understand a lot about a person by meeting their parents, or just interacting with them, even from a distance. When I spoke and corresponded with Christine Hawkins and John Shipton in later years, I observed that Julian Assange had the logical mind of his father and the anti-authoritarianism and independence of his mother.

---

4. Ibid.

Concerned that her son's intelligence and spirit would be ruined by the public school system, Christine encouraged an informal education marked by critical thinking.[5] It was his books and Commodore 64 computer that fueled Assange's mind, not traditional studies.

At 18 years of age he was already the father of a child, Daniel. At 25, he was found guilty of hacking into the Canadian telecommunications corporation, Nortel. The sentence[6] handed down by judge Leslie Ross of the Victoria County Court in Melbourne was a fairly mild reprimand. "Julian Paul Assange, you have pleaded guilty to 24 counts of offences against the Crimes Act of the Commonwealth," reads the sentence, which adds: "the information that you gained and the interference that you caused to various of the computer networks that you accessed did not produce any personal gain. There is no evidence that anything other than your interest in the computer, your desire to access this material to empower you, as it were, to access this particular material was the stimulus to behave as you did."

The judge continued: "Were this exercise embarked upon for the purposes of personal gain, then I would have thought, notwithstanding the matters that go in mitigation, a gaol sentence would have been the only option. You are aware that the more serious of these offences attracts a maximum penalty of ten years' imprisonment."

What were the mitigating factors recognized by Judge Ross? That Assange had acted out of a desire for intellectual knowledge, without motive of financial gain, that he had fully cooperated with the investigation, and even his personal background: "I accept what your counsel said about the unstable personal background that you have had to endure during your formative years and the rather nomadic existence that your mother and yourself were forced to follow and also the personal disruption that occurred within your household." The judge concluded: "That could not have been easy for you. It has had its impact on you obtaining formal educational

---

5. Christine Assange, email to author, February 9, 2019.
6. *The Queen vs. Julian Paul Assange*, ruling by Judge Ross, December 5, 1996.

qualifications which it seems were certainly not beyond you and the submission that you are a highly intelligent individual seems to be well founded [...] These are offences that could only have been committed by intelligent individuals." The relatively lenient sentence was a 2,100 Australian dollars fine.

I learned from the legal documents filed in the Victoria County Court of Melbourne that in 1993, when he was 22 years old, Assange had provided technical assistance to the Australian police unit in charge of fighting online child pornography, the Victoria Police Child Exploitation Unit. He used his computer skills to identify pedophiles publishing and distributing their material on the internet. "Mr Assange's participation was concluded in the mid-nineties," read the documents, "his technical expertise was of value to investigations. Mr Assange received no personal benefit from his contribution, and was pleased to be in a position to assist."[7]

The Cryptome website also proved fundamental in my quest to understand where Julian Assange had come from. Founded by the American John Young in 1996, ten years before WikiLeaks was created, Cryptome was the first to begin routinely releasing confidential or otherwise restricted documents. In those months of 2010 when WikiLeaks' fame was exploding, I tried to contact Young to get his perspective, but my attempts ran up against his considerable wariness.

Cryptome served as an online archive, where Young published files without partnering with traditional media first, as the WikiLeaks organization would instead do systematically and with large teams from the Afghan War Logs onward, so that its media partners could work on investigating the files and confirming their authenticity alongside WikiLeaks. As far as I could tell as an outside observer, Cryptome worked alone, and it was never clear to me how they went about authenticating files. In the case of WikiLeaks, we media partners would carry out further, independent controls before publication. At any rate, Assange told me in our conversations at that time that he believed John Young had done "heroic work."

---

7. County Court of Victoria, Revocation of Prohibition Order, February 11, 2011.

A few weeks after the *Collateral Murder* video was published, Cryptome released the content of Cypherpunk's mailing list.[8] Those email exchanges offered up a portrait of the cultural landscape that had played so large a part in producing the founder of WikiLeaks.

VISIONARIES AND LIBERTARIANS

In the 1990s, Julian Assange was one of them. Visionaries and libertarians, the Cypherpunks included mathematicians like Eric Hughes of the University of California at Berkeley, who had written *A Cypherpunk's manifesto*, and physicist Timothy May, who had worked for the microchip giant Intel. May's solution to a major technical problem had netted him such wealth that he was able to retire at the age of 34, after calculating that he would never have to work again.

There was John Gilmore, who had been employee number five at the software giant Sun Microsystems, and who at less than 30 years of age had also earned enough to go into retirement[9] and devote himself to his personal interests, among them digital rights. Gilmore helped found the Electronic Frontier Foundation (EFF), the influential American organization that would later take WikiLeaks' side in the Julius Baer Swiss bank case.

There was Esther Dyson, an expert in digital technologies and head of the EFF at the time, and John Young, the founder of Cryptome, along with young computer talents like Julian Assange, active in the mailing list since 1995, when he was only 24 years old and the U.S. government's inquiry into Philip Zimmermann and his PGP was fueling the cryptography debate.

All of the Cypherpunks were united by one overriding interest: the impact of surveillance, and the development of tools to defend personal privacy and anonymity, including anonymous payment systems to shield the individual from the absolute control of

---

8. The Cypherpunks mailing list's content is available on the Cryptome website: https://cryptome.org/0001/assange-cpunks.htm (accessed January 17, 2022).
9. John Gilmore, email to author, February 18, 2021.

the state. As explained by Eric Hughes in his "A Cypherpunk's manifesto":[10] "Privacy is necessary for an open society in the electronic age. Privacy is not secrecy. A private matter is something one doesn't want the whole world to know, but a secret matter is something one doesn't want anybody to know. Privacy is the power to selectively reveal oneself to the world." He continues: "When I purchase a magazine at a store and hand cash to the clerk, there is no need to know who I am. [...] When my identity is revealed by the underlying mechanism of the transaction, I have no privacy. I cannot here selectively reveal myself; I must *always* reveal myself. Therefore, privacy in an open society requires anonymous transaction systems. Until now, cash has been the primary such system. An anonymous transaction system is not a secret transaction system. An anonymous system empowers individuals to reveal their identity when desired and only when desired; this is the essence of privacy."

The Cypherpunks were anti-authoritarian, but their political views varied. Timothy May, for example, was a right-leaning anarchist, who did not accept any state interference whatsoever in political, social and economic life and defended a form of capitalism devoid of institutional intervention. Tim May himself had authored one of the more provocative documents, "The Crypto Anarchist manifesto,"[11] whose opening paraphrased *The manifesto of the Communist Party* by Karl Marx and Friedrich Engels: "A specter is haunting the modern world, the specter of crypto anarchy. Computer technology is on the verge of providing the ability for individuals and groups to communicate and interact with each other in a totally anonymous manner. Two persons may exchange messages, conduct business, and negotiate electronic contracts without ever knowing the True Name, or legal identity, of the other."

---

10. "A Cypherpunk's manifesto": www.activism.net/cypherpunk/manifesto.html (accessed January 17, 2022).
11. "The Crypto Anarchist manifesto": https://groups.csail.mit.edu/mac/classes/6.805/articles/crypto/cypherpunks/may-crypto-manifesto.html (accessed January 17, 2022).

May continued: "The State will of course try to slow or halt the spread of this technology, citing national security concerns, use of the technology by drug dealers and tax evaders, and fears of societal disintegration. Many of these concerns will be valid; crypto anarchy will allow national secrets to be trade [*sic*] freely and will allow illicit and stolen materials to be traded. An anonymous computerized market will even make possible abhorrent markets for assassinations and extortion. Various criminal and foreign elements will be active users of CryptoNet. But this will not halt the spread of crypto anarchy."

When I asked Philip Zimmermann what he thought of "The Crypto Anarchist manifesto," he told me he did not believe the crypto anarchy was a plausible prospect: it was a dystopia.[12] And I would later understand that Tim May's dystopia was not Julian Assange's vision of cryptography: he did not want to use it to make drug dealers, tax evaders or assassins unaccountable; he wanted to use it to make state criminals accountable. At any rate, these were the kinds of incitements, news and analysis on the impact of encryption, anonymity and anonymous payment systems fueling the discussions in the Cypherpunks mailing list. It is a debate in which the young Assange participated intensely from 1995 to 2002, when he had yet to create WikiLeaks, which would not be founded until October 4, 2006.

In the discussions hosted by that mailing list, Assange emerged as an unbending libertarian as far as digital rights, like anonymity and encryption, are concerned, but not as a champion of unbridled capitalism like the American libertarians.[13]

In one post, for example, a Cypherpunk by the name of Declan wrote: "One can admit that globalization has ill effects [...] But when responding to claims that factory workers in poorer countries are only being paid $2/hour or whatnot, it makes sense to

---

12. Philip Zimmermann, email to author, June 24, 2011.
13. Robert Manne: "The Cypherpunk revolutionary," *The Monthly*, March 2011: www.themonthly.com.au/issue/2011/february/1324596189/robert-manne/cypherpunk-revolutionary#mtr (accessed January 17, 2022).

ask: Is this worse than their other alternatives, like mud huts in villages?"

Julian Assange's reply: "You don't need a Nobel to realise that the relationship between a large employer and employee is brutally assymetric [*sic*]. One entity knows far more about the rules of the negotiation than the other. There's you as a prospective employee and then there's the local workplace monopoly with hundreds of industrial relations lawyers, psychologists, and other assorted strategists who'll hand you a document thick with legalese and tell you where to sign. Without a legal team, you'll never understand it or the political connections backing it up. And even if you do there's a million other mugs to choose from who won't. To counter this sort of assymetry [*sic*]. Employees naturally start trying to collectivise to increase their information processing and bargaining power. That's right. UNIONS Declan. Those devious entities that first world companies and governments have had a hand in suppressing all over the third world by curtailing freedom of association, speech and other basic political rights we take for granted."

So wrote Assange in October 2001, when he was 30 years old. Politically, that is what he was and what he still is. Anti-war, and a staunch libertarian as far as the individual's right to protect himself from total state surveillance and control are concerned, but not in favor of an unregulated marketplace.

Lastly, the Cypherpunks mailing list highlighted Assange's work on an encryption program called Rubberhose, which he had begun developing in 1997 when he was 26 years old, together with Suelette Dreyfus—a clever Australian researcher with the University of Melbourne, a technology expert and enthusiast[14] who had known Assange since he was very young.

Rubberhose was designed to protect human rights activists and journalists working in authoritarian societies or otherwise hostile settings in the event of their being stopped and searched for incriminating information.

---

14. In partnership with Suelette Dreyfus, Julian Assange authored *Underground: Tales of hacking, madness, and obsession on the electronic frontier* (Kew (Australia), Mandarin, 1997).

The idea behind project Rubberhose was to hide that information in encrypted archives which would be hard to detect, so that if the reporters or activists were threatened with violence—as evoked by the term "rubberhose"—they could plausibly deny having it with them.

Rubberhose was never widely disseminated, but the determination to protect sources in possession of sensitive documents would become central to all of WikiLeaks' work. "We believe that transparency in government activities leads to reduced corruption, better government, and stronger democracies," read the organization's site a few months after its inception.[15] "All governments can benefit from increased scrutiny by the world community, as well as their own people. We believe this scrutiny requires information," WikiLeaks's website continued. "Historically that information has been costly—in terms of human life and human rights. But with technological advances—the Internet, and cryptography—the risks of conveying important information can be lowered."

This was precisely the risk Chelsea Manning had faced in revealing secret files like *Collateral Murder* or the files on the war in Afghanistan. And in those days of October 2010, when I had just published the revelations on Italy's role in the Afghan conflict, I could not know how high a price Chelsea Manning would ultimately have to pay, but I did know that thanks to her exceptional courage, new files of crucial importance would soon be revealed.

---

15.   Quoted from the ACIC document mentioned in chapter 1: "Wikileaks.org—an online reference to foreign intelligence services, insurgents, or terrorist groups?" See: https://file.wikileaks.org/file/us-intel-wikileaks.pdf (accessed May 19, 2022).

5

A Database from Hell:
The Iraq War Logs

THE WORD "DEMOCRACY" ONLY EIGHT TIMES

Not even a month had passed since my meeting with Julian Assange and Kristinn Hrafnsson in Alexanderplatz when WikiLeaks again released files of extraordinary journalistic value: on October 22, 2010, they published 391,832 secret files on the war in Iraq. Like those on Afghanistan, the Iraq War Logs[1] were reports from the battlefield written by American troops, concisely relaying each significant event (SigAct) as it took place in the Iraqi war theater, generally in clipped military jargon full of abbreviations. The reports spanned a period from January 1, 2004 to December 31, 2009, and made it possible to chronicle six years of that conflict through factual reports which, like so many Polaroids, each furnished a snapshot of what had happened in a specific place (latitude and longitude), on a specific day, at a specific time— attacks sustained and undertaken, IEDs, prisoners, dead, wounded, kidnappings, reports and warnings received by the troops from the local population.

The Iraq war is a perfect example of the manipulation of intelligence in pursuit of a political goal. The United States invaded the country on March 20, 2003 on the basis of completely false information, according to which Saddam Hussein's regime possessed weapons of mass destruction and had ties with al-Qaeda. This was a complete fabrication on the part of the George W. Bush administration, in league with the British government of Tony Blair, to

---

1. The 391,832 Iraq War Logs are accessible on the WikiLeaks website: https://wardiaries.wikileaks.org/ (accessed January 19, 2022).

justify the invasion. But their falsified intelligence would have achieved its purpose much less easily if the U.S. media had done its job and treated the secret services and their political bosses with skepticism.

Actually, some media organizations tried to do just that: the newspapers of U.S. publishing company McClatchy, for example, published a series of scoops exposing the Bush administration's falsehoods on the weapons of mass destruction.[2] The *New York Times*, in the meantime, went along with the deception.

Certain reporters with the *New York Times*,[3] it would later turn out, had tried to express doubts after their sources in the U.S. intelligence community had confided their misgivings, but those journalists failed to change the editorial stance of their newspaper. Julian Assange expressed his conviction to me on more than one occasion that if only WikiLeaks had existed before the war in Iraq, then sources with documents exposing the Bush administration's deceit would have had the chance to publish them and force them into the international debate, thanks to WikiLeaks' capacity to make maximum impact with its publications. He also felt that if WikiLeaks had already been active in the very first stages of the Iraq conflict, and had immediately been able to obtain and publish files like *Collateral Murder*, the war would have ended sooner.

Would it really have gone that way? It is hard to say, but WikiLeaks would have at least given the sources possessing evidence of the Bush administration's lies a chance to share their doubts with the global public.

2. "John Walcott receives first I.F. Stone medal for journalistic independence for pre-Iraq War coverage," *Nieman News*, July 23, 2008: https://nieman.harvard.edu/news/2008/07/john-walcott-receives-first-i-f-stone-medal-for-journalistic-independence-for-pre-iraq-war-coverage/ (accessed January 19, 2022).

3. For an inside account of how the *New York Times* helped spread the falsehoods that led to the Iraq war, it is important to read the reconstruction of the Pulitzer Prize winner James Risen, whose reporting set him on a collision course with his newspaper, which he ultimately left. James Risen, "The biggest secret: my life as a New York Times reporter in the shadow of the War on Terror," *The Intercept*, January 3, 2018. For a critique of the role of the American media in building consensus for the Iraq war, see Matt Taibbi, "16 years later, how the press that sold the Iraq war got away with it," *Rolling Stone*, March 22, 2019.

Assange's organization did not exist at the time, however, and the *New York Times* was of tremendous help to Bush and his hawks in supporting their lies. The *New York Times* not only was (and is) the most influential newspaper in the world, it was also politically opposed to the Bush administration, which helped make the untrue claims about the weapons of mass destruction more credible, "corroborated" as they were by an authoritative yet politically hostile newspaper.

The combination of false intelligence and media propaganda produced a war from which the Middle East has yet to recover, not only because it resulted in millions of deaths and refugees, but because it helped generate the barbarities of ISIS, which arose precisely in the Iraqi territories awash with the chaos and violence triggered by the U.S. invasion. From there, its fanatics have struck into Europe and as far as Afghanistan, in a crescendo of beheadings, suicide attacks, crucifixions and mass rapes even more brutal—if possible—than those of al-Qaeda.

The invasion of Iraq began on March 20, 2003, under the name "Operation Iraqi Freedom," and for a superpower like the United States, overthrowing Saddam Hussein's regime was a piece of cake. George W. Bush declared "mission accomplished" on May 1, 2003, and Hussein was captured approximately seven months later. The dictator would be hanged on December 30, 2006, accused of crimes against humanity, including the use of chemical weapons against the Kurdish people of Halabja in northern Iraq in 1988, killing approximately 5,000.

Once Saddam Hussein was overthrown, the country did not in the least take the path foretold by U.S. propaganda, which affirmed that the Iraqis would be grateful to the Americans for liberating them from their dictator and live peacefully in a democratic country at last. In reality, Iraq spiraled into indiscriminate violence from which it has never recovered. The population, overwhelmingly Muslim but divided between Shias and Sunnis,[4] collapsed into sectarian violence.

---

4. The religious schism between Shia and Sunni Muslims dates back fourteen centuries, stemming from a dispute as to who should lead the community after the

The Sunnis were the minority, but had dominated the nation until then under the brutal leadership of Saddam Hussein. Once the dictator fell, Iraq plunged into chaos: Sunnis against Shias, U.S. contractors against the Iraqi population, local militias against the American invader, al-Qaeda against everyone.

The Iraq War Logs detail that inferno day by day. As the weekly *Der Spiegel*[5] immediately commented on the files: "It is neither America's opponents, nor its skeptical allies nor the oppositional media who have compiled these documents describing just how disastrous Operation Iraqi Freedom really was. It was the very people who ousted Saddam."

Many of the reports allow us to retrace, hour by hour, in the course of the same day, armored vehicles blown up by IEDs, women and children decapitated, foreigners kidnapped, contractors shooting with no idea who they are killing, U.S. troops killing men, women and children at checkpoints. An endless cycle of barbarity. It takes a thick skin to read the Iraq War Logs, with their endlessly described horrors.

November 3, 2007, 16:46:00. An Iraqi national reports that "AQI [al-Qaeda in Iraq] came to her house and cut off her babies [*sic*]," reads one of the classified files,[6] which concludes: "Confirms baby is decapitated."

Also appalling are files on the abuse and torture of detainees, sometimes at the hands of the Americans, but mostly by Iraqi forces. There are 1,088 such reports in the database.

December 3, 2008, 11:00:00. A report describes a detainee who died in custody from kidney failure, noting: "There was evidence of some type of unknown surgical procedure on his abdomen [...].

---

death of the Prophet Muhammad in 632. Today, the vast majority of Islam's 1.5 billion adherents are Sunnis, but Iran is Shia and competes for regional dominance with Saudi Arabia, which practices an extremely rigid form of Sunni Islam: Wahhabism.
5.   H. Hoing, C. Meyer, J. Von Mittelstaedt, F. Ott, M. Rosenbach, G.P. Schmitz, H. Stark, "The Iraq War Logs: a protocol of barbarity," *Der Spiegel*, October 25, 2010.
6.   The file is available in a redacted form on the WikiLeaks website: https://wardiaries.wikileaks.org/id/0691646F-0D1C-F0D1-0364DF9D4FFD9438/ (accessed January 19, 2022); the file was originally reported in: Hoing et al., "The Iraq War Logs: a protocol of barbarity."

There was also evidence of bruises on the face, chest, ankle, and back of the body."[7]

In another file, U.S. troops describe the treatment of a prisoner by Iraqi forces who had arrested him at a checkpoint:[8] "[The victim] claims that during the interrogation he was beaten on his hands with a wooded [*sic*] /metal stick, hit with cables and insulted. [The victim] states he was told to lay down on his stomach with his hands behind his back, which is when the Iraqi soldiers allegedly stepped, jumped, urinated, and spit on him. [He] also claims that he was slapped, and hit with a cable. [He] also states he was electrically shocked. He claims this went on for approximately eight hours and repeated two more times."

The report proceeded to explain that the detainee was taken to hospital with injuries that included: "Blurred vision, diminished hearing in left ear, bleeding in ears, bruising on forehead, neck, chest, back, shoulders, arms, hands, and thighs, cuts over the left eye and on the upper and lower lips, hemorrhaging eyes, blood in nasal cavities, and swollen hands/wrists." The report concluded: "Due to no allegation or evidence of US involvement, a US investigation is not being initiated."

It was the Iraq war that begat the atrocities against inmates that would become symbolic of the cruelty of the war on terror: Abu Ghraib. This infamous prison, previously used by Saddam Hussein to imprison and torture his opponents, immediately became the epicenter of the horrors. Saddam's torturers were replaced by American and Iraqi torturers. When WikiLeaks published the Iraq War Logs in October of 2010, the scandal of Abu Ghraib had already been unveiled a full six years earlier[9] by the great inves-

---

7. The file is available in a redacted form on the WikiLeaks website: https://wardiaries.wikileaks.org/id/FC615C05-E517-5C89-78B2CF941B76EDE4/ (accessed January 19, 2022); the file was originally reported in: Nick Davies, Jonathan Steele and David Leigh, "Iraq War Logs: secret files show how US ignored torture," *Guardian*, October 22, 2010.
8. The file is available in a redacted form on the WikiLeaks website: https://wardiaries.wikileaks.org/id/EF414A9C-3EAA-4A7D-8E3B-3D9BAAE09C7E/ (accessed January 19, 2022).
9. Seymour Hersh, "Torture at Abu Ghraib," *New Yorker*, April 30, 2004. The CBS American television station also revealed some of the photos of torture at Abu Ghraib.

tigative reporter Seymour Hersh. But the files provided factual documentation on the torture archipelago and how the United States had tolerated and ignored it.

The invasion, sold by the Bush administration to the public as a war to free Iraq's population from a brutal dictator and create a democratic society that would stand as an example in the Middle East, was revealed as an utter failure in the snapshots taken by the U.S. troops themselves. As German weekly *Der Spiegel*, immediately noted:[10] "In the roughly 400,000 documents, the word 'democracy' appears only eight times. The 'improvised explosive devices' [IEDs] which instilled fear in the hearts of American soldiers, however, are mentioned 146,895 times."

It is only thanks to the Iraq War Logs that a respected organization of researchers, the Iraq Body Count, co-founded by Hamit Dardagan and John Sloboda,[11] was able to confirm the deaths of 15,000 civilian victims of the Iraq war that had never surfaced before. It may seem like merely a statistical matter, but these were fathers, mothers, children. And it took the tenacious work of the Iraq Body Count researchers, like Josh Dougherty, to unearth these previously unknown deaths.[12] Ten years after their publication, the Iraq War Logs remain the only source for a meticulous reconstruction of those deaths.

Iraq Body Count determined that between March 2003 and October 2020, the number of innocent civilians killed in Iraq was between 185,395 and 208,419: these figures represent the victims of direct violence only, and do not include those who died from indirect consequences, such as the collapse of hospitals and healthcare due to the conflict.[13] When the latter are included, the count climbs to around 600,000 victims,[14] although it is impossible to obtain reliable data on such deaths. They are only estimates,

---

10. Hoing et al., "The Iraq War Logs: a protocol of barbarity."
11. Iraq Body Count project: www.iraqbodycount.org/about/ (accessed January 24, 2022).
12. Hamit Dardagan, communication to author, May 20, 2022.
13. Hamit Dardagan, cofounder of Iraq Body Count, email to author, November 17, 2020.
14. Philip Bump, "15 years after the Iraq War began, the death toll is still murky," *Washington Post*, March 20, 2018.

whereas the number of civilian victims registered by Iraq Body Count is an actual tally of verifiable deaths. The war forced 9.2 million Iraqis—that is, 37 per cent of Iraq's population before the U.S. invasion—to flee their homes and seek refuge abroad or be displaced to other areas within their country.[15]

The Iraq War Logs, like the *Collateral Murder* video and the files on Afghanistan, were one of the secret databases that Chelsea Manning found the courage to download from the U.S. Department of Defense networks and hand over to WikiLeaks.

Their publication sparked a fierce reaction from the Pentagon, as had already occurred with the Afghanistan files. "We deplore WikiLeaks for inducing individuals to break the law, leak classified documents and then cavalierly share that secret information with the world, including our enemies," the Pentagon immediately declared,[16] adding: "The only responsible course of action for WikiLeaks at this point is to return the stolen material and expunge it from their Web sites as soon as possible."

But once again, Julian Assange and his organization did not comply. And soon, in addition to the Pentagon, they would also have the *New York Times* on their backs.

LIKE AN ACID THAT CORRODES

A shifty character, who roamed the world like a fugitive from justice, dying his hair, sleeping under false names in hotels, using expensive encrypted telephones, shunning credit cards in favor of cash. A man with an imperious manner who was alienating his own organization and who had become embroiled in a rape and sexual molestation case in Sweden. But most of all, a man who had no qualms about putting other people's lives in danger, casually publishing secret files.

---

15. D. Vine, C. Coffman, K. Khoury, M. Lovasz, H. Bush, R. Leduc, J. Walkup, "Creating refugees: displacement caused by the US post-9/11 wars," Costs of War Project, Brown University, September 21, 2020: https://watson.brown.edu/costsofwar/files/cow/imce/papers/2020/Displacement_Vine%20et%20al_Costs%20of%20War%202020%2009%2008.pdf (accessed January 25, 2022).
16. "The Defense Department's response," *New York Times*, October 22, 2010.

That was how the *New York Times* described Julian Assange, in a long article[17] that came out exactly one day after the Iraq War Logs were released.

Scarcely three months had passed since WikiLeaks' publication of the 76,910 files on Afghanistan had made it a global sensation, and since the German weekly *Der Spiegel* had published the interview with Assange explaining what had motivated him to use his talent not to found a company in Silicon Valley and make money, but to do the WikiLeaks project. "I enjoy helping people who are vulnerable. And I enjoy crushing bastards," he had told *Der Spiegel.*[18]

But now the intellectually gifted 39-year-old[19] anti-authoritarian, who traveled around the world with little more than a backpack and a computer, was being portrayed by the most powerful newspaper in the world as a capricious eccentric who recklessly endangered the lives of others. Were these dangers real or not?

The files on the wars in Iraq and Afghanistan were published in partnership with the *New York Times*, the *Guardian* and *Der Spiegel* and, in the case of the Iraq logs, with the Bureau of Investigative Journalism news organization headquartered in London also. Each of these media organizations helped determine what information to redact. WikiLeaks also set aside 15,000 files on Afghanistan containing some sensitive names. As with the Iraq War Logs, they were so heavily edited[20] that even names that had already been in the news for years, like Blackwater—the company of mercenaries who carried out the Nisour Square massacre in Baghdad in 2007—had been removed.

---

17.   John F. Burns and Ravi Somaiya, "WikiLeaks founder on the run, trailed by notoriety," *New York Times*, October 23, 2010.
18.   John Goetz and Marcel Rosenbach, "I enjoy crushing bastards," *Der Spiegel*, July 26, 2010.
19.   Julian Assange was born July 3, 1971.
20.   The Iraq Body Count cofounder would later testify at Assange's extradition hearing in London about the crucial importance of the Iraq Wars Logs and about Iraq Body Count's contribution to redacting them. Witness Statement of John Sloboda, dated July 17, 2020, submitted before the Westminster Magistrates' Court.

All the precautions taken, the unprecedented security measures, the painstaking journalistic work made it highly unlikely that there was any risk to the sources mentioned in the files.

One thing was already very clear, however. After only three months, the *New York Times* was shaping public opinion along the lines of Pentagon allegations that Assange and WikiLeaks had acted recklessly. But there was one voice in the *Times* article that rose in defense of Julian Assange. It was that of Daniel Ellsberg, the legendary American whistleblower who, in 1971, had risked his neck to bring out the Pentagon Papers, a 7,000-page Pentagon report revealing the U.S. government's falsehoods on the war in Vietnam. Ellsberg said he felt a spiritual kinship with Julian Assange and Chelsea Manning. "They were willing to go to prison for life, or be executed, to put out this information," he told the *New York Times*, confessing: "I've been waiting 40 years for someone to disclose information on a scale that might really make a difference."

Since 1971, Daniel Ellsberg has been an icon of the citizen possessed of exceptional moral courage. To avoid being complicit in a war like Vietnam—which cost 3 million lives—he risked everything to copy the thousands of pages, one by one, using a simple photocopier typical of those years, in secret, at night.[21]

Ellsberg, who was a military analyst and had helped draft the Pentagon Papers, handed all of those top-secret documents over to the American press in order to blow the case open, so the public could finally have proof that the U.S. authorities had lied to their citizens and sent thousands of young men to die in a war they knew perfectly well could not be won, and that would ultimately cost the Vietnamese people millions of lives.

To reveal the Pentagon Papers, not only did Ellsberg have to risk his life and liberty because the files were top-secret, but the *New York Times* and the *Washington Post* had to wage a legal battle all the way to the Supreme Court of the United States, because

---

21. Niraj Chokshi, "Behind the race to publish the top-secret Pentagon Papers," *New York Times*, December 20, 2017.

Richard Nixon's administration tried to block their publication on the grounds that the documents were classified.

Since then, Daniel Ellsberg and the Pentagon Papers have become a symbol of moral integrity and freedom of the press. For Julian Assange and Chelsea Manning, then, there could not have been a more authoritative or admired supporter than Daniel Ellsberg. And yet his defense of Assange and Manning was completely watered down in the *New York Times* article, which conveyed an altogether different message.

In the portrait published by the most influential daily in the world, the founder of WikiLeaks emerged at best as a controversial figure, at times suspicious, if not downright sinister. It was only the beginning of a long media campaign which from 2010 until recently has greatly contributed to alienating the support of public opinion, always the most important shield for those who, like Assange and the WikiLeaks journalists, had (and have) some of the most powerful institutions in the world, like the Pentagon, aligned against them.

It was perfectly legitimate to raise questions about potential risks to the civilians cited in the Iraq and Afghanistan files. But the *New York Times* did not appear to take any note whatsoever of the hard work WikiLeaks had done to protect the sources mentioned in the files. And paradoxically, from that far-off 2010 up until today, all media scrutiny would focus on the figure of Assange and his organization, rather than on the culpability of those who had decimated, tortured and destroyed entire nations.

Like an acid that slowly corrodes even the shiniest metals, so the accusation of putting human lives at risk—leveled by the Pentagon with no proof whatsoever—would be taken up and repeated without question for over a decade, helping to tarnish WikiLeaks' reputation. And it is not hard to imagine how much this must have pleased the Pentagon.

6

Cablegate: Rattling Power
at the Highest Levels

CRIMES, SCANDALS AND POLITICAL PRESSURE

It was one of the biggest scoops in the history of journalism. It rocked the White House and the whole of world politics, from U.S. President Barack Obama and then-Russian Prime Minister Vladimir Putin all the way down to U.S. opinion makers, who went so far as to suggest that extreme measures be taken against Julian Assange, even to "illegally shoot the son of a bitch."[1] On November 28, 2010, just one month after publishing the Iraq War Logs, WikiLeaks began publishing 251,287 U.S. diplomatic cables, in partnership—albeit in some cases a tormented one—with five major international media outlets: the *New York Times*, the *Guardian*, *Der Spiegel*, the French daily *Le Monde* and the Spanish *El País*.

It was the beginning of "Cablegate," so-named in memory of Watergate, the scandal that ultimately led to the 1974 resignation of U.S. President Richard Nixon and that was set in motion by events ensuing from an earlier massive "leak":[2] the Pentagon Papers. After Daniel Ellsberg leaked the documents, Nixon created a special unit of operatives, called "Plumbers," who were supposed to plug the leaks of confidential information that were undermining his administration. The Plumbers first snuck into Ellsberg's psychiatrist's office in search of secrets that they might

1. Huffington Post Staff, "Fox News' Bob Beckel calls for 'illegally' killing Assange: 'a dead man can't leak stuff'," *Huffington Post*, December 7, 2010.
2. As I have already explained, the term "leak" explicitly refers to the release of unauthorized disclosures, hence the name "WikiLeaks."

use to blackmail him into silence,[3] but later went so far as to break into the headquarters of the Democratic Party, based in a building at the Watergate complex in Washington, DC.

Unlike the Pentagon Papers, the cables released by WikiLeaks were not top-secret files; their highest classification level was *secret/noforn*, that is to say, secret and not releasable to any non-U.S. citizen.[4] They consisted of correspondence, sent by 260 U.S. embassies and consulates in 180 different countries, to the Department of State in Washington, the U.S. government body in charge of foreign policy and international relations. In those files, the ambassadors and consulates assigned to each of the 180 countries reported on the most important affairs under way in the relevant country: internal and foreign policy, military issues, organized crime, international trade agreements. The files dated from the end of 2001 to February 2010.

Cables typically remain classified for decades, and usually thirty, forty years or even more go by before their confidentiality lapses, by which point the facts they reveal date so far back in time as to be of interest only to professional historians. But now, for the first time in history, thanks to WikiLeaks and its source, Chelsea Manning, those secrets could be breached and that extremely topical correspondence could be read by all—unveiling state criminality, scandals, and political pressure in every nation in the world. The names of individuals in foreign governments passing on confidential information to U.S. diplomats, diplomats' opinions on politicians from 180 countries, on religious leaders, on the behind-the-scenes in the Vatican under the leadership of two popes, John Paul II and Benedict XVI.

The cables did not impart the absolute truth; they relayed the world through the eyes of U.S. diplomacy. And they did so in a very candid manner. In the secrecy of their correspondence, the diplomats were not in the least diplomatic. At times they were

3. "The Watergate story: timeline," *Washington Post*: www.washingtonpost.com/wp-srv/politics/special/watergate/timeline.html (accessed March 7, 2022); Niraj Chokshi, "Behind the race to publish the top-secret Pentagon Papers," *New York Times*, December 20, 2017.
4. The acronym NOFORN stands for "Not Releasable to Foreign Nationals."

forthright in the extreme, in many cases even Machiavellian, writing as they were in the certainty that their analyses and views would not become public until many decades had passed, when they could no longer embarrass anyone.

The 251,287 files constituted an immense reservoir of information, organized in a way that allowed searching them by keyword. It was a bit like being able to question the magic mirror in the fairy-tale about the secrets of the kingdom. What did the United States really think about Vladimir Putin? What kind of pressure did they use to secure the support of U.S. allies in Afghanistan? What did they really think of Silvio Berlusconi, official declarations aside? And how did they negotiate with the Vatican, in the inner sanctum of diplomacy? And so on … Cuba, Iran, China, Guantánamo, the drone war.

Some of the most interesting revelations were those regarding Russia, which the U.S. diplomats depicted, from their viewpoint of course, very bleakly, referring not only to allegations of serious corruption, but also the analyses of Spanish anti-mafia prosecutor José Grinda González, who described Russia, Belarus and Chechnya as countries virtually in the hands of the mafia. "For each of those countries," he alleged, "one cannot differentiate between the activities of the government and OC [organized crime] groups," adding that Ukraine was going to be another such country.

The Spanish prosecutor, whom the U.S. diplomats considered "a skilled and rigorous professional with deep subject matter expertise," had gone so far as to tell the Americans he agreed with the "thesis" of Aleksandr Litvinenko, the former Russian spy poisoned in London in 2006 with a dose of polonium.

According to Litvinenko, security services like the FSB (Federal Security Service), heir to the KGB, as well as the military intelligence agency, the GRU, and the foreign intelligence service SVR, "control OC in Russia." Going by the cables, the Spanish prosecutor had concluded: "the GOR's [government of Russia's] strategy is to use OC groups to do whatever the GOR cannot acceptably do as a government." These were devastating appraisals, and the *Guardian* reported that its Moscow correspondent, Luke Harding, was expelled from the country after he published these files[5] in the London daily. The cables also chronicled how U.S. diplomats accused Vladimir Putin of using Russian gas and oil as a political weapon against Europe,[6] an accusation that would be at the center of public debate after Russia invaded Ukraine in February 2022. Over a decade after the cables were published, they still inform the public on the origins of this and other major crises the world is experiencing today.

While the portrait of Russia emerging from the cables was a grim one, that of the United States was not particularly uplifting either.

Some of the diplomatic correspondence examined by the U.S. weekly *The Nation*, in partnership with *Haïti Liberté*, Haiti's leading magazine, revealed how textile companies working in that Caribbean country on behalf of U.S. clothing manufacturers, such as Levi's, Fruit of the Loom and Hanes, "worked in close concert with the US Embassy when they aggressively moved to block a minimum wage increase for Haitian assembly zone workers, the lowest-paid in the hemisphere."[7] Using the cables, the two media outlets exposed how U.S. diplomacy ensured strong support for the contractors of those major brands, who refused to raise wages to 62 cents an hour, a level that would have ensured a minimum wage of 5 dollars per day. In a country whose population lives in conditions of extreme poverty and where, according to statistics cited by *The Nation*, a household of three people with one worker and two dependents needed at least 12.50 dollars a day to survive, the refusal to pay a worker 62 cents an hour conveyed a measure

---

5. This cable is available on the WikiLeaks website: https://wikileaks.org/plusd/cables/10MADRID154_a.html (accessed March 7, 2022). Cables on Russia depicted as a mafia state were originally published by the *Guardian*. See: Luke Harding, "WikiLeaks cables condemn Russia as a mafia state," *Guardian*, December 1, 2010. I have published a full reconstruction of the U.S. diplomacy cables on Russia in my book, Maurizi, *Dossier WikiLeaks*.
6. Ibid.
7. Dan Coughlin and Kim Ives, "WikiLeaks Haiti: let them live on $3 a day," *The Nation*, June 1, 2011. The cable in which the U.S. diplomat said the 5 dollars per day minimum "did not take economic reality into account," and was a populist measure, is available on the WikiLeaks website: https://wikileaks.org/plusd/cables/09PORTAUPRINCE881_a.html (accessed March 7, 2022).

of the brutality of U.S. capitalism, backed by the most powerful foreign service in the world.

The Nation and *Haïti Liberté* wrote that one of the U.S. diplomats assigned to Haiti had characterized the bill to raise the minimum wage as one of those populist measures that "did not take economic reality into account but that appealed to the unemployed and underpaid masses."

Equally grim were revelations about the U.S. military-industrial complex, a war machine that was often able to obtain whatever it asked of allied countries like Italy, in part because the public did not have the necessary information to reflect on their country's role in the United States' Forever Wars. Indeed, the debate was (and is) non-existent, and even when dissent did erupt—as in the case of the Italian pacifist groups that opposed the invasion of Iraq in the first months of 2003—disturbing methods were used to neutralize it.[8] Many of the cables revealed facts that were nothing short of explosive, like the order to collect intelligence on the highest-level U.N. officials, including Secretary General Ban Ki-moon. The information requested included biometric data, like DNA, fingerprints and iris scans, and even technical information on their communication systems, including passwords and encryption keys.[9] The order came out of a secret cable dated July 2009, and bore the signature of then Secretary of State Hillary Clinton. It was a directive of dubious legality and one that, as pointed out by the *Guardian*, blurred the line between diplomacy and espionage.

A considerable number of files featured, to put it mildly, uncharitable appraisals of heads of state and politicians; indeed, right before their publication, U.S. authorities flew into a panic and began contacting allied governments to apologize[10] in advance for the embarrassing revelations. The frankness of the cables on

---

8. Stefania Maurizi, "I no global italiani erano spiati," *L'Espresso*, July 16, 2002.

9. Ewen MacAskill and Robert Booth, "WikiLeaks cables: CIA drew up UN spying wishlist for diplomats," *Guardian*, December 2, 2010. The original cable is available on the WikiLeaks website: accessed March 7, 2022: https://wikileaks.org/plusd/cables/09STATE80163_a.html

10. Daniel Kurtz-Phelan, "In his first book, Ronan Farrow laments the decline of diplomacy," *New York Times*, May 9, 2018.

countries like the Tunisia of Zine al-Abidine Ben Ali—portrayed as an entrenched kleptocracy where ordinary citizens lived in misery, amidst repression and economic crisis, while Ben Ali's family wallowed in luxury—contributed to the end of the 23-year regime, such that Amnesty International would later attribute a role to WikiLeaks in sparking the Arab spring.[11]

Assange's organization did not immediately publish the entire database of 251,287 cables, as they had done with the reports on Afghanistan and Iraq. This time the files were released little by little, to give the journalists from the five leading news outlets time to examine the immense database, which required a much more complicated analysis than had the two previous archives. The *New York Times*, the *Guardian*, *Der Spiegel*, *El País* and *Le Monde* examined the files one by one, also in case it was necessary to redact the names of individuals potentially at risk. But although the database did not immediately appear in its entirety online, the reactions of the U.S. government, led at that time by the Democrats, were furious, to say the least.

The White House condemned the release of the cables as "reckless and dangerous action."[12] The Department of State, headed by Hillary Clinton, slammed it as "an attack on the international community." Asked whether Assange was more like a high-tech terrorist or the Pentagon Papers whistleblower, then Vice-President Joe Biden[13]—later elected to the White House as the forty-sixth president of the United States—opted for "hi-tech terrorist" even though, oddly enough, he had stated just one day before that "I don't think there's any substantive damage." As for the American right, they hit the ceiling. Fox television network aired commentator Bob Beckel, who publicly proclaimed that

11. Scott Shane, "Cables from American diplomats portray US ambivalence on Tunisia," *New York Times*, January 15, 2011; Peter Walker, "Amnesty International hails WikiLeaks and Guardian as Arab Spring 'catalysts'," *Guardian*, May 13, 2011.
12. Reuters Staff, "White House condemns latest WikiLeaks release," Reuters, November 28, 2010.
13. Ewen MacAskill, "Julian Assange like a hi-tech terrorist, says Joe Biden," *Guardian*, December 19, 2010.

the matter should be settled through the use of special ops forces. How? Just "illegally shoot the son of a bitch" Assange.

The ultraconservative ex-governor of Alaska, Sarah Palin, suggested hunting him down like an al-Qaeda operative, while Republican Newt Gingrich[14] urged treating him as if he were Bin Laden: "Julian Assange is engaged in terrorism," said Gingrich, adding: "He should be treated as an enemy combatant. WikiLeaks should be closed down permanently and decisively."

The words of condemnation from the Democrats, and the threats from the American right, were followed by concrete actions. WikiLeaks had rocked power at the highest levels. And power reacted. From that November 28, 2010, Julian Assange and his organization would know what it meant to have the full force of the state against them. And not just any state: the most powerful state in the world. The United States.

SURROUNDED

From the Americas to India, from Europe to Russia, in the days between November 28, 2010, and the beginning of December, the name "WikiLeaks" bounced about every media outlet in the world. Revelation upon revelation. They would start from the five major news outlets with exclusive access to the many thousands of cables, and trickle down through newspapers and television stations around the world.

It was an extravaganza for journalism's global age. But shortly after WikiLeaks had begun publishing in partnership with the five newspapers, its website experienced a massive cyber-attack that took it down completely. The attack was a mammoth operation that went on for days, and a declaration of responsibility, or perhaps a fake message, appeared on Twitter: "WikiLeaks.org— TANGO DOWN—for attempting to endanger the lives of our troops, 'other assets' & foreign relations." It bore the signature "th3j35t3r," that is to say "The Jester." As for "tango down," it is an expression used in special forces jargon to indicate the assassination of a terrorist. Whoever was hiding behind that signature also claimed to have attacked hundreds of jihadist sites in the past. Was it just a patriotic zealot?

A copy of the WikiLeaks website appeared on the Amazon servers, but at that point the press reported that politics intervened and WikiLeaks was kicked off.[15] Amazon issued a statement[16] denying they had acted in response to government pressure, claiming it was a problem of violating its terms of service. The protests from WikiLeaks, which appealed to the constitutional protection afforded the press in the United States under the First Amendment, were to little avail, though it was the same formidable shield that had allowed the *New York Times* and the *Washington Post* to win the legal battle for the Pentagon Papers years before. The U.S. Supreme Court had in fact ruled that the Nixon administration could not enjoin the newspapers from publishing them, because the press is protected by the First Amendment, a protection so strong it allows even the revelation of top-secret files.

Invoking the First Amendment was not enough in the case of Cablegate, however, even though the situation was the same. WikiLeaks had published secret files provided by a source, Chelsea Manning, who as an intelligence analyst with clearance to consult those files had legitimate access to them, but who then handed them over to a news organization, that of Julian Assange. This is precisely what had occurred with the *New York Times* and the *Washington Post* in 1971: they had received the Pentagon Papers from a military analyst, Daniel Ellsberg, who had legal access to the documentation, and who decided to leak it to two major news organizations.

But the First Amendment protected (and protects) the press and ordinary citizens from censorship by the government, not from censorship by private companies like Amazon. Jeff Bezos' colossus

---

15. Ewen MacAskill, "WikiLeaks website pulled by Amazon after US political pressure," *Guardian*, December 2, 2010.
16. Amazon Web Services, WikiLeaks: https://aws.amazon.com/it/message/65348/ (accessed March 8, 2022).

could have protected the publication of the cables in the name of freedom of expression, but it did not do so. Just over two years later, the United States authorities probably remembered this gesture when they awarded the company an extremely important contract: construction of the cloud for the CIA's data analysis, processing and storing services.[17] "Amazon had an opportunity to stand up for its customer's right to free expression. Instead, Amazon ran away with its tail between its legs," the Electronic Frontier Foundation stated.[18]

Julian Assange's organization eventually managed to get the site back on its feet and continue publishing, but at that point another offensive intervened. PayPal—the service that enables sending and receiving payments online—suspended the organization's account, and PayPal's vice-president[19] Osama Bedier publicly claimed to have done so at the explicit request of the U.S. Department of State, though the department denied it. This stonewalling by PayPal was followed by that of the lords of credit: Visa, Mastercard, Bank of America and Western Union abruptly cut off any possibility of donating to WikiLeaks, whose only means of subsistence is donations from its readers and supporters. It was an unprecedented siege. For the first time ever, a journalistic organization of international standing faced a banking blockade without the slightest legal measure to justify it. Had this happened to the *New York Times* or *Le Monde*, it would have set off a worldwide scandal: how could a journalistic organization's accounts be closed just like that, from one day to the next, with no legal justification? There were press articles and protests, yet few cried scandal.

Denounced as hi-tech terrorists, threatened, starved by a financial blockade, Julian Assange and his team were cornered. Could things have gotten any worse? Yes, and they did.

---

17. Frank Konkel, "Sources: Amazon and CIA ink cloud deal," *The Business of Federal Technology*, March 18, 2013.
18. Rainey Reitman and Marcia Hofmann, "Amazon and WikiLeaks: online speech is only as strong as the weakest intermediary," Electronic Frontier Foundation, December 2, 2010: www.eff.org/deeplinks/2010/12/amazon-and-wikileaks-first-amendment-only-strong (accessed March 8, 2022).
19. Josh Rogin, "State Department: we did not ask PayPal to cut off WikiLeaks," *Foreign Policy*, December 8, 2010.

Interpol published a *red notice* making the founder of WikiLeaks a wanted man around the world. Swedish prosecutor Marianne Ny had in fact issued a European Arrest Warrant. Assange was only under investigation: Ny requested his extradition to Sweden to question him in relation to rape, sexual molestation and coercion allegations, not in order to stand trial. He had not been indicted, and the case was still in the preliminary stage.

On December 7, 2010, Julian Assange turned himself in to the Metropolitan Police of London, better known as Scotland Yard. He was held in Wandsworth, a men's prison in London with a capacity of 1,600, built during the reign of Queen Victoria. In 1895, the renowned writer Oscar Wilde was incarcerated there, accused of homosexuality and sentenced to two years of forced labor, with devastating consequences for his physical and mental health. He died only three years after his release, at barely 46 years old. It was in fact a famous quote by Wilde that had inspired Assange to work on the concept of WikiLeaks, a creature of the digital age that helps the truth come out by allowing its sources to hide their real identities and send confidential papers anonymously. "Man is least himself when he talks in his own person," Oscar Wilde had said, "Give him a mask, and he will tell you the truth."[20] Wilde could not have imagined that, more than a century later, a journalist who had created a digital mask would end up, like himself, in Wandsworth. Fortunately, Julian Assange did not stay there for long.

A COTTAGE IN THE ENGLISH COUNTRYSIDE

Ten days after handing himself over to Scotland Yard, the founder of WikiLeaks was released on bail, on condition he wore an electronic monitoring ankle bracelet, reported to the police every day and paid 200,000 British pounds to the court. The British authorities had objected to his release, but had not prevailed in court. And so he was able to leave Wandsworth prison.

Julian Assange did not have a home in the United Kingdom where he could stay under house arrest. One of his supporters,

---

20.   Oscar Wilde, *The critic as artist* (1891).

Vaughan Smith, formerly an official with the British Army, a war
reporter and founder of an independent journalism club, the Frontline Club of London, offered to let Assange stay in Ellingham
Hall, his beautiful Georgian-style manor house in the countryside,
about 200 kilometers from the capital. The British press considered Smith a "maverick," a free thinker. And the *Guardian* did not
fail to point out the irony of the journalist who had contributed to
the greatest breach of diplomatic secrets in history, Julian Assange,
being hosted by the son of a "Queen's messenger," a messenger
charged with delivering the kingdom's diplomatic correspondence,
following an almost thousand-year old tradition[21] dating back to
at least 1199 during the reign of King John of England, the king
who signed the Magna Carta.

Assange did not have the hundreds of thousands of pounds
needed to pay his bail either. It was a considerable sum for his financial resources. Among those who helped him collect the necessary
money and guarantees for over 240,000 pounds, each offering
what he could, were the great film director Ken Loach, Nobel prize
winner John Sulston,[22] British actress and activist Tracy Worces-
ter, two British journalists working for WikiLeaks, Sarah Harrison
and Joseph Farrell, and British chef Sarah Saunders.

Saunders, along with her mother, Susan Benn, and her mother's
husband, Gavin MacFadyen—a prominent investigative journalist who founded the Centre for Investigative Journalism (CIJ)
of London—were Assange's "British family" of sorts. In time, I
would come to know them: intelligent, independent, passionate.
And I would forever bear Gavin MacFadyen's lesson in mind:
"Never believe anything, until it is officially denied."

Now that he was out of Wandsworth, Julian Assange could
get back to work, provided he met the terms laid down by the
court. After Christmas 2010, WikiLeaks again reached out to me
through an encrypted message, in the dead of night: "Can you fly

---

21.   A short history of the Queen's Messengers is available on the Foreign Commonwealth Development Office's website: www.fcdoservices.gov.uk/about/our-history/
(accessed March 8, 2022).
22.   Sir John Sulston won the Nobel Prize for Medicine in 2002. He was a leading
figure in defending the public genome against privatization.

to London immediately?" I took a flight on January 10, 2010 and arrived at the arranged meeting in a cottage in the green English countryside, not a mansion like Ellingham Hall. The location was problematic, as it was cut off from all mobile phone communication and lacked internet access.

I knew the organization wanted to do journalistic work on the cables beyond what had been done by the five major media outlets involved initially. The *New York Times*, the *Guardian*, *Der Spiegel*, *El País* and *Le Monde* had not been willing to expand the media club that had exclusive access to the files. Arranging for the coordination of dozens of newspapers throughout the world, from Japan to Argentina, would have been an organizational nightmare, but on the other hand those files did concern every country on earth. It was essential to do more in-depth work, country by country, with investigative journalists having expertise on the local situations and capable of analyzing the U.S. government files as well, removing the names of any individual who might be at risk.

It had been a stroke of brilliance on WikiLeaks' part to invent the international media partnerships formula, to involve journalists from a number of different nations so that each one could dig into the databases, bringing their own specific expertise and seeking out the revelations of importance to their own countries. From the United States to Italy, from France to India: it was an intelligent and unprecedented approach, one that would later be copied by virtually all international journalism consortia. But it was WikiLeaks that invented this strategy, not only to give its revelations maximum impact but also because, as an offspring of the web, it looked at the world and its problems in their entirety.

I arrived at that country cottage where they were expecting me and other reporters from every corner of the world. We were each meeting with Julian Assange and his journalists separately, because we had a complicated job ahead of us. The first thing the WikiLeaks founder did was close the thick curtains, so it was impossible to see through the windows from outside. "It's paradoxical," I said, complaining that neither cell phones nor the internet worked there. We were completely cut off from outside communication. "It's on purpose," Assange told me.

We discussed the cables database, and the extremely strict security conditions I would need to observe while working on the files were explained to me once again. I was familiar with them by then, and knew how completely unheard-of they were; neither I nor any of my foreign colleagues had ever met a single journalist who worked under procedures as strict as those required by Assange.

After analyzing a series of files together, WikiLeaks gave me access to the 4,189 cables on Italy and the Vatican. I would not consult the entire database until later on: with its 251,287 diplomatic cables, I certainly could not save it on a simple flash drive as I did with the 4,000 files dealing with my country and the Holy See.

It was late when I left the cottage. The WikiLeaks staff drove me to one of those decrepit railway stations typical of rural England to catch one of the last trains that would get me back to my hotel in time to pack my bags and fly to Rome the next day. I was completely alone at that Victorian station; there were no railway personnel, no waiting room or café, but at least my phone worked there. I had to wait a long time for the train, because I had just missed the one before it, and I had no choice but to stand outside, numb with the January cold tempered by a few drops of rain. There was not a living soul around. At one point a car drove up and kept shining its headlights at me. I found the high beams disturbing. I began walking away from the station and the car followed me for a short distance, then stopped. As soon as I walked back to the station, however, the car began shining its headlights on me again. It was a commonplace harasser; the kind train stations draw like magnets. I had only to phone the local police, who came quickly and asked him a few questions, to get him to stop. I had decided, back when I first started working on WikiLeaks files, that I would not let myself be intimidated or frightened. It was unlikely that anyone would physically assault the journalists working on the confidential files.

The next day, in the airport, I went through the security controls with great care, just as I had in Berlin when I traveled with the classified files on the Afghanistan war. I boarded the plane, but only a few minutes after take-off it was struck by a bolt of lightning. Nothing serious, but we had to go back to the airport for transfer to another aircraft. At that moment more than ever, I felt grateful to be a journalist in the digital age. The 4,189 cables were stored in a tiny flash drive, protected by encryption, that I kept in my shoulder bag. The cables went completely unnoticed, obviously, and I could carry them around effortlessly. In 1971, to transport the 7,000 photocopied pages of the Pentagon Papers, the reporter with the *Washington Post*—which obtained the pages only after the *New York Times* had already begun publishing them—had to book[23] two first-class airplane tickets: one for himself, and one for the bulky box filled with documents. Forty years later, I was able to fly to Rome with thousands of secret files, corresponding to tens of thousands of pages, in my handbag, and transfer them to another plane with no difficulty at all.

The files were safe, and even in the most extreme of situations, like the threat of violence, no one could force me to decrypt the database so they could access the cables, because not even I knew the password. To add an extra level of protection, WikiLeaks had designed the security procedures so that the databases would fly encrypted without the journalists having the passwords for them. It was only several days after I got back to Italy that I received the instructions for decrypting the files. Now I could discover the Italian secrets.

A DEMOCRACY ON A SHORT LEASH

The password for decrypting the database was very complicated, and typing it in each time called for a great deal of patience. But it was well worth it, considering how topical the 4,189 cables on Italy and the Vatican were. They dated from the end of 2001 to February

---

23. Michael S. Rosenwald, "Fact checking 'The Post': the incredible Pentagon Papers drama Spielberg left out," *Washington Post*, December 23, 2017.

2010. When I was finally able to access the files, in that January of 2011, I could scarcely believe I was reading U.S. diplomatic correspondence unveiling secrets about members of government who were still in office, or at any rate still key players in Italian politics. The names of journalists, cardinals, popes, generals, Italian and foreign state officials were those of the present day. And they were all there; none of the files had been censored in the slightest, as is often the case when the U.S. government issues copies of cables to those petitioning to declassify them thirty or forty years later. No; we could read everything this time.

It was an enormous number of files. Methodically examining them made it possible to "get inside the mind" of the Bush and Obama administrations, to understand exactly how they operated on the global level and what they really thought, beyond their official statements and the vague or distorted media reporting.

It was not hard to confirm the files' authenticity. I could rely on the experience of foreign colleagues who had already worked on them, and I could also rely on the analyses I had done of about 200 U.S. diplomatic exchanges dating from forty years earlier, which I had managed to have declassified after all that time thanks to the expertise of a former diplomat and some American scholars specialized in the government's declassification policies.

The Italy unveiled by the cables was a democracy on a very short leash, where politicians were subject to enormous pressure. From the war in Afghanistan to the foods for which we are famous throughout the world, the United States intervened extensively in Italian affairs. Exposing the pressure this time were not anti-American books or articles or even the ideological *j'accuse* of intellectuals or activists: it was the U.S. diplomats themselves. They spelt it out, in black and white, in their official correspondence with the U.S. Department of State. The 4,189 cables on Italy and the Vatican provided the proof.[24] Some of the most explicit files regarded the war in Iraq. In one dated May 12, 2003, not even two weeks after President George W. Bush had proclaimed victory, the

---

24.   A fully detailed reconstruction of what the cables reveal on Italy is available in my book, Maurizi, *Dossier WikiLeaks*.

U.S. ambassador to Rome, Mel Sembler, offered an analysis of the contribution which Italy, headed at the time by President Carlo Azeglio Ciampi and Prime Minister Silvio Berlusconi, had made to the invasion.[25]

The war had sparked very strong opposition across the entire world, especially in Europe, where Bush's America was shunned and criticized. But Berlusconi's Italy breached the United States' isolation and guaranteed support, even though public opinion was fiercely against it and despite the Constitution, which at article 11 reads: "Italy rejects war as an instrument of aggression against the freedom of other peoples and as a means for the settlement of international disputes."

"The GOI [Government of Italy] made a strategic choice to keep its policy aligned with the U.S. and stuck to it, despite intense internal political pressure to fold," wrote U.S. ambassador Sembler in the cable, explaining: "When president Ciampi seemed on the verge of calling into constitutional question the deployment of the U.S. Army's 173rd Airborne Brigade directly to Iraq from Italian soil, the GOI worked tactics with us to address his concerns. Logistical support to the U.S. military was outstanding. We got what we asked for."[26] Sembler went on to recount how they had been able to use Italy to transport needed war supplies to Iraq: "Italian airfields, ports, and transport infrastructure were placed at our disposal."[27]

One crucial issue the Berlusconi government had played an important role in resolving, according to the U.S. diplomat, was President Ciampi's potential rejection of Italy's cooperation as a violation of the Constitution. Sembler wrote: "GOI ensured that president Ciampi did not challenge constitutionality of 173rd Brigade's deployment from Vicenza to Northern Iraq."[28] The ambassador then relayed how the deployment of the 173rd Brigade had been "the largest combat air drop since WW II [World War

25. The original cable is publicly available on the WikiLeaks website: https://wikileaks.org/plusd/cables/03ROME2045_a.html (accessed March 8, 2022).

26. Ibid.

27. Ibid.

28. Ibid.

II]." After detailing the cooperation received, he affirmed: "The Berlusconi government brought a country roundly opposed to war as close as it could politically to the brink of belligerent status." And Silvio Berlusconi's executive had made everything easier: "had another government been in power—in particular one controlled by the center-left—we would have had a far more difficult situation on our hands," he underlined.

Summing up, he wrote: "Recognizing that Italy can appear frustratingly arcane and byzantine, we are convinced that it is an excellent place to do our political-military business."[29]

In addition to the facts referred to and the brazenness of the language used, also astonishing were revelations about the methods adopted to prevent people—who were demonstrating against a war that would ultimately prove devastating—from "stopping trains and trucks transporting U.S. equipment across Italy." All this was done in a seemingly democratic manner, but the cables gave a glimpse into the real methods employed.

"The GOI," wrote U.S. ambassador Sembler:[30] "impressed us with its ability to balance the political imperative of no violence against anti-war protesters with the need to help the U.S. military to do its job. Although Italian and U.S. methods differ (our hosts prefer late night movements, last minute schedule changes, and general deception), the GOI, working hand-in-glove with the U.S. Army and the Embassy, successfully prevented protesters from stopping trains and vehicles moving our military equipment through Italy."

But how had the peace demonstrators been neutralized, exactly?

Sembler explained it thus in another cable from February 2003, just one month before the invasion of Iraq:[31] "The MOI [Italian Ministry of Interior]'s Department of Public Security has set up a crisis center to monitor events and work tactics together with representatives from the national railroad (Ferrovie di Stato)." He

---

29. Ibid.
30. Ibid.
31. The original cable is publicly available on the WikiLeaks website: https:// wikileaks.org/plusd/cables/03ROME810_a.html (accessed March 8, 2022).

continued: "A system of countermeasures has been activated which includes heavy surveillance of the protester's [*sic*] communications, deployment of hundreds of law enforcement officers at key point along train routes, and moving equipment by night. The GOI, by playing a cat and mouse game with the trains—often shifting routes on short notice—has been able to keep the protesters off balance."

So that was how the Italian Republic worked, then? Outwardly everything was done by the book, but in reality, according to the ambassador's account, the freedom to dissent, the lifeblood of democracy, was sidestepped and protesters spied upon, just like in any authoritarian country. The methods used were to all appearances more respectable, not brutal like those of a dictatorship, but no less reprehensible.

As Chelsea Manning said, describing the content of the confidential files she decided to send to WikiLeaks: "[we Americans are] better in some respects ... we're much more subtle ... use a lot more words and legal techniques to legitimize everything, it's better than disappearing in the middle of the night, but just because something is more subtle, doesn't make it right."

The cables showed that the same verdict could be applied to the Italian institutions. Who had secretly eavesdropped on the Italian pacifists to prevent their blockade of trains carrying equipment for the war in Iraq? The Italian secret services or the U.S. ones? Or maybe Italian police forces? And who had authorized the wiretapping?

The diplomatic correspondence also revealed how the United States viewed Silvio Berlusconi, official statements aside. "His frequent verbal gaffes and poor choice of words have offended nearly every demographic in Italy and many EU [European Union] leaders," wrote ambassador Ronald Spogli, successor to the preceding ambassador, Mel Sembler, in February 2009.[32] Added

---

32. The original cable is publicly available on the WikiLeaks website: https://wikileaks.org/plusd/cables/09ROME128_a.html (accessed March 8, 2022). It was originally reported on in Stefania Maurizi and Gianluca Di Feo, "Ha reso comica l'Italia," *L'Espresso*, February 18, 2011.

Spogli: "His perceived willingness to put personal interests above those of the state, his preference for short-term solutions over long-term investment, and his frequent use of public institutions and resources to gain electoral advantage over his political adversaries has harmed Italy's reputation in Europe and has provided an unfortunately comic tone to Italy's reputation in many quarters of the U.S. government."

A very harsh verdict, but Silvio Berlusconi was not to be dismissed: "The combination of Italy's economic decline and political idiosyncrasies have caused many European leaders to denigrate the contributions of Berlusconi and Italy. We should not. We should recognize that a long-term engagement with Italy and its leaders will provide us important strategic dividends now and in the future," concluded Spogli.

The files indeed chronicled how U.S. diplomacy had an easy time of it during Silvio Berlusconi's government. In 2002, for example, the Bush administration sought to undermine the efficacy of the International Criminal Court—whose mission is to punish those responsible for war crimes, crimes against humanity and genocide—by signing a series of bilateral agreements binding countries like Italy not to hand over U.S. soldiers to the court's judges, to shield them from international law. According to the cables,[33] the Berlusconi government immediately signaled its readiness to sign such an agreement. As the ambassador wrote to Washington: "It appears that once again, when President Bush asks Prime Minister Berlusconi for help, the help is forthcoming."

Not that center-left governments had refused to cooperate with the United States, but, as Spogli wrote[34] on the eve of the Italian general election of April 2006, "If the center-left wins, we can and will work with a [Romano] Prodi government that will provide relative continuity in Italy's foreign policy. But the days of [Berlusconi's] Italy automatically engaging on our behalf will be over as

---

33. The original cable is publicly available on the WikiLeaks website: https://wikileaks.org/plusd/cables/02ROME3796_a.html (accessed March 8, 2022).
34. The original cable is publicly available on the WikiLeaks website: https://wikileaks.org/plusd/cables/06ROME864_a.html (accessed March 8, 2022).

Prodi seeks to deliberately subordinate Italian foreign policy to the EU. To maintain current Italian initiatives, we will have to work much harder and expect more bumps along the road."

The center-left at the time had only one politician who, as far as relations with the U.S. were concerned, felt Silvio Berlusconi had made the right choice: Marco Minniti, whom the *New York Times* would later call "Italy's 'Lord of the Spies'." At least, the database did not mention any others. According to the cables,[35] in March 2006 Minniti "lauded the close relations that PM Berlusconi has built with the U.S. and called that relationship 'an asset that should not be wasted'."

In the many files on Italy and the Vatican, the United States' interventions in Italian politics were documented on an extremely wide variety of issues: from the war in Afghanistan to Italian food. The files unveiled intense pressure[36] from the U.S. against Italy's choice to keep genetically modified organisms (GMOs) out of the country's agriculture and cuisine, Italy's claim to fame around the world. The massive economic interests of multinationals like Monsanto and the chemical giant DuPont's Pioneer were at stake. U.S. diplomats defended these interests with a relentless pressure on the Italian government and a vigorous lobbying effort on the Vatican.

As for Afghanistan, it was an endless request for more: more troops, more Carabinieri to train the Afghan police, more funds, more freedom from the constraints ("caveats") imposed on the Italian soldiers in the war against the Taliban. The pressure was constant, from both the Bush administration and that of Obama.

"When we ask for additional military resources or donor assistance for Afghanistan," wrote a U.S. diplomat in February 2009, when Barack Obama took office:[37] "GOI officials reply that their tight budget prevents them from doing more. We should not accept this excuse. The fact is that the GOI has made a policy

---

35. The original cable is publicly available on the WikiLeaks website: https://wikileaks.org/plusd/cables/06ROME839_a.html (accessed March 8, 2022).
36. Maurizi, *Dossier WikiLeaks*.
37. The original cable is publicly available on the WikiLeaks website: https://wikileaks.org/plusd/cables/09ROME177_a.html (accessed March 8, 2022).

decision to spend less on defense—roughly 1 per cent of GDP—
than is needed to maintain its status as a top-tier NATO ally. We
should push them to put into their defense budget sufficient funds
to meet their responsibilities in Afghanistan."

The Bush administration considered the Italian left very problematic for this reason also. "A strong CL [center-left] win would
bring unions and traditional 'social partners' back into power with
predictable demands for increased social spending that could
erode foreign/defense commitments," wrote U.S. diplomats on the
eve of the April 2006 Italian general election.[38] The resources allo-
cated by Italy for the war in Afghanistan were not the only cause
for dissatisfaction: according to the cables, Italy was suspected of
corrupt practices. "Based on information obtained in 2008 indicating that the Italian intelligence services were paying insurgents
in the Kabul region not to target Italian troops," U.S. diplomats
reported in February 2009,[39] "then-Ambassador Spogli raised the
issue with PM Berlusconi and received assurances that the GOI
would investigate the matter and put a stop to such practices if
the allegations were true. President Bush also reportedly raised the
issue directly with PM Berlusconi, who reiterated that the GOI
would not engage in such activity."

Were these allegations well-founded? Between April 2008 and
February 2009, the files reported these suspicions repeatedly. No
proof of such corruption has surfaced to date, but if confirmation
beyond any reasonable doubt should emerge one day, it would constitute a tremendous scandal.

As I write, Italy has left Afghanistan after twenty years. Italy lost
54 soldiers, brought home about 700 wounded and spent 8.474
billion euros,[40] a remarkable sum considering the dire economic
crisis the country has struggled with for more than a decade. All
this for a failed mission that claimed the life of tens of thousands

---

38. The original cable is publicly available on the WikiLeaks website: https://
wikileaks.org/plusd/cables/06ROME864_a.html (accessed March 8, 2022).
39. The original cable is publicly available on the WikiLeaks website: https://
wikileaks.org/plusd/cables/09ROME177_a.html (accessed March 8, 2022).
40. These statistics comes from the Osservatorio Milex co-founded by Francesco
Vignarca. Vignarca's email to author, November 27, 2020.

of innocent Afghans. And we were supposedly paying off the Taliban and the local warlords too?

The cables on Italy revealed much more than pressure to contribute to the wars in Iraq and Afghanistan. They painted a striking portrait of how Italy had become crucial for the U.S. military-industrial complex and its Forever Wars, after September 11 more than ever. "Italy remains our most important European ally for projecting military power into the Mediterranean, Middle East and North Africa," wrote ambassador Spogli in October 2008:[41] "We have 15,000 U.S. military and DOD [Department of Defense] civilian personnel and 17,000 of their family members on five Italian bases. The GOI has approved the expansion of the base at Vicenza to consolidate the 173rd Airborne Brigade, the deployment of the USAF [U.S. Air Force] Global Hawk UAV [unmanned aerial vehicle, also known as drone] in Sicily, and we are working with the Italians to stand up the AFRICOM Army and Navy Component Commands in Italy."[42]

In the Italian media's general lack of attention to the presence of U.S. and NATO bases in Italy—apart from the rare political quarrel—the country had become "a launching pad for US wars," as the *Guardian*[43] put it in 2013.

The cables made it possible to track this transformation right from its start, providing precise information as to how, very gradually, keeping as low a profile as possible, the United States, with the support of the political establishment, turned Italy into that launching pad.

Without the detailed accounts of the conversations between diplomats and the Italian government on this subject, I could never have acquired the keen awareness that those files conveyed to me—from the secret drone wars to the *boots on the ground* conflicts, like the invasion of Iraq, which featured the city of Vicenza

---

41. The original cable is publicly available on the WikiLeaks website: https://wikileaks.org/plusd/cables/08ROME1226_a.html (accessed March 8, 2022).
42. AFRICOM is the combat command responsible for all U.S. Department of Defense operations, exercises, and security cooperation on the African continent.
43. David Vine, "Italy: home of pizza, pasta, wine and the US military," *Guardian*, October 3, 2013.

at the heart of "the largest combat air drop since WW II." That was how U.S. ambassador Mel Sembler put it, referring to the 173rd Airborne Brigade,[44] the U.S. Army's Contingency Response Force in Europe, which provides rapid forces to the United States European, Africa and Central Commands. The 173rd Airborne Brigade, which has the capacity to deploy in 18 hours,[45] fought in Iraq and in Afghanistan.

The cables not only chronicled how Italy became a launching pad for U.S. wars, they also revealed the inside story of how the U.S. military and intelligence complex was allowed to operate with impunity even when it committed shocking crimes, like kidnapping a human being off the streets of Milan in broad daylight.

LIKE IN CHILE UNDER PINOCHET

He simply disappeared. On February 17, 2003, Hassan Mustafa Osama Nasr, known as Abu Omar, an Egyptian who had come to Italy as a refugee, was abducted at around midday in Milan. He was the imam of the mosque in via Quaranta and was under investigation on suspicion of international terrorism. The Digos—the division of the Italian police countering terrorism and subversion—together with the Milan prosecutors, had been piecing together the mosaic of his contacts.[46]

But on that February day, investigators and magistrates found that their suspect had vanished. According to a woman who had witnessed the scene, he was loaded into a white van in Guerzoni street.

The investigation by the Milan magistrates Ferdinando Pomarici and Armando Spataro into Abu Omar's disappearance was tremendously assisted by telephone metadata: the data showing who phoned who between 11 a.m. and 1 p.m. on February 17, 2003 in the vicinity of Guerzoni street. Analysis of this metadata led the

---

44. The original cable is publicly available on the WikiLeaks website: https://wikileaks.org/plusd/cables/03ROME2045_a.html (accessed March 8, 2022).
45. Nancy Montgomery, "173rd Airborne Brigade troops to deploy to Middle East," *Stars and Stripes*, January 6, 2020.
46. Armando Spataro, *Ne valeva la pena* (Roma-Bari: Laterza, 2010).

anti-terrorism police to identify a suspicious group of telephones. Right after the abduction, some of those telephone users appeared to have traveled along the stretch of motorway leading to Aviano—one of the two military bases where the United States store nuclear weapons in Italy—and to have called, among others, Colonel Joseph Romano, head of the base's security. Crossing this data with the accommodation records of the hotels where some of the telephone users had spent the night, and with credit card transactions, hotel and flight reservations—in some cases made providing the phone numbers present in via Guerzoni—the anti-terrorism agents and the two magistrates, Pomarici and Spataro, were able to trace the identities of the perpetrators of the kidnapping.

The case represented one of the infamous "extraordinary renditions," the secret operations whereby the CIA abducted individuals suspected of terrorism and transferred them to its secret prisons around the world, where they would torture them to extract information.

Abu Omar was first taken to the air base in Aviano and then to Egypt, where he was brutally tortured using various techniques[47] including sexual assault and electric shocks with moistened electrodes placed on his head, chest and genitals.

The inquiry headed by prosecutors Spataro and Pomarici led to the incrimination of 26 United States citizens, almost all of them CIA agents, and several officials with the Italian military secret service, SISMI, including general Nicolò Pollari, head of the service, and Marco Mancini, director of counterintelligence.

The Italian judiciary was efficient: between 2012 and 2014, the 26 Americans were handed definitive sentences of six to nine years. Italy stood as an example to the world, the only country to have carried out justice in the case of an extraordinary rendition. Germany, by contrast, had never reached a final sentence for the CIA agents responsible for the extraordinary rendition of

---

47. Torture techniques used against Abu Omar are described in the sentence of the European Court of Human Rights, *Nasr e Ghali c. Italia*, February 23, 2016: https://hudoc.echr.coe.int/eng#{%22itemid%22:[%22001-162280%22]} (accessed March 8, 2022).

an innocent German citizen, Khaled el-Masri, abducted in 2003 when he was traveling in a bus along the border with Macedonia, brutally beaten, sodomized and transferred to Afghanistan.

And yet all 26 of those convicted have remained as free as air: between 2006 and 2012, six different ministers of justice with center-right and center-left governments—Roberto Castelli, Clemente Mastella, Luigi Scotti, Angelino Alfano, Nitto Palma and Paola Severino—all refused to broaden the searches to the international level in order to arrest them and extradite them to Italy.[48] Furthermore, two presidents of the Italian Republic have issued pardons for four of them: in 2013, Giorgio Napolitano pardoned Colonel Joseph Romano, while a few years later Sergio Mattarella pardoned Robert Seldon Lady, Betnie Medero and Sabrina De Sousa.

In February 2016, the European Court of Human Rights found Italy in violation of articles 3, 5, 8 and 13 of the European Convention on Human Rights. These articles prohibit torture and inhuman and degrading treatment, establish the right to liberty and security, respect for one's private and family life and, finally, the right to an effective remedy before a national authority. Italy, the only country in the world whose magistrates and judges secured a definitive sentence for the CIA agents responsible for an extraordinary rendition, now found itself condemned by the European Court of Human Rights for the manner in which its institutions—including two presidents of the Republic and the Constitutional Court—had handled the Abu Omar case. The court wrote that, insofar as the investigation and trial had not led to the punishment of those responsible, both the CIA agents and top SISMI officials "had ultimately been granted impunity."[49] Although SISMI's General Pollari and the director of the counterintelligence division Mancini were found guilty, they were protected by state secrecy

48.   The Italian Justice Minister Paola Severino agreed to broaden the search to the international level for only one of the twenty-six found guilty: Robert Seldon Lady, the former head of the CIA in Milan.
49.   This is quoted from the sentence handed down by the European Court of Human Rights, *Nasr e Ghali c. Italia*, dated February 23, 2016: https://hudoc.echr.coe.int/eng#{%22itemid%22:[%22001-162280%22]} (accessed March 8, 2022).

and their convictions were nullified. Nevertheless, the sentence handed down by the European Court of Human Rights contained words of high praise for the work carried out by the Italian magistrates, pointing out that, in contrast to cases like that of Khaled el-Masri in Germany, the Italian prosecutors had conducted a thorough investigation to establish the truth.

All of these facts relating to the Abu Omar case were public knowledge, as the investigation had been followed throughout the world by the press and media which, thanks to Spataro and Pomarici's inquests, could finally gain factual information on the CIA's extraordinary renditions program. But it was only thanks to the cables that I was able to obtain proof of the pressure exerted by the U.S. government on Italian politicians not to extradite the twenty-six convicted Americans.

The files made it clear that U.S. diplomats realized they had no chance of influencing Spataro and Pomarici's investigation, inasmuch as they considered Italian magistrates, in general, "fiercely independent." Since they could not pressure the prosecutors directly, they pressured the politicians, on both the left and the right. In one of the files[50] dated May 24, 2006, the Bush administration's ambassador to Rome, Ronald Spogli, described his meeting with Enrico Letta, then undersecretary to the prime minister in the center-left government of Romano Prodi, as follows: "In the context of keeping our excellent bilateral relationship on sound footing, the Ambassador explained to Letta that nothing would damage relations faster or more seriously than a decision by the GOI to forward warrants for arrests of the alleged CIA agents named in connection with the Abu Omar case. This was absolutely critical."

Did Enrico Letta offer any objections to such blatant pressure? Going by the cable, no. "Letta," reads the file, "took note of this and suggested the Ambassador discuss the matter personally with Justice Minister Mastella."

50. The original cable is publicly available on the WikiLeaks website: https://wikileaks.org/plusd/cables/06ROME1590_a.html (accessed March 9, 2022).

A few months later, in August 2006, ambassador Spogli again wrote[51] to Washington: "Justice Minister Mastella has so far kept the lid on recurring judicial demands to extradite presumed CIA officers allegedly involved in a rendition of Muslim cleric Abu Omar, and Prodi declined to release any details about potential Italian knowledge or involvement in the case citing the imperative to protect classified national security information."

The next year it was the turn of Massimo D'Alema, Minister of Foreign Affairs in Romano Prodi's government. The U.S. ambassador relayed their meeting of April 2017 as follows:[52] "D'Alema closed the hour-long meeting by noting that he had asked the Secretary if the Department could send something in writing to him explaining that the U.S. would not act on extradition requests in the Abu Omar case if tendered. This, he explained, could be used pre-emptively by the GOI to fend off action by Italian magistrates to seek the extradition of the implicated Americans."

A year went by and Romano Prodi's center-left government was followed by Berlusconi's center-right one, but the upshot remained the same. "Berlusconi has continued to stand with us as best he can in the trial of twenty-six Americans," wrote U.S. ambassador Ronald Spogli in October 2008.[53]

This pressure from the United States was documented in the cables database up until February of 2010, as the files unfortunately did not go beyond that date. But it was present right until the end of that period. Indeed, at the height of the Obama administration in February 2010, U.S. diplomats continued to lean on both Berlusconi and Minister of Defense Ignazio La Russa: "In relation to the Abu Omar case," they wrote,[54] "SecDef [U.S. Secretary of Defense] requested GOI's advocacy on recognizing U.S. jurisdiction over Colonel Joseph Romano under the NATO SOFA [Status of Forces

---

51. The original cable is publicly available on the WikiLeaks website: https://wikileaks.org/plusd/cables/06ROME2436_a.html (accessed March 9, 2022).
52. The original cable is publicly available on the WikiLeaks website: https://wikileaks.org/plusd/cables/07ROME710_a.html ((accessed March 9, 2022).
53. The original cable is publicly available on the WikiLeaks website: https://wikileaks.org/plusd/cables/08ROME1226_a.html (, accessed March 9, 2022).
54. The original cable is publicly available on the WikiLeaks website: https://wikileaks.org/plusd/cables/10ROME174_a.html (accessed March 9, 2022).

Agreement]. Berlusconi expressed optimism that the matter will be resolved favorably during the appeals process." In a later cable, Gates reiterated the exact same concept with La Russa.[55]

As I write, almost twenty years have passed since the "extraordinary rendition" of Abu Omar. Twenty-six Americans—assisted by Italian secret services—abducted a man in broad daylight to subject him to months of brutal torture. Just like in Chile under Pinochet. Only it happened in the heart of Europe, in the most modern city in Italy. With impunity. And not only in violation of the most basic human rights but, according to Italian prosecutor Armando Spataro, also to the detriment of the investigation which he and his colleague were conducting into Abu Omar, which would have allowed them to identify and arrest his accomplices.

The CIA could have taken the path of respect for human rights. Italian magistrates and police forces managed to nail the CIA agents themselves, even though CIA operatives have far more training, not to mention greater economic and technological resources, than terrorists do. The CIA instead chose the path of criminality and medieval brutality. And the Italian political institutions made sure they went unpunished.

Without the courage of Chelsea Manning and WikiLeaks, we might have been able to imagine how this impunity was achieved, but we would not have had the proof, or perhaps only decades later, when it was no longer of interest to anyone. And this is precisely why Chelsea Manning and Julian Assange have ended up in prison, and why many of the WikiLeaks journalists presumably risk the same fate: because they have revealed classified files like the ones on Abu Omar, where the state secrecy imposed by U.S. authorities served not to protect human lives, but to cover up crimes and ensure impunity for the institutions and individuals that committed them.

When, in February 2010, we began revealing the cables in what was my newspaper at the time, the Italian weekly *L'Espresso*,[56] as

---

55. The original cable is publicly available on the WikiLeaks website: https://wikileaks.org/plusd/cables/10ROME172_a.html (accessed March 9, 2022).
56. Maurizi and Di Feo, "Ha reso comica l'Italia."

well as in the daily *la Repubblica*, the files generated a lot more buzz than the reports on the war in Afghanistan had. And working in partnership with Julian Assange and his WikiLeaks team, we made an immense effort to bring out the files one by one, little by little, only after proper analysis and careful redaction of any information that could even remotely constitute a risk for the sources and individuals mentioned. It meant working around the clock for months.

And yet, despite all our work, and despite the storm the cables generated, not a single political party or Italian association tried to use them to ask the courts to inquire into Italy's collaboration in the Iraq war, or its spying on pacifists, or the pressure applied in the case of Abu Omar, or a great many other important matters.

The only thing worse than the CIA's crimes was the apathy of the Italian public.

7

Guantanamo:
The Black Hole of Civilization

THE WORST OF THE WORST?

In the heart of a glamorous London in the run-up to the royal
wedding between Kate Middleton and Prince William set for
April 29, 2011, a group of journalists had arranged to meet with
WikiLeaks to unveil the secrets of the detention camp that had
become the symbol of U.S. cruelty in the war on terror: Guantanamo. We were all seated around a table in a newsroom, ready to
dive into those files, while the city's streets exuded a festive atmosphere, its parks and gardens in full splendor.

The camp had been opened on January 11, 2002—exactly four
months after September 11—and was not only emblematic of the
torture and brutality inflicted on the detainees. It also represented
an attack on a nearly thousand-year-old principle: *habeas corpus*,
a person's right not to be imprisoned without knowing the crime
of which they are accused, and to appear before a judge to defend
themself.[1]

Habeas corpus was introduced under King John of England with
the Magna Carta in 1215. "No free man shall be seized, imprisoned [...] except by the lawful judgement of his peers and the law
of the land," it read. And ever since that distant year, it is a right
that has remained deeply engrained in Anglo-American jurispru-
dence, becoming a cornerstone of the United States Constitution.[2]

---

1. "Habeas Corpus," Cornell Law School: www.law.cornell.edu/wex/habeas_corpus
(accessed March 10, 2022).
2. "Background on Habeas Corpus," ACLU: www.aclu.org/other/background-
habeas-corpus (accessed March 10, 2022).

The detention camp, also known as "Gitmo," was located in the U.S. naval base of Guantanamo Bay in south-eastern Cuba, and instituted precisely for the purpose of bypassing U.S. and international law in the case of suspected terrorists who, according to the U.S. government, represented an exceptional threat insofar as they were linked to the September 11 attacks, or at any rate were suspected of being high-profile operatives with al-Qaeda.

The Secretary of Defense for the Bush administration at that time, Donald Rumsfeld, had labelled these suspects "the worst of the worst," and the ubiquitous fear that reigned in those months and the secrecy surrounding the facility did the rest. The global public was led to believe that those who ended up in Guantanamo were veritable fiends, who needed to be locked away forever. No one had exact information as to who the prisoners were, or why they had been transferred there.

It took years before any information began to leak out. Julian Assange and his organization had offered a glimpse into the secrecy in November 2007, when they released the operations manual of the military task force running Guantanamo, the "Jtf Gtmo." It was one of the files that had struck me when I first began taking an interest in WikiLeaks.

When Assange and his journalists contacted me in March of 2011, less than three months had passed since our meeting on the cables in London. I was still working night and day on those 4,189 files, publishing investigative reports and articles.

Once again I heard: "Can you fly out here?" WikiLeaks was sitting on thousands of pages of classified documents on Guantanamo and wanted to know if I was interested in being part of the international team of journalists with exclusive access to the files.

I took a flight to London shortly thereafter. We were there all together: Julian Assange and some of the journalists with his organization, along with *Der Spiegel*, *Le Monde*, *El País*, the English daily the *Telegraph*, the Swedish *Aftonbladet*, the *Washington Post*, the U.S. publishing company McClatchy—taking part in the meeting remotely—and myself, working for *L'Espresso* and *la Repubblica* at that time, and Andy Worthington, a British journalist and expert on Guantanamo. Worthington had dedicated many years to compiling a list of everyone who had been locked away in the detention camp.

The *Guardian* and the *New York Times* were off our team this time, after the controversy that had broken out between them and WikiLeaks during publication of the cables, but two major U.S. media organizations did take part: the *Washington Post* and McClatchy. Assange and his journalists held McClatchy in high regard at that time, precisely for the independence its reporters had shown in debunking the lies about Saddam Hussein's weapons of mass destruction, lies deployed by the Bush administration to justify the Iraq invasion. McClatchy could also rely on the expertise of Carol Rosenberg,[3] a journalist who had worked on Guantanamo from the very start; indeed, she was there when the first twenty prisoners arrived, the day it opened. Involving Andy Worthington was another sound choice; he has been pursuing a tireless independent investigation into the camp for years. Julian Assange and WikiLeaks once again evidenced their determination to publish the secret documents in their possession judiciously, painstakingly and with care, in part by sharing them with an international team of journalists experienced in reporting on the CIA's extraordinary renditions, black sites and torture.

The files in question were the Guantanamo prisoner records: the names, surnames and nationalities of 765 of the individuals who had been detained over the years—virtually all of them, since a total of 780 had been confined there. At least twenty-two of them were minors. Omar Khadr, for example, was 16 years old when he was interned in the facility, though not even his tender age saved him from brutal torture and ten years of detention.

The documents consisted of thousands of pages classified as secret and dated back to the Bush years. For the first time, they revealed the reasons the prisoners had been transferred to Guantanamo and locked up there, and revealed their faces in photographs, available for at least 172 of them.

---

3. As I write, Carol Rosenberg works for the *New York Times* and systematically continues to cover Guantanamo.

The files resoundingly gave the lie to the Bush administration's version, that "the worst of the worst" were locked up in Guantanamo. According to research on the 765 records conducted by the British newspaper the *Telegraph*,[4] the "Jtf Gtmo," the U.S. military task force that ran the camp, had itself assessed only 220 of them as dangerous terrorists, while the remaining 395 were labelled as low-level and 150 as completely innocent. At least, that was the assessment as of the date shown in the files; it was subject to change in the future, as the task force reviewed each prisoner's status. But even in the case of prisoners tagged as dangerous, the files made it clear that such assessments were often based on highly unreliable informants, such as prisoners accusing other prisoners after undergoing torture, or in pursuit of personal benefit.

The records exposed the chaos and slapdash choices made by the U.S. authorities in setting up the detention camp, enormously exaggerating the threat posed by the prisoners apart from a very few, relying on unreliable witnesses and on the bounty system, which encouraged the arrest of innocents.

There was the man who had ended up in Guantanamo because his name was similar to that of a former Taliban commander: he was called "Mohammed Nasim," a name that sounded like the one intercepted in a radio communication, "Mullah Nasim."

Mohammed Nasim was a farmer who could neither read nor write, nor did he know his exact age. Nasim had nothing to do with the Taliban, as was written by the U.S. military task force itself: "It is assessed that the detainee is a poor farmer and his arrest was due to mistaken identity." Interned on May 9, 2003, he was still there in February 2005.[5]

There were those who had not the slightest wish to fight, like Asad Ullah,[6] a young Pakistani man 21 years of age "recruited by

4. Christopher Hope, Robert Winnett, Holly Watt and Heidi Blake, "WikiLeaks: Guantanamo Bay terrorist secrets revealed," *Telegraph*, April 25, 2011.
5. The original file is publicly available on the WikiLeaks website: https://wikileaks.org/gitmo/prisoner/958.html (accessed March 11, 2022). It was originally reported in: Stefania Maurizi, "Guantanamo, gli errori e gli orrori," *L'Espresso*, January 11, 2012.
6. The original file is publicly available on the WikiLeaks website: https://wikileaks.org/gitmo/prisoner/47.html (accessed March 11, 2022). Maurizi, "Guantanamo, gli errori e gli orrori."

an individual who convinced detainee to travel to Afghanistan to participate in jihad to repent for his sins of smoking opium and having premarital sex," wrote the Guantanamo task force in his record, concluding that he "does not pose a future threat to the U.S. or its interests."

There was the woodcutter Ezat Khan,[7] who had struggled to pay the "oppressive taxes on the detainee's wood cutting operation making it increasingly difficult for detainee to support his family." He left Afghanistan for Pakistan, but was arrested there and handed over to the U.S. military forces, who transferred him to Guantanamo in June 2002. Why? "[B]ecause of his knowledge of a covert route of travel through the mountains south of Jalalabad, Afghanistan to Parachinar, Pakistan." But six months later, the military concluded that he "has been cooperative, but Joint Task Force Guantanamo considers the information obtained from and about him as not valuable or tactically exploitable."

There was Mohammed Sadiq,[8] born in 1913, transferred to the camp on May 4, 2002, at the tender age of 89. According to the task force files, he was suffering from prostate cancer, senile dementia, severe depression and osteoarthritis. How had he come to be there? Arrested on January 7, 2002, in his house in Afghanistan, he had been found with a Thuraya satellite telephone belonging to a neighbor, and a list of phone numbers associated with individuals suspected of being Taliban. Although the list was not directly linked to him, and the elderly man did not have the slightest idea how to use the telephone, he had been sent to Guantanamo.

Finally, there was a man who had found himself in that inferno because of a lottery. Abdullah Bayanzay,[9] a 42-year-old Afghan, was forcibly enlisted in the Taliban after the elders of his village,

---

7. The original file is publicly available on the WikiLeaks website, accessed March 11, 2022: https://wikileaks.org/gitmo/prisoner/314.html (accessed March 11, 2022). Maurizi, "Guantanamo, gli errori e gli orrori."

8. The original file is publicly available on the WikiLeaks website: https://wikileaks. org/gitmo/prisoner/349.html (accessed March 11, 2022). Originally published in: James Ball, "Guantánamo Bay files: children and senile old men among detainees," *Guardian*, April 25, 2011, and later in: Maurizi, "Guantanamo, gli errori e gli orrori."

9. The original file is publicly accessible on the WikiLeaks website: https://wikileaks. org/gitmo/prisoner/360.html (accessed March 11, 2022). Ths file was originally

knowing they would face horrific reprisals if they failed to provide
new recruits for Taliban military operations, decided in the absence
of volunteers to hold a lottery to select the unlucky winner. After
the United States invaded Afghanistan, Bayanzay was arrested and
transferred to the detention camp in June 2002, but six months
later the task force concluded that he did not pose a threat.

The 765 files on the Guantanamo detainees, like the *Collateral Murder* video and like the reports on the wars in Afghanistan
and Iraq and the U.S. diplomatic cables, had been passed on to
WikiLeaks by Chelsea Manning. Assange and his organization
aimed to publish the files only after we had done all the necessary
investigative work together.

I had been working on those files for several weeks, along with
WikiLeaks and other media partners, when all of a sudden, on
April 25, 2011, the *New York Times*[10] and the *Guardian* published
their own investigations based on the files. Although they had
not been involved in our work, the two newspapers had received
a copy of the files, perhaps from someone previously part of the
organization.

Over a decade later, I would obtain an internal email[11] of the
U.S. State Department revealing it had learned that the *New York
Times* had consulted with the Pentagon before publishing the
Guantanamo files. "On Sunday at 10 p.m., NYT [*New York Times*]
will run 1st stories for Monday print, a 3-4 page 'blowout' with
supporting docs online. They say these are less damaging than the
State cable dump," wrote the State Department in its internal correspondence, adding: "Will provide ammo for those who want to

---

published in: Carlo Bonini and Stefania Maurizi, "Abdullah, il Taliban per caso finito
in carcere dopo una lotteria," *la Repubblica*, April 26, 2011.

10. The *New York Times* published its first article on the night (Central European
Time) of April 24, 2011, the *Guardian* in the very early morning of April 25.

11. Email from Dana S. Smith, U.S. State Department to several redacted and
unredacted recipients, including Jacob J. Sullivan, dated April 23, 2011. I obtained
this email in redacted form thanks to my FOIA litigation against the U.S. State
Department, in which I was initially represented by U.S. FOIA lawyers Kristel Tupja
and Alia Smith of Ballard Spahr. As of this writing, I am represented by Lauren
Russell and Alia Smith of Ballard Spahr. I will discuss my FOIA litigation in chapter
11.

close GTMO [Guantanamo]." The *New York Times* "is sending Gen. [the name of the general and of others is redacted] relevant docs to review," according to the State Department email, which details the U.S. authorities' requests: "We asked for no name of those under the rank of General, no informants, no names of those already resettled/repatriated" and "mentioning someone like Pakistan who visited their detainees after the fact would be fine, but we did not want any of those who helped detain individuals to be outed, for example Eastern European or Middle Eastern countries that helped detain and transfer."

In their email, the U.S. authorities go on to state that the *Times* "would take on board all of our requests and get back to us" and that they had "appreciated the NYT being responsible and coming to us."

They did not show the same appreciation for WikiLeaks; indeed when WikiLeaks and we media partners released the original documents,[12] the Gitmo files, and our investigations based on them—after the *New York Times* and the *Guardian* had already published their articles—the Pentagon strongly condemned the dissemination of those secret files "obtained illegally by WikiLeaks."[13]

Our in-depth analytical work was severely undermined, since we had to rush to publish our pieces within days to keep the two leading newspapers from scooping all of our revelations. It was a shame, because if we had been able to work on them for some months, as we had on the cables, it is likely we would have published much more effective investigations, with the hope of sparking international debate around the inhumane treatment of the detainees, the devastating effects of the wholly false information obtained by U.S. intelligence through torture, and how Guantanamo had itself fanned the flames of Islamic extremism.

---

12. The Gitmo files are publicly available on the WikiLeaks website: https://wikileaks.org/gitmo/ (accessed March 11, 2022).

13. "A statement by the United States government," *New York Times*, April 24, 2011: www.nytimes.com/2011/04/25/world/guantanamo-files-us-government-statement.html (accessed March 11, 2022).

Indeed, as far back as 2004, terrorists had begun to behead Western hostages abducted in Iraq or Syria, videotaping the horrific executions of the prisoners made to wear bright orange uniforms like those worn by the Guantanamo prisoners. It was a clear message to the United States and its allies: the barbarity of the war on terror will be answered in kind. From the CIA's black sites and prisons like Abu Ghraib on up to Guantanamo, the abuses committed by U.S. intelligence and its contractors were potent fuel for terrorist propaganda: they helped create and radicalize far more enemies of the United States than the detention camp could ever hold.

GUANTANAMO'S BARBARITY PERSISTS AND RISKS SETTING A PRECEDENT

It was January 2002 when George W. Bush's Republican administration created the detention camp, and although Barack Obama, a Democrat, ran his presidential campaign promising to close it, and on January 22, 2009—the second day of his presidency—issued an executive order to proceed with its closure within a year,[14] Guantanamo is still open. As I write, it is not clear what Joe Biden's Democratic administration will decide to do about it.

To date, of the 780 detainees interned there since its opening, 9 have come out in a coffin, after dying under unclear circumstances, while 735 have left the facility following authorization of their release by the six major U.S. intelligence agencies[15] because they constituted "no threat to the US or its coalition partners."

As I write, there are still thirty-six prisoners held in Guantanamo, at a cost to the U.S. taxpayer of over 13 million dollars per year each.[16] Of the thirty-six, five have been indicted, accused of

14.   The Executive Order 13492, dated January 22, 2009 is available here: https://irp.fas.org/offdocs/eo/eo-13492.htm (accessed March 11, 2022).
15.   The fact that detainees can be released only after authorization by the six major U.S. intelligence agencies has been confirmed to me by Clive Stafford-Smith, email to author May 21, 2022. Clive Stafford-Smith's work will be discussed later in this chapter.
16.   Carol Rosenberg, "'20th hijacker' is returned to Saudi Arabia for mental health care," *New York Times*, March 7, 2022; Julian Borger, "Guantánamo's last inmates detect a glimmer of hope after 19 years inside," *Guardian*, December 13, 2020.

being directly connected with the September 11 attacks. Their names are Khalid Shaikh Mohammed, the alleged mastermind behind the attacks, Walid bin Attash, Ramzi bin al-Shibh, Ammar al-Baluchi, Mustafa Ahmad al-Hawsawi. They were officially charged in 2008 and have been awaiting trial ever since.

Yes, because ultimately the Bush administration's plan to turn Guantanamo into a judicial black hole—where detainees would remain locked away indefinitely, outside all U.S. and international law, with no judicial review, thus with no judge ever ruling on their innocence or guilt—did not prevail. And if it did not prevail, that is because a number of U.S. lawyers, like the late Michael Ratner of the Center for Constitutional Rights of New York, and Clive Stafford Smith, Joe Margulies and Tom Wilner fought all the way to the United States Supreme Court to win *habeas corpus* for Guantanamo's prisoners.[17]

Despite the climate of fear that came on the heels of September 11, and unlike the many who feared being viewed as enemies of the American people simply for defending the rule of law and the Constitution, these lawyers refused to be intimidated. In June 2004, with the U.S. Supreme Court decision *Rasul v. Bush* they secured *habeas corpus*, giving their detained clients the right to judicial review. The arduous fact-finding efforts of these lawyers over many years had unearthed the unreliability of the informants whose testimony had been used to justify the indefinite detention of their clients.

According to Clive Stafford Smith's research,[18] for example, one prisoner accused ninety-three other prisoners in an 85-minute statement; more than one detainee per minute. His testimony was accepted even though he had been deemed unreliable in a whole series of cases in the past. Another informant had psychological

---

17. Sam Roberts, "Michael Ratner, lawyer who won rights for Guantánamo prisoners, dies at 72," *New York Times*, May 11, 2016; Onnesha Roychoudhuri, "The torn fabric of the law: an interview with Michael Ratner," *Mother Jones*, March 21, 2015; Michael Ratner, "On closing Guantanamo: a Sisyphean struggle," *Huffington Post*, January 23, 2009.
18. Witness statement submitted by Clive Stafford-Smith at the Westminster Magistrates' Court, London, during the extradition hearing of Julian Assange, September 2020.

issues and used his statements to curry favor with the U.S. authorities in the hope of being able to go to the United States for penis
enlargement surgery.

After the attacks on the Twin Towers, that the Western world
did not sink altogether into barbarism and authoritarianism is
thanks to prosecutors like Armando Spataro and Ferdinando
Pomarici, and to lawyers like Ratner, Stafford Smith, Margulies,
Wilner and others. Michael Ratner always maintained that the
United States had all the resources it needed to fight terrorism
using the law instead of torture. Highly experienced Italian prosecutors like Spataro, who has spent his life taking on very dangerous
criminals and terrorists, agree with his view completely.

Their fight for *habeas corpus* was a battle for civilization, to
defend the rights of detainees and the foundations of the rule of
law. And yet, for those among the thirty-six individuals still in
Guantanamo despite never having been charged with any crime,
justice is still very far off.

It is far off for prisoners like Ahmed Rabbani, sold to the United
States in 2002 as a dangerous terrorist by the name of Hassan
Ghul for a 5,000-dollar bounty, tortured for 540 days in a CIA
black site in Afghanistan, then transferred to Guantanamo in
2004. When the real Hassan Ghul was killed by a U.S. drone in
2012, it was clear that Ahmed Rabbani was not the terrorist he
had been mistaken for. Yet at the time of this writing he is still
held in Guantanamo. Since 2013, he has been on a series of hunger
strikes that have brought his weight from 77.1 kilos to 36.3, and
force-fed with methods so brutal that he vomits blood. He has a
son who is 18 years old now whom he has never met, as he was
born some months after Rabbani was handed over to the Americans. Since 2002 he has known only terror, abuse and detention.

The torture techniques introduced after September 11 were
officially banned by the Obama administration, although Donald
Trump threatened to reintroduce them after his election. But as
long as the facility is open, not only does the barbarism continue,
it risks setting a precedent. After every terror attack, there is in fact

no shortage of politicians advocating for the creation of a Guantanamo in Europe.

Indeed, after September 11, the United Kingdom kept a number of foreign nationals suspected of terrorism incarcerated in the maximum-security prison of Belmarsh in London, until December 2004, when the Law Lords—who functioned as the Supreme Court at that time—wiped out any chance of making Belmarsh "Britain's Guantanamo," ruling that the British government—then headed by Prime Minister Tony Blair—could not detain them indefinitely without charging and trying them.[19]

As in the United States, in the United Kingdom the efforts of one lawyer would prove crucial: this time it was Gareth Peirce, who defended the foreign national inmates detained in Belmarsh. Peirce is a living legend. Schooled in the culture of the civil rights battles of Martin Luther King, her dedication to justice and her independence led her to uncover the truth in cases of blatant miscarriage of justice against individuals considered the dregs of society, like the Guildford Four. Three men and a woman suspected of being terrorists with the Irish Republican Army, they were sentenced to life in prison after being found guilty of planting bombs in two pubs frequented by British soldiers. The Guildford Four spent fifteen years in prison, but they were innocent. The case was also portrayed in a film, *In the Name of the Father*, with actress Emma Thompson in the role of Gareth Peirce. Again it was Peirce who represented the British detainees in Guantanamo and made possible their release. The inmates included Shafiq Rasul, the prisoner at the heart of the *Rasul v. Bush* decision, whereby U.S. lawyers Michael Ratner, Clive Stafford Smith, Joe Margulies and Tom Wilner obtained *habeas corpus*.

But while the Supreme Court in the United States ruled in favor of *habeas corpus* but did not close the detention camp, in the UK the Law Lords' decision annulled the "Guantanamo" which

---

19. Lizette Alvarez, "British court strikes down Antiterror Act," *New York Times*, December 17, 2004. One year later, the Law Lords also ruled against the British government's attempt to use evidence obtained through torture. Staff and agencies, "Torture evidence inadmissible in UK courts, Lords rules," *Guardian*, December 8, 2005.

the government was trying to institute in the maximum-security prison of Belmarsh in London.

The egregious human rights violations marking the war on terror—Guantanamo, CIA black sites and extraordinary renditions—will always constitute a moral stain on the United States, and on all governments which to varying degrees contributed to them, like the Italian government in the case of Abu Omar. The torture techniques were so cruel that at times even CIA agents began to weep while witnessing torture sessions like waterboarding.[20] And yet none of the CIA operatives who committed these atrocities have ever paid with even one day in prison. The only CIA agent to end up in prison was John Kiriakou, but not because he tortured anyone. Quite the contrary, in an interview he told me[21] he was one of two agents who refused even to be trained in the techniques introduced after September 11, and later maintained that torture was not the result of abuse by a few bad apples, but the Bush administration's official policy.

In 2014, the Senate Select Committee on Intelligence, the U.S. Senate commission in charge of supervising U.S. intelligence community activities, declassified part of its top-secret report on the use of torture in the war on terror. In the course of five years, the commission studied 6.3 million[22] pages of classified internal CIA files on the so-called "enhanced interrogation techniques," which included waterboarding. The result of that monumental effort was a 6,779-page report, of which only around 520 heavily redacted pages have been made public. The report concludes that, according to the CIA's own documents, the techniques were not effective, and actually produced false information. Khalid Shaikh Mohammed, for example, the alleged mastermind behind the September 11 attacks, subjected among other things to 183 waterboarding

---

20.   Conor Friedersdorf, "The torturers wanted to stop, but the CIA kept going," *The Atlantic*, January 23, 2020.

21.   Stefania Maurizi, "La spia in prigione lancia le sue accuse: Obama ha mancato le promesse," *L'Espresso*, August 1, 2014.

22.   Daniel J. Jones, "Opinion: The CIA tortured prisoners. Americans should know the whole truth," *Washington Post*, December 12, 2019.

sessions, invented[23] information that "led the CIA to capture and detain suspected terrorists who were later found to be innocent."

When it comes to information fabricated under torture, the most shocking case of all is that of Libyan Ibn al-Sheikh al-Libi, thoroughly investigated by the news outlet *Middle East Eye*.[24] After September 11, he was captured in Afghanistan, taken to the Bagram Airbase, then transferred by the CIA to Egypt in a sealed coffin. Like Abu Omar, another infamous "extraordinary rendition," the suspected terrorist was handed over to a regime that could do the United States' dirty work for them. Under torture, Ibn al-Sheikh al-Libi confessed to whatever would satisfy his interrogator: he said that Saddam Hussein's Iraq provided training and assistance to al-Qaeda to build weapons of mass destruction. Once he was handed back to the CIA, Ibn al-Sheikh al-Libi claimed he had invented it all to make the torture stop, but by then it was too late. As revealed in the U.S. Senate Committee report:[25] "Some of this information was cited by Secretary Powell in his speech to the United Nations, and was used as a justification for the 2003 invasion of Iraq."

According to *Middle East Eye*, no other detainee apart from Ibn al-Sheikh al-Libi ever spoke of connections between Iraq and al-Qaeda, let alone for the purpose of building weapons of mass destruction. But that fabricated story was relayed to the British Parliament by British Prime Minister Tony Blair to support the country's invasion.

Thus a piece of false information—which was decisive in sparking a war that annihilated hundreds of thousands of innocent civilians and which helped spawn the horrors of ISIS—was the

23. Report of the Senate Select Committee on Intelligence Committee Study of the Central Intelligence Agency's Detention and Interrogation Program: www. intelligence.senate.gov/sites/default/files/publications/CRPT-113srpt288.pdf (accessed March 12, 2022). Khalid Shaikh Mohammed's quote can be found on p. 485, and was originally reported in: Patrick Cockburn, "CIA torture report: it didn't work then, it doesn't work now," *Independent*, December 14, 2014.
24. Ian Cobain and Clara Usiskin, "EXCLUSIVE: UK spy agencies knew source of false Iraq war intelligence was tortured," *Middle East Eye*, November 7, 2018.
25. Report of the Senate Select Committee on Intelligence Committee Study of the Central Intelligence Agency's Detention and Interrogation Program, p. 141.

result of torture.[26] Yet every time the torture debate resurfaces, so do its staunch defenders. But as pointed out by the prestigious science and technology periodical *Scientific American*,[27] a U.S. Senate Commission study based on 6.3 million pages of secret CIA files was not really necessary: we have known that torture does not work since the Middle Ages. The dark age that Guantanamo, the CIA black sites and extraordinary renditions risked taking us back to.

The Gitmo files, the diplomatic cables, the reports on the wars in Afghanistan and Iraq and the Rules of Engagement for U.S. soldiers in Iraq are the reason Julian Assange risks 175 years in prison in the United States and, as I write, has spent over three years in Belmarsh. The very same prison that could have become the British Guantanamo.

On April 27, 2011, exactly two days after we began releasing the Guantanamo records, U.S. journalist Glenn Greenwald revealed that U.S. authorities had issued a subpoena to compel an individual to testify in relation to a criminal investigation into WikiLeaks for publishing classified U.S. documents.[28] Talk of this had in fact been circulating for a number of months. In January, it was learned that U.S. authorities had ordered Twitter[29] to provide its data on the accounts of WikiLeaks, Julian Assange and other WikiLeaks journalists and supporters. Now the revelations by Glenn Greenwald confirmed that an investigation had indeed been opened.

---

26. Ibn al-Sheikh al-Libi was taken to a very secret area in Gitmo early on, but then moved to CIA black sites, and finally handed over to the Qaddafi regime, which he apparently opposed. He died in prison in Libya, in 2009. The Qaddafi regime characterized his death as "suicide," but international human rights organizations like Human Rights Watch questioned this official version and said it saw photographs of his corpse showing bruising on his body. Cobain and Usiskin, "EXCLUSIVE: UK spy agencies knew source of false Iraq war intelligence was tortured"; Nadine Dahan, "Codename Cuckoo: who was Ibn al-Sheikh al-Libi?," *Middle East Eye*, November 6, 2018.

27. Michael Shermer, "We've known for 400 years that torture doesn't work," *Scientific American*, May 1, 2017.

28. Glenn Greenwald, "FBI serves Grand Jury subpoena likely relating to WikiLeaks," *Salon*, April 27, 2011.

29. Scott Shane and John F. Burns, "US subpoenas Twitter over WikiLeaks supporters," *New York Times*, January 8, 2011.

As legal counsel to represent them in the United States, Assange and his organization had chosen Michael Ratner, while in the United Kingdom Assange's defense was later headed by Gareth Peirce and also included the brilliant human rights lawyer Jennifer Robinson.[30] Ratner would continue to represent Assange and WikiLeaks until his death in 2016. "He was part of a generation of lawyers that was absolutely bold and that understood the political aspects of law," his ex-wife, Margaret Ratner Kunstler, also a prominent lawyer[31] and a leading proponent of human and civil rights in the United States, told the *New York Times* on that occasion. And considering what lay ahead of them, courageous lawyers who understood the political aspects of the law was precisely what Julian Assange and the WikiLeaks journalists would sorely need.

---

30. In the last decade, the Assange and WikiLeaks' legal team has included many high-profile professionals, such as Geoffrey Robertson, Mark Summers, Carey Shenkman, Christophe Marchand, Ben Emmerson, Renata Avila and many others who will be referred to later in this book.

31. Margaret Ratner Kunstler represents Sarah Harrison, who will be introduced later on in this book, and is a WikiLeaks lawyer and adviser to Julian Assange.

8
"The Huffington Post Gang Is Driving Me Nuts"

ELLINGHAM HALL

From the lush green of the English countryside, Ellingham Hall rose discreetly in all its elegant, restrained beauty. An eighteenth-century Georgian-era manor house in the county of Suffolk in southeast England, it is owned by the family of Vaughan Smith.

A former officer with the British Army who later became a war correspondent and founded the Frontline Club, an association for independent journalism based in London, Vaughan Smith invited Julian Assange to serve his house arrest at Ellingham Hall, pending the British court's decision on his extradition to Sweden. It was in part thanks to this offer that on December 16, 2010, Assange was able to leave the old prison of Wandsworth on bail, after ten days of detention by order of the Swedish magistrates, who had issued a European Arrest Warrant for extradition purposes to question him on allegations of rape, sexual molestation and coercion.

After he left Wandsworth, Assange continued to work intensively. In January 2011, I met with him and the WikiLeaks journalists in a house in the English countryside to jointly analyze and publish 4,189 cables on the Vatican and Italy. A few months later, in April, we also worked together on the classified Guantanamo files.

His bail conditions were strict and he wore an electronic ankle bracelet. He was obliged to surrender his passport, so he could not travel abroad, but during the day he was permitted to travel as far as London. In the evening he had to abide by curfew, from 10 p.m. until 8 a.m., sleeping at Ellingham Hall and reporting to nearby

Beccles police station between 8:30 and 11:00 a.m., to sign the register and submit to the routine controls.

That he was a guest in a rich manor home was often stressed by the media, perhaps to depict him as one who, after making the most powerful elite of the world tremble, now led a life of privilege. But everyone familiar with him knew that he actually lived on very little.

Ever since 2010, when the organization's fame exploded worldwide, all criticism against WikiLeaks had focused on Julian Assange. This was not only because he, along with Kristinn Hrafnsson, was the public face of the organization, while the others deliberately remained in the background, but because his charisma and originality both attracted and repelled like a magnet. The media portrayed him as an eccentric hacker, or a self-centered Peter Pan, often as a paranoid, mysterious man at the heart of an international intrigue. But in my dealings with him and his organization, I came to know a journalist who was intellectually gifted, capable of strategic thinking, not motivated by money and, without a doubt, courageous. His passion for technology and its social implications was natural, considering that he had been a hacker as a teenager, but Assange also understood power and its structures. That sort of political intelligence was distinctly less common in people like himself, who live in the world of technology.

And yet WikiLeaks was not just Julian Assange and a technologically advanced platform to which anonymous whistleblowers could submit files. It was a journalistic organization made up of people who could think for themselves, at least those I had come to know or would get to know in the future. Like the mild-mannered Kristinn Hrafnsson, who had solid experience as an investigative reporter behind him. Not in the least "icy," as portrayed at times by the media, Hrafnsson was just as good at dampening controversy as Assange was at igniting it.

British WikiLeaks journalists Joseph Farrell and Sarah Harrison had received their professional training from the Centre for Investigative Journalism of London, founded by Gavin MacFadyen. MacFadyen, harshly critical of the grave decline of mainstream

journalism, had established his center to train investigative journalists who would work in the public interest, conducting
in-depth, critical investigations, not just drafting articles based on
tip-offs from the powerful. Both of them very bright and modest,
Farrell—who still sits on the board of the Centre for Investigative Journalism—was witty and capable of strikingly penetrating
analyses. And only a few years later Sarah Harrison would show
how brave she was and what she was capable of.

I had met talented people both in and around WikiLeaks. Guatemalan lawyer and activist Renata Avila was one of them. She
cultivated an exuberant manner that initially led me to misjudge
her as frivolous, but in reality she was highly impassioned and
intelligent. She did not conceive of the legal profession as a means
to amass money and prestigious clients; rather, she was inspired by
lawyers like Michael Ratner, who had used his profession and civic
passion to help change the world for the better, for example by
winning *habeas corpus* for the most wretched on earth.

I was not as familiar with Stella Moris, who worked on the
Swedish case and only opened up to other people little by little; it
took some time to get to know her better. And I gradually came to
know the Guatemalan film-maker and journalist of Italian origin
and sunny disposition, Juan Passarelli, who filmed some of the particularly crucial stages of the work.

There was no shortage of passion and brilliance within and
around WikiLeaks. But in the summer of 2011, something
happened that would have a profound effect on the organization's
future.

WHOSE FAULT WAS IT?

Seven months after we published the Guantanamo files, I went
to visit Julian Assange in Ellingham Hall to discuss the journalistic work I had been doing for some time on the U.S. diplomatic
cables. By then I could search the entire database of 251,287 files,
not just those on Italy and the Vatican. It was August 26, 2011, a
summer Friday. WikiLeaks was in full swing, and Assange's staff

had scheduled a weekend appointment for me so that I could spend two days at Ellingham Hall.

As I walked in, I saw a magnificent stuffed tiger trapped in a dome-shaped glass case. It must have been more than a century old, but the vivid color of its coat and its powerful paws made it look ready to pounce on whoever entered the house. There were others like it throughout Ellingham Hall, even in front of the room with a fireplace in which WikiLeaks had arranged for me to spend the night. The stuffed tigers and long-antlered deer heads mounted on the walls were only a part of the legacy of the Smith family, which included soldiers and queen's messengers but had also produced a descendant like Vaughan Smith, who never failed to lend his support to Assange, a man despised by the establishment.

Ellingham Hall was beautiful, but it was an old country house, with taps that spouted cold water even in that English August, and rather uncomfortable beds. Vaughan Smith and his family had shown great generosity in hosting not only the founder of WikiLeaks, but all of his staff and even the visitors and journalists like myself who encroached on that residence. But Ellingham Hall was not the Versailles that the media implied, hinting at a new privileged life led by Julian Assange.

A curious scene met my eyes in a large room on the ground floor, where a number of portraits of Smith family ancestors hung from the walls and a maze of electric cables, cameras, backpacks and computer chargers amassed by WikiLeaks lay scattered about the floor. I almost seemed to see the stern features of the Smith family ancestors frowning down at the arrival of Julian Assange and his journalists, who were disturbing the centuries-old peace of the house. I was struck by the irony of the whole situation. The founder of WikiLeaks and his staff seemed like a group of rebels camped out in establishment headquarters.

When I arrived at Ellingham Hall that day, I found Julian Assange and his journalists in great distress. The day before, the German weekly *Der Freitag* had disclosed[1] that the cables database

---

1. Steffen Kraft, "Leck bei Wikileaks," *Der Freitag*, August 25, 2011: www.freitag. de/autoren/steffen-kraft/leck-bei-wikileaks (accessed March 19, 2022).

was available in full online, with none of the names redacted of persons who might be at risk. That enormous trove of files was encrypted, but *Der Freitag* let everyone know that the password was available to the public, one needed only know where to look for it. The weekly did not reveal any details, but for those who had followed the entire case closely, it was not impossible to connect the dots. By now it was only a matter of time before all the cables would be fully available on the internet, with the names of sources, politicians and activists, in both democratic countries and authoritarian ones, who had spoken with U.S. diplomats in confidence.

We were all in shock. Since November 28, 2010, WikiLeaks had been publishing the cables a drop at a time: I was one of the journalists who had been working on them for a good eight months, analyzing the content and redacting names when necessary. That was why the organization had not already published the entire database on its site, as it had done with the other archives.

The journalistic work required for the cables was particularly demanding; indeed, our publications were proceeding very slowly. And now everything was about to end up willy-nilly on the internet, nullifying all our efforts to protect some of the individuals who might be at risk? It did not seem real.

WikiLeaks had begun publishing the cables in November 2010. Now, at the end of August 2011, it was reasonable to assume that the U.S. Department of State, the heart of United States foreign policy, had deployed strategies to minimize the risk, like alerting all the individuals potentially affected and, if necessary, providing them with assistance. But the U.S. authorities never fully and publicly discussed such strategies. In any case, neither WikiLeaks nor journalists like myself, who had worked so hard on the cables while observing the strict security protocols required of us, had ever wanted to see all the files published online without the sensitive names redacted beforehand. How had this happened? Understanding it requires diving into the inner workings of WikiLeaks' file publication operations.

After the German spokesman at the time, Daniel Domscheit-Berg, was suspended by Assange in the summer of 2010, he publicly described his clash with the founder of WikiLeaks as a profound, irreconcilable difference of opinion on how to manage the organization. He announced the creation of his own WikiLeaks, called "OpenLeaks." According to Domscheit-Berg, his new organization would have media partners too: newspapers and traditional media with whom he would exclusively share all secret files received, just like WikiLeaks did. One of OpenLeaks' media partners would be *Der Freitag*, the very same weekly which on August 26, 2011 disclosed that the entire encrypted cables database was available on the internet, and that the password was public also.

Domscheit-Berg's criticism of Julian Assange was extensively taken up by the bulk of the international press, which—with the exception of *Der Spiegel*—did not dig into the crisis very deeply. But their clash in fact concerned some very serious matters.

When he was suspended from the organization, Domscheit-Berg had taken over 3,000 files with him which had been sent to WikiLeaks but had not yet been published, along with, from what *Der Spiegel*[2] was able to piece together, the submission server on which files arrived from sources anonymously, as well as another server with all of WikiLeaks' old publications. Apparently the latter contained not only documents already revealed before then, but also an encrypted archive with the 251,287 U.S. diplomatic cables. The file had an insignificant name in a hard-to-find sub-folder.

I have relayed what was chronicled by *Der Spiegel*, since I was not present when these events occurred. I can only relate what happened at Ellingham Hall on August 26, 2011, and in the days immediately afterwards.

In an attempt to recover those extremely important materials after Domscheit-Berg took them, WikiLeaks relied on the mediation of the German computer security expert and journalist Andy Müller-Maguhn, one of the spokespersons for the Chaos Computer Club (CCC) at that time, and a member of its board of directors. Based in Berlin, the CCC has always been one of

---

2.   Christian Stöcker, "A dispatch disaster in six acts," *Der Spiegel*, September 1, 2011.

the most respected hacker organizations in the world. By "hacker" they do not mean "cybercriminal": the CCC is a reference point for a global galaxy of individuals and organizations passionate about technology, privacy and encryption and its political and social implications. The CCC was a sort of family for Assange and WikiLeaks, so they might have been able to arbitrate the situation, since Domscheit-Berg was a member.

In actual fact, it did not go well. The organization never did manage to obtain the 3,000 or so files Domscheit-Berg had taken with him. However, they did regain the server with the old publications.

A few days after Julian Assange and WikiLeaks began to reveal the U.S. diplomatic correspondence, they were targeted by a massive cyber-attack which shut down their website and computer infrastructure completely. "Quickly, several mirror servers were set up to prevent WikiLeaks from disappearing completely from the Internet. Well-meaning WikiLeaks supporters also put online a compressed version of all data that had been published by WikiLeaks until that time via the filesharing protocol BitTorrent," wrote *Der Spiegel*. This made censoring them very difficult. Because BitTorrent is a file sharing protocol, anyone could now download a copy of the data Domscheit-Berg had taken away with him and store it on their own computer. What supporters did not know is that the dataset did not contain old publications alone, it also included a password-protected copy of all the diplomatic cables.

At any rate, although the complete trove of cables had inadvertently ended up online, and had in all likelihood been downloaded by thousands of supporters throughout the world completely unawares, it was nevertheless encrypted, and the password was not public. Furthermore, the password was so strong that when I later asked internet security guru Bruce Schneier if it was strong enough, he told me:[3] "Without the key, no one would have been able to brute force the file. No one, probably not even aliens with planet sized computers."

---

3.   Bruce Schneier, email to author, September 5, 2011.

But in February 2011, two journalists with the *Guardian*, David Leigh and Luke Harding, published the password in their book,[4] claiming that when the WikiLeaks founder gave them access to the encrypted database, he wrote "ACollectionOfHistorySince_1966_ ToThe_PresentDay#" on a slip of paper. "That's the password," he told David Leigh: "But you have to put in the world 'Diplomatic' before the word 'History'. Can you remember that?"

It was an additional security measure; if the slip of paper ended up in the hands of someone not authorized to access the files, but who knew where to go look for them, he still would not have been able to decrypt the database, because the password was incomplete. It was staggering that the two journalists with the *Guardian* had made the entire password public.

It was just the kind of file protection information that should never be revealed. Assange had been absolutely clear with me about that and, as far as I know, no other media partner has ever disclosed a WikiLeaks password.

However, even though the passphrase had been divulged, the public did not seem to have grasped the importance of that information. And WikiLeaks probably kept quiet to avoid drawing attention to it. But when on August 25, 2011, the German weekly *Der Freitag* revealed that the encrypted documents were available online and that the password had been published also, everything changed. Now anyone who knew where to go look for the archive could decrypt it and access the entire set of unredacted cables.

Technically, there was no longer anything WikiLeaks could do to keep the files from being revealed. They could not remove the database, because after being distributed through file sharing systems like BitTorrent, it had probably already been downloaded by tens of thousands of supporters and detractors. The same was true for the password: it had been published in the book by the two *Guardian* journalists. It could not be erased from the mind of those who had read it.

4. David Leigh and Luke Harding, *Inside Julian Assange's war on secrecy* (London: Guardian Books, 2011).

I arrived at Ellingham Hall the day after that article came out in *Der Freitag* and found myself a witness to the crisis, which unfolded before my eyes throughout the weekend I was there. Julian Assange as well as Sarah Harrison, who worked as a journalist for WikiLeaks at that time, tried repeatedly to contact the U.S. Department of State to alert them to the imminent risk of the files being published online, with the names unredacted. I witnessed their repeated attempts to alert the U.S. authorities and to seek their cooperation.

I left Ellingham Hall on Saturday, August 27, concerned that it was only a matter of days. Whoever found the files first would publish them.

On September 1, 2011, Cryptome, the New York-based website founded by Cypherpunk John Young, published the entire database of unredacted cables.[5] The very next day, September 2, WikiLeaks republished the files by then available on Cryptome.[6]

WikiLeaks promptly published an editorial on how the *Guardian* had "negligently disclosed the Cablegate password."[7] But far from admitting any responsibility, the London daily accused WikiLeaks of recklessness in publishing the unredacted cables, even though the cables had been fully available on Cryptome since the day before. Many international media quickly aligned with their version and condemnation,[8] without making the slightest attempt to understand what had really happened. I would witness this same attitude toward Julian Assange and WikiLeaks in the majority of

---

5. The U.S. diplomacy cables published on John Young's website, Cryptome, are still available there: http://cryptome.org/z/z.7z (accessed March 20, 2022). In September 2020, John Young testified at Westminster Magistrates' Court in London during the extradition hearing of Julian Assange: he confirmed that he published the full database of unredacted cables on September 1, 2011 and revealed crucial information which will be discussed further on in this book.
6. The U.S. diplomacy cables are available on the WikiLeaks website: www.wikileaks.org/plusd/ (accessed March 20, 2022).
7. "Guardian journalist negligently disclosed Cablegate passwords," WikiLeaks, September 1, 2011: https://wikileaks.org/Guardian-journalist-negligently.html (accessed May 2022).
8. James Ball, "WikiLeaks publishes full cache of unredacted cables," *Guardian*, September 2, 2011.

international media for over a decade, as they uncritically echoed the accusation of the moment.

Not even a year earlier, right after Assange and his organization began publishing the cables, they had attained worldwide fame comparable to that of rock stars.[9] "Just my instinct, I believe Assange will be TIME's Man of the Year," U.S. State Department spokesperson, Philip J. Crowley had written in an email I would obtain a decade later.[10] Alec Ross, senior adviser for innovation to then Secretary of State Hillary Clinton, wrote in his internal correspondence: "The HuffPo [Huffington Post] /Open government gang is driving me nuts. They think Assange is some sort of hero."[11]

But a mere eight months after these emails, much of the media had downgraded Julian Assange and WikiLeaks from rock stars to reckless.

ISOLATED

Who had alerted *Der Freitag* to the fact that the encrypted archive was online and that the password was public also? Of course the German weekly never revealed its source, but it must have been someone very familiar with the internal dynamics of WikiLeaks: how many people knew that the database had inadvertently ended up online?

---

9. Nick Squires, "WikiLeaks: Julian Assange crowned 'Rock Star of the Year' by Italian Rolling Stone," *Telegraph*, December 14, 2010; *Hindustan Times* Correspondent Rome, "Assange elected 'Rockstar of the Year'," *Hindustan Times*, December 15, 2010.

10. Email from Philip J. Crowley to Harold Hongju Kho and several others recipients, including Jacob J. Sullivan, December 9, 2010. I obtained this email in heavily redacted form thanks to my FOIA litigation against the U.S. State Department. I will discuss my FOIA battle later, in chapter 11 of this book. Philip J. Crowley would later resign over his comments on the treatment of Chelsea Manning. *Time*'s editors chose the founder and CEO of Facebook, Mark Zuckerberg, as *Time* Magazine's Person of the Year, but Julian Assange won the popular online vote for the accolade. Daniel Trotta, "Time names Mark Zuckerberg 2010 Person of the Year," Reuters, December 15, 2010.

11. Email from Alec J. Ross to Jared Cohen, December 4, 2010. I obtained this email in a heavily redacted form thanks to my FOIA litigation against the U.S. State Department.

Whoever it was, they had in all likelihood done so for two reasons: first, to undermine the publication work WikiLeaks was pursuing with us media partners to release the cables gradually and securely, and, second, to tarnish the reputation of Julian Assange and his organization, so that public opinion would conclude that they were irresponsible, putting lives in danger.

The U.S. authorities most likely considered the incident a point in their favor. After all, what had they done to prevent publication of the unredacted files, once they were alerted by WikiLeaks? It was only later that I learned how hard the organization had tried to seek the U.S. State Department's collaboration—in August 2011, when Julian Assange and Sarah Harrison were contacting them and I was present during some of their phone calls; besides the attempts I witnessed, they also made others. Nonetheless, all media condemnation focused on WikiLeaks. And, to date, no one seems to have asked any questions. Why, for example, did Daniel Domscheit-Berg take more than 3,000 unpublished files away with him and then, as reported by *Der Spiegel*, claim to have destroyed them? Assange later told me[12] that those files were their "greatest loss." Nor does anyone seem to have asked what happened to the alternative organization, OpenLeaks, which Domscheit-Berg had heralded as an improved version of WikiLeaks. So far, it has never materialized.

The media's demonization campaign, which made Assange and his journalists seem responsible for endangering thousands of people throughout the world because the cables contained names to "strictly protect," immediately struck me as exaggerated. Having worked on those documents night and day for eight months, I knew that the label "strictly protect" did not necessarily apply to sources who might be at risk: it was also used simply to shield senior officials in foreign governments from political embarrassment, or even for entities which were not actual persons, like the Italian police.

---

12. Stefania Maurizi, "Julian Assange: WikiLeaks will go ahead," *L'Espresso*, November 30, 2012.

Not only did the media campaign uncritically contribute to the U.S. authorities' campaign against WikiLeaks, but the clash between the former German spokesperson and Julian Assange created a rift in the prestigious Chaos Computer Club of Berlin, after the club decided to expel Domscheit-Berg.

As lawyer and activist Renata Avila would help me understand later, many different civil society groups inspired and supported Assange and his organization between 2007 and 2011. Avila was acquainted with many of those groups, because she was part of them. There was the large and diverse community that advocated free software and privacy protection, and revolved around the CCC and the Wau Holland Foundation and their contacts of reference, like Andy Müller-Maguhn. There was the community that aspired to democratize the media and expand access to information and knowledge, wrenching it from the grip of the oligarchies who have always controlled the newspapers, television and radio. There were communities from Latin America to Africa fighting to hold the perpetrators of genocides and gross human rights violations accountable to the law for their crimes. These groups were different from each other, but they shared certain passions and projects: the democratization of technology, the media, and internet access, the defense of privacy and encryption, the fight for justice.

The conflict between Assange and Domscheit-Berg, and the expulsion of the latter from the CCC, created rifts and ill feeling in the club which had been like a family to Assange and WikiLeaks. In the meantime, the demonization campaign further alienated media support and public opinion. A few months earlier, in February 2011, a plan aimed at undermining the reputation of WikiLeaks, disrupting its journalistic work and destroying its public support, had also surfaced. It was based on the techniques of dirty war.

DIVIDE, DISCREDIT, SABOTAGE

The plan was called "The WikiLeaks Threat" and was outlined in a document bearing the logos of three U.S. companies: HBGary

Federal, Berico Technologies and Palantir, the company cofounded by German-American billionaire Peter Thiel, who had also cofounded PayPal, among the first online payment services to cut off WikiLeaks access to donations immediately after they began publishing the cables. Palantir would later become well known for its work for the NSA and the CIA, and for having been backed by the CIA in the initial stages of its creation, via the In-Q-Tel fund[13] through which the U.S. intelligence community financially invests in hi-tech firms it considers strategic.

According to U.S. press reports, the HBGary Federal company worked for a legal firm representing one of the largest banks in the United States: Bank of America. In November 2010, in an interview with the U.S. magazine *Forbes*, Julian Assange announced that he would be publishing files regarding "one or two banks," without giving their names.

The document revealing the plan against WikiLeaks had only emerged thanks to hacking activities attributed to Anonymous, a movement of internet activists whose identities are in fact anonymous and who hide behind the famous Guy Fawkes mask. Anonymous was a collective, not a media organization like WikiLeaks, but shared some of the same supporters. In December 2010, when Assange's organization began publishing the cables and all donations were blocked by the Visa and Mastercard credit card companies, as well as the PayPal, Western Union and Bank of America payment systems, Anonymous launched a series of online attacks against Visa, Mastercard and PayPal in an act of protest. After the attacks, the CEO of HBGary Federal went about boasting that he could unmask the activists in the collective. At that point, Anonymous hacked that company's website, and the files they took revealed a number of internal documents, including the plan to cripple WikiLeaks.[14]

---

13. In-Q-Tel is the venture capital fund which the U.S. intelligence community relies on to invest in cutting-edge technologies in support of its missions. The name In-Q-Tel comes from the word "intel," i.e. intelligence, and "Q," the fictional character of the James Bond saga, who provides high-tech gadgets to James Bond. The website of In-Q-Tel is available at this link: www.iqt.org/ (accessed March 21, 2022).
14. The plan "The WikiLeaks Threat" is available in Nate Anderson, "Spy games: inside the convoluted plot to bring down WikiLeaks," *Wired*, February 14, 2011,

The dirty war strategy called for sabotage activities on a number of levels: "Feed the fuel between the feuding groups. Disinformation"; "Submit fake documents and then call out the error"; "Create concern over the security of the infrastructure. Create exposure stories. If the process is believed to not be secure they are done"; "Cyber attacks against the infrastructure to get data on document submitters. This would kill the project"; "Media campaign to push the radical and reckless nature of wikileaks activities. Sustained pressure." And, finally, sabotage techniques aimed at undermining the support of journalists like Glenn Greenwald. "It is this level of support that needs to be disrupted," read the document, concluding: "These are established professionals that have a liberal bent, but ultimately most of them if pushed will choose professional preservation over cause, such is the mentality of most business professionals. Without the support of journalists like Greenwald wikileaks would fold."

There is no evidence that these dirty war strategies were ever implemented by the three companies that had cooked up the plan, and as soon as they were made public, Bank of America denied knowing of them and having enlisted HBGary Federal. As for Palantir, whose logo was on every single page of the document outlining the strategy, they issued a public apology. One thing is certain, however: from 2010 until today, there has been a protracted media campaign against WikiLeaks and continuous pressure, just as posited in the plan.

In the course of that year, between April 2010 and 2011, Julian Assange and the WikiLeaks journalists had pulled off some of the biggest scoops in journalism history, publishing the *Collateral Murder* video, the Afghan and Iraq War Logs, the diplomatic cables and the Guantanamo files. Yet they found themselves accused of endangering lives, cut off from donations by the credit giants, and harshly attacked by the same leading newspapers that had greatly benefited from the WikiLeaks scoops, like the *New York Times* and the *Guardian*. The Swedish case would do the rest.

---

as well as on the WikiLeaks website: https://wikileaks.org/IMG/pdf/WikiLeaks_Response_v6.pdf (accessed March 21, 2022).

9

From Sweden to Ecuador

"HE NEEDS HIS HEAD DUNKED IN
A FULL TOILET BOWL AT GITMO"

Five months after the cables were published in full, including
the names of U.S. diplomatic contacts and sources, a legal ruling
changed Julian Assange's fate forever. On May 30, 2012, the
Supreme Court of the United Kingdom ruled that he should be
extradited to Sweden at the request of prosecutor Marianne Ny,
who had ordered his extradition to question him on the allegations
of rape, sexual molestation and coercion.

Ever since December 2010, the WikiLeaks founder had been
under house arrest in the English countryside with an electronic
bracelet around his ankle, awaiting the verdict of the courts.
Assange had been fighting extradition to Sweden all along, convinced that it would pave the way to his extradition to the United
States. In the British courts, he had appealed all the way up to the
Supreme Court. There was no public request from U.S. authorities,
but this did not at all mean that one had not been made, under seal.
Until such time as they are made public, extradition proceedings
remain shrouded in secrecy, precisely so that presumed criminals
will not be tipped off and attempt to flee.

Since at least the end of 2010, it was common knowledge that
the United States had opened an investigation into the publication of classified U.S. government files by WikiLeaks, and in
April 2011 Glenn Greenwald revealed that the FBI had issued a
subpoena on a Cambridge, Massachusetts resident, whose identity
was not made public, to appear in court to testify before the Grand
Jury in Alexandria, Virginia.

The Grand Jury is an institution enshrined in the U.S. Constitution, but it plays a controversial role in the American criminal

justice system. It is not a jury that rules on the innocence or guilt of a defendant on trial, rather it is a jury called upon to decide whether or not there are sufficient grounds to charge an individual. Closed to the public, to the press and to the lawyers of the persons summoned to testify, the Grand Jury operates in secrecy.

The revelations by Greenwald confirmed the rumors that had been going around for some time about the opening of a U.S. investigation. But no one knew how it was proceeding, precisely by reason of the secrecy in which the Grand Jury operates.

Two months before the British Supreme Court ruling, WikiLeaks, together with us media partners, had revealed 5.3 million internal emails[1] of the Stratfor company. A private U.S. intelligence firm that buys and sells information for wealthy and influential clients like multinational corporations, government agencies and the media, Stratfor has close ties with the FBI and the U.S. intelligence agencies. In an email dated July 26, 2010— the day after WikiLeaks began publishing the classified files on the Afghanistan war—the Vice-President for Counterterrorism at Stratfor at the time, Fred Burton, commented:[2] "The owner [of WikiLeaks] is a peacenik. He needs his head dunked in a full toilet bowl at Gitmo."

And again, on December 14, 2010, just one week after Assange was arrested in London at the request of Swedish prosecutor Marianne Ny, Burton wrote:[3] "Death penalty case for Manning. Assange is looking at life imprisonment w/Ramzi Yousef @ The SuperMax. We won't be able to extradite for the death penalty but will be able to hold w/the sealed indictment."

---

1. Stratfor's internal emails are available on the WikiLeaks website: https://search. wikileaks.org/gifiles/ (accessed March 24, 2022). My exclusive based on these files: Stefania Maurizi, "WikiLeaks, la nuova ondata," *L'Espresso*, February 27, 2012.
2. Fred Burton's email dated July 26, 2010 is available on the WikiLeaks website: https://search.wikileaks.org/gifiles/emailid/364817 (accessed March 24, 2022).
3. Fred Burton's email dated December 14, 2010 is available on the WikiLeaks website: https://search.wikileaks.org/gifiles/emailid/1645706 (accessed March 24, 2022). As for Ramzi Yousef, he has been convicted as the mastermind behind the 1993 World Trade Center bombing. He is serving a life sentence at the United States maximum security prison ADX Florence, in Colorado.

As for Chelsea Manning, Burton also cited remarks by one of his highest-level sources in the FBI: "Manning should fry and hopefully will,"[4] explaining that by "fry" the FBI source meant she should be given an extremely harsh sentence, perhaps even the death penalty.

And finally, on January 26, 2011, Burton wrote to his colleagues:[5] " Not for Pub—We have a sealed indictment on Assange. Pls protect."

Stratfor's internal emails not only laid bare the animus which people with close ties to U.S. intelligence harbored toward Assange, WikiLeaks and Manning, but also that there was a sealed indictment. Was it true?

The head of Stratfor definitely had sources with access to that kind of confidential news: he had been a special agent with the U.S. Department of State, specializing in anti-terrorism, and he had participated in high-profile operations like the arrest of Ramzi Yousef, considered the mastermind behind the attacks on the World Trade Center in New York in 1993.

In the uncertainty around how the investigation of WikiLeaks was proceeding, one thing was certain: Assange would fight the risk of extradition to the United States with every available resource. But the ruling by the Supreme Court of the United Kingdom had left him with no way out. Within only a few days, the British authorities would transfer him to Stockholm and, from that moment on, no one knew what fate awaited him.

AN INVESTIGATION OPENED,
CLOSED AND REOPENED

Sweden is renowned for its culture of women's rights, and of human rights in general.

But after 9/11, Sweden's reputation was considerably tainted by its cooperation with the CIA's extraordinary renditions program,

---

4. Stratfor's email mentioning Chelsea Manning is available on the WikiLeaks website: https://search.wikileaks.org/gifiles/emailid/1522200 (accessed March 24, 2022).

5. Fred Burton's email dated January 26, 2011 is available on the WikiLeaks website: https://search.wikileaks.org/gifiles/emailid/1112549 (accessed March 24, 2022).

when Swedish secret services consigned asylum seekers suspected of terrorism to the Agency, who then transferred them to Egypt, where they were brutally tortured.[6] And yet Sweden's culture of transparency and freedom of expression had made it a country WikiLeaks had looked upon with interest, hoping to find in it a place where the organization could enjoy protection.

In August 2010, two weeks after publishing the classified reports on the war in Afghanistan, Julian Assange travelled to Sweden to hold a conference at the invitation of a local social democratic association. While he was there, he had sexual intercourse, on separate occasions, with two Swedish women:[7] Anna A., who worked for the organization that had invited him and who hosted him in her home, and Sofia W. The two women did not know each other. It was only after they came into contact and realized they had both had sexual relations with Assange that they went to the police together. Why was that?

According to the reconstruction of the facts agreed upon by both the prosecution and Assange's defense in the appeal to the Supreme Court of the United Kingdom,[8] the two women went to the Swedish police for advice, insofar as Sofia W. wanted the WikiLeaks founder to be tested for sexually transmitted diseases. After listening to them, however, the police proceeded *ex officio* with filing two formal reports: one for the rape of Sofia W. and the other for the sexual molestation of Anna A.[9]

According to the report filed by the Swedish police, the rape incident had gone as follows: on August 17, Sofia W. and Julian Assange had sexual intercourse more than once protected by a condom and, after one of these instances: "They dozed off and she

6. "Sweden violated torture ban in CIA rendition," Human Rights Watch, November 9, 2006: www.hrw.org/news/2006/11/09/sweden-violated-torture-ban-cia-rendition (accessed March 24, 2022).

7. The violation of the two women's privacy, and that of Julian Assange, which we commit by describing their sexual relations, is done exclusively to reconstruct the legal case.

8. "Agreed statement of facts and issues": www.scribd.com/document/80912442/ Agreed-Facts-Assange-Case (accessed March 24, 2022).

9. The reports were filed as Case N. K246314-10 for the allegations of rape of Sofia W. and Case N. K246336-10 for the allegations of sexual molestation of Anna A.

awoke and felt him penetrating her." She immediately asked: "Are you wearing anything?" To Assange's negative reply she answered: "You better not have HIV," and he replied: "Of course not." The police report continues: "She felt that it was too late. He was already inside her and she let him continue. She didn't have the energy to tell him one more time. She had gone on and on about condoms all night long. She has never had unprotected sex before. He said he wanted to come inside her; he did not say when he did, but he did it. A lot ran out of her afterward."[10]

In the molestation episode, according to the police report, Anna A. and Julian Assange had consensual intercourse, but he molested her "during an act of copulation—which was begun and conducted under the express condition that a condom would be used—by purposely damaging the condom and continuing the copulation until he ejaculated in her vagina."[11]

There were at least two striking things in the police report on the alleged rape: Sofia W. had not signed the report, and had interrupted her interview when she was informed that Assange would be arrested. Furthermore, after the police officer held an interview with her in person on August 20, 2010, which was not recorded but only summarized, the police officer was instructed by her superior to create and sign a new interview in the Swedish police computer system, which was done on August 26 "with the necessary changes."[12]

---

10.   The two reports filed by the Swedish police as Case N. K246314-10 and N. K246336-10 are in Swedish. All of my attempts to obtain a copy under FOIA from the Swedish Police Authority were rejected. I was able to consult a copy of the two reports from other sources. A reconstruction of the Swedish police documents was published in: Nick Davies, "10 days in Sweden: the full allegations against Julian Assange," *Guardian*, December 17, 2010. The *Guardian's* article does not contain any reference, however, to the sentence, "she let him continue," which is present in the police report. According to Davies, the sentence was included in his original draft, but then his piece was rewritten in the *Guardian* office to include the comments by Julian Assange's lawyer, hence a lot of detail was cut out in order to make space for it. Nick Davies, email to author March 28, 2022. Whereas the sentence is correctly reported in: Nils Melzer (with Oliver Kobold), *The trial of Julian Assange: A story of persecution* (London: Verso Books, 2022).
11.   Ibid.
12.   I will discuss the matter of the interview having been modified in chapter 18, referring to the official letter from the UN Special Rapporteur on Torture, Nils Melzer,

After Sofia W. and Anna A. went to the police station on the afternoon of August 20, 2010, the police officers opened the two investigations *ex officio* and immediately phoned the public prosecutor on duty, who ordered Julian Assange's arrest that day. Not even four weeks had passed since publication of the classified files on the war in Afghanistan, and WikiLeaks and Julian Assange were now famous and celebrated for the *Collateral Murder* video and the Afghan War Logs. Assange had just won the Sam Adams Award[13] for Integrity: one in a long list of prestigious prizes he and WikiLeaks have received in over a decade.

News of the arrest warrant for rape was immediately passed on to the Swedish tabloid *Expressen*, in violation of the privacy of the two women and of Assange. *Expressen* then published it, and the news swept around the world.

The next day, August 21, the case was taken up by Stockholm's chief prosecutor Eva Finné who, after examining the facts, decided to revoke the arrest warrant for Julian Assange and closed the rape investigation on August 25 because, in her judgement, the suspect's conduct disclosed no crime at all.[14] But she decided to keep open the investigation into the alleged misconduct against Anna A.

On August 30, the WikiLeaks founder was questioned on this allegation. He claimed not to have torn the condom at all, nor to have even noticed that it was broken, adding that, during the entire week he spent as a guest in A's home, she never spoke of that episode to him and only mentioned the accusations on August 20, the day she went to the police.

---

and the Swedish government, dated September 12, 2019, as well as my questions to the Swedish police.

13. The Sam Adams Award is an award for journalists and whistleblowers who showed integrity in exposing crimes and lies of the military-intelligence complex. Sam Adams Award website: https://samadamsaward.ch/ (accessed May 22, 2022); Craig Murray, "Julian Assange wins Sam Adams Award for Integrity," Craig Murray blog, August 19, 2010: www.craigmurray.org.uk/archives/2010/08/julian_assange/ (accessed May 22, 2022).

14. "Agreed statement of facts and issues": www.scribd.com/document/80912442/ Agreed-Facts-Assange-Case. See also Eva Finné's statement: "I don't think there is reason to suspect that he has committed rape," reported by BBC: "Swedish rape warrant for Wikileaks' Assange cancelled," BBC, August 21, 2010: www.bbc.com/ news/world-europe-11049316 (accessed March 27, 2022).

Only two days after Assange was questioned, on September 1, a different magistrate, the Director of Public Prosecution in Gothenburg, Marianne Ny, decided to reopen the rape investigation and to expand the molestation investigation after the counsel for the two women, Claes Borgström, appealed the Stockholm chief prosecutor's decision to drop the rape case.

Assange remained in Sweden for several weeks, until September 27 when he flew to Berlin to meet with me and other journalists interested in publishing the Afghan and Iraq war reports. Before he left the country, his Swedish lawyer at the time, Björn Hurtig, checked with Marianne Ny to make sure he had permission to do so. Julian Assange arrived at my hotel in Berlin on the evening of September 27, 2010 without any luggage, apart from his shoulder bag. That same day, Ny issued an arrest warrant.

In the two months that followed, while WikiLeaks with its media partners was revealing hundreds of thousands of classified U.S. government files, Assange's lawyers were proposing various options to prosecutor Ny to question him on the allegations. They asked to conduct the interview by telephone or video conference, in writing or an in-person interview in the Australian embassy. All of these options were perfectly permissible according to Swedish law, but she rejected all of them.[15]

On November 18, ten days before WikiLeaks began publishing the U.S. diplomacy cables, Marianne Ny ordered his detention on suspicion of rape, unlawful coercion and three instances of sexual molestation. The detention order was *in absentia*, since Assange was no longer in Sweden. Assange's defense appealed, but the Swedish Court of Appeals upheld the order, though it did reduce the molestation accusations to two episodes rather than three and, more importantly, established that the alleged rape should be low-

---

15. I will discuss how Assange tried repeatedly to be questioned by Swedish prosecutor Marianne Ny in chapter 11, using documentation I have obtained from the Swedish and British authorities. The fact that Assange asked to be questioned via phone, videolink, written statement or in person at the Australian embassy is also documented in the reconstruction of the facts agreed upon by both the prosecution and Assange's defense in the appeal to the Supreme Court of the United Kingdom: "Agreed statement of facts and issues": www.scribd.com/document/80912442/Agreed-Facts-Assange-Case.

ered to *minor rape*, the less serious offense, since in 2010 Swedish law provided for essentially three degrees of the crime: *gross rape*, *rape* and *minor rape*. The maximum sentence for the first category was ten years, for the second six years, and for the third category four years. Minor rape, also called *less serious* [*rape*], could apply in cases as follows: an individual has consensual sexual intercourse with a partner and then, without consent having been withdrawn, has intercourse in another situation wherein the same partner is vulnerable, because asleep or unconscious, hence in a helpless state.

On December 2, 2010, five days after WikiLeaks began publishing the cables with *The Guardian* and its other media partners, Marianne Ny issued a European Arrest Warrant for Assange, who was in London at the time to work on the files. The warrant requested his extradition to Sweden for questioning on suspicion of rape (*minor rape*), molestation and coercion. In the meantime, Sweden had already activated Interpol, which issued a *red notice*, making the founder of WikiLeaks wanted throughout the world.[16] Five days later, he turned himself in to Scotland Yard, a DNA sample was taken, and he was imprisoned in Wandsworth, in solitary confinement for ten days, until he was released on bail on December 16. He spent the next 18 months in British courts fighting his extradition, arguing in particular that the European Arrest Warrant ordering extradition of a suspect simply to question him—not to send him to trial, as he had not been charged—was a disproportionate measure, and that it had been requested by the same prosecutor, Marianne Ny, who was conducting the preliminary investigation, and not by a judge.

He lost every appeal. On May 30, 2012, the Supreme Court of the United Kingdom ruled that a public prosecutor was a judicial authority who could legally issue a European warrant for arrest.

In the Stratfor emails, which WikiLeaks had revealed together with us media partners two months before this ruling, the analysts

---

16. "Sweden authorizes INTERPOL to make public Red Notice for WikiLeaks founder": www.interpol.int/en/News-and-Events/News/2010/Sweden-authorizes-INTERPOL-to-make-public-Red-Notice-for-WikiLeaks-founder (accessed March 28, 2022).

working with the private U.S. intelligence company had commented[17] on Assange's arrest in December 2010, in the midst of publishing the cables, as follows: "Charges of sexual assault rarely are passed through Interpol red notices, like this case, so this is no doubt about trying to disrupt WikiLeaks release of government documents."

Stratfor spoke of "charges," but in reality Swedish prosecutor Ny never charged Julian Assange. He was only under investigation, which made Interpol issuing a red notice for him even more anomalous. But he was already stuck with the rape narrative: as far as much of the media was concerned, Assange was no longer just a paranoid, enigmatic man at the heart of an international intrigue who might have put people's lives in danger. He was also a rape suspect trying to escape the justice of a highly civilized country like Sweden, and therefore doubly suspected of being guilty.

After the Supreme Court ruling[18] on May 30, 2012, Assange's defense applied to have his appeal reopened, but on June 14 their application was rejected. The verdict was final.

The British Supreme Court has the last letter in the Greek alphabet, "omega," as its symbol because, for those appealing to the court, it is their last chance to obtain justice on British soil. Julian Assange had run out of chances. It was only a matter of days before he would be transferred to Sweden. But he never did arrive in that Scandinavian country.

WHEN ECUADOR SAID:
"COLONIAL TIMES ARE OVER"

Disguised as a motorcyclist to elude the inevitable surveillance—he was under house arrest with an electronic ankle tag, pending his

17. The Stratfor email dated December 7, 2010, is available on the WikiLeaks website: https://search.wikileaks.org/gifiles/emailid/1092001 (accessed March 28, 2022).
18. The Supreme Court ruling is at: www.supremecourt.uk/cases/docs/uksc-2011-0264-judgment.pdf (accessed March 28, 2022). The Supreme Court's press release on its decision to dismiss Julian Assange defense's request to reopen the appeal is at: www.supremecourt.uk/news/julian-assange-v-swedish-prosecution-authority.html (accessed March 28, 2022).

imminent extradition to Sweden—on June 19, 2012, five days after the United Kingdom Supreme Court's final verdict, the founder of WikiLeaks violated his bail conditions, took refuge in Ecuador's embassy in London and requested asylum.

The news astonished everyone and many found it bizarre, to say the least, not to mention distinctly suspicious: if he was innocent like he said he was, why had he run away? Very few believed his stated motives, namely that he had applied for asylum not to escape Sweden, but to seek protection from the United States. Officially there was no extradition request, or even an indictment from U.S. authorities, so many wrote him off as a fugitive from Swedish justice. But then, many wondered, why Ecuador?

In 2012, Latin America was in the midst of the "pink tide," the wave of left-wing governments coming to power, from Lula and Dilma Rousseff's Brazil to Hugo Chávez's Venezuela and Evo Morales' Bolivia, fighting the devastating neoliberal economic model and U.S. interference throughout the entire region. Ecuador, led at the time by progressive president Rafael Correa, had as its main economic partner the United States, so it was not in Correa's interests to ruin his country's relations with the U.S. superpower. Correa had himself maintained strong economic ties with the United States, but he had also made a number of independent choices, like refusing to enter free trade agreements that he did not consider to be in his country's interests, and asking U.S. troops to leave the Manta military base in the Pacific Ocean. These policies had placed Correa at the center of a heated clash with the old oligarchies who dominated the country's politics and economy, and who controlled a large part of the national media.

In 2011, the WikiLeaks journalists mentioned to me how surprised they were when Ecuadorian authorities contacted the organization with a request to make public all the cables on their country. Their request was opposite to that of most governments, which most certainly did not want to see their affairs exposed in the public square, including the embarrassing appraisals of their politicians by U.S. diplomats.

When Julian Assange took refuge in the Ecuadorian embassy in London to seek asylum, Correa's government did not say no. In the darkest years of dictatorships and political violence in Latin America countries, foreign embassies, including Italy's embassy in Chile during Augusto Pinochet's coup d'état, had been a place of salvation for thousands. Many countries in the region, including Ecuador, had signed and ratified the Caracas Convention on Diplomatic Asylum, which allows refugees to apply for protection from a member nation even if the refugee is not at that nation's borders, but has succeeded in reaching one of its embassies. That is what Julian Assange had done.

Decisive in all this was Ecuador's consul in London at the time, Fidel Narváez, who would never fail to support Assange even during the difficult phases of his presence in the embassy, and former Spanish judge and now lawyer Baltasar Garzón, who has headed Assange's legal team ever since.

Garzón is an icon of the fight for justice in some of the most harrowing cases of crimes against humanity, like those committed by the Chilean and Argentine dictatorships. In 1998, he ordered the arrest of Pinochet—who had flown to London for a surgical operation—via a red notice issued by Interpol: the same tool used by Sweden to make Julian Assange a wanted man internationally. Garzón fought tenaciously to extradite the dictator to Spain and try him for torturing and assassinating Spanish citizens in Chile during his ferocious regime. But after 503 days under house arrest in a luxurious manor in Surrey, soothed by the refined Scotch sent him by Margaret Thatcher, Pinochet was able to return to Chile undisturbed, after Britain's Home Secretary at the time, Labour's Jack Straw, refused his extradition on medical grounds. On March 3, 2000, he left London in a wheelchair, like an old man too ill and frail to take the stand. Upon disembarking in Santiago, Chile, he was walking on his own two legs again, welcomed as a hero by the military and his supporters.[19]

---

19. David Connett, John Hooper and Peter Beaumont, "Pinochet arrested in London," *Guardian*, October 18, 1998; Clare Dyer, "Extradition refused as 'unjust and oppressive'," *Guardian*, January 13, 2000; Mat Youkee, "Thatcher sent Pinochet

The United Kingdom was not so benevolent towards Julian Assange. There was no Scotch. On August 15, 2012, the day before Ecuador officially granted him asylum, the British authorities threatened to raid the embassy to arrest him. An unthinkable scenario: embassies are inviolable even in wartime. The reply from Rafael Correa's small Latin American country was firm. "We want to be very clear, we're not a British colony. The colonial times are over," Ecuador's Foreign Minister, Ricardo Patiño, publicly declared.[20] The British authorities took a step back, but deployed a large contingent of police around the embassy and closed the access road to the public. "The night the British threatened the embassy was probably the tensest" Fidel Narváez, Ecuador's consul at the time would later tell me,[21] recalling how there were agents everywhere: "they were outside every window and they were even inside the building, because there was an interior patio."

Ecuador was not cowed: on August 16, 2012, they granted the WikiLeaks founder diplomatic asylum, deeming Julian Assange's fears of facing political persecution in the United States well founded. Patiño expressed his hope for a diplomatic solution to the case, a safe-conduct that would allow Assange to leave the embassy, but the British authorities immediately made it known that they would not concede this, claiming that they were legally obliged to extradite him to Sweden.

Even before granting him asylum, Ecuador offered the Scandinavian country its cooperation. In diplomatic correspondence dated July 25, 2012, the Ecuadorian authorities wrote to the Swedish Ministry for Foreign Affairs:[22] "Mr. Julian Assange,

finest Scotch during former dictator's UK house arrest," *Guardian*, October 4, 2019; "Pinochet retreats to luxury estate," *BBC News*, December 2, 1998: http://news.bbc. co.uk/2/hi/225567.stm (accessed March 28, 2022); Alex Bellos and Jonathan Franklin, "Pinochet receives a hero's welcome on his return," *Guardian*, March 4, 2000; Warren Hoge, "After 16 months of house arrest, Pinochet quits England," *New York Times*, March 3, 2000.

20. Eduardo Garcia and Alessandra Prentice, "Britain threatens to storm Ecuador embassy to get Assange," *Reuters*, August 16, 2012.

21. Stefania Maurizi, "I was fired for helping Julian Assange, and I have no regrets," *Jacobin*, October 25, 2019: www.jacobinmag.com/2019/10/julian-assange-fidel-narvaez-ecuador-moreno (accessed March 28, 2022).

22. The diplomatic correspondence was sent from the "Embajada del Ecuador, Estocolmo, Suecia" to the "Ministry for Foreign Affairs of Sweden, Americas

through his lawyers, has made known to the Swedish Prosecution's Office his availability to be interrogated in the facilities of the Embassy of Ecuador in London. In this context, the Embassy of Ecuador makes patent the National Government's willingness to provide the cooperation that would be necessary accordingly with the decision of the relevant Swedish authorities."

The Swedish ministry did not even answer.

CONFINED TO 20 SQUARE METERS

I went to visit him almost immediately.[23] On November 15, 2012, I headed to the Ecuadorian embassy in London, in the exclusive Knightsbridge district, right behind Harrods department store. The building was guarded night and day by Scotland Yard agents. At times there were one or more police vans in the immediate vicinity, equipped with cameras keeping a watchful eye and other technologies I could not identify. Once inside, I even saw an officer's head peering through the bathroom window, at eye-level, so the curtain had to be kept closed to avoid close encounters and the tense feeling of being watched. Apart from that, the atmosphere in the embassy was relaxed and the diplomatic staff were kind. The building was nothing like the large facilities that typically house diplomatic headquarters; it was a normal apartment, and did not even have a small garden or courtyard where Assange might safely go to take a breath of fresh air and enjoy a bit of sunlight.

That first time I visited him there, he was confined to a room of about 20 square meters, with just one window. The area was divided by a bookshelf separating his bed from the portion where he worked. That small space crammed with books, binders, computers, bookshelf, bed, table and chairs gave an oppressive feeling,

---

Department, Stockholm". Note No. 4-2 154/2012, dated July 25, 2012. A copy of this letter was released to me under FOIA by the Ministry for Foreign Affairs of Sweden, which confirmed to me that the ministry's archives contain no reply to this letter from the Swedish authorities. Utrikesdepartementet, Rättssekretariatet, email to author, March 12, 2021.

23.   I recounted my visit in my article: Stefania Maurizi, "Julian Assange: WikiLeaks will go ahead," *L'Espresso*, November 30, 2012.

intensified by the lack of fresh air and natural light. The only way he could get physical exercise was on a treadmill. Assange had been there for scarcely five months, but a careful observer could already see the effects of his confinement. I had last met him in February, when we worked together on the Stratfor files; only nine months had gone by. He had lost a lot of weight since then, almost 10 kilograms. His face was too white and he had a dry cough. Hanging on the wall, I noticed a small blackboard with a list of instructions in case he experienced any medical emergencies.

Assange told me that WikiLeaks would carry on. Indeed in July, while he was in the embassy awaiting Ecuador's decision on his asylum, the organization had revealed the Syria files,[24] again in cooperation with us media partners: over 2 million emails on the Syrian regime of Bashar al-Assad. This was a declaration of WikiLeaks' determination and capacity to keep publishing despite the founder's situation, despite the threats from the U.S. authorities, despite the Grand Jury investigation and the banking blockade on donations. They were under siege, but they were not defeated. Quite the contrary, Assange told me: "The Pentagon and White House multiple times made public demands of us to destroy everything. We published everything successfully. We faced down the threats made by the Pentagon, we took the heat and we won." Once again, his courage impressed me, as it always had.

When I left the embassy that November day and felt the pleasantly crisp air on my face once out on the street again, I wondered what it felt like for him never to be able to go out for even one minute, and to know he would be arrested if he ever fell ill and tried to go to hospital. The British authorities had stationed Scotland Yard agents all around the building for the explicit purpose of capturing him immediately the moment took a step outdoors.

Six months later, in May 2013, I went to visit him again, and that time I brought him a bright yellow and orange coloured mask in the shape of the sun. It had been crafted in the same Venetian

---

24. The Syria files are available on the WikiLeaks website: https://search.wikileaks.org/syria-files/ (accessed March 28, 2022).

workshop that film director Stanley Kubrick had engaged for the famous masked orgy scene in his film *Eyes Wide Shut*.

I could not know that for the next six years, it would be the only sun Julian Assange would ever see.

10

No Place for Protection

NSA: THE "NO SUCH AGENCY"

It was picked up by every newspaper, television network, and news outlet in the world. One of the biggest scoops in journalism history. On June 6, 2013, the *Guardian* published an investigation by Glenn Greenwald revealing that the National Security Agency (NSA) was collecting the telephone metadata of millions of U.S. citizens, namely the customers of Verizon, one of the biggest telecoms companies in the United States. The evidence was a top-secret document obtained by Greenwald, who wrote: "The document shows for the first time that under the Obama administration the communication records of millions of US citizens are being collected indiscriminately and in bulk—regardless of whether they are suspected of any wrongdoing."[1]

The NSA is the U.S. government agency responsible for gathering intelligence from telephone, satellite and internet communications, for protecting the communications of U.S. authorities through encryption, and for decrypting the communications of other countries' foreign leaders and citizens in order to extract information. Unlike the CIA, which sends its spies throughout the world to buy or extort secrets from human sources, the NSA does not have field operatives; they obtain secrets by spying on phones and computers. According to Chelsea Manning in her chat with Adrian Lamo, the half-a-million messages collected on September 11 and published by WikiLeaks in 2009, which had drawn Manning's attention to Assange's organization, came from an NSA database.

---

1. Glenn Greenwald, "NSA collecting phone records of millions of Verizon customers daily," *Guardian*, June 6, 2013.

The NSA has been characterized as "the largest, most costly, and most technologically sophisticated spy organization the world has ever known."[2] Three times as big as the CIA, it absorbs one-third of the U.S. intelligence budget, which in 2020 was 85.8 billion dollars.[3] It professes to be the biggest employer of mathematicians in the country,[4] who are hired to encrypt and decrypt communications. It is the most secret of the U. S. intelligence agencies, so much so that the acronym is jokingly deciphered as "No Such Agency." But now it had lost control of its secrets.

For the NSA, it was an unprecedented shock: seeing its top-secret documents in the global media was like seeing blood gushing from its veins. But there were those who downplayed the news, stressing that, at bottom, Glenn Greenwald's revelations only regarded metadata, and not the actual content of the conversations of millions of people.

Telephone metadata is the data that indicates who called whom, from where, at what time and for how long. The value of this kind of information is often underestimated, as it does not reveal what people actually say to each other in the course of a phone call. But when an intelligence agency holds enormous amounts of metadata, it does not really need to know the content of the conversation to find out who we are. Metadata reveals so much about our lives and social contacts that former NSA director general Michael Hayden

---

2. This quote comes from the book by American investigative journalist, James Bamford, entitled *The shadow factory*, and referred to in Jane Mayer's article, "The secret sharer," *New Yorker*, May 23, 2011. During the Vietnam War, James Bamford spent some years in the US Navy, and was assigned to an NSA unit. He then became a journalist and wrote the first book ever on the NSA: *The puzzle palace*. He has spent his life reporting on the NSA and interviewed Edward Snowden: James Bamford, "Edward Snowden: the untold story," *Wired*, August 22, 2014.

3. Steven Aftergood, email to the author, February 4, 2021. US intelligence budget data are available on the Federation of American Scientists' website: https://irp.fas.org/budget/index.html (accessed April 1, 2022).

4. At the Joint Mathematics Meetings in 2021, the NSA held a session entitled: "The National Security Agency needs you." The agency claims: "We are the largest employer of mathematicians in the country and work in a dynamic culture that welcomes diversity, encourages intellectual exploration, demands unbreakable ethics and covets the pursuit of the greater good": https://meetings.ams.org/math/jmm2021/meetingapp.cgi/Session/2975 (accessed April 1, 2022).

went so far as to say[5] "we kill people based on metadata." Indeed, it is used by U.S. intelligence to identify suspected terrorists in countries like Pakistan in order to kill them with drones.[6]

Right after this scoop, Glenn Greenwald and Ewen MacAskill in the *Guardian*,[7] and U.S. journalists Laura Poitras and Barton Gellman in the *Washington Post*, published a new top-secret NSA document revealing that the agency had direct access to the servers of the Silicon Valley giants—Google, Apple, Facebook, Microsoft, Yahoo, YouTube, Skype, AOL, Paltalk—through a program called "Prism," whereby the NSA could collect all the content of emails, file transfers, live chats and internet searches of millions of people. According to the file, the Prism program was run in cooperation with those nine companies, though they publicly denied it. As with the revelation on Verizon, the Prism revelation made headlines around the world.

How many top-secret NSA documents were still out there, and who had sent them to the journalists?

THE EXCEPTIONAL COURAGE OF EDWARD SNOWDEN

On June 9, 2013, the source of the top-secret documents was revealed in an interview published by the *Guardian* and filmed by documentary film-maker and journalist Laura Poitras. His name was Edward Snowden. He was 29 years old and he had been working for the NSA in that natural paradise known as the U.S. state of Hawaii as an employee of private defense contractor Booz Allen Hamilton, after previously working as a technical expert for the CIA.

---

5. Cora Currier, Glenn Greenwald and Andrew Fishman, "U.S. government designated prominent Al Jazeera journalist as 'Member of al Qaeda'," *The Intercept*, May 8, 2015.
6. Extrajudicial killings by drones are conducted on the basis of top secret information collected by intelligence agencies, but such information often proves faulty and those targeted are completely innocent.
7. Glenn Greenwald and Ewen MacAskill, "NSA Prism program taps into user data of Apple, Google and others," *Guardian*, June 7, 2013; Barton Gellman and Laura Poitras, "U.S., British intelligence mining data from nine U.S. internet companies in broad secret program," *Washington Post*, June 6, 2013.

Using PGP, Philip Zimmermann's famous program, and other encrypted chats, Snowden had contacted Greenwald and Poitras and asked them to meet him in Hong Kong. He had flown from Hawaii to speak with them there, realizing that if he tried to reveal the NSA secrets to the journalists on U.S. soil, he would risk being arrested before he had even finished his work with them.

He had also chosen Hong Kong, he told[8] Greenwald and Poitras, for another reason: in those years, the former British colony, which had returned to Chinese rule in 1997, enjoyed a freedom and protection of political dissent not found on Chinese soil. "There were other places he could have gone to, affording greater protection from potential US action, including mainland China. And there were certainly countries that enjoyed more political freedom," Greenwald explained, "But Hong Kong, he felt, provided the best mix of physical security and political strength."

Snowden had chosen the two journalists because they were both independent. He was skeptical towards media outlets like the *New York Times*, which in 2004—under editor-in-chief Bill Keller— had delayed publishing[9] a huge scoop on NSA eavesdropping on U.S. citizens without warrants for more than a year, a scandal that might have endangered the re-election of George W. Bush. Mindful of this, Snowden chose not to share the top-secret NSA documents with the powerful U.S. newspaper, though he did agree to share some of the files with Barton Gellman, then freelancing for the *Washington Post*.

Poitras, together with Greenwald, who worked as a columnist for the *Guardian* at the time, flew to Hong Kong, accompanied by Ewen MacAskill, a seasoned reporter with the same newspaper. They verified Snowden's account of his personal history and his work for the NSA, and were given access to a large database of top-secret documents.

---

8. Glenn Greenwald, *No place to hide: Edward Snowden, the NSA and the U.S. surveillance state* (New York: Metropolitan Books, 2014).
9. James Risen, "The biggest secret: my life as a New York Times reporter in the shadow of the War on Terror," *The Intercept*, January 3, 2018.

After 9/11, the NSA did not implement a targeted monitoring of terrorist networks, but had instead embarked on the path of mass surveillance.

A year before Snowden's revelations, I had flown to the United States to meet with Thomas Drake and Bill Binney, who had worked for the NSA for many years. Binney in particular had spent thirty-six years with the agency, and was considered one of the best codebreakers it had ever had. Codebreakers decrypt the encrypted communication of a foreign country, a suspected terrorist, or any other target, in order to extract intelligence.

Immediately following September 11, Binney had left the NSA and, together with Drake and other colleagues, blown the whistle on the mass surveillance path the agency had taken. In so doing, Drake risked thirty-five years in prison. Binney told me that after deciding to talk about his own case with U.S. attorney Jesselyn Radack, he wrote and signed a statement with the words: "If something happens to me, I did not commit suicide."

It was deeply unsettling to hear Binney, a politically conservative mathematician who had worked at the NSA for a lifetime, expressing his fear that if NSA's surveillance system were to end up in the hands of a political authoritarian, a new Hitler, dissenters would not stand a chance. Binney also explained[10] to me why, in his analysis, indiscriminate collection of the communications and data of billions of people rather than a targeted surveillance of terrorist networks fails to prevent attacks: the NSA was drowning in a sea of data so large that it was impossible to see threats before they materialized, so the agency was unable to alert the authorities before terrorists struck.

Thomas Drake, Bill Binney and a number of their colleagues had blown the whistle on the NSA abuses before Edward Snowden did, but it was only thanks to the latter that the public was able to learn the sheer extent, the pervasiveness of its mass surveillance, and to engage in an open debate on its failure in preventing ter-

---

10. Five years after our meeting in the United States, Bill Binney released an in-depth interview to me in which he discussed the NSA's mass surveillance programs revealed by the Snowden files: Stefania Maurizi, "NSA, Bill Binney: 'Things won't change until we put these people in jail'," *la Repubblica*, February 11, 2017.

rorist attacks. Indeed, Snowden provided Glenn Greenwald and Laura Poitras with a trove of top-secret documents describing NSA programs like Prism, and revealing the countries targeted.

Under the Bush administration, the system had become a leviathan. Rather than going to look for terrorists like needles in the haystack, it aimed to collect the entire haystack, every form of human communication, under a "collect it all" strategy.[11] Working for the agency, Snowden found this profoundly troubling.

"I could watch drones in real time as they surveilled the people they might kill. You could watch entire villages and see what everyone was doing," he told Greenwald,[12] adding: "I watched NSA tracking people's Internet activities as they typed. I became aware of just how invasive US surveillance capabilities had become. I realized the true breadth of this system. And almost nobody knew it was happening."

Snowden had hoped that with the election of Barack Obama, who promised change, those Bush administration excesses would be corrected. But no. And like Chelsea Manning, he could have pretended not to see and simply carried on. He had powerful incentives to look the other way: he was not even 30 years old, an intellectually gifted young man with a high-profile job, a good salary, living in a paradise like Hawaii with his young girlfriend. Why risk his neck and ruin everything? "I couldn't keep it all to myself. I felt it would be wrong to, in effect, help conceal all of this from the public," he told[13] Glenn Greenwald.

Snowden, like Chelsea Manning, was a whistleblower, who risked his life to rip a gaping hole in secret power, that power whose crimes and abuses the public has no chance of knowing unless an insider steps out of the darkness of state secrecy and reveals them to us.

But after the interview that made him famous throughout the world, Edward Snowden had vanished. Where was he?

---

11. Glenn Greenwald, "The crux of the NSA story in one phrase: 'collect it all'," *Guardian*, July 15, 2013.
12. Greenwald, *No place to hide.*
13. Ibid.

A BRUTAL LAW FROM WORLD WAR I:
THE ESPIONAGE ACT

Everyone was trying to hunt him down. His face was on every TV channel, every website, every newspaper on the planet. Hundreds of reporters were looking for him. But most of all, the NSA and the U.S. government were looking for him. Where could someone like that hide, after leaving the five-star Mira Hotel?

In the poorest quarters of Hong Kong, among people even more vulnerable than he. Two local attorneys, Robert Tibbo and Jonathan Man, gave him legal assistance, and Tibbo arranged for him to stay for a few days with some refugee families,[14] who welcomed them into their humble homes: Vanessa Rodel and her daughter Keana Kellapatha; the family of Supun Kellapatha, his partner Nadeeka Nonis and their two daughters; and, finally, the Ajith Pushpa Kumara family. They could have reported him and gone on to collect their reward: they were poor and seeking protection, and the U.S. government would very likely have shown its gratitude. But they did not betray him.

The United States did not waste any time. On June 21, 2013, the exact day of his thirtieth birthday, the *Washington Post* revealed that federal prosecutors had filed a criminal complaint against Edward Snowden.[15] The most serious charge was alleged[16] violation of the Espionage Act, a draconian 1917 law used by U.S. authorities on a massive scale during World War I to target individuals who were opposed to the conflict, as well as political leaders despised by the government and business community, such as socialists William Haywood and Eugene Debs. It was the same law that the United

---

14. The revelations on how Edward Snowden was protected by asylum seekers in Hong Kong, dubbed "Snowden's guardian angels," emerged thanks to research conducted by Oliver Stone for his film on Edward Snowden. It was reported by the Canadian outlet the *National Post* as well as by Ewen MacAskill, "Hong Kong refugees helped hide Edward Snowden after NSA leak," *Guardian*, September 7, 2016. Finally, it was reported in Edward Snowden, *Permanent record* (New York: Metropolitan Books, 2019).

15. Peter Finn and Sari Horwitz, "US charges Snowden with espionage," *Washington Post*, June 21, 2013.

16. I use "alleged" to stress the concept that charges should not be taken at face value: an individual charged with a crime remains innocent until he has been proven guilty.

States used to charge Daniel Ellsberg for handing the Pentagon
Papers to the press, the same law under which they had indicted
Chelsea Manning for sending classified documents to WikiLeaks
and, finally, the same law under which Julian Assange and his
organization were being investigated by the Grand Jury in Alexandria, Virginia.

The Espionage Act has been used to inflict harsh punishment
on those who reveal classified information. It is a highly controversial law, as it makes no distinction between whistleblowers and
spies.[17] Between those who act out of conscience and reveal secrets
to the press to expose the truth about war crimes and torture, and
those who hand over national secrets to the agents of another
country. It does not distinguish between the person who seeks to
blow the whistle on state criminality and the one who seeks to
harm the United States. The Espionage Act does not even allow a
public interest defense. The accused cannot defend himself before
a judge, saying: "It's true that I revealed classified information, but
I did so for reasons of conscience and in the interest of the collec-
tivity and of justice, to inform the press of very serious facts that
the public should know."

After the U.S. authorities announced the indictment of
Snowden, it was clear that he risked spending at least 30 years in
that special hell in the United States known as maximum-security
prison, provided that no further charges would be added, which
would entomb him in prison for life.

The treatment of Chelsea Manning at the hands of the U.S.
government led one to fear the worst.

THE CRUEL AND INHUMANE TREATMENT OF CHELSEA MANNING

After her arrest in 2010, Chelsea Manning had been imprisoned
first in Kuwait and then in the Quantico marine base in Virginia,
where her treatment was extremely harsh. Held in solitary con-

---

17. Jameel Jaffer, "The Espionage Act and a growing threat to press freedom," *New
Yorker*, June 25, 2019.

finement twenty-three hours a day, she was stripped naked; sleep-deprived because forced to respond to continuous checks by the guards throughout the night; deprived of any physical exercise, even in her own cell, and of her glasses, so she could not read. Even the spokesman for the Department of State at the time, Philip J. Crowley, defined her detention conditions as "counterproductive and stupid," a remark that would ultimately bring him to resign.[18]

It was only after an international campaign that Chelsea Manning was transferred to a less restrictive prison, that of Fort Leavenworth in Kansas. The United Nations Special Rapporteur on Torture, Juan Mendez,[19] established that during her eleven months in solitary confinement, her treatment by the U.S. government had been cruel, degrading and inhumane.

On June 3, 2013, three days before Glenn Greenwald published his explosive NSA scoop based on the Snowden documents, Chelsea Manning's trial by court martial began. It was held at Fort Meade in Maryland, where the NSA has its headquarters. Manning was accused, among other things, of violating the Espionage Act, just as Snowden would be a few weeks later, and of aiding the enemy, a crime punishable by death, though as reported by the *Guardian*, the U.S. authorities did not intend to seek the death penalty.[20] If found guilty, however, she risked life in prison, without possibility of parole.

The United States never accused Chelsea Manning of passing classified files to the enemy, but they tried to bolster the argument that since she had sent them to WikiLeaks, and Julian Assange's

---

18. "ACLU calls military treatment of accused WikiLeaks supporter Pfc. Manning cruel and unusual," ACLU, March 16, 2011, accessed April 4, 2022: www.aclu.org/press-releases/aclu-calls-military-treatment-accused-wikileaks-supporter-pfc-manning-cruel-and
19. The report of the UN Special Rapporteur on Torture, Juan Mendez, is available at: www.ohchr.org/Documents/HRBodies/HRCouncil/RegularSession/Session19/A_HRC_19_61_Add.4_EFSonly.pdf (accessed April 4, 2022).
20. Ed Pilkington, "US government claims it has proof of Bradley Manning aiding the enemy," *Guardian*, July 16, 2012; "The Chelsea Manning case: a timeline," ACLU, May 9, 2017: www.aclu.org/blog/free-speech/employee-speech-and-whistleblowers/chelsea-manning-case-timeline (accessed April 4, 2022).

organization published them online, that meant that enemies of the United States, like al-Qaeda, were able to read them.

The exceedingly harsh treatment of the WikiLeaks source suggested that Edward Snowden risked the same fate at best, and probably an even worse one.

First of all, the documents Chelsea Manning had revealed were at the most classified as *secret*, while those revealed by Snowden were *top secret*, so even more sensitive. Furthermore, it was not hard to imagine the fury and embarrassment of U.S. authorities when, only three years after Manning's disclosure of 700,000 Pentagon and State Department files, a new whistleblower had now leaked the records of their most secret agency.

On June 23, Snowden left Hong Kong. But he was not alone.

EXILE

A woman of sharp intelligence, strong organizational skills and a sunny disposition, Sarah Harrison was not only a serious and motivated professional, she was also a very courageous individual who did not let anyone push her around. A British journalist then working for WikiLeaks, it was Harrison who accompanied Snowden the day he left Hong Kong.

I knew her very well, not only directly, but also through Gavin MacFadyen, co-founder of the Centre for Investigative Journalism of London, who held her in high regard on both the professional and personal level.

Having followed Julian Assange's legal and diplomatic case very closely, she knew how to go about seeking international protection under asylum, and was familiar with the city of Hong Kong, where she had friends and family. She also knew how to use encryption to protect her communications.

Assange was trapped in a room in the Ecuadorian embassy and Sarah Harrison was in Hong Kong. It seemed like "mission impossible," but WikiLeaks managed to save Snowden from arrest and prison.

After the interview that brought him to the entire world's attention, Snowden was left on his own. Neither the *Guardian* nor the *Washington Post*, which published his top-secret files and landed scoops that would later win them the Pulitzer Prize, took it upon themselves to protect him. This was not because the three journalists who had worked with him on the ground were indifferent to his fate, but because the two media giants did not want to deal with the legal risks. The *Washington Post* had not even wanted to send Barton Gellman to Hong Kong to meet Snowden and obtain one of the biggest scoops of all time.

Sitting as they were on NSA secrets, the two newspapers had considerable bargaining power, but did nothing to help their source. Only WikiLeaks was there for Edward Snowden. The American writer Bruce Sterling summed it up nicely:[21] "It's incredible to me that, among the eight zillion civil society groups on the planet that hate and fear spooks and police spies, not one of them could offer Snowden practical help, except WikiLeaks."

If the whistleblower had remained in Hong Kong and sought asylum there, the procedure would have been lengthy and uncertain. The local authorities would have assessed both his asylum request and the United States' application for his arrest for extradition purposes. He would have spent several years awaiting their decision, most likely in prison. In prison he would have been isolated and prevented from contributing to the public debate on mass surveillance that he had just sparked. And he would most likely have been at risk as well: prisons are dangerous places in every part of the world.

That Sunday, June 23, Edward Snowden and Sarah Harrison were holding plane tickets for a flight from Hong Kong to Quito, the capital of Ecuador, to which Snowden had applied for asylum. Ecuador's consul in London, Fidel Narváez, had issued Snowden a safe-conduct pass attesting to his status, so he would be able to travel with a minimum of protection.

---

21. "The Ecuadorian library or The blast shack after three years," Bruce Sterling, August 3, 2013: https://bruces.medium.com/the-ecuadorian-library-a1ebd2b4a0e5 (accessed April 5, 2022).

No direct flights from Hong Kong to Quito existed, but there were a number of possible routes. The only way to avoid transiting through U.S. airspace was to fly from Hong Kong to Moscow, then on to Havana, Caracas and finally Quito.[22]

When he arrived in Moscow, however, Edward Snowden was informed that the United States had revoked his passport. This move by his government put him in a trap; he was stuck in Russia. Snowden and Harrison remained in Moscow's Sheremetyevo airport for 39 days and 39 nights, in a windowless room with no shower, eating food from Burger King.

WikiLeaks announced that Snowden had applied to over twenty countries for asylum:[23] from Austria to China, from Cuba to Germany, on up to Italy. Some, like Cuba, did not answer, while others, like China, denied any knowledge of his request, and still others, like India, said "no" without further explanation. Most of the countries, Italy included,[24] rejected his application for asylum on the grounds that it needed to be presented at that nation's border or within its territory.

Rafael Correa's Ecuador, at first willing to grant Snowden asylum provided that, as initially planned, he reached the country or one of its embassies, as Julian Assange had, was no longer willing to organize the trip to bring him out of Russia now that he was trapped in the Moscow airport.

On July 2, an incident took place that underscored how tricky it would be to get Edward Snowden to Latin America, even if WikiLeaks could find a way to get him on an airplane with a revoked passport. Bolivia's president, Evo Morales, who had made no secret of his willingness to grant Snowden asylum, was flying home on the presidential airplane after a summit in Moscow.

---

22. Edward Snowden, *Permanent record*.
23. The list has been made public by WikiLeaks, accessed April 5, 2022: https://wikileaks.org/Edward-Snowden-submits-asylum.html.
24. The then Italian Minister of Foreign Affairs, Emma Bonino, declared: "As a result the legal conditions do not exist to accept such a request, which in the government's view would not be acceptable on a political level either." "Italy rejects Snowden asylum request", Reuters Staff, July 4, 2013. For a full reconstruction of the Italian Minister of Foreign Affairs' reply to the asylum request, see: Stefania Maurizi, "Bonino, perché non risponde?" *L'Espresso*, July 9, 2013.

To reach his destination, Morales had to transit through Italian, French, Spanish and Portuguese airspace, and indeed was authorized to do so. But before reaching Italian territory, he was forced to re-route to Vienna, since the airspace of all four European countries had been closed. Hiding behind "technical reasons" or silence, the four countries denied Morales access to their airspace. Snowden had never boarded that flight.

Presidential airplanes are inviolable under international law. After that flagrant violation, it was clear that even though Venezuela, Bolivia and Nicaragua had offered Snowden protection, flying from Moscow to Latin America would entail the risk of being forced to land and being arrested. Not everything that a superpower has the means to do—directly or through its allies—always proves a smart move in the end; the Morales "incident" showed the world how far the United States was prepared to go to get its hands on Snowden, confirming his status as a victim of persecution in the eyes of the global public.

For Vladimir Putin's Russia, offering Snowden protection became a cause for national pride and a fantastic opportunity. In a single stroke, Putin could poke a finger in the United States' eye, could take credit for saving an important whistleblower, could show the global public, critical towards his authoritarian government, the need for a country that could say "no" to the United States when it did something wrong and, finally, could expose the hypocrisy of Western democracies that preached freedom of the press only to abandon and persecute one of the greatest journalistic sources of all time.

On August 1, 2013, Russia granted Edward Snowden temporary asylum. He was finally able to leave the airport with Sarah Harrison after thirty-nine days and thirty-nine nights. Harrison stayed on with him for four months in Moscow.

It was with great bitterness that I watched as Snowden was completely forsaken by Europe and driven into the arms of Vladimir Putin. Was it not paradoxical that, after risking his life to reveal a monstrous threat to democracy like the NSA's program of mass surveillance, he could escape Chelsea Manning's fate only by going into exile in an authoritarian country? What Snowden had revealed was of exceptional public interest; indeed, his revelations continue to be a wake-up call for our democracies. As Daniel Ellsberg would later explain to me:[25] "We could be East Germany from one day to the next, and have a police state that the East Germans couldn't even dream of, because they didn't have this kind of capability then. We don't have that yet, because they [the NSA and the U.S. intelligence agencies] haven't used the information they are collecting, but they have the private information [...] and that means, as Snowden has put it, we're a 'turnkey tyranny': in other words, turn a switch, and we could be a total police state."

I spoke with the WikiLeaks journalists a number of times to find out what had driven them to try to help Edward Snowden, to embark on such a risky endeavor from both the legal and extra-legal standpoint. After all, he was not one of their sources; they had no direct professional or ethical obligation towards him. The media focused a great deal on the notion that Julian Assange had primarily acted with a view to self-promotion: after a few years of publishing less explosive scoops than those of 2010, he was now back in the limelight.

Like all journalistic organizations that value their image, WikiLeaks certainly did not shrink from worldwide prestige and fame. There is nothing untoward about that. But they told me they had wanted to try to do for Snowden what they had been unable to do for Chelsea Manning.

Years later, this would be confirmed by Snowden himself. Indeed, now that Julian Assange risks spending his life in prison, the NSA whistleblower has become very vocal in Assange's defense. Though he may have criticized the WikiLeaks founder in the past, he has always felt that Assange's commitment to the public's right to know and to whistleblowers is genuine. "It's true that Assange can be self-interested and vain, moody and even bullying," Snowden wrote in his book,[26] "but he also sincerely conceives of himself as a fighter in a historic battle for the public's right to know, a battle

---

25. Daniel Ellsberg, interview with author, February 7, 2022.
26. Snowden, *Permanent record.*

he will do anything to win. It's for this reason that I regard it as too reductive to interpret his assistance as merely an instance of scheming or self-promotion. More important to him, I believe, was the opportunity to establish a counterexample to the case of the organization's most famous source, US Army Private Chelsea Manning."

But for those who expose the abuses of secret power, like Manning, Snowden, Assange and the WikiLeaks journalists, could there be a happy ending?

IN PRISON, IN EXILE OR CONFINED

With Edward Snowden safe in Russia, at least for the moment, his top-secret files continued to yield scoop after scoop, offering revelations on every country and on the role of the NSA's British counterpart, the Government Communications Headquarters (GCHQ), which ran programs of mass surveillance in partnership with the U.S. agency. Indeed, it was the British authorities who launched two of the more troubling attacks against journalists working on the files.

At Heathrow airport in London, just two weeks after Snowden was granted temporary asylum, British authorities detained David Miranda, Glenn Greenwald's husband, who was traveling with some copies of the Snowden documents. Miranda was held in the airport for nine hours, questioned without the assistance of a lawyer, and all of his electronic devices were confiscated: telephones, computer, USB sticks.[27]

To detain him, the British authorities used the controversial "Schedule 7" of the Terrorism Act 2000, which authorizes them to stop anyone who is transiting through international ports, airports or train terminals to determine if they are involved in preparing or instigating acts of terrorism. Besides detaining the suspect, they can question them and seize their personal belongings, including electronic devices, and copy their content. The person held is

---

27. Glenn Greenwald, "Glenn Greenwald: detaining my partner was a failed attempt at intimidation," *Guardian*, August 19, 2013.

required to cooperate—they cannot invoke their right to remain silent—and to disclose the passwords to their devices, or risk being jailed.

It was obvious that David Miranda was not a terrorist: his detention was a blatant act of intimidation.

Two days later, another sobering incident came to light. The *Guardian* admitted[28] that one month earlier, in its offices in London, it had been forced, under the GCHQ's supervision, to destroy the hard drives containing the top-secret files, after repeated pressure on the newspaper to halt the publications. Rather than publicly denouncing this pressure, the daily had unfortunately lowered itself to that gesture of submission to the British secret services. It is true that the *Guardian* then proceeded to publish a number of other investigations based on the files, but at the end of 2013 its editor-in-chief, Alan Rusbridger, affirmed that it had only released 1 per cent of the files.[29] As of today, the complete database has never been published by anyone, neither the London daily nor Glenn Greenwald nor Laura Poitras.

The British authorities were not the only ones to hector reporters. During my work on the case and the Snowden files on Italy—which I ultimately published[30] in the newspaper I was working for, *L'Espresso*—I too found myself in out of the ordinary situations, though nothing comparable to the intimidation targeting David Miranda and the *Guardian*.

During the weeks I was traveling to meet with sources and contacts, I found myself undergoing an inspection at the Rome Fiumicino airport. Before boarding my flight for London, I was summoned over the loudspeaker and asked to submit to additional security checks, during which my luggage was carefully inspected and questions were asked about my trip. When I asked to know

---

28.   Julian Borger, "NSA files: why the Guardian in London destroyed hard drives of leaked files," *Guardian*, August 20, 2013.

29.   "Only 1% of Snowden files published—Guardian editor," *BBC News*, December 3, 2013: www.bbc.com/news/uk-25205846 (accessed April 5, 2022).

30.   Glenn Greenwald and Stefania Maurizi, "Revealed: how the NSA targets Italy," *L'Espresso*, December 5, 2013.

why I was being inspected again—was I by chance on a black list?—I received only vague replies.

The first time I met Laura Poitras, during my visit to Ellingham Hall in August 2011, she told me she had undergone 40 such airport inspections, which in the U.S. are called "secondary screenings." They had been much more aggressive in her case, however, including full-scale interrogations and confiscation of her electronic devices. But she was not the only one. Over the years, many of the talents orbiting Julian Assange and WikiLeaks had been detained, questioned and intimidated in U.S. airports. They included the gifted French computer science engineer and digital rights activist Jérémie Zimmermann and American journalist and computer security expert Jake Appelbaum. I was acquainted with both of them. Appelbaum, who had worked on the Snowden files with the German weekly *Der Spiegel*, would later earn his PhD in cryptography with no prior university degree. As for Zimmermann, his technical skill was joined by a passion for technology, how it works and how it can be used to change the world for the better, rather than in uncritical, commoditized ways.

In the summer of 2010, Appelbaum spoke at a conference in place of Julian Assange, after which he began experiencing hassles in airports. During an interview with independent U.S. news organization Democracy Now!, he spoke of being repeatedly detained in U.S. airports by border control officers and questioned about his political ideas, about the war in Afghanistan and Iraq, and whether he was associated in some way with Assange and WikiLeaks. "They didn't ask me anything about terrorism. They didn't ask me anything about smuggling or drugs or any of the customs things that you would expect customs to be doing," Appelbaum told Democracy Now!, adding: "They did it purely for political reasons and to intimidate me, denied me a lawyer. They gave me water, but refused me a bathroom, to give you an idea about what they were doing."[31]

---

31. "'We don't live in a free country': Jacob Appelbaum on being a target of widespread Gov't surveillance," *Democracy Now!*, April 20, 2012: www.democracynow.org/2012/4/20/we_do_not_live_in_a (accessed April 6, 2022).

Jérémie Zimmermann, on the other hand, was detained in the Washington-Dulles airport in 2012 by two individuals who introduced themselves as FBI, though they did not show him any badges. They told him that his name had surfaced in the U.S. investigation of WikiLeaks, and that they wanted information on its internal workings. They gave him an anonymous Yahoo email address and asked him to contact them—a clear intimidation tactic, in the attempt to make him an informant.

For investigative journalists, continuous inspections in airports entails risks for their sources. In those intensive months of work on the Snowden case and documents, I traveled to London solely with encrypted memory sticks that did not contain sensitive files. I carried with me only Sandro Pertini's speeches and letters. If I had been stopped under Schedule 7, like David Miranda, and forced to furnish the passwords, the British authorities would have found a surprise in the decrypted files. They would have read a missive that went something like this: "Mother, how could you have done that? I've had no peace since they gave me the news, that you asked for my pardon." It was one of the politically impassioned letters written by Pertini,[32] a beloved president of the Italian Republic who fought fascism at an immense personal cost, amidst arrests, internal exile and harsh prison conditions. Yet he reproached his mother for applying to the Mussolini regime for his pardon. Pertini deeply understood that mass surveillance lies at the foundation of any authoritarian state.

I encountered difficulties traveling not only in London but in Berlin also; while I was on my way to meet a source, I found myself being brazenly followed. It was an obvious attempt to frighten me, but nothing like the difficulties faced by Sarah Harrison, who for a long time after helping Snowden could not go back to London.

---

32. "Pertini's character has been deeply marked by his fight against fascism and the personal suffering which resulted from it—eight months in jail, flight to France and, after returning to Italy, 15 further years of imprisonment," a U.S. diplomat wrote in a cable declassified by the U.S. government and republished by WikiLeaks. The cable, which dates back to 1978, states: "The experience inflamed his already-existent commitment to individual liberty and his concern for the underdog, the victim, the non-conformist, the dissenter." Available at: https://wikileaks.org/plusd/cables/1978ROME13249_d.html (accessed May 4, 2022).

Considering that she risked at the very least being detained at the United Kingdom's border, like David Miranda,[33] she settled in Berlin. In 2015, Germany's center-left SPD party awarded her the Willy Brandt Prize[34] for "special political courage."

The Edward Snowden case showed how far Western democracies were prepared to go to target journalists and their sources when they strike at the heart of secret power. Further confirmation of just how far would soon follow.

THE "BLOOD ON THEIR HANDS" THAT NEVER WAS

Just twenty days after Snowden was granted temporary asylum, on August 21, 2013, Chelsea Manning was condemned to 35 years in prison for leaking 700,000 classified U.S. government documents to WikiLeaks, including the *Collateral Murder* video, the reports on the wars in Iraq and Afghanistan, the U.S. diplomatic cables and the Guantanamo detainee records. Manning was found guilty of violating the Espionage Act, but was acquitted of the charge of aiding the enemy.

The court martial trial, presided over by military judge Colonel Denise Lind, was almost completely eclipsed by the explosive NSA revelations.

During the court martial proceedings, Brigadier General Robert Carr was called on to testify. As reported by the *Guardian*,[35] Carr headed the Information Review Task Force assigned to investigate the consequences of the publication of those secret files. Carr testified that his task force's investigations had not unearthed even one case of an individual who was killed as a result of the revelations.

In the course of the court hearings, Manning described[36] the measures she had adopted to select documents whose publica-

---

33.   Sarah Harrison, "Britain is treating journalists as terrorists—believe me, I know," *Guardian*, March 14, 2014.
34.   *Spiegel* staff, "SPD ehrt Snowden-Vertraute für 'politischen Mut'," *Der Spiegel*, September 17, 2015.
35.   Ed Pilkington, "Bradley Manning leak did not result in deaths by enemy forces, court hears," *Guardian*, July 31, 2013.
36.   Glenn Greenwald, "Finally: hear Bradley Manning in his own voice," *Guardian*, March 12, 2013.

tion would not harm the United States, but at the most cause it embarrassment, revealing scandals, political pressure and interference. Her caution was then joined by that of WikiLeaks and its media partners in publishing the files, redacting them as we, the team, deemed fit. With Carr's conclusions, the Pentagon's "blood on their hands" campaign, used for years to demonize WikiLeaks and its source, melted like snow in the sun.

As pointed out by the *New York Times*,[37] Manning's thirty-five-year sentence was the longest ever inflicted on a source for revealing classified U.S. government documents to the press. One hundred and twelve days of her sentence were waived for the eleven months she had spent detained in cruel, inhumane and degrading conditions.

Manning—who had acted out of conscience, who had not caused the death or injury of anyone, and who had not been driven by any motive of personal gain—was handed a draconian punishment based on a 1917 law that does not distinguish between spies and whistleblowers.

It was Barack Obama who launched recourse to the Espionage Act on a massive scale to target whistleblowers who reveal secret information to the press just as if they were traitors passing secrets to the enemy.

Julian Assange, the journalists with WikiLeaks, Chelsea Manning and Edward Snowden had exposed crimes committed by the highest levels of power. Assange was confined in an embassy, Manning had been sentenced to 35 years in prison and Snowden was stuck in Russia. Of the three, only two had found places of refuge, and that at a very high price; Snowden was forced to live in exile, and Assange would soon discover that his asylum had no way out.

---

37.   Charlie Savage and Emmarie Huetteman, "Manning sentenced to 35 years for a pivotal leak of US files," *New York Times*, August 21, 2013.

11
My Trench Warfare to Unearth the Truth

WHEN GOOGLE HANDED OVER WIKILEAKS' DATA

It was moving forward in secret. The criminal investigation into Julian Assange and the WikiLeaks journalists opened by the U.S. authorities in 2010 had been under seal ever since, as the United States treated the publication of classified documents as a national security threat on the level of al-Qaeda. The investigation was being conducted by a Grand Jury in Virginia, "home to the Pentagon, CIA, and the world's largest naval base," wrote the *Washington Post*,[1] noting that, since September 11, it was the court of the Eastern District of Virginia that investigated the more high-profile national security cases, WikiLeaks included.

Despite the secrecy, scraps of information surfaced every now and then, like the court order issued by a judge with the Eastern District of Virginia in December 2010 to acquire the data on the Twitter accounts of WikiLeaks, Julian Assange,[2] Chelsea Manning, Jake Appelbaum—who had spoken on behalf of Assange at a public conference[3] in New York—and others, like Icelandic activist and then parliamentarian Birgitta Jónsdóttir, who worked on publication of the *Collateral Murder* video and later became critical of Assange and WikiLeaks.

1. Sari Horwitz, "In Va.'s Eastern District, US attorney's reach transcends geographic bounds," *Washington Post*, December 15, 2012.
2. Scott Shane and John F. Burns, "U.S. subpoenas Twitter over WikiLeaks supporters," *New York Times*, January 8, 2011. At the time of the court order, there was no Twitter handle publicly known to belong to Julian Assange.
3. "Affidavit of Julian Paul Assange," Julian Assange: https://wikileaks.org/IMG/html/Affidavit_of_Julian_Assange.html (accessed April 8, 2022); Eric Schmitt and David E. Sanger, "Gates cites peril in leak of Afghan War Logs by WikiLeaks," *New York Times*, August 1, 2010.

Crucial information also emerged from the subpoena published by Glenn Greenwald in April 2011, and above all from the court martial trial of Chelsea Manning. Another piece in the puzzle came to light in January 2015. WikiLeaks had just been informed[4] that U.S. authorities had ordered Google to hand over the data of three of its journalists: Kristinn Hrafnsson, Sarah Harrison and Joseph Farrell.

The internet giant was ordered[5] to provide all email addresses, email dates, message content, sources of payment, credit card and bank account numbers associated with the Google accounts, every draft email, every deleted email, all metadata and contact lists, all photos and files. As in the case of Twitter, the search and seizure warrant was very broad. Unlike Google, however, Twitter had promptly challenged the court order, thus allowing some WikiLeaks collaborators and volunteers to learn of its existence and appeal against it. In the case of Google, on the other hand, the warrant, which dated back to 2012, had been kept secret for almost three years. According to the Silicon Valley giant, a gag order issued by the U.S. authorities, which its lawyers had tried to contest to no avail,[6] had prevented their disclosing it. WikiLeaks was only notified of the warrant in December 2014, just three months after Julian Assange published an insightful book on Google.[7]

Signed by the same Eastern District of Virginia prosecutor who would charge Edward Snowden a year later, the search and seizure

---

4. Stefania Maurizi, "Il governo USA ha ottenuto da Google le email e tutti i dati relativi ai giornalisti di WikiLeaks," *L'Espresso*, January 23, 2015; Ed Pilkington and Dominic Rushe, "WikiLeaks demands answers after Google hands staff emails to US government," *Guardian*, January 26, 2015.
5. The three search and seizure warrants issued by Judge John F. Anderson are available on the WikiLeaks website: https://wikileaks.org/google-warrant/227-harrison.html; https://wikileaks.org/google-warrant/228-farrell.html; https://wikileaks.org/google-warrant/229-hrafnsson.html (accessed April 10, 2022).
6. Ellen Nakashima and Julie Tate, "Google says it fought gag orders in WikiLeaks investigation," *Washington Post*, January 28, 2015.
7. Julian Assange, *When Google met WikiLeaks* (New York: O/R Books, 2014). The book tells the story of Julian Assange's meeting with the then-chairmen of Google and "Google Ideas", Eric Schmidt and Jared Cohen respectively, at Ellingham Hall, in 2011. A meeting of men and minds who are poles apart. Their visions of the internet are poles apart as well. For Assange, "the liberating power of the internet is based on its freedom and statelessness." For Schmidt, "emancipation is at one with US foreign policy," writes Assange.

warrant proved that the U.S. investigation into WikiLeaks was going forward and was focused on alleged violations of the Espionage Act. When reporters are put under investigation for violating a law which is completely blind to the public interest, and when their communications, which may reveal interactions with their sources, can be acquired by the state in complete secrecy, how can they do aggressive and independent work?

I was keeping a close eye on the criminal case against WikiLeaks as it unfolded in the United States. In Sweden, by contrast, the investigation of Julian Assange had been at a standstill for years. Far too long.

A SUSPICIOUS IMPASSE IN SWEDEN

It was August 2015 when I reached the determination that the complete lack of progress in the Swedish case called for a thorough journalistic investigation. Almost five years had passed since prosecutor Marianne Ny had reopened the case on September 1, 2010. Julian Assange was still under investigation for minor rape—the least serious category of rape under the Swedish laws at the time—and for sexual molestation and coercion. The investigation was completely stalled in the preliminary stage: he had neither been charged for those offenses, nor had the case been dropped.

The WikiLeaks founder had been confined to the embassy since June 19, 2012, the day he entered it. In August 2015, the building was still surrounded night and day by Scotland Yard agents. Every time I visited him, there were more signs that his confinement was eroding his health. Besides living in a space of about 20 square meters, he could never go outside for even an hour a day, unlike prisoners who have committed the most heinous crimes, like Italian mobsters convicted of strangling a teenager and dissolving his body in acid.

Inside the embassy, Julian Assange kept on working. WikiLeaks continued with its revelations, sometimes on its own, but most often with us media partners. Newspapers like the *New York Times* and the *Guardian* had been cold towards WikiLeaks for some time, if not openly hostile, after the conflicts over the cables, such as when the two *Guardian* journalists published the password to decrypt the diplomatic cables. But WikiLeaks continued to partner with quality media outlets, including the German daily *Süddeutsche Zeitung*, the French online investigative newspaper *Mediapart* and the Italian weekly *L'Espresso*, which I worked for at the time.

Publishing kept Assange feeling alive. Every time we revealed documents that caused a stir and were picked up by others, he was radiant, like all journalists when they score a scoop. But from up close, it was sad to witness his physical and mental suffering. He never wanted to appear weak. When we met, his attitude was always stoic. And yet his confinement was having an undeniable impact on him. It was a slow and gradual process, but in my regular visits to the embassy I could see his health slowly ebbing away. One day I spoke to him of Ravello, the town on the Amalfi coast beloved by the great American intellectual Gore Vidal. As I described the sapphire blue of the sea, I saw that he was closing his eyes. He told me he was trying to remember what it was like to be out in the wide open space of the sea. He was buried within four walls, with no end in sight.

It was an Italian prosecutor who made me realize how anomalous the Swedish legal paralysis was. "Why isn't the investigation going forward?" he asked me in early 2015, during casual conversation. I explained to him that the investigation had been stuck in the preliminary phase since that far-off September 1, 2010, because prosecutor Marianne Ny did not want to go to London to question Assange before deciding whether to charge him or clear his name once and for all, she only wanted to question him after he had been extradited to Sweden.

Assange had been fighting extradition tooth and nail since 2010, certain that once he was transferred to Sweden, he would risk being sent on to the United States. Through his lawyers, he had tried to obtain diplomatic guarantees from the Swedish authorities to the effect that he would not be sent to the United States if he agreed to go to Stockholm for questioning. Such assurances are standard practice in the case of individuals who risk torture or inhumane treatment if they should end up in a given country, and the risk for Assange was real, considering the rage evidenced by U.S. authorities following the WikiLeaks publications.

Technically speaking, the prohibition on transferring an individual to a country where he risks serious harm is called the "principle of non-refoulement," and is a pillar of international law, from the Geneva Convention on Refugees to the United Nations Convention against Torture. It is true that diplomatic assurances are far from reliable, as the Scandinavian country itself has proved,[8] but the fact that Swedish authorities were not willing to provide the WikiLeaks founder with any such guarantees confirmed his fear of possible extradition.

I have never been privy to the advice Assange was given by his legal counsel on the Swedish case, as it is protected by confidentiality. But after the death of Michael Ratner—the pre-eminent lawyer key in bringing *habeas corpus* to Guantánamo—I read in his book, published posthumously,[9] that in October 2010, right after the Iraq War Logs were published, Ratner flew to London along with a colleague, Leonard Weinglass, to meet with Assange.

During that meeting, Ratner and Weinglass predicted what would happen in 2019: the WikiLeaks founder would be indicted under the Espionage Act for publishing classified U.S. government files, and the U.S. authorities would attempt to implicate him in a criminal conspiracy with Chelsea Manning. "No matter if it's Nixon or Bush or Obama, Republican or Democrat in the White House," they told him, "The U.S. government will try to stop you from publishing its ugly secrets. And if they have to destroy you and the First Amendment and the rights of publishers with you, they are willing to do it." As for the Swedish case, in that far-off 2010 Ratner advised Assange: "My guess is that you

8.   After September 11, Sweden handed two asylum seekers over to the U.S. authorities who transferred them to Egypt, after receiving diplomatic assurances that Egypt would not torture them. It was a mere fig leaf: they were subsequently tortured. "Sweden violated torture ban with U.S. help," Human Rights Watch, May 19, 2005: www.hrw.org/news/2005/05/19/sweden-violated-torture-ban-us-help (accessed April 12, 2022).
9.   Michael Ratner, *Moving the bar: My life as a radical lawyer* (New York and London: O/R Books, 2021).

would probably have the most support and the best legal team in a bigger country like the U.K. In a smaller country like Sweden, the U.S. can use its power to pressure the government, so it would be easier to extradite you from there." Ratner then told Assange, who was listening closely though he showed no emotion: "It's far less risky to ask the Swedish prosecutor to question you in London."

The problem was that Marianne Ny was completely unwilling to do so.

"Try to understand why the Swedish prosecutor doesn't want to go to London to question him," the Italian magistrate advised me in early 2015, explaining that unless Assange made himself unavailable to Swedish justice, Marianne Ny had only to employ the international judicial cooperation agreements, take a two-hour flight from Stockholm to London to question him, and then decide whether to charge him and send him to trial or definitively drop her investigation.

It was not the first time someone had voiced such misgivings to me on how his case was being handled. A few months earlier, Eva Joly—a French public prosecutor whose investigations into the corruption of France's financial giants had rocked the establishment—told me,[10] without mincing words: "I traveled all around Europe to conduct interrogations, on the basis of European Mutual Legal Assistance agreements drafted around 1959, and since then we have [developed] much better conventions. It is not very difficult for the Swedish prosecutors to interrogate Assange in London and I think they are wrong [not to have done so], that they are not informed, they have not attended updating courses for twenty years." Joly also told me, and later confirmed, that had Ny decided to charge Assange after questioning him, she could even have found a way to put him on trial without extraditing him, such as by delegating it all to an Ecuadorian prosecutor.

---

10. Stefania Maurizi, "Julian Assange, sfida per la libertà," *L'Espresso*, July 15, 2014: https://espresso.repubblica.it/inchieste/2014/07/15/news/Julian-assange-dopo-quattro-anni-di-impassegiudiziario-l-udienza-per-la-revoca-dell-arresto-1.173268 (accessed April 15, 2022). In a phone conversation we had on May 27, 2019, Eva Joly also explained to me that the Swedish prosecutors could have even put Julian Assange on trial without extraditing him to Sweden.

Of course a magistrate has every right to choose how to question a suspect, but why did the authorities of a country where human rights are supposed to matter, like Sweden, show such complete disregard for Assange's legitimate concerns? The rage fueling the assertions of U.S. politicians that he should be killed, or hunted down like an al-Qaeda terrorist, gave a measure of how the United States would treat him if it ever managed to get its hands on him.

For his part, the WikiLeaks founder had not made himself unavailable to Swedish justice. Indeed, he had asked to be questioned ever since he had been in that country. Even when he took refuge in the embassy in June 2012, before granting him asylum Ecuador had officially communicated to the Swedish authorities[11] Assange's readiness, and that of the government of Quito, to arrange for his questioning in the embassy. The paralysis stemmed entirely from Marianne Ny's decision not to use the judicial cooperation procedures, but rather to insist on extradition at all costs before questioning him.

Only a few weeks after my conversation with the Italian magistrate, Ny suddenly announced, in March 2015, that she would in fact question Assange in London. After almost five years, she had finally agreed to do what she could have done in 2010, when the suspect's memories, not to mention those of his alleged victims and various witness, were still fresh. Back when they had not yet been influenced by thousands of articles on the case, it would have been much easier to establish the facts, and of course much faster.

Rafael Correa's Ecuador immediately issued a press release[12] stating : "We welcome the decision of the Swedish authorities to finally interview Julian Assange in our London embassy. The government of Ecuador has repeatedly made this offer since 2012," adding: "This decision could have been taken from the beginning, and not only when the case is about to be subject to statute of limitation." Indeed, in mid-August 2015, the statute of limitations for

11.   I referred the content of this official letter from the Ecuadorian authorities to the Sweden authorities in chapter 9.
12.   Ministerio de Relaciones Exteriores y Movilidad Humana del Ecuador, Comunicado Oficial, March 13, 2015, 14:40.

at least two of the allegations—molestation and coercion—would have expired.

Despite Marianne Ny's announcement, and although several months had passed since then, the questioning had not occurred. Bewildered by the never-ending standstill, I decided the time had come to try to dig into the case by obtaining the full documentation.

TO LOOK OUT THE WINDOW

It seemed to me intolerable that a journalist who had revealed war crimes and torture was shut up inside an embassy in increasingly poor health, while not a single reporter had ever tried to investigate the highly anomalous handling of the Swedish case, to rigorously piece it together and contribute to its resolution. Julian Assange was not locked up in the embassy of North Korea or some other far-off country. He was in the heart of Europe. Hundreds of national and international newspapers, press agencies, television and radio stations around the world had covered his case, simply reporting on the defense and the prosecution's opposing arguments. It was disheartening that, despite all the resources available to these major newspapers and television stations, no one ever tried to dig any deeper.

There is a famous phrase[13] that encapsulates the task of journalism: "If someone says it's raining and another person says it's dry, it's not your job to quote them both. Your job is to look out the window and find out which is true."

On August 3, 2015, I submitted a Freedom of Information Act (FOIA) request to the Swedish Prosecution Authority in charge of the investigation, in order to access the full set of documents on the Assange case. Immediately thereafter, I presented an analogous request to the Crown Prosecution Service, the British public authority which prosecutes criminal cases in England and Wales, and which was providing assistance to the Swedish authority. Since the founder of WikiLeaks was under investigation in Sweden but

---

13. The quote is attributed to Jonathan Foster, a British journalist and lecturer in journalism.

physically in London, Marianne Ny had to rely on the cooperation of her British counterparts. Later on, I also submitted FOIA
requests on the Assange case in the United States and Australia,
and one to Scotland Yard to access its full correspondence with
the U.S. Department of Justice on the three WikiLeaks journalists targeted by the Google search and seizure warrants: Kristinn
Hrafnsson, Sarah Harrison and Joseph Farrell. Since Harrison
and Farrell are British citizens, it was reasonable to assume that
the U.S. authorities had communicated with those in the UK, and
Scotland Yard was a natural interlocutor for them.

I could never have imagined how opening that window would
engulf me in a journalistic investigation that is still going at full
intensity even as I write. Seven years have gone by, and represented
by seven different lawyers,[14] I am still fighting a legal battle in
Sweden, the United Kingdom, the United States and Australia,
as all four governments continue to deny me access to the documentation. On my own, with the backing of no one, as not even
my newspaper at the time was interested when I embarked on this
endeavor. At first I paid the lawyers' fees out of my own pocket, for
as long as I could afford them, then went in search of funding[15] to
meet the legal expenses. I have been working on this FOIA-based
investigation completely without pay since 2015, but it absolutely
had to be done: someone needed to do the hard work of digging
for the facts.

The few documents I have managed to obtain thus far are only
the tip of the iceberg. But they have made it possible to find out
what was going on behind the Swedish paralysis.

NOT JUST ANOTHER EXTRADITION REQUEST

Two hundred and twenty-six pages. That was all the Swedish
Prosecution Authority released to me under my FOIA application

---

14. Later on in this book, I will discuss the important contribution of my FOIA
lawyers.
15. In the acknowledgments of this book, I discuss the funding of my FOIA
litigation.

in those summer months of 2015. But when I read those documents, I could scarcely believe what had been handed over to me.

Sweden is a country with strong laws on transparency in public
affairs. And I had a strategy: use them as a crowbar to pry documents on the Assange case from other countries like the United
Kingdom, where accessing them is much more arduous. Indeed, I
was immediately forced to sue the Crown Prosecution Service just
to obtain 551 pages in seven years, many of which were censored
completely. In Sweden, by contrast, it was easy at first. Whether
I had Sweden's transparency to thank, or just the distraction of
some office worker, the upshot was that the Swedish Prosecution
Authority gave me the documents that made it possible to learn
the reasons for the legal paralysis.

After Marianne Ny reopened the rape case on September 1,
2010, Julian Assange voluntarily remained in Sweden to cooperate with the investigation, and his Swedish lawyer at the time,
Björn Hurtig, promptly requested that his client be questioned.
But the prosecutor postponed an interview with him.[16] On September 27, Assange flew to Berlin to meet with some journalists,
including myself. Before leaving Sweden, however, he made sure
that there were no objections to his departure. On September 14,
his Swedish lawyer contacted Marianne Ny for confirmation. "By
telephone," wrote[17] public prosecutor Ny in her correspondence
with the Crown Prosecution Service, "Mr. Hurtig was informed
that there were some investigative measures still outstanding

---

16.   The fact that Julian Assange had asked Marianne Ny to be questioned from
the very beginning is confirmed both by a communication from Björn Hurtig to Ny
dated November 12, 2010, which was released to me under the FOIA by the Swedish
Prosecution Authority, and by the "Agreed Statement of Facts and Issues" document,
which states: "The Appellant [Julian Assange] instructed Mr Hurtig to act for him as
counsel. Between 8th – 14th September 2010, the Appellant's counsel requested that
he be interviewed. That request was deferred by the prosecutor." "Agreed statement of
facts and issues": www.scribd.com/document/80912442/Agreed-Facts-Assange-Case
(accessed March 24, 2022).
17.   Letter from Marianne Ny to the Crown Prosecution Service's lawyer, Paul Close,
dated January 19, 2011. I obtained a copy of this letter thanks to my FOIA litigation
against the UK authorities at the Crown Prosecution Service. The documentation can
be published in this book according to the Open Government Licence v3.0: www.
nationalarchives.gov.uk/doc/open-government-licence/version/3/ (accessed April 18,
2022).

before a new interview with Julian Assange would be relevant and that there was no arrest warrant issued for him."

Satisfied that there were no objections to his leaving Sweden, on September 27 the WikiLeaks founder flew to Berlin and arrived at my hotel with no luggage; it had vanished during his direct flight. Ny planned to question him the next day, but Hurtig told her he had not been able to speak with his client. That same day, September 27, the prosecutor ordered his arrest.

It was a very intense time. WikiLeaks was working on publication of the classified Iraq war reports. Nevertheless, through his lawyer Assange conveyed to Marianne Ny his readiness to be questioned on Sunday, October 10, 2010, or any day of the following week, that of October 11. "Neither the times we had then suggested nor another occasion suggested were acceptable to you; on some occasions, our proposed times were too far in the future (a few weeks' time); another occasion, one of your investigators was ill," Hurtig wrote to the prosecutor. "It must therefore seem strange" he concluded, "that a hearing could not take place because an investigator was ill."[18]

Thereafter, every means proposed by Julian Assange's lawyers to question their client, whether by telephone or video conference, in writing or an in-person interview in the Australian embassy—he was, after all, an Australian citizen—was rejected by the prosecutor. Under Swedish law, they were all perfectly legitimate avenues for questioning a suspect, but Ny only wanted to question him in person, in Sweden.

On December 2, 2010, when WikiLeaks was in the midst of publishing the cables, Marianne Ny issued a European Arrest Warrant for extradition. Assange, who was in London to work on the files, handed himself over to Scotland Yard on December 7. He was held in solitary confinement for ten days in Wandsworth prison, then released under house arrest.

---

18. Letter from Hurtig to Marianne Ny, dated November 12, 2012. I obtained it under the FOIA from the Swedish Prosecution Authority. I originally published this letter in my investigation: Stefania Maurizi, "Five years confined: new FOIA documents shed light on the Julian Assange case," *L'Espresso*, October 19, 2015.

The Swedish Prosecution Authority documents released to me included the letter written by Hurtig to the London lawyers who had taken over the case, now that the founder of WikiLeaks was in the United Kingdom. "The case is one of the weakest cases I have ever seen in my professional career," wrote[19] Hurtig. "I should add here that I have not been provided with the complete case-file relating to Mr. Assange. There is no requirement under Swedish law to provide the full case-file, but it can be requested, and I have requested it in writing and orally. I have been refused access to this file orally by Ms. Ny, the Swedish Prosecutor. I know that the full file contains extremely important exculpatory material, for example showing fundamental inconsistencies in the complainants' accounts of the key events." He went on to explain: "I have been asked about the likely outcome of the proceedings if Mr. Assange is extradited to Sweden. In my opinion, it is highly uncertain whether Mr. Assange will be prosecuted at all, if extradited."

Hurtig added that he considered it "highly unlikely that he will be convicted" and continued: "in the extremely unlikely event that he would receive a sentence of immediate imprisonment, I would estimate a sentence in the range of 8 – 12 months, which would in practice, with two-thirds remission of sentence under Swedish law, mean a sentence of 6 – 8 months actually being served (with credit, of course, being given for time spent in custody in the UK)."

So wrote Assange's lawyer in December 2010, when his client was under investigation for *minor rape*, for which the maximum sentence is four years, two episodes of sexual molestation and one of coercion, each punishable by a maximum of two years in prison. One could object that Hurtig's assessment was biased, coming as it was from Assange's legal counsel, but the allegation of rape was so weak that Stockholm's chief prosecutor, Eva Finné, had immediately dismissed it, concluding: "I don't think there is reason to suspect that he has committed rape."[20]

---

19. Letter from the then Swedish legal counsel of Julian Assange, Björn Hurtig, to the then British legal counsel of Assange, Mark Stephens of the British law firm Finers Stephens Innocent LLP, dated December 14, 2010. I obtained a copy of this letter under the FOIA from the Swedish Prosecution Authority.
20. "Agreed statement of facts and issues": www.scribd.com/document/80912442/ Agreed-Facts-Assange-Case. See also Eva Finné's statement: "I don't think there

By the end of December, Assange was in London under house arrest at Ellingham Hall, with an electronic tag around his ankle. Prosecutor Ny could have decided to question him in the United Kingdom under the mutual legal cooperation agreements, but did not wish to do so; she only wanted to question him after extraditing him to Sweden.

On January 13, 2011 Paul Close, a British lawyer with the Crown Prosecution Service, wrote[21] to the Swedish magistrates: "It is simply amazing how much work this case is generating. It sometimes seems like an industry. It is certainly non stop. Please do not think that the case is being dealt with as just another extradition request."

How odd that a routine legal case regarding alleged sexual offenses was generating the work of "an industry." And what was so special about it, such that it was not "just another extradition request"? The Crown Prosecution Service lawyer gave no further explanation. In a previous email, he had also expressed his satisfaction with the small amount of media interest generated by one of the hearing sessions on the case:[22] "I believe the press was disappointed that it was all rather boring and technical, which of course is precisely what I wanted to happen." A few days after these emails, Close would give the Swedish Prosecution Authority some crucial advice.

HOW KEIR STARMER'S CROWN PROSECUTION SERVICE HELPED CREATE THE QUAGMIRE

On January 25, 2011, Paul Close gave his Swedish counterparts his opinion on the case, apparently not for the first time. "My

is reason to suspect that he has committed rape," reported by BBC: "Swedish rape warrant for Wikileaks' Assange cancelled," BBC, August 21, 2010: www.bbc.com/news/world-europe-11049316 (accessed March 27, 2022).
21.   Email from Paul Close to Ola Löfgren and copied to Marianne Ny dated January 13, 2011, 19:24. I obtained a copy of this email through an FOIA request to the Swedish Prosecution Authority.
22.   Email from Paul Close to Ola Löfgren and copied to Marianne Ny dated January 11, 2011, 15:48. I obtained a copy of this email through an FOIA request to the Swedish Prosecution Authority.

earlier advice remains, that in my view it would not be prudent for the Swedish authorities to try to interview the defendant in the UK," wrote[23] Close, adding: "Even if the defendant was to consent to such an interview [by appointment] on a mutually agreed basis, the defence would without any doubt seek to turn the event to its advantage. It would inevitably allege it was conclusive proof that the Swedish authorities had no case whatsoever against him and hence the interview was in the hope that he would make a full and frank confession. He would of course have no obligation [under English law] to answer any questions put to him. Any attempt to interview him under strict Swedish law would invariably be fraught with problems." The Crown Prosecution's lawyer continued: "General experience has also shown that attempts by foreign authorities to interview defendants in the UK, frequently leads to the defence retort that that [sic] some inducements or threats were made by the interviewers [such as the prosecutors' approach to bail on the defendant's surrender to the foreign state]. Thus I suggest you interview him only on his surrender to Sweden and in accordance with the Swedish law. As we have discussed your prosecution is well based on the existing evidence and is sufficient to proceed to trial, which is the prosecution's intention. The obtaining by you of a DNA sample from the Defendant in the UK is an operational matter for you and your colleagues to determine. A letter of request would be required. I believe you could only seek a non intimate sample from him. I am not sure if this evidence is really critical [or there are time issues involved]. Again you may on balance conclude that the obtaining of such evidence could have a greater propensity for harm or mischief by the defense, than it would benefit the prosecution case. You have the evidence of the complainants."

---

23. Email from Paul Close to Ola Löfgren copied to Marianna Ny and dated January 25, 2011, 17:36. I obtained a copy of this email through an FOIA request to the Swedish Prosecution Authority in 2015. However, the Swedish Prosecution Authority released this email to me in full only in 2021, after several appeals in the Swedish courts to try to access the full correspondence on the Assange case: the previous release had the paragraph on DNA fully redacted.

My FOIA investigation in Sweden promptly cleared up one of the mysteries at the very heart of the case. It was the British authorities with the Crown Prosecution Service who had advised the Swedes against the only legal strategy that could have brought the case to a rapid resolution, namely questioning Julian Assange in London, rather than insisting on his extradition. It is true that Marianne Ny had insisted on interviewing him in person in Sweden from the very start, but given the lack of progress in the preliminary investigation, she could have reassessed her strategy and decided to use the legal cooperation procedures to question Julian Assange in person in London. Unfortunately, she did not do so: she continued to insist on extradition at all costs. In advising the Swedes not to question him in the United Kingdom, the Crown Prosecution Service had helped create the legal paralysis trapping the WikiLeaks founder in Britain since 2010. After all options to oppose his transfer to Sweden were exhausted and Assange took refuge in the Ecuadorian embassy, that legal paralysis was compounded by a diplomatic impasse involving five countries— Australia, Sweden, Britain, Ecuador and the United States. This quagmire had left him in a legal limbo, under investigation for years, suspected of being a rapist but never either charged or cleared once and for all.

One of the anomalies in Paul Close's message was his use of the term "defendant,"[24] when Assange was only under investigation: he had not been charged. His reference to the Swedish authorities' intention to send him to trial was also odd since, on January 19, 2011, only six days before that email, prosecutor Ny had in fact explained[25] to Close: "According to Swedish law, a decision to prosecute may not be taken at the stage that the preliminary investigation is currently at."

Faced with Marianne Ny's refusal to question him in London, Assange fought extradition to Sweden all the way up to the United Kingdom's Supreme Court. Two days before his appeal

---

24. The term "defendant" means someone who has been charged.
25. Letter from Marianne Ny to Paul Close dated January 19, 2011. I obtained a copy of this email through an FOIA request to the Swedish Prosecution Authority.

to the court, the Crown Prosecution Service again wrote[26] to the Swedish prosecutor: "I do not believe anything like this has ever happened, either in terms of speed or in the informal nature of the procedures. I suppose this case never ceases to amaze."

Once again the British authorities alluded to a special situation, without explaining what made it so special.

As soon as the WikiLeaks founder was granted permission to appeal to the Supreme Court of the United Kingdom, the Swedish member of Eurojust—the European Union's agency for criminal justice cooperation—contacted his British counterpart, expressing his optimism that the court would rule against Julian Assange and exploring tactics to extradite him to Sweden before he could appeal to the European Court of Human Rights for protective measures. He wrote an email with the subject "Assange pick up," and the text read precisely as follows:[27] "As Sweden has to be ready to pick up Mr Asange [sic] asap after a positive decision it is extremely important to have a very good dialogue with UK authorities. It is my experience in similar situations from Eurojust it is important with a pick [sic] as close to the decision as possible to avoid conflicts with an expected appeal to the European Court of Human Rights. After the 10 days time frame [sic] there are no longer a possibility [sic] to have coercive measures against Mr A."

On May 30, 2012, the Supreme Court ruled that Assange should be extradited. Once the sentence became definitive, the WikiLeaks founder did not sit around and wait; just five days later, he took refuge in Ecuador's embassy in London, and was granted asylum on August 16.

Fifteen days after he received asylum, a press article came out entitled: "Sweden could drop case says Assange." Commenting on

26. Email from the Crown Prosecution Service to Marianne Ny, dated December 13, 2011, 14:30. I obtained a copy of this email thanks to my FOIA litigation against the Crown Prosecution Service.
27. Correspondence between Eurojust's National Member for Sweden and the UK authorities at Eurojust and at the Crown Prosecution Service, dated December 8, 2011, 01:10 pm. I obtained a copy of this email thanks to my FOIA litigation against the Crown Prosecution Service. I published this document in my article: Stefania Maurizi, "Will Assange be able to appeal to the European Court of Human Rights to fight his extradition to the US?," *il Fatto Quotidiano,* January 6, 2021.

the article, the Crown Prosecution Service wrote[28] to Marianne Ny: "Journalists!!! Don't you dare get cold feet!!." And again, in November 2012 British attorney Paul Close wrote[29] to the Swedish prosecutor: "I have no idea why the Brit Vice-Ambassador wants to meet with you. I can but assume that as you mix in those social circles it is hardly surprising!"

What interest did the British authorities have in the Swedish investigation, to the point of telling Ny "don't you dare" close it? And why did the British deputy ambassador want to meet with her?

One thing is certain: Julian Assange's human rights and health conditions seemed to be the last thing on the London authorities' minds. Towards the end of 2012, when the WikiLeaks founder had been confined for five months, the Crown Prosecution Service remarked[30] in an email to prosecutor Ny as follows: "There is no question of him being allowed out of the Ecuadorian embassy, treated and then allowed to go back. He would be arrested as soon as was appropriate. His concern seems to stem from living in a confined space [surely just good practice], having very little daylight in London and needing lots of good fresh air [again useful practice for going to the healthiest country in the world]. As for the weight loss, there are many people of my acquaintance [obviously just women] who would always welcome this."

On the very day the Crown Prosecution Service was writing these words, I paid my first visit to Julian Assange in the embassy: he had already lost a lot of weight, as I immediately reported in my article.[31]

---

28. Email from the Crown Prosecution Service to Marianne Ny dated August 31, 2012, 12:07. I obtained a copy of this email thanks to my litigation against the Crown Prosecution Service.

29. Email from Paul Close to Marianne Ny, dated November 2012, 11:28. I obtained a copy of this email through a FOIA request to the Swedish Prosecution Authority.

30. Email from the Crown Prosecution Service to Marianne Ny, dated November 29, 2012, 11:28. I obtained a copy of this email thanks to my litigation against the Crown Prosecution Service.

31. Stefania Maurizi, "Julian Assange: WikiLeaks will go ahead," *L'Espresso*, November 30, 2012.

A full year went by, and even the Swedish authorities began to question the dead end into which they had waded at the advice of the British authorities, by insisting on extradition. In October 2013, Marianne Ny wrote[32] to the CPS: "It seems that Julian Assange is absolutely determined not to go to Sweden, whatsoever," and "the chance of the judgement to extradite Assange being enforced within a reasonable time seems [to] be small." She therefore concluded: "There is a demand in Swedish law for coercive measures to be proportionate. The time passing, the costs and how severe the crime is to be taken into account together with the intrusion or detriment to the suspect. Against this background we have found us to be obliged to consider to lift the detention order (court order) and to withdraw the European arrest warrant. If so this should be done in a couple of weeks. This would affect not only us but you too in a significant way."

The next sentence was redacted, so it offered no help in understanding why revocation of the European Arrest Warrant would also have effects on the British. Was it not a Swedish investigation? At any rate, this email provides the proof that little more than one year after Julian Assange took refuge in the embassy, Marianne Ny was considering dropping the extradition proceedings. It was her investigation; she had the power to do so. So why didn't she? And why did the Crown Prosecution Service reply:[33] "I would like to consider all the angles over the weekend." What angles did the British authorities have in a Swedish sex case? "I hope it didn't ruin your weekend," Ny replied.[34] It is unclear why a Swedish prosecutor dropping an extradition would ruin the weekend of Crown Prosecution Service's authorities.

---

32. Email from Marianne Ny to the Crown Prosecution Service, dated October 18, 2013, 12:01. I obtained a copy of this email thanks to my litigation against the Crown Prosecution Service.

33. Email from the Crown Prosecution Service to Marianne Ny, dated October 18, 2013, 16:45. I obtained a copy of this email thanks to my litigation against the Crown Prosecution Service.

34. Email from Marianne Ny to the Crown Prosecution Service, dated October 21, 2013, 08:55. I obtained a copy of this email thanks to my litigation against the Crown Prosecution Service.

Two months after this email exchange, Marianne Ny again wrote to the Crown Prosecution Service, no longer mentioning the possibility of dropping the extradition, but rather inquiring into the costs of the Scotland Yard agents guarding the embassy day and night. It was rumored in Sweden that they were becoming "unreasonably high." But for the British authorities this was not a problem; they replied[35] that they "do not consider costs are a relevant factor in this matter."

In the years between 2010 and 2013, the Crown Prosecution Service made crucial decisions, like advising Marianne Ny against the only legal strategy that could have brought the case to a rapid close: questioning Assange in London. It was advice that helped create an impasse which would gravely undermine Julian Assange's health, deny justice to everyone, and cost millions of pounds of public money. Why did the Crown Prosecution Service take that route?

During that time, the Crown Prosecution was headed by Keir Starmer,[36] who would later be elected leader of the British Labour Party, replacing Jeremy Corbyn, a politician deeply disliked by the British establishment, especially the military industrial complex, for his leftist and pacifist positions. What role, if any, did Keir Starmer play in the Julian Assange case?

Ever since 2015, when I first opened the window of my FOIA investigation, I have been fighting to find answers to these questions. It would require accessing all the relevant documents, but, despite seven years of effort and six appeals in United Kingdom and Swedish tribunals and courts, to date all my attempts have failed.

It was only thanks to my trench warfare, however, that I would also unearth the fact that the Crown Prosecution Service had

---

35. Email from the Crown Prosecution Service to Marianne Ny, dated December 10, 2013, 16:29. I obtained a copy of this email thanks to my litigation against the Crown Prosecution Service.
36. Keir Starmer took up his post as head of the Crown Prosecution Service on November 1, 2008 and his last day was October 31, 2013. Paul Close's advice to the Swedish Prosecution Authority not to question Julian Assange in London is documented in my files obtained under the FOIA from at least January 2011, but he provided such advice even earlier. Keir Starmer was elected leader of the British Labour Party in April 2020.

destroyed key emails on the Julian Assange case. But before I went down that rabbit hole, the quagmire got even worse.

WHEN MARIANNE NY FINALLY CHANGED HER MIND

After Marianne Ny's email to the Crown Prosecution Service dated October 2013 indicating that she was considering dropping the extradition proceedings, another full year went by without progress until, on March 13, 2015, the prosecutor announced that she would question Julian Assange in London. What had driven Sweden to finally break free from its paralysis? First of all, the allegations of sexual molestation and coercion would legally expire in only five months' time due to the statute of limitations. And in the meantime, there had been two important developments.

The WikiLeaks founder had asked the Swedish Court of Appeal to lift the arrest warrant. In November 2014, the court rejected his appeal, but for the first time also criticized the judicial paralysis in no uncertain terms:[37] "The Court of Appeal notes, however, that the investigation into the suspected crimes has come to a halt and considers that the failure of the prosecutors to examine alternative avenues is not in line with their obligation—in the interests of everyone concerned—to move the preliminary investigation forward."

And that was not all. On September 16, 2014, the United Nations Working Group on Arbitrary Detention (UNWGAD) officially communicated to the Swedish and UK authorities that they had received a complaint on Julian Assange's conditions and asked the two countries for explanations.

These three factors constituted a wake-up call for the Swedish authorities. But the questioning that had been pending for almost five years did not take place, and in August 2015 the period in which the allegations of molestation and coercion could be acted upon expired.

---

37. Maurizi, "Five years confined ... "; David Crouch, "Julian Assange: Swedish court rejects appeal to lift arrest warrant," *Guardian*, November 20, 2014.

Ny stated[38] on that occasion "Since the autumn of 2010, I have tried to gain permission to interview Julian Assange, but he has consistently refused to appear. When the statute of limitation approached, we chose to attempt to interview him in London. A request to interview him on the premises of the Embassy of Ecuador was submitted in the beginning of June, but a permission has yet to be received."

No mention on Ny's part of having taken too long, as revealed by the FOIA documents. With five years at their disposal, the Swedish authorities decided to question him only five months before the statute of limitations expired, and sent a request for legal cooperation to the United Kingdom on May 29, 2015. The British authorities received it on June 2. The questioning was scheduled for June 17 and 18; time was running out. On June 12, Ny learned that Quito had not yet received the request and wrote to the Ecuadorian ambassador to London, Juan Falconí Puig:[39] "I regret that the Letter of Request for legal assistance in the matter of Julian Assange has not been transmitted yet to the Ecuadorian Embassy. As far as I could find out early this morning the necessary process of Authentication of the documents still was not accomplished last night. I am now awaiting information when this will be and when the documents can be transmitted."

On June 16, the afternoon before the questioning, Ecuador's ambassador informed Ny that there was no longer enough time to receive a response from the Foreign Ministry in Quito. Ny had already sent her investigators to London, but in the absence of the government's authorization, Juan Falconí Puig did not give the go-ahead. "My decision to let my investigative team go to London," wrote Marianne Ny to the diplomat,[40] "was to be prepared in case the Republic of Ecuador, in spite of the formal

38. Maurizi, "Five years confined...."
39. Email from Marianne Ny to Embajada del Ecuador Gran Bretana, dated June 12, 2015, 12:49. I obtained a copy of this email through my FOIA request to the Swedish Prosecution Authority.
40. Email from Marianne Ny to Embajada del Ecuador Gran Bretana, dated June 18, 2015, 12:38. I obtained a copy of this email through my FOIA request to the Swedish Prosecution Authority.

request being handed over at such a late stage, would decide to grant permission."

The questioning so long awaited and scheduled for June 17 and 18, 2015, fell through. And since Juan Falconí Puig had been assigned to another position, and the new ambassador would be arriving in July, the statute of limitations expired in August. Neither the alleged victim of the crimes, Anna A., nor the founder of WikiLeaks received justice. In fact, according to Swedish law, a suspect cannot waive the statute of limitations in an attempt to prove his innocence and clear his name. The allegations of sexual molestation and coercion would stick to Julian Assange forever.

The day before the statute of limitations expired, Claes Borgström, legal counsel for the two women at the time, remarked[41] to the *New York Times*: "Mr. Assange has now been in London for many years, probably for longer that he would have been in Sweden had he come here—even if he had been charged and found guilty."

Did it not occur to him and the Swedish authorities that if Julian Assange had chosen to remain inside the embassy for longer than the punishment he risked in Sweden—had he ever been charged and found guilty—perhaps it really was because he feared extradition to the United States? That his fears were real, and not merely an excuse to escape Swedish justice?

In October 2015, two months after the statute of limitations on the molestation and coercion allegations expired, Scotland Yard removed the agents who had been surrounding the building day and night since June 2012, explaining that their permanent presence was "no longer proportionate."[42] And the numbers backed them up: according to the UK government's own estimates, in three years that siege of a defenseless man had cost the taxpayers 13.2 million pounds.[43] Assange was still under investigation for rape in Sweden however, so the European Arrest Warrant for extradition purposes was still valid. Despite having removed its

---

41.   Stephen Castle, "Time is running out on part of Assange sex assault investigation," *New York Times*, August 12, 2015.
42.   Maurizi, "Five years confined...."
43.   Mayor of London, Questions and Answers Julian Assange: www.london.gov.uk/questions/2020/0144 (accessed April 22, 2022).

agents, Scotland Yard announced it would continue to "make every effort to arrest him," using "a number of overt and covert tactics."[44]

That the British authorities were quite serious was made clear only a few days later, when Ecuador's Foreign Minister reported[45] having asked the United Kingdom for a safe passage to let Julian Assange leave the embassy for a few hours to get an MRI for a shoulder problem that had been causing him pain. The British government replied that he could leave whenever he wished, but he would be arrested.

Assange remained in the embassy, forgoing medical treatment. A short time later, however, an authoritative United Nations body, the Working Group on Arbitrary Detention, took his side.

44. Maurizi, "Five years confined...."; Jamie Grierson, "Julian Assange: police removed from outside Ecuadorian embassy," *Guardian*, October 12, 2015.

45. Ben Quinn, "Britain unmoved by Ecuadorian request to give Julian Assange 'safe passage' for MRI scan," *Guardian*, October 15, 2015.

12
Arbitrarily Detained

ONE INTERNATIONAL LAW FOR US AND ONE FOR
THEM: HOW SWEDEN AND THE UK IGNORED THE
UNITED NATIONS WORKING GROUP

They go about their work unobtrusively and seldom attract the spotlight. The United Nations Working Group on Arbitrary Detention has the mandate to establish when individuals are being arbitrarily deprived of their liberty: political activists and journalists persecuted by regimes, refugees and asylum seekers detained with no end in sight. It concerns itself with some of the most vulnerable people on the planet. Julian Assange had filed a complaint to the Working Group represented by a number of lawyers, including high-profile Australian legal counsel Melinda Taylor, expert in international law and human rights, and herself once a victim of arbitrary detention in Libya.

In February 2016 the Working Group released its opinion: the founder of WikiLeaks was in fact being arbitrarily detained by Sweden and the United Kingdom. The group called on the two countries to end Assange's deprivation of liberty and afford him the right to compensation. Among the reasons for the UN body's finding of arbitrary detention, the Working Group indicated five crucial factors.

"Mr. Assange has been denied the opportunity to provide a statement" and "access to exculpatory evidence and thus the opportunity to defend himself against the allegations," evidence like the SMS messages sent by the two women in 2010 at the time of the alleged offenses. For years, the WikiLeaks founder had denounced the fact that his Swedish lawyers had only been allowed to read them, but not to obtain any copies or take notes on them.[1] And then, according to the Working Group, "the duration of such detention is *ipso facto* incompatible with the presumption of innocence."

Also making his deprivation of liberty arbitrary was "the indefinite nature of this detention, and the absence of an effective form of judicial review or remedy," as well as the fact that "the Embassy of the Republic of Ecuador in London is not and far less than a house or detention centre equipped for prolonged pre-trial detention and lacks appropriate and necessary medical equipment or facilities."[2] The Working Group underlined: "It is valid to assume, after 5 years of deprivation of liberty, Mr. Assange's health could have been deteriorated to a level that anything more than a superficial illness would put his health at a serious risk and he was denied his access to a medical institution for a proper diagnosis, including taking a MRI test."

Finally, the United Nations body took one last, by no means minor factor into account: "With regard to the legality of the EAW [European Arrest Warrant], since the final decision by the Supreme Court of the United Kingdom in Mr. Assange's case, UK domestic law on the determinative issues had been drastically changed, including as a result of perceived abuses raised by Sweden's EAW, so that if requested, Mr. Assange's extradition would not have been permitted by the UK. Nevertheless, the Government of the United Kingdom has stated in relation to Mr. Assange that these changes are "not retrospective" and so may not benefit him."

What was the Working Group referring to?

---

1. The fact that the full case file contained "extremely important exculpatory material" was promptly noted in a letter dated December 14, 2010 from Assange's Swedish lawyer at the time, Björn Hurtig, to Assange's then British lawyer, Mark Stephens, as I explained in chapter 11. Hurtig did not clarify what kind of material he was referring to, but wrote that he "was permitted to inspect but not to take copies or notes of sms/text messages from the complainants' mobile telephones."
2. "The Working Group on Arbitrary Detention deems the deprivation of liberty of Mr. Julian Assange as arbitrary," Office of the United Nations High Commissioner for Human Rights, February 5, 2016: www.ohchr.org/en/statements/2016/02/working-group-arbitrary-detention-deems-deprivation-liberty-mr-julian-assange (accessed April 22, 2022). The Working Group's opinion No. 54/2015 on Assange is available in the body of the press release.

From 2014 on, with the introduction of "Section 12 A," the United Kingdom would no longer grant extradition of a suspect solely for the purpose of questioning, as was done in the case of Assange. From then on, extradition would only be granted if the foreign judicial authority issuing the European Arrest Warrant had already charged the suspect and was therefore requesting their transfer in order to send them to trial. This was a legal argument raised repeatedly by Assange's defense in fighting Sweden's warrant, contending that the measure was disproportionate; prosecutor Ny had requested his extradition only to question him as a suspect, not as a defendant who needed to stand trial. But WikiLeaks' founder had lost his appeal in all of the British courts, which upheld the legality of the measure. Two years after the Supreme Court's sentence on Assange, the United Kingdom changed its laws, but it was too late for him.

The Working Group's decision was well argued, but was rejected by both Sweden and the United Kingdom. According to the two governments, Julian Assange had entered the embassy and remained there voluntarily, and could leave whenever he wished, so it was not even a matter of detention, much less arbitrary detention. The Swedish authorities did not appeal the Working Group's decision; they simply ignored it. It was the first time in its history[3] that the Scandinavian country had been found to detain an individual arbitrarily. Britain, on the other hand, dismissed it with disdain: then Foreign Secretary Philip Hammond labeled it as "frankly ridiculous,"[4] after which the British authorities tried to appeal it, and lost. "The UK reacts in the way that certain states do that one does not want to be compared to," Mads Andenas told me[5] on that occasion. Andenas, a highly regarded Norwegian diplomat and professor of law at the University of Oslo, had previ-

---

3. This information was confirmed to me by Katarina Fabian, deputy director of the Department for International Law, Human Rights and Treaty Law, Ministry of Foreign Affairs, Government of Sweden. Email to author, February 5, 2016.
4. Matthew Weaver, "Julian Assange hails 'sweet victory' of UN report—as it happened," *Guardian*, February 5, 2016.
5. Stefania Maurizi, "Pressioni politiche sulle Nazioni Unite per la decisione su Julian Assange," *L'Espresso*, February 9, 2016.

ously headed the United Nations Working Group and handled the initial stages of the procedure on Assange. Andenas added: "I can confirm that there is strong pressure on the Working Group when they are issuing an opinion against a large state like the UK, and a state with such a good human rights record like Sweden."

When authoritarian countries arbitrarily deprive activists, journalists or political opponents of their freedom, the Western democracies normally call upon such countries to respect the Working Group's decisions. In January 2016, a few days before the United Nations body made public its opinion on Julian Assange, Prime Minister David Cameron's Conservative UK government threatened the Maldives with sanctions[6] for arbitrarily detaining former president Mohamed Nasheed. And in 2009, the United Kingdom and European Union upheld the sanctions previously approved against Myanmar, citing the arbitrary detention of activist and Nobel Peace Prize winner Aung San Suu Kyi.[7]

In the Assange case, by contrast, not only did the British authorities react with scorn, they ignored the deliberation completely, dismissing it as not binding. From a strictly technical standpoint, they were right, in the sense that the Working Group is not a judicial authority. "The Working Group is not just an NGO, it is the highest institution in the United Nations system, which had been created by member states to deal with differences between citizens and their government when it comes to addressing issues of the legality of detention and the legitimacy of detention," Christophe Peschoux[8] explained to me. Peschoux, a courageous and unassuming man within the United Nations Secretariat, pointed out that the Working Group's decisions are binding in the sense that they are based on international laws and conventions which countries like the United Kingdom have ratified, and are therefore obliged to uphold. Indeed, in the face of these reactions from British authorities and certain media treating the decision like

6. Reuters Staff, "Britain could use sanctions to pressure Maldives government," Reuters, January 27, 2016.
7. Jared Genser, *The Working Group on Arbitrary Detention: Commentary and guide to practice* (Cambridge: Cambridge University Press, 2020).
8. Christophe Peschoux, communication to author, May 9, 2021.

just another opinion, the body issued a statement[9] with a "Note to editors" to underscore: "The Opinions of the Working Group on Arbitrary Detention are legally-binding to the extent that they are based on binding international human rights law [...]. The Opinions of the WGAD are also considered as authoritative by prominent international and regional judicial institutions, including the European Court of Human Rights."

As pointed out in the *Guardian*[10] by human rights organizations like Human Rights Watch, the stance taken by Sweden and the United Kingdom not only harmed Assange, it also undermined the credibility of the United Nations body, which defends some of the most defenseless people on earth, like prisoners in the hands of brutal regimes. If democracies like the United Kingdom publicly dismiss its decisions, defining them as ridiculous, how could they then turn around and expect authoritarian countries to comply with them and free political prisoners, human rights activities, journalists or refugees?

The United Nations body had shown great courage, Professor Mads Andenas also told me:[11] "This case is special: there are such strong interests that it was a very courageous decision by the people in the Working Group and in the Secretariat, who made it possible. These people did impressive work and no one is going to thank them. The campaign against Assange is a highly sophisticated one."

In light of the United Nations body's opinion, the founder of WikiLeaks again appealed to the Swedish courts, requesting revocation of the detention order issued by prosecutor Ny. Once again, he lost both at first instance and on appeal. Despite the Working Group's decision, the risk of extradition continued to hang over his head, since Sweden had decided to ignore it, just as an authoritarian country would have done.

9.　The press release with a Note to Editors is available on the OHCHR's website: www.ohchr.org/en/press-releases/2016/02/julian-assange-arbitrarily-detained-sweden-and-uk-un-expert-panel-finds (accessed April 24, 2022).

10.　Owen Bowcott, "Britain 'sets dangerous precedent' by defying UN report on Assange," *Guardian*, February 24, 2016.

11.　Stefania Maurizi, "Pressioni politiche sulle Nazioni Unite per la decisione su Julian Assange," *L'Espresso*, February 9, 2016.

JUSTICE FOR NO ONE

It was not until November 14, 2016, over six years after reopening the rape investigation, that the Swedish prosecutors questioned Julian Assange inside the Ecuadorian embassy. Marianne Ny did not go to London in person; she sent another prosecutor accompanied by a police officer. The list of questions for the suspect had been prepared in advance and sent to an Ecuadorian prosecutor, who asked Assange the questions that day in the presence of the Swedish prosecutor and the police officer. His answers were then sent to the Swedish authorities by the Ecuadorian authorities.

This manner of questioning a suspect met with plenty of insinuations and suspicions, but when I later asked the Swedish authorities about it, they replied that the procedure was provided for in the judicial cooperation agreement[12] between Stockholm and Quito. Signed months earlier, precisely to provide a clear regulatory framework, it applied to any individual subjected to questioning. "The deal is general and not tailormade for Mr. Assange," the Swedish Ministry of Justice clarified to me.[13] Hence despite the insinuations by some media outlets, the founder of WikiLeaks did not receive special treatment. Quite the opposite; the Ecuadorian prosecutor barred Per Samuelsson,[14] who together with his colleague, Thomas Olsson, represented Julian Assange in Sweden. Samuelsson was not allowed to enter the embassy.

After all his work on the case, Samuelsson could not advise his client during the most crucial stage: his questioning, which had been six years in coming. "It is a serious breach of Julian's rights as a suspect under Swedish law," Samuelsson told me, "It is a decision taken by the Ecuadorian prosecutor. Why I do not know. Assange felt compelled to do the statement anyway otherwise they would blame him."

12.   The bilateral judicial cooperation agreement between Sweden and Ecuador is publicly available: www.regeringen.se/sveriges-regering/justitiedepartementet/internationellt-rattsligt-samarbete/rattslig-hjalp-i-brottmal/ (accessed April 24, 2022).
13.   The fact that the bilateral agreement was not "tailor-made" for Assange was confirmed to me by the press office of the Swedish Ministry of Justice. Email to author, May 10, 2019.
14.   Per Samuelsson email to author, November 14, 2016.

Stressing that for six years he had made himself available for questioning, and repeatedly invoking the opinion of the United Nations Working Group, Assange answered the Ecuadorian prosecutor's fifty-seven questions and read a statement[15] retracing the sexual relations with Sofia W. at the heart of the preliminary rape investigation, the relations that took place the night of August 16–17, 2010, not even four weeks after publication of the Afghan War Logs.

The document reads:[16] "During that night and again in the morning, we had consensual sexual intercourse on four or five occasions: it was obvious to me through her words, her expressions and her physical reactions that she encouraged and enjoyed our interactions." He continued: "In the morning she went out to pick up breakfast for us. After enjoying breakfast together, I left her home on good terms. At no stage when I was with her did she express that I had disrespected her in any way or acted contrary to her wishes other than to not be interested in her enough. She even took me to the train station on her bicycle and we kissed each other goodbye."

Assange told of how, after leaving her that morning, they had talked on the phone the next day, or perhaps the day after: "She made friendly small talk." They spoke again on August 20: Sofia W. told him that she was in the hospital and asked him to get tested for sexually transmitted diseases. Assange remembered his reply as follows: "But I was very busy dealing with the political and legal threats against me from the Pentagon which had sharply increased and said I couldn't do anything until the next day. She said that the police could help her to force me to get STD [sexually transmitted disease] test results if I didn't come down to the hospital. I told her I found this strange and threatening. She stated that it was normal in Sweden to go to the police with all sorts of problems and that it meant nothing."

---

15.   I obtained a copy of the 57 questions, the answers and the statement by Julian Assange through my FOIA litigation against the Swedish Prosecution Authority.
16.   These quotes come from the questioning of Julian Assange and from his statement, November 14, 2016.

According to Assange, he was willing to get tested: "I said I was happy to get tests to assure her out of good will, but it could not be until the next day, Saturday. She agreed to my suggestion to meet her the following day in a nearby park at noon and said that she was now fine and seemed at ease. You can imagine my disbelief when I woke the next morning to the news that I had been arrested in my absence for 'rape' and police were 'hunting' all over Stockholm for me."

On August 20, 2010, Sofia W. went with Anna A. to the police. According to the facts agreed upon by the prosecution and defense on the occasion of the 2012 appeal to the UK Supreme Court,[17] "SW wanted the Appellant [Julian Assange] to get tested for disease. On 20th August 2010 SW went to the police to seek advice. AA [Anna A.] accompanied her for support. The police treated their visit as the filing of formal reports for rape of SW and molestation of AA." The police questioning of Sofia W. on August 20 was never recorded, only summarized by the interviewing officer, Irmeli Krans, who noted that, after she was informed that Assange had been arrested *in absentia*, "Sofia had difficulty concentrating, as a result of which I made the judgement that it was best to terminate the interview." Sofia W. left the police station without even confirming or signing the report.

In the course of his questioning in November 2016, the founder of WikiLeaks quoted some of the messages sent by the two women on those days. They were SMS messages that his defense had never been able to obtain a copy of or transcribe: only to read and memorize. Like the one sent the day Sofia W. and Anna A. went to the police station: "On 20 August [SW][18] wrote that she 'did not want to put any charges [*sic*] on Julian Assange, but that the police were keen on getting their hands on him (14:26); and that she was chocked [*sic, shocked*] when they arrested him because she only wanted him to take a test (17:06).'" And the day after

---

17. "Agreed statement of facts and issues": www.scribd.com/document/80912442/Agreed-Facts-Assange-Case (accessed March 24, 2022).
18. In the statement given by Assange, which I obtained thanks to my FOIA litigation, Sofia's name has been redacted. I use "SW" when referring to the content of her SMS messages for clarity.

Sofia went to the police: "On 21 August [SW] wrote that she 'did not want to accuse Julian Assange for anything', (07:27); and that it was the 'police who made up the suspicions' (22:25)."

The entire *minor rape* case was based on one allegation: "Assange, with intention, had sexual intercourse with her by abusing the fact that she was asleep and thereby in a helpless state." During his questioning, Assange stated that this was not true: "[SW] was not asleep and I was certain she expressly consent [*sic*] to unprotected sex before such intercourse started. This is also evidenced by [SW]'s own text messages," such as the message sent the next day in which she wrote that she was "half asleep."[19]

Six months after the questioning in the embassy, on May 19, 2017, Marianne Ny dropped the rape investigation, releasing this statement:[20] "According to Swedish legislation, a criminal investigation is to be conducted as quickly as possible. At the point when a prosecutor has exhausted the possibilities to continue the investigation, the prosecutor is obliged to discontinue the investigation. At this point, all possibilities to conduct the investigation are exhausted. In order to proceed with the case, Julian Assange would have to be formally notified of the criminal suspicions against him. We cannot expect to receive assistance from Ecuador regarding this. Therefore the investigation is discontinued."

After almost seven years, the Swedish case had reached its conclusion, with justice for no one: neither the two women, nor Assange, nor the public, especially the British and Swedish citizens whose government had spent substantial public resources pursuing the case. And with the blame for all this dumped on Assange and Ecuador, and Assange's health undermined, his reputation deeply tarnished, and a decision by the United Nations Working Group on Arbitrary Detention completely ignored by the two democracies of the United Kingdom and Sweden.

19. This quote, like previous Assange quotes, comes from the questioning of Julian Assange and from his statement, November 14, 2016.
20. Marianne Ny's statement is available on the Swedish Prosecution Authority's website: www.aklagare.se/en/media/press-releases/2017/may/1/january/the-investigation-against-julian-assange-is-discontinued2/ (accessed April 25, 2022).

The statute of limitations for the *minor rape* allegation would expire in August 2020, so the investigation could be reopened until that time. And two years later, that is exactly what the Swedish authorities would do.

13
A Russian Connection?

He did not leave the Ecuadorian embassy. Although the Swedish investigation had been dropped and the European Arrest Warrant issued by Marianne Ny no longer hung over his head, Julian Assange did not set foot outside the red-brick building in the elegant district of Knightsbridge.

He had always claimed he took refuge there out of fear of being arrested, extradited to the United States and convicted for publishing the classified documents on the Afghanistan and Iraq wars, the diplomatic cables and the Guantanamo detainee records: the 700,000 files that had earned Chelsea Manning a thirty-five-year prison sentence. Rafael Correa's Ecuador had deemed Assange's concerns for his life and freedom well-founded, to the point of granting him diplomatic asylum, but few others believed him. Everyone treated him as a fugitive trying to escape Swedish justice.

The WikiLeaks founder stayed in the embassy because the risk of arrest remained, despite withdrawal of the Swedish warrant. To enter the building and seek asylum he had breached the conditions of his bail, which obliged him to stay under house arrest with an electronic tag, and of course to surrender to Scotland Yard for extradition after losing his Supreme Court appeal. He had violated those conditions to exercise a legitimate right recognized by international law, namely the right to apply for asylum, but neither the United Kingdom nor Sweden ever showed any regard for the decision taken by another sovereign nation, Ecuador, to grant him asylum. In those two governments' eyes, Julian Assange had always been a fugitive. In consequence, if he dared step over the embassy's threshold to go outside, Scotland Yard would arrest him for breach of bail.

The punishment would have been relatively mild; at most fifty-two weeks in prison. But once in the hands of the British authorities, he would again risk being extradited to the United States, either directly by the United Kingdom or, once again, indirectly by Sweden. Although the rape investigation had been closed, prosecutor Ny could always reopen it for the third time, since the statute of limitations on the allegations would not expire until August 2020. The British authorities had treated the decision by the United Nations Working Group on Arbitrary Detention— that Julian Assange should be released and compensated—with complete disdain, never taking it into the slightest consideration. And for international and British media, this attitude was apparently not a problem. From the BBC to the *New York Times*, from the *Guardian* to the *Washington Post*, no one raised the issue of the British authorities' treatment of the WikiLeaks founder. Whether because of the rape allegation or the allegation that he had put lives in danger, there was always a good reason to ignore Assange's condition. And in May 2017, when the Swedish investigation was dropped, there was another reason, one of gargantuan proportions.

Between July and October 2016, in the thick of the U.S. presidential election campaign in which Hillary Clinton ran as the Democratic candidate and Donald Trump as the Republican, WikiLeaks published the internal emails of the Democratic National Committee (DNC)—the governing body of the United States Democratic Party—and those of John Podesta, the chairman of Clinton's presidential campaign.

Assange and his organization were ultimately accused of helping the Republican candidate win, in collusion with the men working for Trump's election and the Russian government. All hell broke loose. But what is true?

I had witnessed the birth of this demonization campaign back in 2012, when the *Guardian* accused Julian Assange of being the

Kremlin's useful idiot.[1] His crime? Hosting the show "The World Tomorrow"—a series of interviews with a range of individuals, from leading figures in international politics to Guantanamo detainees, from activists to cryptography experts—which was also broadcast by the Russia Today television network, later known as "RT." The British newspaper's criticism was cutting: "The World Tomorrow confirms he is no fearless revolutionary. Instead he is a useful idiot."

This reaction was rather over-the-top. *The World Tomorrow* was not a partnership between WikiLeaks and RT; it was an independent production. RT, like my own media group,[2] had acquired the license to broadcast the show; it purchased the television rights and broadcast all the episodes in the series. Journalists with other European television networks had considered acquiring the rights as well.

The *Guardian*'s criticism was also overblown considering that only one-and-a-half years earlier, WikiLeaks had revealed cables wherein U.S. diplomacy painted Russia as "a mafia state," files which the London daily had published with great fanfare, and only thanks to WikiLeaks and its source, Chelsea Manning. When the article on *The World Tomorrow* show calling Assange a useful idiot was published in the *Guardian*, nothing WikiLeaks had published up to that point could be even remotely linked or traced back to Russia.

In point of fact, WikiLeaks had by that time released: the 700,000 files from Manning, then the Spy Files, a series of company brochures on the surveillance industry, which were not classified U.S. government files, but rather the kind of documents of interest to the galaxy of individuals and organizations that defend privacy, and finally, the Stratfor emails.

---

1. Luke Harding, "The World Tomorrow: Julian Assange proves a useful idiot," *Guardian*, April 17, 2012.
2. My media group acquired the license from Journeyman Pictures, a British film distribution company. The media group I worked for at the time was the Italy-based L'Espresso Group, with 1,950 employees, operating in national newspapers, local newspapers, periodicals, radio, internet and internet television. It owned two of the most important media outlets in Italy: the weekly *L'Espresso* and the daily *la Repubblica*.

I have no inside information on how WikiLeaks obtained the Stratfor emails. According to the U.S. Department of Justice, they were hacked by a branch of Anonymous activists infiltrated by an FBI agent provocateur under the cover name "Sabu." The year after the *Guardian* article, political activist and American pacifist Jeremy Hammond, accused of the hacking, would be sentenced to ten years in prison,[3] despite never having benefited from the files in any way, financially or otherwise, and even though the Stratfor files revealed information of undeniable public interest. Hammond had been inspired by Chelsea Manning.

The vitriolic attack by the *Guardian* kicked off a full-scale demonization campaign. When WikiLeaks later helped Snowden seek asylum in 2013, the accusations intensified. But after the U.S. government itself had trapped Snowden in Putin's Russia by cancelling his passport, did helping him really make WikiLeaks a tool of the Kremlin? All the leading newspapers with the Snowden files in hand, first among them the *Guardian*, could have sought a way to save one of the greatest journalistic sources of all time, thanks to whom the London daily would win its first Pulitzer Prize. And yet, after securing their scoop, they abandoned him to his fate. The *Washington Post*, after winning the Pulitzer together with the *Guardian* for the revelations based on Snowden's files, went so far as to publish an editorial[4] opposing a presidential pardon, calling for the punishment of its own source.[5]

In their attempt to aid Snowden, Julian Assange's organization had sought asylum for him from numerous European countries—in vain. It is an embarrassing truth, but with all its glorification of press freedom, Europe utterly deserted one of the most important sources in history. And to realize what Snowden had risked, we need only remember the words of former CIA director James

---

3. Ed Pilkington, "Lawyers in Stratfor leak case present letters of support ahead of sentencing," *Guardian*, November 4, 2013. As reported in this *Guardian* article, I was among the journalists, lawyers and activists who petitioned the judge for clemency for Jeremy Hammond, insofar as the revelations from the Stratfor files were definitely in the public interest and Hammond obtained no personal gain from them.

4. Editorial Board, "No pardon for Snowden," *Washington Post*, September 17, 2016.

5. Glenn Greenwald, "WashPost makes history: first paper to call for prosecution of its own source (after accepting Pulitzer)," *The Intercept*, September 18, 2016.

Woolsey, in 2015. Baselessly crediting him with part of the responsibility for the terrorist attacks in France in November 2015, Woolsey said[6] of Snowden: "I would give him the death sentence, and I would prefer to see him hanged by the neck until he's dead, rather than merely electrocuted."

It is true that Julian Assange and WikiLeaks often agreed to interviews on the RT television network, but they worked far more with Western media, and, in all my years partnering with them for my newspaper, I never witnessed a situation in which they obtained files on Russia and did not publish them. Indeed, I noted that the Kremlin's media were not allowed to work with WikiLeaks as media partners. To the best of my knowledge, they only partnered with WikiLeaks on one publication, the Spy Files released in 2013[7]—the company brochures on the surveillance industry—but no classified files, including U.S. government files.

The repeated accusations of being the Kremlin's useful idiots would reach their peak with the U.S. presidential elections in 2016.

THE INFORMATION TRUMPS ALL

Julian Assange publicly[8] announced that WikiLeaks would be publishing files on Hillary Clinton on June 12, 2016. Two days later, the *Washington Post*[9] revealed for the first time that IT security experts recruited by the Democrats had determined that the party's networks had been penetrated by Russian government cyber criminals.[10]

---

6.   Bradford Richardson, "Ex-CIA director: Snowden should be 'hanged' for Paris," *The Hill*, November 19, 2015.
7.   The Spy Files are available on the WikiLeaks website: https://wikileaks.org/spyfiles/ (accessed April 29, 2022).
8.   Mark Tran, "WikiLeaks to publish more Hillary Clinton emails—Julian Assange," *Guardian*, June 12, 2016.
9.   Ellen Nakashima, "Russian government hackers penetrated DNC, stole opposition research on Trump," *Washington Post*, June 14, 2016.
10.   While media reports use the term "Russian hackers," I prefer to use "Russian government cyber criminals," to draw a line between "hackers," like the teenage Julian Assange who hacked Nortel networks for "intellectual inquisitiveness," as established by the judge, or the Chaos Computer Club of hackers, that is, individuals who are passionate about technology and how it works and impacts society, and the "Russian

Apart from this vague information disseminated by the media, there was no proof of such hacking at that time. Four days after WikiLeaks published the Democratic National Committee emails, the *New York Times* reported:[11] "American intelligence agencies have told the White House they now have 'high confidence' that the Russian government was behind the theft of emails and documents from the Democratic National Committee," adding: "But intelligence officials have cautioned that they are uncertain whether the electronic break-in at the committee's computer systems was intended as fairly routine cyberespionage— of the kind the United States also conducts around the world—or as part of an effort to manipulate the 2016 presidential election."

This was the uncertain situation in July 2016, when WikiLeaks published the first batch of U.S. Democratic Party files. It was not until October 6, the day before the organization revealed those of John Podesta, the chairman of Clinton's election campaign, that James Clapper, director of National Intelligence, head of the U.S. intelligence community, released an official statement[12] accusing Moscow of interfering with the U.S. election process.

But if Clapper's statements had been released even earlier, promptly alerting the public of an alleged Russian attempt to interfere with the U.S. elections, would that have really justified WikiLeaks stopping the publication of those emails, and the media not reporting on them?

We all remembered when, in 2014, the *Washington Post*—a newspaper certainly not hostile to the U.S. intelligence community—published an article[13] asking President Obama to fire then-CIA director John Brennan for lying. Brennan had denied that his agency had penetrated the computers of the Senate committee charged with investigating CIA torture. But it had. He later

---

government cyber criminals" who penetrate networks to conduct espionage activities for financial or political gain.

11.   David E. Sanger and Eric Schmitt, "Spy agency consensus grows that Russia hacked DNC," *New York Times*, June 26, 2016.

12.   David E. Sanger and Charlie Savage, "US says Russia directed hacks to influence elections," *New York Times*, October 7, 2016.

13.   James Downie, "Obama should fire John Brennan," *Washington Post*, July 31, 2014.

apologized, but it was not the first time he had not told the truth. He had also claimed in the past that drone attacks had not caused a single civilian casualty. Another falsehood. And the *Washington Post* noted that Brennan was not the only intelligence director to have lied: James Clapper "had lied[14] under oath to Congress" when he declared that the National Security Agency (NSA) did not collect the telephone metadata of U.S. citizens, after which, thanks to Edward Snowden, we learned that it most definitely did.

But regardless of whether or not U.S. intelligence was telling the truth about the Democratic emails being hacked by the Russians, journalists are duty-bound to publish everything that is true and in the public interest, whatever the source. And that is what WikiLeaks did. As a matter of fact, dozens of prominent U.S. and international media organizations covered the documents once they had been published by WikiLeaks, first and foremost the *New York Times*.

On July 22, 2016, the organization revealed thousands of the Democratic National Committee's internal emails. There were only three days to go before the convention that would name Hillary Clinton the presidential nominee and mark the defeat of Bernie Sanders. The messages exposed[15] how the committee, rather than remaining neutral in the primaries as it was supposed to, boycotted left-wing candidate Sanders and favored Clinton, a democrat far to the right of Sanders. That the party establishment favored a candidate with considerable ties to Wall Street and support from Silicon Valley and the military-industrial complex, rather than a candidate who spoke to the more vulnerable segments of the population, confirmed the suspicions of Sanders' supporters. The revelations set off a political firestorm. Echoed by U.S. and interna-

---

14. The general counsel of the Office of the Director of National Intelligence would later deny that James Clapper lied and, while acknowledging that his testimony "was inaccurate," he said, "it could not be corrected publicly because the program involved was classified." Martin Pengelly, "Clapper did not lie to Congress on NSA, says national intelligence counsel," *Guardian*, January 4, 2014.
15. The emails of the Democratic National Committee are available on the WikiLeaks website: https://wikileaks.org//dnc-emails/ (accessed May 1, 2022).

tional media, they ultimately led to the resignation of Democratic National Committee chairwoman Debbie Wasserman Schultz.[16]

The files had been published without media partners, and the WikiLeaks journalists were criticized for releasing thousands of documents onto the web in one fell swoop. With the John Podesta emails, they wanted to do it differently. They told me that this time they would release the materials in several batches, to allow room for a more in-depth analysis, and would do so together with interested media partners. I decided I would work on them also: U.S. elections have always had an impact on every country in the world, Italy included. I was alone, however; the other media partners kept their distance. I was in contact with the organization on an almost daily basis, and witnessed their attempts to obtain files on Donald Trump as well. I remember WikiLeaks asking us media partners to help analyze four files on the Republican candidate's business affairs. Unfortunately, we discovered that the material was already public.

On October 6, the WikiLeaks journalists informed me that they would be publishing the first batch of Podesta emails the next day. That choice of date did not surprise me: the second presidential debate between Trump and Clinton was to be held on October 9. In my many years of partnering with them, I had seen how WikiLeaks chose their publication dates strategically, to ensure maximum impact for their revelations. We arranged to talk again the following day. I knew they would be publishing either late in the morning or early in the afternoon: Podesta's emails were aimed at U.S. public opinion in particular, so it made little sense to bring them out when America was sleeping.

They published[17] a short time after the *Washington Post* revealed a 2005 clip from the television show *Access Hollywood*, featuring Donald Trump making extremely vulgar remarks about women.

16. Jonathan Martin and Alan Rappeport, "Debbie Wasserman Schultz to resign D.N.C. post," *New York Times*, July 24, 2016.
17. The Podesta emails are available on the WikiLeaks website: https://wikileaks. org/podesta-emails/ (accessed May 1, 2022).

WikiLeaks was excoriated. They were accused of carefully coordinating the release of the emails with Trump's campaign to offset the negative effect of the video, in order to help the Republican candidate. The choice to release the emails in batches was attacked as well. In the case of the Democratic National Committee emails, they had been wrong to publish them all together. Now, in the case of Podesta's emails, they were wrong to publish them in waves. It was interpreted as a malevolent strategy: to wear Hillary Clinton down through a steady trickle of revelations over the four weeks leading up to the election. By now the fury against Julian Assange and his organization was so fierce that whatever they did was perceived as suspect. The atmosphere was so charged that, for the first time ever, Rafael Correa's Ecuador went so far as to cut off Assange's access to internet: his only means of staying in touch with the world, confined as he was within the four walls of the embassy.

I do not pretend to know the truth about what really happened; I can only report the facts as I experienced them. The decision to publish the first Podesta emails was not made at the last second; it was made at least one day before, when I was informed of the decision. Unfortunately, to the best of my knowledge, no other WikiLeaks media partner can confirm my testimony, as no other media partner was present. And yet the emails were in the public interest, and those that I worked on and was able to verify were unquestionably authentic.[18] They depicted an elitist Democratic Party establishment, one that glided effortlessly among Wall Street bankers and the lords of Silicon Valley, light years away from the American middle class that had been brought to its knees by the economic crisis.[19] They also chronicled their relationships and contacts with the centrist parties of other countries, like Italy.

Important files included speeches given by Hillary Clinton to financial giants behind closed doors. During the primaries, Bernie

18. Stefania Maurizi, "WikiLeaks, per Hillary conta più papa Francesco che Renzi," *la Repubblica*, November 8, 2016.
19. Thomas Frank, "Forget the FBI cache; the Podesta emails show how America is run," *Guardian*, October 31, 2016.

Sanders had criticized her sharply for those conferences and urged her to reveal their content. The *New York Times* had also asked her to make public those "richly paid speeches to big banks, which many middle-class Americans still blame for their economic pain."[20] But Hillary Clinton had steered clear of any such transparency during her electoral campaign and, when WikiLeaks published her speeches[21] and leading U.S. media reported on them, it was clear why. They contained statements like:[22] "I'm kind of far removed" from the struggles of the middle class, "because [of] the life I've lived and the economic, you know, fortunes that my husband and I now enjoy." According to the *New York Times*:[23] "The Clintons have made more than $120 million in speeches to Wall Street and special interests since Bill Clinton left the White House in 2001."

Didn't the U.S. public have as much right to know what Clinton said to the financial giants behind closed doors as they did to know the content of Trump's tax returns?

Hillary Clinton was defeated in the November 2016 elections. Julian Assange and his organization were pilloried, accused of contributing to the election of Trump. They were especially attacked after Trump declared "*I love WikiLeaks*" in the course of his presidential campaign, and after Twitter exchanges surfaced between WikiLeaks and both Donald Trump Jr., one of the president's sons, and Roger Stone, a controversial lobbyist and strategist who had long been close to Trump. Although the exchanges took place when WikiLeaks had already published all the Democratic emails of July 2016, in reporting on them the media hinted at collusion between Assange's organization and Trump's campaign for the purpose of damaging Clinton.

---

20. The Editorial Board, "Mrs. Clinton, show voters those transcripts," *New York Times*, February 25, 2016.
21. The Podesta email containing the Hillary Clinton's speeches to financial giants is available on the WikiLeaks website: https://wikileaks.org/podesta-emails/emailid/927 (accessed May 1, 2022).
22. Ibid.
23. Amy Chozick, Nicholas Confessore and Michael Barbaro, "Leaked speech excerpts show a Hillary Clinton at ease with Wall Street," *New York Times*, October 7, 2016.

In May 2017, the U.S. Department of Justice appointed special prosecutor Robert S. Mueller to investigate "Russiagate," the alleged Russian operations aimed at influencing the 2016 U.S. presidential elections. After almost two years of inquiries, in April 2019 the "Mueller Report" was released, summarizing the results of the investigation. The report found that Russia had interfered in the elections, hacking the Democratic Party's emails, but the prosecutor did not find evidence of a conspiracy or cooperation between Trump's campaign and Russia, the core of the Russiagate theory.

According to the report, the GRU Russian intelligence services, concealed behind two false online identities, "DCLeaks" and "Guccifer 2.0," contacted WikiLeaks through direct Twitter messages to offer the files, then sent them via PGP-encrypted emails. The report did not accuse Assange's organization of knowing that it was Russia behind the two identities, however, nor did it explain a glaring inconsistency: how could the WikiLeaks founder have announced to the whole world on June 12, 2016, that the emails would be published when, according to Mueller's investigations, the first contact with DCLeaks had occurred on June 14, and with Guccifer 2.0 on June 22? The document also failed to clarify why, in almost two years of inquiries, and with a team of nineteen lawyers assisted by a good forty FBI agents, intelligence analysts and IT experts, the special prosecutor had never questioned Assange and WikiLeaks. Publication of the Democratic Party's emails was considered the incident at the heart of Russiagate. Mueller interviewed 500 people. Why did he never question the journalists who had actually published the files?

To this day, whatever one may think of prosecutor Mueller's investigation and final report, there are still a great many points to clarify, and inexplicable contradictions. Nor does the report seem to offer any certainty as to who sent the emails, and exactly how they did so.

Despite all this, the report did make it clear that Mueller had considered indicting WikiLeaks, Assange or even Stone for criminal conspiracy to hack the emails, but decided against it because "This Office determined the admissible evidence to be insufficient"[24] to prove that they played an active role in the theft, or even that they were aware of it. Furthermore, publication of the files could enjoy constitutional protection under the First Amendment. Mueller wrote:[25] "Under the Supreme Court's decision in Bartnicki v. Vopper, 532 U.S. 514 (2001), the First Amendment protects a party's publication of illegally intercepted communications on a matter of public concern, even when the publishing parties knew or had reason to know of the intercepts' unlawful origin." Finally, the report concluded:[26] "There is also insufficient evidence at the present time to establish beyond a reasonable doubt that Roger Stone or any other persons associated with the Campaign coordinated with WikiLeaks on the release of the emails."

As I write, these conclusions to special prosecutor Robert S. Mueller's investigation still hold true: WikiLeaks and Julian Assange were not indicted for publishing the Democratic Party's emails, and the investigation failed to identify any collusion between Donald Trump's campaign and Assange's organization.

I do not claim to know the truth about the case, and I never learned the source of the emails. If they really did come from Guccifer 2.0, WikiLeaks was not the only media outlet to publish documents from that account. The influential online U.S. newspaper *The Hill* also received files from Guccifer 2.0, as it revealed to its readers.[27] Personally, I did not appreciate the direct messages exchanged between Donald Trump Jr. or Roger Stone and the organization, but I defend the publication of the Democratic National Committee and Podesta files, which I still consult today for the interesting nuggets they contain.

---

24. This quote comes from pp. 177 and 178 of volume I of the Mueller Report released under FOIA to the American journalist Jason Leopold and to the Electronic Privacy Information Center (EPIC): www.documentcloud.org/documents/20401632-updated-mueller-report-leopold-foia-11220 (accessed May 1, 2022).
25. Ibid.
26. This quote comes from p. 189 of volume I of the Mueller Report released under FOIA to the American journalist Jason Leopold and EPIC.
27. Joe Uchill, "Guccifer 2.0 leaks docs from 'Pelosi's PC'," *The Hill*, August 31, 2016.

One month after Trump won the election, the BBC interviewed[28] Dean Baquet, director of the *New York Times*, which published a string of articles based on the Podesta and Democratic National Committee emails WikiLeaks had revealed. Baquet said that "the thought that he might be doing Vladimir Putin's bidding was one that sometimes kept him up at night," but added: "It would keep me up at night worse or at least longer if I had information from a hack that I knew was accurate, that voters and citizens needed to know. That would make me really uncomfortable.... Will I lose a little sleep because I'm being manipulated? Yeah. But I lose a lot more sleep if I sit that stuff in a safe."

The BBC recapitulated the *New York Times* director's thinking as follows: "In Baquet's view, the information trumps all, no matter how it has been obtained." And yet the demonization campaign unleashed by WikiLeaks' publication of the Democratic Party emails was only a sampling of what the next two years had in store.

---

28. Ian Katz, "Hacking: truth or treason?," BBC News, December 15, 2016: www.bbc.com/news/world-us-canada-38303381 (accessed May 1, 2022).

14
The Fury of the CIA

A ROBBERY IN ROME

I took no notes in my notebook, always kept close to me, to avoid leaving any written trace for anyone. I did no Google searches on the terms mentioned in the files. I took every possible precaution. I was working on classified CIA files which WikiLeaks had not yet published. And one year earlier, an incident had occurred that left me acutely aware of how vulnerable written notes are.

Between the summer of 2015 and February 2016, Julian Assange's organization, together with us media partners, had published[1] top-secret documents revealing how, in previous years, the NSA had spied on major world leaders. These included, among others, three presidents of the French Republic: François Hollande, Nicolas Sarkozy and Jacques Chirac; German Chancellor Angela Merkel and other heads of German institutions; Brazil's political and financial leadership, including then-president Dilma Rousseff; and, finally, Italian Prime Minister Silvio Berlusconi and his top aides. Berlusconi was secretly intercepted by the NSA in the autumn of 2011, when Italy was struggling with a severe economic crisis and Berlusconi's "bunga bunga" sex party scandals were hitting headlines around the world, after which the collapse of Berlusconi's coalition led to Mario Monti's technocratic government.

Three months before the top-secret files on Italy were revealed, I was on a train heading to Rome from the city's Fiumicino airport

---

1. The top-secret documents revealed by WikiLeaks on the NSA's spying on world leaders are available on the WikiLeaks website: https://wikileaks.org/nsa-france/ (accessed May 3, 2022). One of my most important exclusives based on these documents is: Stefania Maurizi, "WikiLeaks reveals the NSA spied on Berlusconi and his closest advisers," *L'Espresso*, February 23, 2016.

when my backpack was violently wrenched away from me, in broad daylight. In my backpack I had been carrying notebooks, telephones, a digital recorder and a number of flash drives containing important files. They were journalistic materials that had nothing to do with WikiLeaks, and were not from Snowden's or any other U.S. database, but they were still very sensitive files. Shocked at my backpack being ripped away from me, I screamed, but the moment the train stopped at the Magliana station, the robber leapt out of the train. I ran after him for a short distance between the railway tracks, but in vain. Only the certainty that I had carefully encrypted the files and erased certain data—including metadata that could identify the sources of the information—was able to allay my fears.

At the police station where I went to report what I thought was a mugging—one of the many happening every week in Rome— the officer who filed my criminal report told me that the tactics used to physically attack me and steal my bag were not those of an ordinary mugging, but rather of an "atypical robbery." Although the central police station in Rome immediately took action, my criminal complaint came to naught. My backpack and the important journalistic materials it contained never surfaced again, nor did I ever hear back from the Italian police or any prosecutor regarding my criminal complaint. Did they ever investigate the "atypical robbery," as Italian law would require? That episode brought home to me how defenseless notebooks and recorders are. Since they are not encrypted, their content can be accessed effortlessly, by anyone.

As far as Google searches are concerned, from Snowden's files I had learned that through programs like Prism, the NSA can monitor searches being conducted by a targeted individual in real time.[2] This is extremely important information for journalists, who must protect the sources who discuss sensitive information with us. When I later learned of an emblematic experience recounted by James Risen, the Pulitzer prize-winning[3] U.S. reporter, I was

2. Glenn Greenwald and Ewen MacAskill, "NSA Prism program taps in to user data of Apple, Google and others," *The Intercept*, June 7, 2013.
3. J. Risen, "The biggest secret. My life as a New York Times reporter in the shadow of the war on terror," *The Intercept*, January 3, 2018.

not at all surprised. After meeting a source through an intermediary, Risen had set about doing some searches on him. An hour later, the intermediary called him on the phone. "Stop Googling his name," he said.

Working on the complicated topics outlined by the top-secret CIA documents without doing any web searches, without being able to freely speak with anyone, without taking any notes or drawing any diagrams or graphs, was a nightmare. With each hour that passed, I wondered if WikiLeaks and we media partners would really be able to publish our journalistic work on those files without the CIA discovering us first. I understood how Glenn Greenwald, Laura Poitras and Ewen MacAskill must have felt, when they were about to reveal Snowden's files. Did the CIA know everything already?

THE INVISIBLE ARSENAL: VAULT 7

If they did know, they did not stop us. On March 7, 2017, two months before prosecutor Marianne Ny dropped the rape investigation, WikiLeaks published[4] the first 8,761 CIA documents, and as a media partner I concurrently released the more important revelations in my daily at the time, *la Repubblica*.[5]

Julian Assange's organization had named the series of documents "Vault 7." As acknowledged by the agency itself,[6] it was the "largest data loss in CIA history." For the first time ever, they

---

4. The first batch of CIA documents are available on the WikiLeaks website: https://wikileaks.org/ciav7p1/ (accessed May 3, 2022). The full series of Vault 7 files is available on the WikiLeaks website.
5. Stefania Maurizi, "WikiLeaks' files reveal major security breach at the CIA," *la Repubblica*, March 7, 2017. *Der Spiegel* also published an article on Vault 7: Michael Sontheimer, "CIA spies may also operate in Frankfurt," *Der Spiegel*, March 7, 2017.
6. The CIA admitted it was the largest data loss in: "WikiLeaks Task Force Final Report," dated October 17, 2017, obtained by U.S. Senator Ron Wyden, a member of the U.S. Senate Select Committee on Intelligence, which oversees the U.S. intelligence community. The document is available on Wyden's website: www.wyden.senate.gov/imo/media/doc/wyden-cybersecurity-lapses-letter-to-dni.pdf (accessed May 3, 2022). It was originally reported by Ellen Nakashima and Shane Harris, "Elite CIA unit that developed hacking tools failed to secure its own systems, allowing massive leak, an internal report found," *Washington Post*, June 16, 2020.

revealed the agency's cyberweapons: the software programs the CIA used to hack their targets' computers, telephones, electronic devices and computer networks in order to steal information. Malicious software, also known as malware, viruses, Trojans: Vault 7 exposed a vast hacking arsenal.

Three years earlier, a scandal had broken out after the agency penetrated[7] a computer network of the U.S. Senate Intelligence Committee then investigating the brutal torture techniques used by the CIA after 9/11. The Vault 7 documents did not disclose illegal operations of that kind, but detailed the specific weapons in the CIA's cyber arsenal. One such weapon was "Weeping Angel," a program whereby the agency could plant malware in a specific Samsung smart TV model that could then be used to eavesdrop on conversations taking place in the room where the screen was located. Concerns about televisions connected to the internet had been circulating for some time, but now the files offered proof revealing how Weeping Angel transformed televisions by that major brand into tools of espionage.

The classified documents in the Vault 7 database were of a technical nature that particularly sparked the interest of individuals and organizations opposed to surveillance, one of the "communities" that had given birth to WikiLeaks and from which it drew its life blood. The world had discovered the power of cyberweapons in 2010, when the public learned of Stuxnet, the virus created by the NSA and its Israeli counterpart, Unit 8200, to sabotage the Iranian nuclear program by infecting the computer systems controlling the centrifuges used to enrich uranium. The next year, Julian Assange's organization began revealing documents on the private surveillance industry.

In fact ever since 2011, often together with us media partners, WikiLeaks had been publishing the so-called Spy Files:[8] large databases of files on surveillance technologies and cyberweapons

---

7. Spencer Ackerman, "CIA admits to spying on Senate staffers," *Guardian*, July 31, 2014.
8. The Spy Files are available on the WikiLeaks website: https://wikileaks.org/spyfiles/ (accessed May 3, 2022). The Spy Files Russia are available on the WikiLeaks website: https://wikileaks.org//spyfiles/russia/ (accessed May 3, 2022).

created and marketed by both Western and Russian companies. They also revealed more than 1 million internal emails of the Hacking Team,[9] an Italian company which had sold such weapons to some of the most infamous regimes on the planet, helping them spy on dissidents, activists and journalists.[10]

One such case straight out of a horror film was that of Jamal Khashoggi, the Saudi journalist who lived in the United States and was a columnist for the *Washington Post*, authoring editorials highly critical of Saudi Arabia's prince Mohammed bin Salman. After entering the Saudi consulate in Istanbul in October 2018, Khashoggi never came out. He was killed and cut into pieces by Saudi officials.[11] From what information has emerged so far, we know that before his assassination some of his close contacts were targeted by one of the cyber weapons marketed by NSO Group, an Israeli company.[12] Thanks to the Hacking Team emails revealed by WikiLeaks three years before Khashoggi's murder, I documented[13] that two of the top Saudis implicated in the atrocious execution, Saud al-Qahtani, a senior official with the Saudi Arabia government, and Maher Mutreb, believed to have coordinated and performed the entire operation, had respectively been in contact

9. The Hacking Team emails are available on the WikiLeaks website: https://wikileaks.org//hackingteam/emails/ (accessed May 3, 2022).
10. Stefania Maurizi, "Silence and mysteries: did Hacking Team play any role in the Khashoggi murder?" *la Repubblica*, April 8, 2019; Stefania Maurizi, "Gli affari di Hacking Team in Sudan: vendeva tecnologia ai servizi segreti," *L'Espresso*, July 29, 2015.
11. An investigation by the UN Special Rapporteur on Extrajudicial, Summary or Arbitrary Executions, Agnès Callamard, concluded that "Mr. Khashoggi's killing constituted an extrajudicial killing for which the State of the Kingdom of Saudi Arabia is responsible," and that "there is credible evidence, warranting further investigation of high-level Saudi Officials' individual liability, including the Crown Prince's." The report is available in: "Khashoggi killing: UN human rights expert says Saudi Arabia is responsible for 'premeditated execution'," OHCHR, June 19, 2019: www.ohchr.org/en/press-releases/2019/06/khashoggi-killing-un-human-rights-expert-says-saudi-arabia-responsible?LangID=E&NewsID=24713 (accessed May 4, 2022).
12. Dana Priest, "A UAE agency put Pegasus spyware on phone of Jamal Khashoggi's wife months before her murder, new forensics show," *Washington Post*, December 21, 2021; Oliver Holmes and Stephanie Kirchgaessner, "Israeli spyware firm fails to get hacking case dismissed," *Guardian*, January 16, 2020.
13. Maurizi, "Silence and mysteries." The contacts between al-Qahtani and Hacking Team were first revealed by David Ignatius, "How chilling Saudi cyberwar ensnared Jamal Kashoggi," *Washington Post*, December 7, 2018.

with the Italian company in 2015 and 2011. Hacking Team had provided the Saudis with its cyberweapons and training courses since at least 2010.

The surveillance industry files brought me to the realization that whereas in the past, the opponents of fascism and Nazism could escape to other countries—as Italian president and partisan fighter Sandro Pertini had done, taking refuge in France—in the cyberweapons era, there is no escape. Even when persecuted dissidents and journalists somehow manage to find a place to hide, the spies of regimes can, with little effort and few resources, spy on them, eavesdrop on them, stalk them at a distance, even from the other side of the world. And once their movements and contacts are tracked, it is not difficult to eliminate them, as shown by the Khashoggi case.

The Spy Files and the Hacking Team emails revealed by WikiLeaks helped spark a worldwide debate on the surveillance industry, raising awareness among journalists, human rights activists and political opponents. The files were also key in inspiring the efforts of software experts who, from at least 2011 on, began a scientific and methodical examination of the industry, exposing its abuses through their forensic analyses and calling for strict control and laws on the export of such weapons to authoritarian countries.

Important as they were, the Spy Files and Hacking Team emails dealt with cyberweapons manufactured and marketed by private companies. Vault 7, on the other hand, revealed a portion of the arsenal of a nation, or rather of a superpower, the United States. Unlike warplanes and warships, bombs and drones, weapons that are visible, cyberweapons are software: intangible and invisible, they can be created, stored and exported to foreign countries without the public being aware of their existence or how they are used. As Julian Assange explained:[14] "There is an extreme proliferation risk in the development of cyber 'weapons'. Comparisons can be drawn between the uncontrolled proliferation of such 'weapons', which

---

14. WikiLeaks press release on Vault 7: https://wikileaks.org/ciav7p1/ (accessed May 4, 2022).

results from the inability to contain them, combined with their high market value, and the global arms trade."

The documents revealed by WikiLeaks had now made an informed debate on such weapons possible. Before publishing the files the organization redacted them, and they did not release the actual cyberweapons—which could have been used by foreign powers and criminal organizations—but the related documentation.

A few months after the first publications, the media revealed that a young American software engineer who had worked for the CIA in the past, Joshua Schulte, had been arrested, accused of being the source of the Vault 7 files. He was charged under the Espionage Act, the same brutal 1917 law used to indict Chelsea Manning and Edward Snowden, and which was the basis for the investigation of Julian Assange and the WikiLeaks journalists by the Grand Jury in Alexandria, Virginia.

Little is known about Schulte: to date it is not at all certain that he really is the source of Vault 7, as the U.S. authorities sustain. The first attempt to try him for the charge of passing the files to WikiLeaks collapsed; the proof against him did not convince the jury. But one thing is certain: he has been in prison since his arrest in August 2017, and as of this writing a new trial is underway.

He was incarcerated for over three years at the Metropolitan Correctional Center[15] of New York under a brutal isolation regime called Special Administrative Measures (SAMs), and reported being treated like an animal.[16] "Inmates are locked in concrete boxes the size of parking spaces with purposefully obstructed views of outside," his lawyers complained. "[T]he cages are filthy and infested with rodents, rodent droppings, cockroaches and mold;

---

15. The MCC is the prison where Jeffrey Epstein died after allegedly committing suicide.
16. The complaint filed by Joshua Schulte's lawyers describing his detention conditions is publicly available: https://storage.courtlistener.com/recap/gov.uscourts. nysd.480183/gov.uscourts.nysd.480183.447.0.pdf (accessed May 4, 2022). See also press reports: Larry Neumeister, "Ex-CIA engineer tells judge he's incarcerated like an animal," Associated Press, January 24, 2021; Kevin Gosztola, "US Justice Department tries to stifle alleged WikiLeaks source's challenge to cruel confinement," *Shadow-Proof*, January 29, 2021.

there is no heating or air conditioning in the cages, there is no functioning plumbing, the lights burn brightly 24 hours per day, and the inmates are denied outside recreation, normal commissary, normal visitation, access to books and legal material, medical care, and dental care. All attorney–client privilege is also void to SAMs inmates as the prison confiscates, opens, and reads all legal mail; inmates are forbidden from transferring legal material to and from their attorneys." Inmates "are not given any cups or silverware to drink or eat with" and consequently "are forced to eat and drink with their hands like the caged animals that they are."

Finally, the complaint reads: "in the winter the cages reach the freezing level and in the summer the heat is unbearable. Currently, Mr. Schulte wears 4 sets of clothing, 5 sets of socks, a sweatshirt and sweatpants, two blankets, 3 sets of socks on his hands, and still freezes when the temperature in his cell plummets below freezing and water literally freezes in his cell. The warden and MCC [Metropolitan Correctional Center] staff are aware and indifferent to this barbaric torture."

Although he has been transferred to another prison,[17] he has continued to denounce his detention conditions, including sleep deprivation and exposure to extremely cold temperatures, as "torturous."[18]

I have no idea if Joshua Schulte really was WikiLeaks' source for Vault 7. Whether he was or not, no one should be incarcerated in such conditions. And whoever the source, it is indisputable that the revelations were in the public interest.

All my fears of being discovered before we could publish proved unfounded. The CIA did not realize it had lost control of its cyber arsenal until March 7, 2017, the day WikiLeaks and we media partners began publishing the first batch of Vault 7 documents and revelations. Only later would we learn what had happened behind the scenes.

17. Matthew Russell Lee, "In CIA leak case Schulte is moved to MDC after Oct 25 trial canceled and reassigned," *Inner City Press*, October 19, 2021: www.innercitypress. com/sdnylive77schultefurman101921.html (accessed May 5, 2022).
18. Luc Cohen, "Ghislaine Maxwell sex crimes trial highlights conditions at Brooklyn jail", Reuters, November 18, 2021.

A SPINE-CHILLING SPEECH

Immediately following the Vault 7 publication, the CIA created a task force to investigate the leak. That internal investigation revealed dramatic flaws in the agency's security, detailed in black and white in the task force report. Only ten pages of the report have been declassified,[19] most of which are heavily redacted, but the few legible paragraphs are disconcerting.

The CIA had apparently lost control of the files one year earlier: "We assess that in spring 2016 a CIA employee stole at least 180 gigabytes to as much as 34 terabytes of information," the task force report said, adding: "This is roughly equivalent to 11.6 million to 2.2 billion pages in Microsoft Word." Ultimately, however, the agency could not even be sure exactly how many files it had lost, because the software development network where this data was stored "did not require user activity monitoring or other safeguards that exist on our enterprise system."

The internal inquiry concluded: "Because the stolen data resided on a mission system that lacked user activity monitoring and a robust server audit capability, we did not realize the loss had occurred until a year later, when WikiLeaks publicly announced it in March 2017. Had the data been stolen for the benefit of a state adversary and not published, we might still be unaware of the loss—as would be true for the vast majority of data on Agency mission systems."

It was a troubling conclusion: how could the CIA protect the security of U.S. citizens if it was not even capable of protecting its own networks? And we are not talking about agencies with limited funds: in the 2017 fiscal year alone, the United States spent 73 billion dollars[20] on intelligence, a colossal sum.

Vault 7 not only enabled an informed debate on cyberweapons, especially among the individuals and organizations opposed to

---

19. "WikiLeaks Task Force Final Report," accessible at: www.wyden.senate.gov/imo/media/doc/wyden-cybersecurity-lapses-letter-to-dni.pdf (accessed May 3, 2022).
20. These statistics come from the Project on Government Secrecy of the Federation of American Scientists, directed for two decades by secrecy guru Steven Aftergood: https://irp.fas.org/budget/index.html (accessed May 5, 2022).

surveillance, it also unearthed glaring holes in the agency's security which, had they not been exposed publicly, would most likely have been covered up.

Did the U.S. taxpayer not have the right to know that despite such massive government spending on intelligence agencies, their security was so defective? Did the global public not have the right to know that the cyber weapons arsenal of a superpower was handled so carelessly that a hostile nation or criminal organization could have stolen it without the CIA even noticing? The revelations of Vault 7 were unquestionably in the public interest.

But the CIA was furious. On April 13, 2017, the CIA's new director, Mike Pompeo, gave his first public speech. It came barely five weeks after WikiLeaks began revealing the files and just two days after the *Washington Post* published a forthright editorial by Julian Assange[21] arguing that WikiLeaks' motive for revealing Vault 7 was "identical to that claimed by the New York Times and The Post—to publish newsworthy content."

Pompeo had been appointed by Donald Trump, who had taken office in the White House just three months earlier after winning the 2016 elections and declaring *"I love WikiLeaks."* This love had faded quickly, it would seem, as always happened when it came to Assange's organization; political leaders might fleetingly sympathize when its publications were to their advantage, only to resume warring with WikiLeaks soon after.

In the first speech given by the new head of the CIA, one might have expected Pompeo to address the more serious threats facing the world: nuclear terrorism, for example, which in the time of ISIS represents a threat to all of humankind. Instead he lashed out at a small journalistic organization whose director was buried in a 20 square-meter room and could not even go to hospital for an MRI scan. "It's time to call out WikiLeaks for what it really is," said Pompeo, "a non-state hostile intelligence service often abetted

21. Julian Assange, "Julian Assange: WikiLeaks has the same mission as The Post and the Times," *Washington Post*, April 15, 2017.

by state actors like Russia."[22] Then he got personal: "Assange is a narcissist who has created nothing of value. He relies on the dirty work of others to make himself famous. He's a fraud, a coward hiding behind a screen."

It was a vindictive, malevolent attack; it was not the venting of a politician. It was an attack coming from an organization that could literally disappear Julian Assange and the WikiLeaks journalists in the dead of night. And it came at a time of considerable isolation for them, after the political upheaval of the U.S. presidential elections and after Rafael Correa, the president who had provided Assange with protection since 2012, had completed his presidential term. Everything was about to change. And yet another harrowing incident had transpired in that fall of 2017.

For the second time, Chelsea Manning tried to kill herself. Ever since her sentencing to thirty-five years in prison for sending the 700,000 classified U.S. government files, she had been in the all-male military prison of Fort Leavenworth, in Kansas. Just after entering prison, she announced that she would take the name Chelsea and that she intended to fight to obtain hormone therapy for her transition. The Pentagon denied her the therapy, however, asserting they do "not provide hormone therapy or sex-reassignment surgery for gender identity disorder."[23] Manning did not give up, and took the U.S. Department of Defense to court, represented by the American Civil Liberties Union. As a result of her legal battle, she became "the first person to receive health care related to gender transition while in military prison."[24] But although the Pentagon agreed to provide her hormone therapy, it forbade her to wear female clothing or to wear her hair long, which was also part of the therapy.

---

22. "A discussion on national security with CIA Director Mike Pompeo," Center for Strategic & International Studies, April 13, 2017: www.csis.org/analysis/discussion-national-security-cia-director-mike-pompeo (accessed May 5, 2022).; Stefania Maurizi, "Usa, nuovo direttore Cia attacca Wikileaks: 'È un servizio segreto ostile'," *la Repubblica*, April 14, 2017.
23. "The Chelsea Manning case: a timeline", ACLU, May 9, 2017: www.aclu.org/blog/free-speech/employee-speech-and-whistleblowers/chelsea-manning-case-timeline (accessed May 5, 2022).
24. Ibid.

After her first suicide attempt in July 2016, the military had put her in solitary confinement as punishment for trying to kill herself. In October, she tried again.[25]

Only after these suicide attempts, on January 17, 2017, just three days before Donald Trump entered the White House as 45th president of the United States, Barack Obama announced that Chelsea Manning's sentence would be commuted from thirty-five years in prison to the seven she had already served, and that she would therefore be leaving prison on May 17, 2017.[26]

Obama ended his presidency with a bleak record: he had used the Espionage Act to prosecute more whistleblowers and sources for revealing secret documents to the press than had all the U.S. presidents before him combined. He had indicted eight such whistleblowers, including Chelsea Manning, Edward Snowden, Thomas Drake and John Kiriakou, the CIA operative who had refused to torture and had blown the whistle on the practice. But by commuting Manning's sentence, President Obama at least made it possible for her to leave that prison which was killing her. Julian Assange's ordeal, on the other hand, was not only not coming to an end, it was about to get much worse.

25.   Charlie Savage, "Chelsea Manning tried committing suicide a second time in October," *New York Times*, November 4, 2016.
26.   Ed Pilkington, David Smith and Lauren Gambino, "Chelsea Manning's prison sentence commuted by Barack Obama," *Guardian*, January 18, 2017.

15
Under Siege

FROM PROTECTION UNDER CORREA
TO OPPRESSION UNDER MORENO

The tiny embassy had always made us feel welcome. Now, it seemed like a prison. With the end of Rafael Correa's presidency, everything changed. His successor, Lenín Moreno, took office in May 2017 promising to continue Correa's leftist policies, at least in part, but instead quickly moved away from them. Each time I entered the red-brick building in Knightsbridge, I noticed a change that told me Julian Assange would not remain there much longer. His life inside the embassy had never been easy. The siege by Scotland Yard, which continued without pause up to October 2015, was a daily reminder that if he should ever step outside, he would be arrested. Even after the agents surrounding the building were removed, the risk remained; surveillance cameras installed all around the entrance were a constant visual reminder.

But as long as Rafael Correa was in power, Assange was protected inside the embassy. There had been tense periods, like when his internet connection was cut off during publication of the U.S. Democratic Party emails. There had been ambassadors who were less "friendly" than others, but Correa's Ecuador had never questioned, for example, whether he could receive visitors. Good friends came and went continuously. So did academics, reporters, diplomats, politicians and stars. From renowned U.S. intellectual Noam Chomsky to civil rights icon Reverend Jesse Jackson, from British rapper M.I.A. and U.S. singer Lady Gaga to Puerto Rican rapper Resident, from actor and activist Pamela Anderson to Vivienne Westwood, the iconic fashion designer with a keen social conscience. And journalists from dozens of media outlets; Italian MPs from the Five Star Movement; Argentina's ambassador to the

United Kingdom, Alicia Castro; Yanis Varoufakis, Greece's former
Minister of Finance, and Croatian philosopher Srećko Horvat,
co-founders of the DiEM25 progressive political movement who
have always supported Julian Assange, even when it was not politically convenient to do so.

Friends and visitors did what they could to provide some relief
from the sensory deprivation caused by never being able to go
outside that building. One day they brought Assange a new kind
of coffee he had never tried before; on another, a cheese he had
never tasted. Books, music, chocolate, *empanadas* and Argentine
wine. Legendary British director Ken Loach gave him a treadmill, one of the few ways he could get some physical exercise in
the embassy. The WikiLeaks founder not only lacked sunlight and
fresh air, but also the chance to take a walk in the midst of nature,
as he loved to do.

Presidents and political cycles came and went and Assange was
still there, holed up inside those four walls. And the superpower
was still out there too, with Assange still on its radar.

Shortly before Correa's term ended, another guest arrived in
the embassy. This time it was a feline: the Embassy Cat.[1] Julian
Assange and his cat became inseparable. He brought a bit of diver-
sion and light-heartedness, with his fierce sallies on the baubles
hanging from the Christmas tree, or his parading to and fro in
front of the window with a serious look on his face. He drew pho-
tographers like a celebrity, and jokes from journalists. In November
2016, when the Swedish prosecutors finally came to question
Assange on the rape allegations, the cat peeked out the window
wearing a shirt collar and red-and-white striped tie. At the sight
of the feline, Twitter abounded with comments like: "Things got
serious at the embassy today: even the cat wore a tie" and "Julian
Assange's cat was dressed to impress on his big day."

But with the end of Correa's presidency, any fun or light-
heartedness came to an end too. With Lenín Moreno, the
atmosphere inside the building was at first uncertain, then openly
hostile.

---

1.   The cat even had a Twitter account: @embassycat.

Between November and December 2017, just six months after Ecuador's new president took office, I went to visit Assange on two occasions. I wanted to discuss, among other things, an astounding discovery I had unearthed through my FOIA litigation.

WHY DID THE UK CROWN PROSECUTION SERVICE DESTROY KEY DOCUMENTS?

The pages were so heavily redacted that they revealed very little information. The number of pages was truly tiny,[2] only 439. To obtain them I had been forced to sue the British authorities with the Crown Prosecution Service (CPS), as they had refused to release the documents on the Assange case to me despite my FOIA request. But my legal battle had been worth it. It had allowed me to discover that it was the Crown Prosecution Service, a public authority then headed by Keir Starmer, which had helped create the legal paralysis and diplomatic quagmire responsible for Julian Assange's arbitrary detention.

Why had the Swedish and British authorities handled the rape investigation, dropped in May of 2017, so senselessly? The only hope of obtaining an answer lay in accessing the full documentation on the case, especially every exchange between the British and Swedish authorities. The CPS had told me that they had given me the full correspondence.

I soon realized, however, that this was not true; it was most assuredly not the full correspondence. It contained no email exchanges during crucial stages in the case, for example when the Swedish prosecutor issued the European Arrest Warrant, or when Assange took refuge in the embassy, or in the period when he was granted asylum. It was simply not plausible that London and Stockholm had not communicated with each other on those occasions. There must have been important documentation which the British authorities had not released to me. Together with my two London lawyers—Estelle Dehon, a first-rate FOIA specialist, and

---

2. I would obtain a few more pages later on, though a very limited number: a total of 551 pages in the seven years of my FOIA battle, as mentioned in chapter 11.

Jennifer Robinson, a top-notch human rights lawyer who has also represented Julian Assange since 2010, and who has never stopped working on his case even when it would have been convenient to do so—we decided to put up a fight in the London tribunals to try to obtain the full correspondence.

When I sought an explanation for the gaps corresponding to crucial stages in the case, the Crown Prosecution Service replied: "All the data associated with Paul Close's account was deleted when he retired and cannot be recovered."[3] Close, a lawyer with the CPS's Special Crime Division—the division responsible for prosecuting high-profile cases—was the same official who had advised Swedish prosecutor Marianne Ny from early on not to question Julian Assange in London. It was Paul Close who told Ny: "Please do not think that the case is being dealt with as just another extradition request." His messages were essential to clarify the many question marks around the Swedish investigation.

By deleting his account, the Crown Prosecution Service had destroyed key documents on a case that was high-profile, controversial and ongoing. Why? And what did the CPS destroy exactly, and on whose instructions? The documents had not disappeared by accident: they had been erased by the same public authority that had helped create the impasse ensnaring Assange since 2010. The CPS did not tell me the exact date they were destroyed, but Close retired in 2014, so it must have occurred around that time, and when Keir Starmer was no longer head of the Crown Prosecution Service.

A few days after uncovering this fact, I shared this information with two *Guardian* journalists: seasoned legal correspondent Owen Bowcott, and the superb but unassuming Ewen MacAskill, who had won a Pulitzer Prize for his work on the Snowden files. We published the revelations on the CPS destruction of documents in partnership.[4] When contacted by the *Guardian*, the Crown Pros-

---

3.   This statement by the CPS comes from: "In the matter of an appeal to the Information Tribunal between Stefania Maurizi and (1) The Information Commissioner (2) Crown Prosecution Service," EA/2017/2014, dated November 2, 2017.
4.   Stefania Maurizi, "Seven years confined: how a FOIA litigation is shedding light on the case of Julian Assange," *la Repubblica*, November 10, 2017; Ewen MacAskill

ecution Service stated: "We have no way of knowing the content of email accounts once they have been deleted." A disconcerting statement to say the least: a public authority had destroyed documentation but had no clue as to what it had destroyed. They added that the email account was deleted "in accordance with standard procedure." I would later discover that this procedure was by no means standard. The destruction of key emails was distinctly suspicious.

This was definitely something to discuss with Julian Assange. I flew to London in both November and December 2017. I could not in my wildest dreams have imagined what was going on in the embassy behind the scenes.

THE LIVES OF OTHERS

I had been in the embassy numerous times, a small apartment with an entrance hall where the guards employed by a private security company were stationed. It was a Spanish company called UC Global, and had been providing security for the embassy—previously a subcontracted service—since 2012.[5] The security firm had arrived two months after WikiLeaks' founder took refuge there.[6] Ecuador of course realized it was protecting one of the most despised, beloved and surveilled journalists on the planet. Lacking the most rudimentary security equipment, the embassy was vulnerable; at the very least, it needed protection from physical intrusion. The Correa administration had opted for UC Global—which also provided security for the president's daughters when they were in Europe—because unlike an Ecuadorian company, a Spanish company could operate in London without having to obtain visas for its employees.[7]

---

and Owen Bowcott, "UK prosecutors admit destroying key emails in Julian Assange case," *Guardian*, November 10, 2017.

5. In 2012, security was handled by a company called Blue Cell, which subcontracted to UC Global. In 2015, the contract went directly to UC Global.

6. Stefania Maurizi, "'I was fired for helping Julian Assange, and I have no regrets': an interview with Fidel Narvaez," *Jacobin*, October 25, 2019.

7. In the years in which Julian Assange was in the Ecuadorian embassy, the United Kingdom was a member of the European Union. It withdrew from the European Union on January 31, 2020, after the Brexit referendum.

UC Global's headquarters were in fact in Puerto Real and Jerez de la Frontera, in the province of Cádiz in southern Spain, and its owner was a Spanish citizen. David Morales was a former Spanish marine, and his contract with the Quito government was handled by Senain, Ecuador's intelligence services at the time.

Every time I entered the embassy, the routine was the same. Security asked all visitors for their passports, in order to register their entrance and exit, and to hand over their cell phones. For obvious security reasons, visitors could not go into the rooms of the embassy with electronic devices that could take photos or videos. After going through those controls, as well as a metal detector, I had always been allowed to take my backpacks, handbags, note-books, pens and digital recorders with me. But on that December day in 2017, something unprecedented happened.

When I went inside, only one other person was present besides Assange: a security guard. He confiscated my backpack with all my journalistic materials, something that had never been done before. I happened to be carrying very important information with me that day: not classified U.S. government documents; they were files of another kind, but highly confidential. I had not been able to leave them with a trusted third party because it was December 29, the middle of the Christmas season. I protested, but to no avail. Everything I had with me was confiscated, including my non-dig-ital wristwatch. I was not even allowed to take a pen with me. As soon as I left the embassy, in fact, I had to inform the editors of *la Repubblica*, my newspaper at the time, that I had not been able to conduct my interview with Assange as planned. While he and I chatted in the conference room, my mind was in a panic; some of the most sensitive materials I had ever handled in my professional life were, at that moment, in a stranger's hands. The only thing that could comfort me, at least in part, was that I had encrypted them, so they were protected.

Two years would go by before I learned what happened that day while Assange and I were having our chat. Someone, presumably the guard with UC Global, secretly photographed the journal-istic materials contained in my backpack. I had an iPod Touch with me and two cell phones, one encrypted and one a dumb-phone, that is to say, a cell phone without the internet capacity of a smartphone. Whoever performed this operation did not stop at taking photographs. They also made video and audio record-ings of my meeting with Assange, and they took the SIM card out of my dumbphone and photographed its IMEI code, the unique number that identifies a phone and can also be used to intercept it. I was shocked when I learned of these spying activities two years after our December 2017 appointment, and obtained some photos and videos documenting them which had been found among UC Global's materials.

Julian Assange had always worried about being spied on inside the building. Only one year after his arrival, Correa's government reported that a microphone had been found concealed inside the ambassador's office. Ricardo Patiño, Ecuador's Minister of Foreign Affairs at the time, publicly affirmed that he held the Surveillance Group, a British company specializing in surveillance, responsible for planting it, but they denied his accusation.[8] The incident forever remained a mystery,[9] as I was told by Fidel Narváez, the Ecuador-ian consul who spent six years with Assange in the embassy in London, up until July 2018. But with the end of Correa's pres-idency, WikiLeaks' surveillance concerns intensified, as I had occasion to observe during my visits to London.

For his part, Assange deployed every means imaginable—at least as far as his confinement permitted—to protect himself and his visitors. Before starting a conversation, he always turned on a white noise device, whose rustling sound made it harder to pick up conversations. Furthermore, instead of talking, we would often write. Every time I left the embassy, I found myself mulling over the absurd conditions we were now forced to work under, and when, years later, I saw the photos of my cell phone taken apart and the video and audio of some of our conversations, I was flooded

8. BBC News Staff, "Ecuador asks UK for help on embassy bug," July 4, 2013.
9. Fidel Narvaez told me this in an interview with me on September 16, 2019. An edited version of our conversation appeared in the U.S. magazine *Jacobin*. Maurizi, "I was fired for helping Julian Assange."

with rage. It was the kind of surveillance used against journalists by the worst regimes on earth. And it had not been deployed in North Korea or China, but in London, in the heart of the democratic Europe that claims to defend freedom of the press. Who had ordered these operations? Whoever had tampered with my phone in all likelihood had tried to access my encrypted files as well. Had they succeeded?

As I write, the case is under investigation by the Audiencia Nacional, the Spanish judicial body in charge of investigating the most serious offenses, from organized crime to terrorism and drug trafficking. Initially coordinated by Judge José de la Mata, as revealed by the Spanish daily *El País*[10]—which broke the story and was able to access some of the recorded videos and audio files[11]— and later by Santiago Pedraz, the inquiry concerns the owner of UC Global, David Morales, under investigation for alleged crimes against privacy, violation of attorney–client privilege, misappropriation, bribery and money laundering. Morales was arrested and then released on bail. It was the investigation by the Spanish police and judiciary that allowed me to discover, among other materials, the photos of my cell phone unscrewed and opened in two. I am one of the victims who opted to file a criminal complaint, as did John Goetz—an outstanding investigative reporter with the German state television network ARD, who had worked with WikiLeaks as a media partner since 2010—and some of his colleagues.

The Audiencia Nacional's investigation relies on search and seizure activities conducted by the Spanish police to acquire documentation, video and audio recordings, and on the testimony of former UC Global employees, who are protected witnesses. From here on I refer to their reconstruction of the facts, currently under examination by the Spanish judiciary.

It all started after the election of Donald Trump: early in December 2017, the company replaced the security cameras inside

---

10.   José María Irujo, "Spanish security company spied on Julian Assange's meetings with lawyers," *El País*, July 9, 2019; José María Irujo, "Director of Spanish security company that spied on Julian Assange arrested," *El País*, October 9, 2019.
11.   José Manuel Abad Liñán, "The life of Julian Assange, according to the Spaniards who watched over him," *El País*, April 14, 2019.

the embassy. While the old ones recorded only images, to detect possible break-ins, the new, much more sophisticated cameras could record not only video, but audio as well.[12] Assange repeatedly asked if they picked up sound also, and UC Global always denied it, but in fact they did. "From that moment on," one of the protected witnesses recalled,[13] "the cameras began to record sound regularly, so every meeting that the asylee held was captured." A microphone had also been planted in the base of the fire extinguisher in the conference room. That was the room where visitors normally met with Assange, and he often sat at the head of the table, near the door, the spot closest to the fire extinguisher.

WikiLeaks' founder had always been considered paranoid; indeed, his own legal team found his request to hold their meetings in the women's lavatory excessive. In one of the security camera clips I obtained, two of his lawyers, Gareth Peirce and the excellent Aitor Martinez, are seen going into the toilet for a private conversation with their client. But that lavatory had also been bugged, according to the witnesses.[14]

The security personnel were expected to write detailed profiles of the targets of these espionage activities, and "special attention had to be given to Mr. Assange's lawyers."[15] The security guards were ordered to photograph "their documentation, the electronic equipment that had to be left at the entrance of the embassy, and as far as possible, the visitors' conversations with the asylee [Assange] listened to. In some cases, this involved following them, tracking their every move."[16] Morales instructed his employees to prioritize lawyer Baltasar Garzón, the coordinator of Julian Assange's legal team. "I possess numerous photos taken with a mobile phone of

12. Anonymous Witness 2. The witness statements of protected witnesses "Anonymous Witness 1" and "Anonymous Witness 2" were submitted to Westminster Magistrates' Court during the extradition hearing of Julian Assange. They are available in a summarized form in: *The Government of the US of America–v–Julian Paul Assange*, Consolidated Annex, accessed May 7, 2022: www.judiciary.uk/wp-content/uploads/2021/01/USA-v-Assange-annex-040121.pdf

13. Anonymous Witness 2.
14. Ibid.
15. Ibid.
16. Ibid.

Secret Power

Mr. Garzon when he collected the former president of Ecuador, Rafael Correa, from Madrid-Barajas airport," one of the protected witnesses recalled.[17]

It was only after the Spanish prosecutors in Madrid launched their investigation of the company and I had the chance to see some of the videos and UC Global's internal correspondence that I realized how vast the surveillance operation really was. In one of the emails, Morales asked his employees for "Embassy wifi data (if we have the password or whatever). I need to see the composition of the walls surrounding the Guest's room (brick, masonry, cement)."[18] Apparently, the company was considering planting microphones that could pick up conversations through the walls.

The visitors who had top priority for surveillance included Julian Assange's lawyers: Baltasar Garzón, Jennifer Robinson, Renata Avila, Melinda Taylor and Carlos Poveda; journalist and documentary filmmaker Juan Passarelli and his brother José; Sarah Harrison, and Croatian philosopher Srećko Horvat. And even British chef Sarah Saunders, who together with her mother, Susan Benn, assisted Assange with some of the more practical aspects of his daily life, like eating properly.

Special attention was also reserved for visitors like the German Bernd Fix and Andy Müller-Maguhn. I knew both of them. Fix, outwardly gruff but kind, was one of the founding members of the Wau Holland Foundation. Established in memory of Herwart Holland-Moritz, known as "Wau" Holland, a visionary computer expert who deeply understood the role of data in contemporary society and co-founded the Chaos Computer Club to promote the hacker ethic and public debate on technology, the Wau Holland Foundation[19] was one of the organizations that had helped WikiLeaks fight the blockade on donations. As for Müller-Maguhn, besides sitting on the board of Wau Holland and mediating

---

17. Ibid.

18. Email from David Morales to Cyberseguridad UC Global, dated September 21, 2017, 22:41. Originally reported in: Stefania Maurizi, "A massive scandal: how Assange, his doctors, lawyers and visitors were all spied on for the U.S.," *la Repubblica*, November 18, 2019.

19. Wau Holland Foundation: https://wauland.de/en/about/ (accessed May 7, 2022).

between Julian Assange and Daniel Domscheit-Berg when he was suspended from WikiLeaks in 2010, he was also a freelance journalist with solid expertise in computer security and privacy. Warm and always ready to help, he had worked[20] on important investigations like the Snowden files for *Der Spiegel* together with Laura Poitras and the staff of the German weekly. Other computer experts appeared to have been targeted as well, like the Swede Ola Bini and Australian Felicity Ruby, who served as adviser to Australian Greens senator Scott Ludlam and to the United Nations Development Fund for Women.

But there was one person the Spanish company came to focus on in particular.

A LOVE BORN IN HELL

"Special attention to STELLA MORRIS … we believe that this is a false name," David Morales wrote[21] to his employees on September 21, 2017, adding: "she is the one who supposedly in a rumor spread recently said she had a baby of the guest. She is supposed to be Uruguayan, but we managed to identify a person related to her (her mother) in Catalonia. If necessary I want a person dedicated to this activity fully, so if you have to hire someone for it tell me. All this has to be considered top secret."

I knew Stella Moris as a very bright, thoughtful and affable woman. Initially she had worked on the Swedish case as legal adviser. In late 2016 and early 2017, I sensed that she and Assange were romantically involved, but in my presence, at least, they never indulged in any displays of affection, nor did they ever speak to me of, or even hint at, their relationship. I noticed that Assange, a very independent man, had become increasingly dependent on her, but his private life was a sphere I did not want to intrude

---

20.   Andy Müller-Maguhn, Laura Poitras, Marcel Rosenbach, Michael Sontheimer and Christian Grothoff, "The NSA breach of Telekom and other German firms," *Der Spiegel*, September 14, 2014.
21.   The correct spelling is Stella Moris, but in his email Morales wrote MORRIS. Email from David Morales to Cyberseguridad UC Global, dated September 21, 2017, 22:41. I obtained this email from a journalistic source.

on. The public had the right to know a great many things about WikiLeaks, but not to pry into the personal lives of their journalists, so I kept my impression that they had entered into a romantic relationship to myself, without asking any questions to confirm it.

When I later discovered that they had had two children together, Gabriel and Max, conceived in the embassy and born respectively in 2017 and 2019, I was very surprised. Like all journalists, I learned this news when Moris disclosed it in an interview with the *Daily Mail*.[22] I had never seen Julian Assange interact with children, but I had heard more than once that he was good with them. That did not surprise me: he would certainly know how to stimulate their curiosity. And after all, his first son was born when Assange was only 18 years old, so he had experience with children. I had noticed that Stella Moris disappeared for a long time, then reappeared with a few extra kilos and a tired air, little details that caught my attention, but only because over the years she had always looked the same. I wondered if she might have had a child. I did not find it particularly odd that she had changed her name from Sara Gonzalez Devant to Stella Moris. Daniel Domscheit-Berg used a cover identity too: Daniel Schmitt.

Moris had an excellent academic background: she held a Master of Science in Forced Migration from Oxford University's Refugee Studies Centre, whose director, Matthew J. Gibney, told me:[23] "She was a serious, determined, driven, mature and intelligent student. She came to Oxford with some important practical experience because she had worked in the Office of the President of East Timor in the early 2000s."

The camera recordings I later had the chance to see showed that Julian Assange and Stella Moris took a range of precautions to keep the birth of their first child, Gabriel, private. The clips

22.   Sarah Oliver, "WikiLeaks boss Julian Assange fathered two children inside the Ecuadorian embassy with lawyer, 37, who fell in love with him while helping his fight against extradition to the US," *Daily Mail*, April 11, 2020.
23.   Matthew J. Gibney, email to author, April 16, 2020. Originally reported in: Stefania Maurizi, "Assange è il padre dei miei figli: rischia di nuovo la morte," *il Fatto Quotidiano*, April 16, 2020. Sara Gonzalez Devant's MSc dissertation, accessed May 7, 2022: www.rsc.ox.ac.uk/publications/displacement-in-the-2006-dili-crisis-dynamics-of-an-ongoing-conflict

showed a friend of theirs, actor Stephen Hoo, bringing the infant into the embassy in a baby carrier, so that an outside observer would not immediately link Gabriel to his parents.[24] And according to UC Global's internal emails, Hoo introduced the baby as his son. But the fact that Stella Moris always came to the embassy shortly before or after the baby had led the company to suspect that he was Moris and Assange's child. According to one of the witnesses,[25] to determine whether or not this was true, David Morales actually asked him to steal one of Gabriel's nappies, in an attempt to extract his DNA for a paternity test. The plan fell through, however, because the guard warned Moris not to bring the newborn to the embassy again.

I do not know why Julian Assange and Stella Moris decided to have two children in such a complicated situation. In her interview with the *Daily Mail*, Moris explained their choice like this: "Being in love, getting engaged, having children while he was in the embassy, it was an act of rebellion."

If that pregnancy was an attempt to get their lives back, to move forward somehow and to defy those who had wanted to destroy Assange for years, an attempt to achieve a modicum of normality for a couple whose lives had very little by way of normality, then the nappy episode was a sinister wake-up call: a normal life was very far off indeed. As soon as he was born, their first son was already a target of spies.

THE AMERICAN FRIENDS

It had all started with a trade fair. In 2016, when Donald Trump had yet to win the presidential election, Morales travelled to the U.S. city of Las Vegas to participate in the SHOT Show, a trade exhibition for the security, hunting, and firearms industries. At that time, UC Global could boast only one major job: its contract

---

24. The videos of Stephen Hoo carrying Gabriel Assange to the embassy were recorded by the security cameras inside and outside the building. José María Irujo, "Spanish firm that spied on Julian Assange tried to find out if he fathered a child at Ecuadorian embassy," *El País*, April 15, 2020.
25. Anonymous Witness 2.

with the Ecuadorian government to guard that country's embassy in London. A small job, but one that could open big doors. After all, the Spanish company was in charge of security for the embassy housing one of the most despised enemies of the U.S. military-intelligence complex. In the roulette of the business world, betting on the military-industrial complex is virtually a guarantee: a colossus with vast resources at its disposal, it can award lavish contracts and foster a network of relations like no other.

According to the protected witnesses, after participating in the trade fair, Morales acquired a hefty contract with the Las Vegas Sands company owned by billionaire Sheldon Adelson. Aged 87 years when he died in January 2021, Adelson had built up the largest empire of casinos on the planet, with premises in Macao, Singapore and Las Vegas, where he had built an ultra-fake replica of Venice in his "The Venetian Resort,"[26] complete with St. Mark's campanile and the Rialto bridge. "A tribute to Italian opulence," proclaimed the hotel's website. And certainly a tribute to the opulence of Sheldon Adelson who, according to Forbes estimates in 2014, was the eighth or ninth richest man in the world,[27] but hardly a respectful homage to the renowned art and beauty of Italy, though the resort was inaugurated by a stunning Sophia Loren.[28] Politically, Adelson was the biggest donor to the Donald Trump campaign, not to mention a staunch Zionist, opposed to a Palestinian state, an advocate of Benjamin Netanyahu's right-wing Israel and of Israeli settlements in the occupied territories.

As reported by the protected witnesses, after his travels in the United States, Morales summoned his staff and told them that from then on they would be "playing in the big league,"[29] with the major players, and that he had switched over "to the dark side." As

26.   After the death of Sheldon Adelson, La Vegas Sands Corporation sold "The Venetian Resort."
27.   Robert D. McFadden, "Sheldon Adelson, billionaire donor to G.O.P. and Israel, is dead at 87," *New York Times,* January 12, 2021.
28.   "In pictures: casino magnate Sheldon Adelson," *CNN,* January 12, 2021.
29.   Anonymous witness 1.

a result of this collaboration with the U.S. authorities, he said, "the Americans will get us contracts all over the world."[30]

At the security fair in Las Vegas, Morales had come into contact with Zohar Lahav, the chief of security for Sheldon Adelson's company, who negotiated a contract with Morales.[31] It seems unlikely that the Las Vegas Sands—already equipped with a considerable security apparatus headed by a former U.S. secret service agent named Brian Nagel—really needed David Morales to provide security for Adelson's yacht, *Queen Miri*, when it was sailing in the Mediterranean Sea.

"My understanding is that this person offered to cooperate with the U.S. intelligence authorities by supplying information about Mr. Assange," one of the witnesses recalled,[32] adding that Morales told him "he was traveling to talk with 'our American friends'." When he asked him exactly who those "friends" were, he simply replied: "U.S. intelligence."

It was "the Americans" who wanted to establish Gabriel Assange's paternity. They were also the ones who proposed the list of targets to monitor. Andy Müller-Maguhn "was one of the targets that David Morales had instructed to be prioritised on behalf of US intelligence,"[33] and the head of UC Global "showed at times a real obsession in relation to monitoring and recording the lawyers who met with the 'guest' (Julian Assange) because 'our American friends' were requesting it."[34] It was on the Americans' behalf that Morales asked his employees for cameras with streaming capabilities so that "our friends in the United States" would be able to see what was happening inside the embassy in real time, minute by minute, as if in a reality show. But when Morales asked one of his men—later a protected witness—to create the remote access, the employee initially balked, saying it was not techni-

30. Ibid.
31. Ibid.
32. Ibid.
33. Anonymous Witness 2.
34. Anonymous Witness 1.

cally feasible, then refused to collaborate "in an illegal act of this magnitude."[35]

Again, it was "the Americans" who asked Morales to apply stiff little stickers to the windows so that their laser microphones outside the embassy could pick up the conversations inside the building through the vibrations produced by words on the glass. Julian Assange's use of a white noise device, which also created a vibration, made it hard to intercept conversations. By applying the stickers, the problem was solved. Curiously, the stickers bore the symbol of security cameras in operation. To an outside observer, the symbol looked harmless enough; far from arousing suspicion, it seemed perfectly natural to flag the cameras' presence.

As the concerns of the protected witnesses grew, they also noted that from mid-2017 to mid-2018, Morales "displayed a noticeable increment in his assets,"[36] to the point that he was able to buy a luxury car and a home that cost, in their estimation, around 1 million euros. Word went around in the company that the United States was paying him 200,000 euros a month, and when one of the witnesses confronted him for passing information to the Americans, he bared his chest and replied: "I am a mercenary through and through."[37]

As of this writing, the Audiencia Nacional is examining these reports and testimony from the protected witnesses as well as other witnesses and materials. David Morales is under investigation: he has not been formally charged. The inquiry is based, among other things, on a high number of security cam videos and photographs, including the ones of my telephone opened in two. Was it pure coincidence that I was heavily targeted right after I learned that crucial documents on the Julian Assange case had been destroyed by the Crown Prosecution Service?

The judge with the Audiencia Nacional has requested cooperation from a number of judicial authorities. Specifically, he has asked U.S. authorities to provide information on IP addresses allegedly

---

35. Anonymous Witness 2.
36. Ibid.
37. Anonymous Witness 1.

indicating that Morales sent emails from Sheldon Adelson's "Venetian Resort" and from Alexandria, Virginia, where the U.S. Grand Jury investigation on WikiLeaks was being conducted.[38]

The testimony from the protected witnesses also revealed that in December 2017, *"the Americans"* were so desperate that Julian Assange was still holed up in the embassy—where they could not get their hands on him—that they discussed with Morales the possibility of leaving the door open so they could kidnap him, and even the possibility of poisoning him.[39]

They did not carry out their extreme schemes; ultimately, another kind of poison would create the conditions for the United States to get its hands on Assange. But evidence would emerge that the proposals for killing Assange had not been idle chit-chat. They were in dead earnest.

38. José María Irujo, "Three protected witnesses accuse Spanish ex-marine of spying on Julian Assange," *El País*, January 21, 2020.
39. Anonymous Witness 2.

16
The Final Attempts

THE DIPLOMATIC ROUTE

Even when he was vice-president, Lenín Moreno had never liked the founder of WikiLeaks. "He doesn't understand what WikiLeaks is or what they do," the former consul of Ecuador, Fidel Narváez would later tell me.[1] Still, at the beginning of Moreno's administration Assange could at least count on the support of his Minister of Foreign Affairs, María Fernanda Espinosa, who sought to protect him through a range of measures, such as giving him Ecuadorian citizenship or attempting to grant him diplomatic status. Had the latter venture met with success, Assange could have left the embassy without risking arrest. But it did not go as planned.

The attempt was immediately rebuffed by the British authorities. In December 2017, Quito tried to appoint Assange to a diplomatic position in the United Kingdom, but the British Foreign Office rejected his appointment. "Ecuador knows that the way to resolve this issue is for Julian Assange to leave the embassy to face justice," a spokesperson told the *Guardian*.[2]

From the very start, the British authorities played a key role in creating the impasse that would be identified by the United Nations Working Group as arbitrary detention. They ignored the UN decision, they ignored the WikiLeaks founder's right to benefit from asylum, they ignored the detrimental effects of his confinement on his health. They showed no regard for Ecuador's sovereign decision to give him asylum, nor to grant him diplomatic protection. The procedure of appointing him to a diplomatic

1. Stefania Maurizi, "'I was fired for helping Julian Assange, and I have no regrets': an interview with Fidel Narvaez," *Jacobin*, October 25, 2019.
2. Owen Bowcott, "Julian Assange's bid for diplomatic status rejected by Britain," *Guardian*, January 10, 2018.

position was perfectly legitimate; two years later, in March 2019, the United Kingdom attempted a similar, though not identical tactic,[3] granting diplomatic protection to Nazanin Zaghari-Ratcliffe, a British-Iranian dual citizen arbitrarily detained by Iran since 2016, according to the UN Working Group, and finally released in March 2022.

Not only did the attempt to appoint Assange to a diplomatic post in the United Kingdom fail, but the attempt to assign him to such a post in some other country which, unlike Britain, would accept him, also fell through. If he had been successfully appointed as a diplomatic agent to a third state, upon leaving the embassy his immunities and inviolability would have had to be respected while in transit to that country, as established by the Vienna Convention on Diplomatic Relations.[4]

As of this writing, despite my FOIA battle I have been unable to obtain the documentation on how this failed attempt unfolded behind the scenes, nor was I present when the events occurred. I can only report what I was told by Baltasar Garzón, the coordinator of Julian Assange's legal team, since only an extremely limited number of people were cognizant of the details, and he was one of them.

The diplomatic passport operation was conceived by Julian Assange's lawyers and a few Ecuadorian authorities. Various countries were considered. Fidel Narváez, then Ecuadorian consul to London, told me that Ecuador considered Russia to be one possible option. But the legal counsel of WikiLeaks' founder did not. Garzón put it to me like this: "We considered countries such as Greece, Serbia, Bolivia, Venezuela and China, always ruling out Russia and making it clear to the Ecuadorian authorities that this country was not viable because it would fuel conspiracy theories."[5]

It was a perfectly licit plan from the standpoint of international law: as a sovereign nation, Ecuador had the right to grant Julian

---

3. Patrick Wintour, "Foreign Office grants Zaghari-Ratcliffe diplomatic protection," *Guardian*, March 8, 2019.
4. Art. 40 of the Vienna Convention on Diplomatic Relations, United Nations, 1961: https://legal.un.org/ilc/texts/instruments/english/conventions/9_1_1961.pdf (accessed May 8, 2022).
5. Baltasar Garzón, communication to the author via Aitor Martinez, April 14, 2022.

Assange diplomatic status and to appoint him to a post in a third country, if that country should approve the appointment. But once the U.S. authorities learned of this plan, the risk to Assange of leaving the embassy became too great. Very few people knew of the operation—how had the United States learned of it? "The plan was found out by UC Global due to the surveillance on [the] meeting between Julian Assange and [his] lawyers," Garzón explained to me, referring to a visit that he and Aitor Martinez had paid to Assange on December 18, 2017 in which they discussed the matter.

After the two Spanish lawyers returned to Madrid, four masked men broke into Garzón's office that same night: "They did not take anything (not even the money at the office). They were looking for the server and searched [for] documents," Baltasar Garzón told me. According to the protected witnesses, the head of UC Global had considered entering the Spanish lawyer's law offices. "Morales spoke about the possibility of entering the legal offices of ILOCAD, the law firm which is headed by Baltasar Garzón in Madrid" one of them stated,[6] adding "This would allow us to obtain information concerning Mr. Assange for the Americans. Two weeks after this conversation, the national media reported that men in balaclavas had entered Garzón's law offices."

As I write, the UC Global case is still under investigation by the Spanish judge with the Audiencia Nacional. One thing is certain, however: as soon as the U.S. authorities learned about the plan to appoint Julian Assange to a diplomatic post, they leaped into action. On December 21, 2017, they issued a criminal complaint, filed under seal, for the alleged offense of conspiracy to commit computer intrusion in violation of the United States Computer Fraud and Abuse Act (CFAA). What exactly was WikiLeaks' founder accused of? Of agreeing in 2010 to help Chelsea Manning crack a password "hash"[7] stored on Pentagon computers connected

---

6. Anonymous Witness 2.
7. Computers do not store users' passwords in plain text for security reasons. Passwords get "scrambled" through a mathematical algorithm, which produces a hash value for a password. It is the hash value which is stored on the computer, instead of the password itself.

to SIPRnet, the network used to store classified files, to which she, as an intelligence analyst, had legitimate access. The U.S. authorities alleged that if Chelsea Manning had succeeded in cracking the password hash, she could have logged into those computers with a username that did not belong to her, thus making it harder to identify her as the source of the documents.

The day after they issued the criminal complaint, December 22, 2017, the U.S. authorities sent an arrest request to the United Kingdom authorities via diplomatic channels. But since the criminal complaint and the arrest request were secret, neither Assange nor the public were aware of it. This occurred right around the time I went to visit him, December 29, 2017, when the guard with UC Global confiscated my backpack. The bid to get the WikiLeaks founder out of the embassy safely, protected by diplomatic immunity, had failed. But there was still another route to try.

THE LEGAL ROUTE

Unaware of the U.S. authorities' decisions, Julian Assange and his lawyers appealed to the Westminster Magistrates' Court in London, requesting withdrawal of the arrest warrant which British authorities had issued for breach of bail when, in 2012, he did not surrender to Scotland Yard and submit to extradition, and instead took refuge in the embassy and sought asylum. Since prosecutor Ny had dropped the rape investigation in May 2017 and revoked the European Arrest Warrant, highly regarded legal counsel Mark Summers of Julian Assange's defense team held that the arrest ordered by the British had no independent life outside the extradition proceeding, and that it was no longer a proportionate measure since Assange had lost his freedom a full seven years before.

But the Westminster Magistrates' Court judge, Emma Arbuthnot, rejected the request and upheld the arrest warrant. In her February 2018 ruling, Arbuthnot argued that the measure was proportionate and that the founder of WikiLeaks should come to court and face the consequences of his choices.[8]

---

8. Judge Emma Arbuthnot issued two rulings on the case: one dated February 6, 2018, and another February 13, 2018: www.judiciary.uk/wp-content/uploads/2018/02/

Assange's defense had shown—to no avail—that he had cooperated with the Swedish investigation, and that the British
authorities had advised the Swedish authorities not to question
him in London, thus helping to create the legal and diplomatic
quagmire in which he had been embroiled since 2010. As proof of
this, Assange's legal team submitted to the court some of the documents I had procured through my FOIA battle, the ones that had
not been destroyed and that I had managed to obtain and publish in
my newspaper. But it was to no purpose; quite the contrary, Judge
Arbuthnot made it clear that she too did not hold the decision by
the UN Working Group on Arbitrary Detention in high regard. "I
do not find that Mr Assange's stay in the Embassy is inappropriate,
unjust, unpredictable, unreasonable, unnecessary or disproportionate," she ruled.[9] Arbuthnot added: "I have read the medical reports.
Mr Assange is fortunately in relatively good physical health. He
has a serious tooth problem and is in need of dental treatment
and needs an MRI scan on a shoulder which has been described
as frozen. I accept he has depression and suffers respiratory infec-
tions. Mr Sommers [sic] contends he has been punished enough.
I do not accept there is no sunlight; there are a number of photographs of him on a balcony connected to the premises he inhabits.
Mr. Assange's health problems could be much worse."[10]

In all the seven years of his confinement in the embassy, the
founder of WikiLeaks had been able to go out on the balcony six
times. Nonetheless, his condition did not strike Judge Arbuthnot
as a problem. The treatment of a human being who, from June
2012 to February 2018—when she issued her ruling—had not
been able to breathe in fresh air, enjoy sunlight or receive medical
treatment, was neither unjust nor disproportionate, in Arbuthnot's eyes. And it mattered little that only a few days earlier, in
the pages of the *Guardian*, three high-profile physicians, Sondra

Assange-Ruling.pdf; www.judiciary.uk/wp-content/uploads/2018/02/assange-ruling-
2-feb2018.pdf (accessed May 9, 2022).
9.   The quote comes from the ruling dated February 13, 2018: www.judiciary.uk/
wp-content/uploads/2018/02/assange-ruling-2-feb2018.pdf (accessed May 9, 2022).
10.   Ibid.

Crosby, Brock Chisholm and Sean Love, had affirmed:[11] "It is our professional opinion that Mr. Assange's physical and psychological circumstances at the embassy are in violation of the spirit of the UN standard minimum rules for the treatment of prisoners."

In her ruling, Arbuthnot wrote in black and white:[12] "I give little weight to the views of the Working Group." And no one raised any objections.

The judge was the wife of Lord James Arbuthnot, who had served as Minister for Defense Procurement, as chair of the advisory board of the UK division of the multinational defense and security systems manufacturer Thales and, until December 2017, as a board member of the private intelligence firm SC Strategy Limited.[13] According to Matt Kennard and Mark Curtis, two of the very few British journalists who have dug into the case,[14] both before and after Judge Arbuthnot's ruling on Assange, her husband was working closely with the neoconservative Henry Jackson Society. An influential British pressure group very critical of WikiLeaks, the Henry Jackson Society included among its international supporters former head of the CIA James Woolsey,[15] the one who wanted to see Snowden "hanged by the neck until he's dead." The affiliations and connections of Emma Arbuthnot's husband raised the issue of conflict of interest in a case like that of Assange. But in a statement to journalists Kennard and Curtis, the British judiciary denied that Judge Arbuthnot had shown any bias.

---

11.   Sondra S. Crosby, Brock Chisholm and Sean Love, "We examined Julian Assange, and he badly needs care—but he can't get it," *Guardian*, January 24, 2018.
12.   The quote comes from Arbuthnot's ruling dated February 13, 2018.
13.   "Appointment of Lord Arbuthnot to the Chair of the Thales UK Advisory Board," Thales Group, May 12, 2016: www.thalesgroup.com/en/united-kingdom/news/appointment-lord-arbuthnot-chair-thales-uk-advisory-board (accessed May 9, 2022); Jamie Doward, "Judge in Uber's London legal battle steps aside over husband's links to firm," *Guardian*, August 18, 2018.
14.   Matt Kennard and Mark Curtis, "As British judge made rulings against Julian Assange, her husband was involved with right-wing lobby group briefing against WikiLeaks founder," *Declassified UK*, September 4, 2020: www.dailymaverick.co.za/article/2020-09-04-as-british-judge-made-rulings-against-julian-assange-her-husband-was-involved-with-right-wing-lobby-group-briefing-against-wikileaks-founder/ (accessed May 9, 2022).
15.   The fact that James Woolsey was one of the international patrons of the Henry Jackson Society can be easily verified on its website: https://henryjacksonsociety.org/%20international-patrons/ (accessed May 10, 2022).

After that February 2018 ruling, which upheld the arrest warrant the British authorities had issued for violating the conditions of his bail, Assange remained inside the embassy. Indeed, had he left it, he would have been captured by Scotland Yard. The prison sentence for such a violation would have been mild, at most one year in prison but, once in the hands of the British authorities, he would have risked extradition to the United States; ever since December 22, 2017, a U.S. arrest request had been hanging over his head. Assange could not know this, as it was secret, but it was what he had always feared, and what had led him to seek protection from Ecuador and to remain in the embassy even after Marianne Ny dropped the rape investigation. But it would soon no longer be just a fear, it would become a certainty.

THE POISON

Five weeks after Judge Arbuthnot's ruling, I visited him again in March 2018. I wanted to interview Assange and that time, unlike three months earlier, the security checks went smoothly, just as they always had. I was able to interview him without any difficulties. We were in the midst of the Russiagate investigation, and many media outlets were portraying WikiLeaks as the key player in every political drama. Assange had tweeted, for example, about the referendum on Catalonian independence held in October 2017: some press articles depicted his tweets as part of a Russian influence operation in support of independence. Nigel Farage, a strong proponent of Brexit, had visited Assange in the embassy: proof of his role in the great conspiracy, from Trump to Brexit. These articles provided no factual evidence of Assange's or WikiLeaks' role in these affairs, they were merely based on who had contacted or met with him. To me, as a journalist, all this made very little sense; we meet all sorts of people in doing our job, but going by certain media, it seemed that Assange and WikiLeaks would at any moment be arrested for Russiagate and put on trial. And yet, as of this writing, they have never been incriminated.

This climate of continuous scandal, sparked by article upon article about these suspicions and accusations, severely undermined WikiLeaks' reputation. During one of our conversations in those months, Assange joked: "We are in the business of crucifixion."[16] But it was no laughing matter. On March 27, 2018, Lenín Moreno's Ecuador cut Assange off from the world. He was no longer permitted to receive visitors, apart from his lawyers, and he could no longer access the internet. For a human being who at that point had been holed up inside an apartment for six years, with no way out, the ban on visitors was a very harsh form of isolation. The ban on internet access was also cruel. For Assange, the web is not simply a tool for work and leisure, as it is for most people; it is part of his identity. His world. Disconnecting him from the internet was like killing him socially and intellectually.

He was cut off from everyone. And the lack of internet access also made it hard to communicate with the people in Assange's physical vicinity, because the Ecuadorian authorities had installed jammers—electronic devices that block the use of telephones and computers—inside the embassy.

Three weeks after his isolation began, U.S. media outlet *The Intercept* wrote:[17] "Evidence has now emerged that the cutting off of Assange's communications with the outside world is the byproduct of serious diplomatic pressure being applied to the new Ecuadorian president, pressure that may very well lead, perhaps imminently, to Assange being expelled from the embassy altogether. The pressure is coming from the Spanish government in Madrid and its NATO allies, furious that Assange has expressed opposition to some of the repressive measures used to try to crush activists in support of Catalan independence." The article was authored by Glenn Greenwald and M.C. McGrath, a brilliant researcher on open data, and was based on a thorough analysis of the Twitter data.

Up until 1830, Ecuador had been a Spanish colony; the pressure from the Spanish government was a very serious matter for the Latin American country. The fury from Madrid had to do with

---

16.   Stefania Maurizi, "Julian Assange: 'I want to testify on Cambridge Analytica, but there has been political pressure'," *la Repubblica*, March 27, 2018.

17.   M.C. McGrath and Glenn Greenwald, "How shoddy reporting and anti-Russian propaganda coerced Ecuador to silence Julian Assange," *The Intercept*, April 20, 2018.

an independence referendum held in Catalonia in October 2017. WikiLeaks' founder had always been a keen commentator on international affairs, and via Twitter had condemned the Spanish government's repression of the Catalans supporting the referendum, considered illegal by Madrid. A media campaign immediately erupted, associating Assange's tweets on Catalonia with a Russian influence operation to spread disinformation in support of independence. *The Intercept* dismantled these accusations, however, publishing a technical analysis of the social network data to show that the dissemination of Assange's tweets on Catalonia had not been in the least anomalous, as claimed by certain media.

The Intercept additionally pointed out in its article that the media campaign was extensively based on information from a group called Hamilton 68, which claimed to study the influence operations through an analysis of 600 accounts the group believed to be linked to propaganda from the Kremlin. "But from its inception, the dubiousness of Hamilton 68 was self-evident," wrote Greenwald and McGrath, noting that Hamilton 68 was originally created "by the exact people with the worst records of lying and militarism in Washington: Bill Kristol, former CIA officials, GOP [Republican] hawks, and Democratic Party neocons." Besides having this background, "Hamilton 68 was, and remains, incredibly opaque about its methodology, refusing even to identify which accounts they designate as 'promoting Russian influence online'," wrote *The Intercept*.

Greenwald and McGrath represented a rare critical voice. "If, as appears to be true, these unsupported allegations about spreading disinformation during the referendum in Catalonia are being used as a tool for political manipulation in the case of Julian Assange, it is working," they wrote, adding: "The escalation of tensions with Spain, which has strong diplomatic ties to Ecuador, threatens Assange's asylum in a way that the longstanding pressure from the United States and United Kingdom could not." And so it did. Although my information on what was happening inside the embassy was sketchy at best, owing to Assange's forced isolation, I knew that his situation was growing increasingly precarious.

After all the attempts to get him out without his being arrested had failed, now even the attempt to protect him within those four walls was tottering.

The Catalonia affair was only one of the campaigns to demonize Assange. Another such extremely harmful campaign was based on a *Guardian* article that made its way around the world[18] claiming that the founder of WikiLeaks had received a visit from Paul Manafort, former chairman of Donald Trump's election campaign. The meeting was said to have taken place around March 2016, and there had allegedly been two prior meetings as well, in 2013 and 2015. If true, it was proof of direct contact with a Trump associate, before WikiLeaks had revealed the Democratic Party documents. But did it really happen?

This time, the doubts expressed about the *Guardian* revelations came from the *Washington Post*,[19] definitely not a newspaper suspected of sympathizing with Julian Assange.

The *Guardian's* online article on Manafort was signed by two reporters: Luke Harding and Dan Collyns. Harding had always been acerbic in his portrayals of Julian Assange. The *Washington Post* emphasized that the piece on Manafort was based solely on anonymous sources, and that the journalists had not published any supporting documents. The name of one of the reporters indicated in the print edition of the *Guardian* article—that of Ecuadorian journalist and political activist Fernando Villavicencio—had been removed from the version online. According to the *Washington Post*, "a government ministry under Ecuador's previous government accused Villavicencio of fabricating documents." The U.S. daily underscored how the *Guardian* had subsequently altered the language used in its original report to make its conclusions sound less firm. The original article spoke of a "meeting," but revised this to an "apparent meeting." The *Washington Post* also noted that "No other news organization has been able to corroborate the Guard-

---

18. Luke Harding and Dan Collyns, "Manafort held secret talks with Assange in Ecuadorian embassy, sources say," *Guardian*, November 27, 2018.
19. Paul Farhi, "The Guardian offered a bombshell story about Paul Manafort. It still hasn't detonated," *Washington Post*, December 4, 2018.

ian's reporting to substantiate its central claim of a meeting,"
adding: "News organizations typically do such independent
reporting to confirm important stories." Finally, the *Post* quoted
Glenn Greenwald, who pointed out that Ecuador's embassy was
surrounded by cameras that recorded whoever entered and exited.
"If Paul Manafort got anywhere near that building, let alone three
times, there would be mountains of evidence." On the contrary, to
date not a single photo or video of his presence has emerged, and
one can readily imagine that dozens of reporters have tried to track
down such images.

Both Manafort and WikiLeaks denied the meeting. Manafort's
name does not appear in the register of people who visited Julian
Assange in the embassy over the years. To this day, no proof of his
presence has ever surfaced, photographic or otherwise. And yet, as
I write, the *Guardian* article is still online. The climate of suspicion created over the years by articles like these has contributed to
a smear campaign against Assange and WikiLeaks which has ultimately robbed them of public empathy. The poison spread by the
media has worked.

THE LAST MEETING

I had written ten emails to the Ecuadorian authorities. Ten. I had
phoned them repeatedly, even the Ministry of Foreign Affairs in
Quito. Ever since Julian Assange had been cut off from the world,
in March 2018, I had again and again sought permission to enter
the embassy. After eight months of trying, I succeeded. I met with
him on November 19, 2018. It was the first visit with a journalist to be authorized since his complete isolation. And to grant it,
the Ecuadorian authorities had required me to fill in the "Registro
de Visitas," a form in which, among other personal information,
I was asked for "Brand, model, serial number, IMEI number and
telephone number (if applicable) of each of the telephone sets,
computers, cameras and other electronic equipment that the appli-
cant wants to enter with to the Embassy and keep during their
interview." Providing that technical information on my electronic

devices exposed me to the risk of having my communications spied on, but to obtain the permission I shared that data, hoping that, as stated in their form, they would let me keep my dumb phone and encrypted telephone with me.

As soon as I entered the embassy I was struck by the cold, hostile atmosphere. The UC Global company had been replaced by another security firm called Promsecurity. I went inside the conference room with my backpack and phones, since no one at the entrance had asked me to hand them over, as the guards with UC Global always had. I pulled them out to see if they were working, or if the jammers that kept electronic devices from making calls and connecting to internet were still active. My phones appeared to be completely blocked. While I was checking them, a security man suddenly opened the door. He asked me to hand over my phones, even though I had provided all the technical information they wanted. It was obvious that they had been watching me in real time through the security cameras in the room, because otherwise they could not have seen me with the door closed.

A short time earlier, Lenín Moreno's Ecuador had laid down a strict set of rules to make Assange's life as uncomfortable as possible. It was very clear that Assange no longer enjoyed any protection. María Fernanda Espinosa, the Minister of Foreign Affairs who had toiled to grant him citizenship and diplomatic status, had left the government and taken the position of President of the United Nations General Assembly. The consul to London who had been with him in the embassy for a full six years, Fidel Narváez, had been removed. Even the cat, who had brought a bit of cheer and distraction, was gone.

I was shocked when I saw Julian Assange. Just three days before my visit, U.S. media had revealed[20] that charges had been filed against him by the U.S. government. Though the charges were under seal, the news had apparently emerged inadvertently due to a bureaucratic error. It was known only that there was an indictment; the offense of which he was accused remained secret.

---

20. Charlie Savage, Adam Goldman and Michael S. Schmidt, "Assange is secretly charged in US, prosecutors mistakenly reveal," *New York Times*, November 16, 2018.

Speaking softly to avoid being heard, he reviewed the various options that might present themselves in the months to come. He was lucid and rational, but clearly experiencing the anxiety of a person who no longer had any control over his life. He could not formally give me any statements; he feared that if he made any statements that were reported by the press, Moreno's Ecuador would accuse him of violating his restrictions and use it to justify throwing him out of the embassy. His isolation and the new rules were designed to make his life unbearable, and their effect on him was palpable. Either he remained in there indefinitely, until his physical and mental collapse, or he decided to leave the embassy, triggering the beginning of his end.

I had never seen him like that before. The great tension in his face, the extreme weight loss that not even his thick winter jumper could hide. And when, to lighten the mood, I asked him where the cat had gone off to, he told me that he had decided to entrust the cat to some friends who could take care of it. But whenever the cat went outside, it was afraid of everything. He said this sadly. He always wanted to appear strong, but his physical and psychological suffering were evident.

I went out of the embassy and wrote this message to *la Repubblica*, my newspaper at the time: "Julian Assange is slowly dying, and this is no exaggeration: he must have lost 12 kilos in the eight months since I last saw him (I had last seen him March 23): he has lost so much weight that his shoulders seem small, like an emaciated fashion model. He has the beard and hair of a hermit. I wonder how his brain can still work, because it's clear that it still does."

When I got back from London, I described[21] our meeting in an article. My editors at *la Repubblica* told me they had been trying to contact me for two days. "Why didn't you answer?" they asked me. There was no trace of any phone calls, SMS message or emails on my telephones or computer. It was not the first time I had experi-

---

21. Stefania Maurizi, "The detention and isolation from the world of Julian Assange," *la Repubblica*, November 26, 2018.

enced problems with my communications. But it was the last time I ever met with Julian Assange in the embassy.

Five months later, I saw him outside that red-brick building in Knightsbridge where he had been holed up for six years and ten months. And so did the whole world, with the same hermit's white beard and hair that he had worn the last time I saw him. He was shouting *"UK must resist."*

17
In the Would-be Guantanamo

A BRUTAL ARREST

Seven agents dragged him out, lifting him by his legs and arms as he struggled, gesticulating and shouting. The Metropolitan Police, known to the world as Scotland Yard, were in plainclothes. Had they been wearing uniforms, it would probably have made for a grimmer scene, more suggestive of an authoritarian country. For Lenín Moreno's Ecuador, it would also have been an embarrassing symbol of submission. The images were brutal enough in themselves. And the whole world was watching. A defenseless journalist, his health sapped by nine years of confinement and arbitrary detention, forcibly removed by the police, in handcuffs, his face ghostly white, that hermit's white hair and beard. While a uniformed officer in the foreground could barely hold back his laughter.

On April 11, 2019, around 10:50 in the morning London time, Scotland Yard was allowed to enter the embassy on the authorization of Moreno, who withdrew Assange's asylum, complaining, among other things, of alleged violations of the strict conditions that had been designed to make his life as hard as possible, as I had noted during my last visit in November 2018.

Two months earlier, the *Financial Times* reported[1] that the Latin American country had obtained a 4.2 billion dollar-loan from the International Monetary Fund. Many had connected it to Moreno's choice to expel Assange, though Ecuador's president had already realigned the country with the United States for some time, distancing himself from Correa and signing military and security

---

1. John Paul Rathbone and Colby Smith, "IMF agrees to $4.2bn fund for Ecuador," *Financial Times*, February 21, 2019.

deals. After U.S. Vice-President Mike Pence's visit[2] to Ecuador in June 2018, rumors of Assange's impending eviction had become increasingly insistent.

In view of the threat of expulsion, Assange's legal team, coordinated by Baltasar Garzón, had sought every means to protect him, appealing[3] to the Inter-American Court of Human Rights. The latter had advised Ecuador that the Latin American country had an obligation of non-refoulement, namely not to transfer him, directly or indirectly, to the United States, where he risked torture or inhumane and degrading treatment. But Ecuador nonetheless let the British authorities arrest him.

At the very same time Scotland Yard was getting its hands on Assange, the Ecuadorian police were arresting Swedish programmer Ola Bini, a well-known software developer whose work focuses on privacy and cryptography. Bini had been living in Quito for some time. I have never met him, but according to his lawyers[4] he was a personal friend of Julian Assange, though not part of WikiLeaks. His name was included in the list of people that UC Global wanted information about. Moreno's government publicly accused him of "cooperating with attempts to destabilize the government." As of this writing, Bini is still on trial. Amnesty International has publicly stated[5] that "The work of people like Ola Bini who defend the right to privacy on digital media is fundamental for the protection of human rights around the world."

---

2. "Fact sheet on cooperation between the United States and Ecuador," US Mission Ecuador, June 28, 2018: https://ec.usembassy.gov/fact-sheet-on-cooperation-between-the-united-states-and-ecuador/ (accessed May 11, 2022).

3. Jennifer Robinson, Sidney Conference for International Law (SCIL), February 26, 2021. See the Inter-American Court of Human Rights' Advisory Opinion OC-25/18 dated May 30, 2018: www.refworld.org/pdfid/5c87ec454.pdf (accessed May 11, 2022).

4. Reuters Staff, "Ecuadorean judge orders Swedish citizen close to Assange jailed pending trial," April 13, 2019: www.reuters.com/article/us-ecuador-wikileaks-idUSKCN1RPoHA (accessed May 11, 2022).

5. "Ecuador: Authorities must monitor trial against digital defender Ola Bini," Amnesty International, March 3, 2020: www.amnesty.org/en/latest/news/2020/03/ecuador-authorities-must-monitor-trial-digital-defender-ola-bini/ (accessed May 11, 2022).

The day of his arrest, as he was being lifted bodily and hauled outside, despite his handcuffs Assange was clutching a book in his hands. And it was not just any book.

THE STATE WITHIN THE STATE

It was called *History of the National Security State* and was based on a series of interviews with Gore Vidal conducted by independent American journalist Paul Jay.[6] It was one of the books I had given[7] Assange over the years to help keep his mind active during his isolation in the embassy.

History of the National Security State is a small gem. In it, Vidal concisely chronicles how the United States, after the end of World War II, rather than dismantling its war machine, dramatically expanded its military-industrial complex. It did this by exploiting the fear of an enemy portrayed as an omnipotent, existential threat, the Soviet Union, and setting up the National Security State, which after September 11, 2001, became a leviathan. A state within the state, with its own agencies, from the CIA and the NSA to the Pentagon, entities which are essentially in practice accountable to no one, shielded by secrecy, allotted a grotesque budget for weapons and endless wars.

Attempting to understand why, on the day of his arrest, Assange had chosen that book in particular, the *Washington Post* interviewed[8] its author, Paul Jay. Jay did not know the WikiLeaks founder, so he could not know exactly why Assange chose it, but he defined the heart of his conversations with Gore Vidal as follows: "The essence of the book is that this is not in the interests of the American people or people anywhere, this kind of security state." He went on to say: "I guess the fundamental point of what Vidal was saying is that the American empire is not good for the

---

6.   Paul Jay, *Gore Vidal, History of the National Security State: Includes Vidal on America* (Toronto: The Real News Network, 2014).
7.   Stefania Maurizi, "I've known Julian Assange for 10 years. His confinement and arrest are a scandal," *Newsweek*, April 30, 2019.
8.   Stephanie Merry, "Julian Assange carried a book during his arrest. He may have been sending a message," *Washington Post*, April 11, 2019.

American people. The way it's sold to the American people is that this is good for all Americans because we're all in the same boat, but it's quite the opposite. It's good for an elite, especially arms manufacturers and the fossil fuel industry and others that cash in on this kind of foreign policy. But it's young working people, men and women, that die for this, and they go off and die in these foreign wars."

I have no idea if Julian Assange was carrying Vidal's book with him to send that message to the world, but among the many enemies of WikiLeaks, the U.S. National Security State was certainly the behemoth determined to destroy Assange and the WikiLeaks journalists right from the early stages of their work. I had given him that book thinking he might find it interesting to look at the origins of the behemoth through the erudition and analytical faculties of an intellectual like Gore Vidal.

I remember that, besides the book, I had also brought him some lemons from the Amalfi Coast where the American writer loved to live, amidst the blue of the sea of Ravello and the citrus gardens. I had guarded those lemons with great care during my Rome to London flight. "Not because I was afraid someone might poison them," I told Assange, "but one must be careful about food brought into the embassy." Even a minor case of food poisoning could be disastrous for him, since he could not go to hospital without being arrested. When I later learned that, according to the protected witnesses, U.S. intelligence had discussed with the head of UC Global the possibility of poisoning him, I remembered how we had joked about poisoned lemons.

We do not know how the CIA, NSA and the Pentagon, the heart of the U.S. National Security State, celebrated the arrest of Julian Assange. We do know that then British Prime Minister Theresa May welcomed the arrest, saying that "it showed that no one was above the law."[9] Of course, that is, no one apart from the

9. Reuters Staff, "UK PM May says Assange arrest shows no one above the law," Reuters, April 11, 2019: www.reuters.com/article/us-ecuador-assange-may-idUSKCN1RN1OA (accessed May 2022).

state criminals who were responsible for the horrors revealed by the WikiLeaks publications.

Some scraps of information revealing the British establishment's delight at the scene are also found in the diaries[10] of Sir Alan Duncan, Boris Johnson's former deputy at the Foreign Office, who was apparently a key player in "Operation Pelican," the eviction of Julian Assange from the Ecuadorian embassy.

Duncan, who in 2018 called[11] the founder of WikiLeaks "a miserable little worm," wrote that getting to his arrest had "taken many months of patient diplomatic negotiation, and in the end it went off without a hitch."[12] Back in 2016, he had met with Guillaume Long,[13] the Foreign Minister in Rafael Correa's government, who "defends the supposed human rights of Julian Assange," Duncan wrote in his diary, without hiding his antipathy for Long. But with the end of the Correa government, and the arrival of Moreno, there had been plenty of opportunities to negotiate. Moreno "exudes goodwill and warmth. He loves the UK and I gave him a beautiful porcelain plate from the Buckingham Palace gift shop. Job done,"[14] wrote Sir Duncan, relaying that he had met Moreno in Ecuador three months after the operation succeeded. In his diaries, Duncan does not hide his profound satisfaction with Assange's arrest: "I do millions of interviews, trying to keep the smirk off my face."[15]

Such was the British establishment's respect for pesky journalists like those with WikiLeaks. Forcibly removed from the four walls of the embassy, which for six years and ten months had protected him, Julian Assange was soon confined by four different walls: those of the would-be British Guantanamo.

---

10. Alan Duncan, *In the thick of it: The private diaries of a minister* (London: William Collins, 2021).
11. Samuel Osborne, "Julian Assange branded 'miserable little worm' by UK minister," *The Independent*, March 27, 2018.
12. Alan Duncan, "Theresa's like a flaking old pit prop everyone knows will collapse … we are in meltdown … ****-A-DOODLE-DOO!," *Daily Mail*, April 5, 2021.
13. Matt Kennard, "Revealed: the UK government campaign to force Julian Assange from the Ecuadorian embassy," *Declassified UK*, April 28, 2021.
14. Ibid.
15. Ibid.

FIFTY WEEKS

He was sent to the maximum-security prison of Belmarsh, where Tony Blair's government had made its unsuccessful attempt to indefinitely detain suspected terrorists after 9/11, just as the Americans had done in Guantanamo.

The very day of his arrest, he was brought before Judge Michael Snow[16] of Westminster Magistrates' Court in London, who found him guilty of breaching the conditions of his bail in 2012, when instead of surrendering to Scotland Yard for extradition to Sweden for questioning on rape allegations, he took refuge in the Ecuadorian embassy and sought asylum.

In February 2018, Julian Assange's defense had petitioned for withdrawal of that mandate for arrest issued by British authorities in 2012. If the appeal had been successful, Assange could have left the embassy without risking arrest and enjoyed the right to asylum in Ecuador. But the attempt had failed, when Judge Emma Arbuthnot—wife of Lord Arbuthnot—had turned down the appeal.

When, on the day of his arrest, Assange's legal counsel raised doubts as to Judge Arbuthnot's impartiality, Snow scornfully rejected them. He also called Assange "a narcissist who cannot get beyond his own selfish interests."

Why a journalist arbitrarily detained for almost a decade deserved such contemptuous public treatment was not clear. But it was clear that day that Julian Assange had been right from the very beginning.

Once he had been arrested for breach of his bail terms, the United States immediately requested his extradition, charging him with conspiracy to commit computer intrusion, the crime for which they had issued an arrest warrant under seal in December 2017. It was an alleged violation of the United States Computer Fraud and Abuse Act (CFAA). If extradited and found guilty of this crime, he faced a maximum sentence of five years in prison.

---

16. Simon Murphy, "Assange branded a 'narcissist' by judge who found him guilty," *Guardian*, April 11, 2019.

Upon his arrest by Scotland Yard, he was notified of the indictment[17] that had been returned by the Eastern District of Virginia, the court in the same state where the CIA and Pentagon have their headquarters and which investigates some of the most high-profile terrorism and national security cases.

Meanwhile, British justice moved swiftly. On May 1, 2019, British judge Deborah Taylor sentenced[18] the founder of WikiLeaks to fifty weeks in prison for violating his bail conditions in 2012. Taylor did not evince any consideration of either the decision of the United Nations Working Group on Arbitrary Detention or the fact that Assange's concerns about extradition to the United States had proven well-founded. She also put to him that his continued residence in the embassy had cost the United Kingdom the "expenditure of £16 million of taxpayers' money." And it was of little moment that—as the documents obtained through my FOIA litigation showed—the British authorities with the Crown Prosecution Service helped create that legal paralysis and had also told[19] the Swedes that they did "not consider costs [to be] a relevant factor in this matter."

The fifty-week sentence was near the maximum penalty for that crime, which was fifty-two weeks. The Working Group publicly declared it "a disproportionate sentence" and again called on[20] the United Kingdom to free him: "The Working Group regrets that the Government has not complied with its Opinion and has now furthered the arbitrary deprivation of liberty of Mr. Assange." London ignored the Working Group, as it had since December 2015.

---

17. The indictment is available on the U.S. Department of Justice website: www. justice.gov/opa/press-release/file/1153486/download (accessed May 12, 2022).
18. Sentencing Remarks of HHJ Deborah Taylor: www.judiciary.uk/wp-content/ uploads/2019/05/sentencing-remarks-assange-010519.pdf (accessed May 12, 2022).
19. Email from the Crown Prosecution Service to Marianne Ny, dated December 10, 2013, 16:29. I obtained a copy of this email thanks to my litigation against the Crown Prosecution Service. I have quoted it in chapter 11.
20. "United Kingdom: Working Group on Arbitrary Detention expresses concern about Assange proceedings," UN OHCHR, May 3, 2019: www.ohchr.org/en/ news/2019/05/united-kingdom-working-group-arbitrary-detention-expresses-concern-about-assange (accessed May 12, 2022).

After U.S. and British justice, Swedish justice went into action. Little more than one month after Assange's arrest, on May 13, 2019 the Swedish Prosecution Authority reopened the rape investigation for the third time, at the request of Elisabeth Massi Fritz, the legal counsel of the alleged victim, Sofia W.

But the reopening of the Swedish investigation paled in comparison to what befell Julian Assange and Chelsea Manning immediately afterwards.

THE LAW AS A SWORD

On May 16, 2019, around two weeks after Assange was sentenced to fifty weeks in prison, Chelsea Manning was locked up once again for refusing to testify before the Grand Jury in Alexandria, in the court of the Eastern District of Virginia, where the U.S. investigation into Assange and WikiLeaks had been opened almost ten years earlier. She had already been sent to prison in March for the same reason, and had spent two months behind bars. This time, she was risking a long prison term. Released in May 2017 after serving seven years in a military prison and after two suicide attempts, Manning was now locked up again for an act of civil disobedience.

Grand Juries are so controversial as an institution that their abolition has been advocated[21] for years. They have a lengthy history of persecuting political activists and systematically pardoning policemen responsible for violent deaths, including that of black U.S. citizen Eric Garner, whose murder sparked huge protests linked to the Black Lives Matter movement.[22]

They work in secret: they are formed by a prosecutor who presents the evidence to the jury, questions the witnesses, issues

---

21. Mary Turck, "It is time to abolish the grand jury system," *Al Jazeera*, January 11, 2016; LaDoris Hazzard Cordell, "Grand juries should be abolished," *Slate*, December 9, 2014.
22. Harry Bruinius, "Eric Garner case 101: why grand juries rarely indict police officers," *Christian Science Monitor*, December 9, 2014; Katie Benner, "Eric Garner's death will not lead to federal charges for N.Y.P.D. officer," *New York Times*, July 16, 2019.

subpoenas for documents and witnesses, and offers witnesses
immunity from any criminal consequences of their testimony. At
the end of this process, the jury must decide if there is sufficient
evidence to indict the individual under investigation. The task of
the Grand Jury is not to establish innocence or guilt: it is to decide
whether or not the suspect should be indicted, that is to say, if
there is sufficient evidence to send them to trial. All of this takes
place with no exchange between prosecution and defense, because
the Grand Jury does not unfold in the presence of a judge, nor of
the suspect's lawyers nor witnesses.

What happens behind the closed doors of a Grand Jury remains
a mystery. It is the prosecutor who decides what evidence to
present to the members of the jury who, as ordinary people, do not
necessarily have any legal expertise: they must base their decision
on what the prosecutor tells them. In selecting which evidence to
present and which to omit, which witnesses to question and which
to leave out, the prosecutor enjoys great discretion in the introduction of evidence that may incriminate or exonerate the suspect. In
short, the prosecutor is the one who "leads the orchestra." As the
adage in U.S. legal circles goes: "A prosecutor could get a Grand
Jury to indict a ham sandwich, if he or she wanted."

Precisely because it works in secret, we do not know the Grand
Jury's aim in its subpoena of Chelsea Manning, but Manning
once again proved unwilling to compromise on her principles. She
refused to testify, despite being offered immunity in exchange for
her testimony. At that point, Judge Anthony Trenga not only sent
her to jail for contempt of court, he also ordered her to be fined:
after her first thirty days in custody, 500 dollars each day that she
continued to refuse to testify, doubling to 1,000 dollars each day
after two months.

In a letter to Judge Trenga, Manning explained that her refusal
stemmed from the secret nature of the proceedings and their use
in the past for political ends, to victimize activists and more vulnerable social groups, for example, while letting policemen go
unpunished: "The secrecy of grand jury proceedings fuels paranoia
and fear, running contrary to our ideals of open courts." She went

on to close her letter as follows: "Each person must make the world we want to live in around us where we stand. I believe in due process, freedom of the press, and a transparent court system. I object to the use of grand juries as tools to tear apart vulnerable communities. I object to this grand jury in particular as an effort to frighten journalists and publishers, who serve a crucial public good. I have had these values since I was a child, and I've had years of confinement to reflect on them. For much of that time, I depended for survival on my values, my decisions, and my conscience. I will not abandon them now."[23] Despite her imprisonment and heavy fines, Chelsea Manning did not give in, and once again, she paid the price.

After sending WikiLeaks' source back to prison, U.S. justice came down hard on its founder.

23. "Letter from Chelsea Manning to Judge Anthony Trenga," dated May 28, 2019: www.releasechelsea.com/statements_by_chelsea/chelsea_letter_to_judge_trenga/ (accessed May 12, 2022).

18

175 Years for the Crime of Journalism

THE FIRST TIME IN UNITED STATES HISTORY

He had been accused of being paranoid, of being a narcissist who fancied himself the target of international intrigues, of invoking fear of extradition to the United States as an excuse to escape Swedish justice. And now everything he had feared and anticipated had come to pass.

On May 23, 2019, the same Grand Jury before which Manning had refused to testify charged[1] Julian Assange with criminal conspiracy to obtain classified U.S. government documents from her: the Rules of Engagement for U.S. soldiers in Iraq—published in conjunction with the *Collateral Murder* video—the diplomatic cables, and the Guantanamo detainee records.

Besides indicting Assange for his role in obtaining the files, the U.S. authorities indicted him for publishing the diplomacy cables and the documents on the wars in Afghanistan and Iraq, accusing him of putting the sources cited in them at risk.

He was charged on seventeen counts of alleged violations of the Espionage Act, which were added to the charge of agreeing to help Chelsea Manning crack a password hash. If extradited to the United States and found guilty, Assange risked 175 years in prison. The news came while he was in the hospital wing of Belmarsh prison for dramatic weight loss and severe depression.

The U.S. government wanted to lock him up for life for obtaining and publishing documents which had uncovered war crimes, torture, appalling abuses. It was the first time, in the 102 years

---

1. The superseding indictment dated May 23, 2019 is available on the website of the U.S. Department of Justice: www.justice.gov/opa/press-release/file/1165556/ download (accessed May 12, 2022).

since enactment of that draconian law, that a journalist was being brought to trial under the Espionage Act.

While the Obama administration had investigated Assange and WikiLeaks from 2010 to 2016 but ultimately did not indict them, the Trump administration had now crossed the Rubicon.

The U.S. authorities accused Assange of not receiving the documents passively but rather of actively seeking them out. According to the indictment, Chelsea Manning did not act entirely on her own, but had taken action in response to a wish list published by WikiLeaks on its site at the end of 2009 under the title "The Most Wanted Leaks of 2009," specifying the documents it would like to receive. These were secrets every journalist and newsroom in the world were on the hunt for: the Rules of Engagement in Iraq and Afghanistan, the Guantanamo operating procedures, the CIA videos showing interrogations, later destroyed by the agency. But the prosecution interpreted the list as a solicitation to steal classified documents and therefore a criminal conspiracy. Even the comments in the chats between Manning and the person the U.S. authorities claimed was Julian Assange were portrayed as evidence of encouragement to steal documents. Comments like "*curious eyes never run dry*" were adjudged as incitement to continue extracting classified files. Even extremely common journalistic source protection techniques, like the use of encrypted Jabber chat and "measures to conceal Manning as the source of the disclosure of classified records to WikiLeaks, including by removing usernames from the disclosed information" were portrayed as part of the criminal conspiracy.

U.S. lawyers Michael Ratner and Leonard Weinglass had foreseen it all as far back as October 2010, when they flew to London to tell Assange that he would be indicted under the Espionage Act for publishing those secret files, and that the U.S. authorities would seek to pass off the contact between WikiLeaks and Chelsea Manning as a criminal conspiracy, rather than a source passing documents to a journalist. Nine years later, that is exactly what happened.

The same day the U.S. authorities published these accusations against Julian Assange, Chelsea Manning issued a statement.[2] After repeating that she had already expressed everything she had to say about the files in the course of her court martial trial in 2013 and would therefore not testify before the Grand Jury, she stressed "I continue to accept full and sole responsibility for those disclosures in 2010," hence denying that she had done so under the direction of Assange and WikiLeaks. She concluded: "This administration describes the press as the opposition party and an enemy of the people. Today, they use the law as a sword, and have shown their willingness to bring the full power of the state against the very institution intended to shield us from such excesses."

Since 2010, the sword of the law had been brought down hard upon Manning, Assange and WikiLeaks. This use of the law as a weapon is called "lawfare." And the lawfare was far from over.

THE FULL FORCE OF THE STATE

One hundred and seventy-five years in prison for obtaining and publishing the U.S. government documents provided by Manning, exposing war crimes and torture. I had revealed the exact same documents in my newspaper, and from 2010 onward I have continued to consult and publish them every time I find information relevant to my investigations. Yet I have never been questioned, arrested or imprisoned. And none of the journalists who, like me, have worked on those secret files as media partners—from New York to New Zealand, from London to Argentina—have been subject to repercussions. But the full force of the state had come down on the source of those revelations, Chelsea Manning, and on Julian Assange and the WikiLeaks journalists who had made it possible for the public to know about them.

---

2. Chelsea Manning's statement is available on the website of "The Sparrow Project": https://sparrowmedia.net/2019/05/statement-from-chelsea-manning-her-lawyer-regarding-todays-superseding-indictment/ (accessed May 13, 2022).

Manning had been handed the longest[3] sentence ever inflicted by U.S. justice on a U.S. citizen for revealing classified documents to the press: thirty-five years. She had spent seven of them in a military prison, the first eleven months in cruel, inhumane and degrading conditions, attempted suicide twice, and was now back in prison. Assange had lost his liberty on December 7, 2010, and had never known freedom again. He had gone from Wandsworth prison to house arrest, from confinement in Ecuador's embassy to the maximum-security prison of Belmarsh. His physical and mental health had been gravely undermined. The WikiLeaks journalists had been living under constant investigation. U.S. authorities had in fact seized the Google emails of at least three of them: Kristinn Hrafnsson, Sarah Harrison and Joseph Farrell. And yet the organization and its founder have won some of the most prestigious awards in journalism: from *The Economist* New Media Award to the Amnesty International New Media Award,[4] from the Walkley Award for Most Outstanding Contribution to Journalism to the Martha Gellhorn Prize,[5] from the "Piero Passetti" journalism prize of the national union of Italian journalists[6] to the Günter Wallraff Prize awarded in 2022.[7]

The same day they announced the indictment of Assange for Espionage Act violations, the United States Department of Justice stated, "The Department takes seriously the role of journalists in our democracy and we thank you for it. It is not and has never been

3. Charlie Savage, "Chelsea Manning ordered back to jail for refusal to testify in WikiLeaks inquiry," *New York Times*, May 16, 2019; Charlie Savage, "Chelsea Manning to be released early as Obama commutes sentence," *New York Times*, January 17, 2017.
4. "Amnesty International Media Awards 2009: full list of winners," *Guardian*, January 3, 2009.
5. Jason Deans, "Julian Assange wins Martha Gellhorn journalism prize," *Guardian*, June 2, 2011.
6. Roberto Borghi, "Giornalisti: Premio Cronista, anche New Media e WikiLeaks," *PrimaOnline*, March 21, 2011: www.primaonline.it/2011/03/21/90338/giornalisti-premio-cronista-anche-new-media-e-wikileaks/ (accessed May 13, 2022).
7. *Die Zeit* Staff, "Wikileaks-Gründer Assange erhält Günter-Wallraff-Preis," Zeit Online: www.zeit.de/news/2022-05/18/wikileaks-gruender-assange-erhaelt-guenter-wallraff-preis?utm_referrer=https%3A%2F%2Fwww.google.com%2F (accessed May 25, 2022).

the Department's policy to target them for their reporting. Julian Assange is no journalist."[8]

For obvious reasons, it is not up to those in power to decide who is and who is not a journalist. The mission of journalism is to serve as a watchdog to power. If power decides who can rightfully be defined as a "journalist", then there is no hope of independent oversight. Indeed the statements by the Department of Justice were a wake-up call even to the media that had been demonizing WikiLeaks for almost a decade. This time they recognized the unprecedented threat represented by the path the Trump administration had taken.

The most influential newspaper in the world, the *New York Times*, authored an article[9] pointing out the risks for press freedom: "Though he is not a conventional journalist, much of what Mr. Assange does at WikiLeaks is difficult to distinguish in a legally meaningful way from what traditional news organizations like The Times do: seek and publish information that officials want to be secret, including classified national security matters, and take steps to protect the confidentiality of sources."

The influential American Civil Liberties Union (ACLU) also raised[10] the alarm. "For the first time in the history of our country, the government has brought criminal charges against a publisher for the publication of truthful information. This is an extraordinary escalation of the Trump administration's attacks on journalism, and a direct assault on the First Amendment," said Ben Wizner, director of the ACLU's Speech, Privacy and Technology Project.

Wizner went on: "It establishes a dangerous precedent that can be used to target all news organizations that hold the government accountable by publishing its secrets," concluding: "it is equally dangerous for U.S. journalists who uncover the secrets of other

---

8. "Remark from the briefing announcing the superseding indictment of Julian Assange," U.S. Department of Justice, May 23, 2019: www.justice.gov/opa/press-release/file/1165636/download (accessed May 12, 2022).
9. Charlie Savage, "Assange indicted under Espionage Act, raising First Amendments issues," *New York Times*, May 23, 2019.
10. "ACLU comment on Julian Assange indictment," ACLU, May 23, 2019: www.aclu.org/press-releases/aclu-comment-julian-assange-indictment (accessed May 12, 2022).

nations. If the US can prosecute a foreign publisher for violating our secrecy laws, there's nothing preventing China, or Russia, from doing the same."

Wizner sought to underscore that when the U.S. authorities presume to assert their jurisdiction over an Australian journalist, Julian Assange, indicting him on the charge of violating an American law, it opens a Pandora's box. Russia, China, Saudi Arabia might attempt to do the same, prosecuting foreign reporters who reveal their secrets, with a domino effect on press freedom.

Although in the past prosecution of publishers and journalists for publishing secrets had in some cases been considered by U.S. authorities, such attempts had ultimately always been abandoned. In any case, all known attempts concerned American publishers and journalists subject to American laws.[11] The indictment of a non-U.S. journalist under the Espionage Act had no precedent in all of U.S. history. And the difference between the way this law has been applied to whistleblowers and publishers and how it has been applied to government officials and spymasters has been stark. As Julian Assange told[12] me in an interview before he was indicted: "There is not any pretense any more that there is equality before the law."

THE ESPIONAGE ACT FOR WHISTLEBLOWERS: PRISON, CRUELTY, BANKRUPTCY

Introduced in 1917, a few weeks after the country entered World War I, the Espionage Act immediately became a tool used to bludgeon political dissent, which was perceived as a threat to the war effort. The Espionage Act was in fact used to indict around

11. "Report of Carey Shenkman regarding US Espionage Act of 1917 and Computer and Fraud Act," submitted to Westminster Magistrates' Court in the extradition hearing of Julian Assange, September 2020. The report is available in a summarized form in: *The Government of the US of America-v-Julian Paul Assange*, Consolidated Annex: www.judiciary.uk/wp-content/uploads/2021/01/USA-v-Assange-annex-040121.pdf (accessed May 7, 2022); Jameel Jaffer, "The Espionage Act and the growing threat to press freedom," *The New Yorker*, June 25, 2019.
12. Stefania Maurizi, "Julian Assange: 'I still enjoy crushing bastards'," *L'Espresso*, April 2, 2015.

2,000 Americans for their political speeches in opposition to U.S. participation in World War I.[13]

It is a brutal law insofar as it makes no distinction between spies who pass secret documents to the enemy to harm their nation, and whistleblowers and journalists who reveal documents to the public to expose atrocities, war crimes, torture, extrajudicial killings. It puts them all on the same level. It does not provide for a public interest defense either. It does not allow a journalist or whistleblower to say "Yes, I broke the law, but I did so to bring out extremely troubling facts that the public in a democracy ought to know." Deprived of the capacity to invoke the public interest, they have no other shield with which to defend themselves.

One of the most infamous attempts to charge sources and whistleblowers under the Espionage Act was the indictment against Daniel Ellsberg for revealing the Pentagon Papers. The case collapsed, however, when gross government misconduct emerged. The illegal wiretapping of his telephone calls; President Richard Nixon's "plumbers" sneaking into Ellsberg's psychiatrist's office in search of information to blackmail him into silence; CIA assets being ordered to "incapacitate Ellsberg, totally," which in the language of covert operations meant killing him.[14] All of these abuses of power led the judge to dismiss the case.

Despite the repeated attempts to use it, in all of the twentieth century only one[15] journalistic source was ever actually indicted and found guilty under the Espionage Act: Samuel Loring Morison, a U.S. intelligence analyst who gave classified files to *Jane's Defence Weekly*, a military magazine. Loring Morison was handed a two-year prison sentence in 1985 and was pardoned by U.S. President Bill Clinton in 2001.

It was Barack Obama who took the unfortunate path of normalizing use of the Espionage Act against whistleblowers and

13.   "Report of Carey Shenkman regarding US Espionage Act of 1917 and Computer and Fraud Act."
14.   Stefania Maurizi, "Daniel Ellsberg: 'It is outrageous that Biden has continued to pursue Julian Assange's prosecution'," *Il Fatto Quotidiano*, March 22, 2022.
15.   Jaffer, "The Espionage Act and the growing threat to press freedom"; "Pardon—Samuel Loring Morison," Clinton Digital Library: https://clinton.presidentiallibraries.us/items/show/36273 (accessed May 12, 2022).

journalistic sources as if they were spies and traitors. After promising to create the most transparent government in history, his administration indicted more whistleblowers and sources than all U.S. presidents before him combined: eight in all. Thomas Drake, Shamai Leibowitz, Stephen Kim, Chelsea Manning, Donald Sachtleben, Jeffrey Sterling, John Kiriakou and finally Edward Snowden.

Drake, a cryptolinguist who worked as a senior executive for the NSA and tried to report the agency's abuses even before Snowden did, risked a thirty-five-year sentence. The judicial case eventually crumbled, but he emerged with his life in tatters, almost bankrupt and reduced to working in an Apple store.[16]

John Kiriakou, an ex-CIA operative in the forefront of anti-terrorism operations after 9/11, refused to use the torture techniques that were introduced in the immediate aftermath of the attack on the Twin Towers. When he publicly discussed the CIA's use of waterboarding in 2007, he found himself indicted under the Espionage Act, sentenced to thirty months in prison, financially ruined and unable to find a job to support his five children.

I interviewed[17] him by mail in 2014 while he was incarcerated in the Loretto prison, in Pennsylvania, where he was serving his sentence. In a hand-written letter he told me of refusing to be trained in the torture techniques owing to moral qualms about them, and that he was "one of two people who refused." In conversation with me, he was able to clarify the ethical motivations that had prompted him to come forward and blow the whistle, but for U.S. justice, his motivations were completely irrelevant. The Espionage Act puts a conscientious objector who reveals classified information to the press for moral reasons on the same level as a spy who sells it to the enemy.

Then there was Chelsea Manning, punished like no other, to the point of trying to kill herself on two separate occasions.

16. Stefania Maurizi, "Così spiavamo le vite degli altri," *L'Espresso*, June 17, 2013; Timothy Bella, "NSA whistleblower Thomas Drake: 'I've had to create a whole new life'," *Al Jazeera*, November 12, 2015.

17. Stefania Maurizi, "La spia in prigione lancia le sue accuse: Obama ha mancato le promesse," *L'Espresso*, August 1, 2014.

And finally Snowden, who was forced to live in exile in Russia, with the prospect of having to look over his shoulder for the rest of his life. Why did he not return to the United States, as he would have liked to do, and face U.S. justice? Daniel Ellsberg explained[18] why very effectively: since Snowden would not be allowed to defend himself by claiming and demonstrating that he had acted in the public interest when he revealed the Orwellian surveillance system put in place by the NSA, he would have no chance of a fair trial. In returning to the United States, he would sentence himself to life in prison, in all likelihood, in solitary confinement.

And yet the essential debate he ignited had not only brought to light that the NSA was secretly collecting billions of phone metadata of American citizens—though U.S. intelligence publicly denied it—it also revealed that such metadata collection had not helped avert even one terrorist attack, ever.[19] Thanks solely to his whistleblowing, in 2015 the United States Congress put an end to this indiscriminate collection through the USA Freedom Act. From the U.S. Federal Court of Appeals for the 9th Circuit[20] on up to the European Court of Human Rights,[21] numerous sentences have established that the NSA's bulk surveillance and that of its

---

18.   Daniel Ellsberg, "Daniel Ellsberg: Snowden would not get a fair trial—and Kerry is wrong," *Guardian*, May 30, 2014.

19.   As soon as journalists began revealing the NSA surveillance programs thanks to the Snowden files, U.S. authorities claimed that those programs, which included the collection of telephone metadata, had enabled the prevention of 54 terror attacks. But they later stated that the metadata collection had actually allowed prevention of just one instance of terroristic activity, on the part of Basaaly Moalin, a Somali citizen living in the United States, accused of transferring 10,900 dollars to the Shabaab. However, a ruling by Judge Berzon of the United States Court of Appeals for the Ninth Circuit clarified that the collection of metadata had not been crucial, so even the one case in which metadata collection was defended by U.S. authorities as playing a pivotal role in thwarting terroristic activities crumbled. For a reconstruction of the case, see Mattathias Schwartz, "The whole haystack," *The New Yorker*, January 26, 2015; Charlie Savage, "Disputed NSA phone program is shut down, aide says," *New York Times*, March 4, 2019; Josh Gerstein, "Court rules NSA phone snooping illegal—after 7-year delay," *Politico*, September 2, 2020.

20.   The ruling of the United States Court of Appeals for the Ninth Circuit: https://cdn.ca9.uscourts.gov/datastore/opinions/2020/09/02/13-50572.pdf (accessed May 12, 2022).

21.   The judgment of the European Court of Human Rights is available on the ECHR website: https://hudoc.echr.coe.int/eng#{%22itemid%22:[%22001-210077%22]} (accessed May 12, 2022).

British counterpart, the GCHQ, is illegal. Without the courage of Edward Snowden, this would not have been possible. And yet, as of this writing, he remains in exile in Russia.

This was the treatment reserved for journalists, sources and whistleblowers when they revealed classified documents to report crimes and abuses at the highest levels of power. They were incarcerated, driven to mental breakdown, brought to the brink of suicide, financially ruined, forced to live in exile.

THE ESPIONAGE ACT FOR GENERALS AND SPYMASTERS: IMPUNITY

While the lives of Chelsea Manning, Edward Snowden and other conscientious whistleblowers have been torn asunder by the Espionage Act charges, senior officials and spymasters have faced few or no major consequences. When they reveal classified documents, and do so to manipulate the public debate or claim credit for important operations, impunity is assured.

In 2011, for example, no one indicted then-CIA director Leon Panetta and his men under the Espionage Act for letting Mark Boal, screenwriter for the film *Zero Dark Thirty* directed by Kathryn Bigelow, attend a ceremony, closed to the public, honoring the team that conducted the raid on Osama bin Laden.

By participating in that event, the screenwriter was able to draw on information classified as *secret/noforn*.[22] "I hope they get Pacino to play [Leon Panetta]. That's what he wants, no joke!" wrote senior officials in the Public Affairs offices of the CIA and the Pentagon in their emails.[23] Instead of Al Pacino, another Italian American star was chosen: James Gandolfini. Bigelow's film would be sharply criticized for justifying forms of torture like waterboarding, sending the message that such torture was vital for

22. "Secret/noforn" means that the information is secret and not releasable to foreign nationals.
23. Inspector General, United States Department of Defense, available on the Project on Government Oversight website: www.pogo.org/investigation/2013/06/ unreleased-probe-finds-cia-honcho-disclosed-top-secret-info-to-hollywood (accessed July 12, 2022).

obtaining the information necessary to get to Bin Laden. This was simply not true.[24]

Things also turned out fine for General James E. Cartwright, considered Obama's favorite general. In 2013 he was involved in an investigation into the leak of classified information on use of the Stuxnet cyber weapon to sabotage Iran's nuclear program. U.S. prosecutors sought a two-year sentence, but in January 2017, the same day President Obama commuted Chelsea Manning's sentence, he pardoned Cartwright.[25] While Manning got out after seven years of military prison and two suicide attempts, Cartwright did not serve a single day in prison.

All went equally well for General David Howell Petraeus in 2015. Petraeus gave his biographer and lover, Paula Broadwell, eight notebooks he had filled during his service as ISAF mission commander in the war in Afghanistan. When the FBI questioned him, he denied having given her access to classified information.[26] But he had. He was charged and the indictment described the content of the eight notebooks as follows:[27] "classified information regarding the identities of covert officers, war strategy, intelligence capabilities and mechanisms, diplomatic discussions, quotes and deliberative discussions from high-level National Security Council meetings, and defendant DAVID HOWELL PETRAEUS's discussions with the President of the United States of America."

24. Glenn Greenwald, "Zero Dark Thirty: CIA hagiography, pernicious propaganda," *Guardian*, December 14, 2012; Jane Mayer, "Zero conscience in 'Zero Dark Thirty'," *The New Yorker*, December 14, 2012.
25. Savage, "Chelsea Manning to be released early as Obama commutes sentence"; Charlie Savage, "Obama pardons James Cartwright, general who lied to FBI in leak case," *New York Times*, January 17, 2017.
26. Michael S. Schmidt and Matt Apuzzo, "Petraeus reaches plea deal over giving classified data to his lover," *New York Times*, March 3, 2015.
27. The indictment of David H. Petraeus is available on the Federation of American Scientists website: https://sgp.fas.org/news/2015/03/petraeus.pdf (accessed May 12, 2022); "Statement from the Justice Department on the criminal charges against David Petraeus," U.S. Department of Justice, March 3, 2015: www.justice.gov/opa/pr/statement-justice-department-criminal-charges-against-david-petraeus (accessed May 12, 2022). Factual information on the case can be found in the "Factual Basis" filed in support of the Plea Agreement: www.justice.gov/sites/default/files/opa/press-releases/attachments/2015/03/03/petraeus-factual-basis.pdf (accessed May 12, 2022).

Although the notebooks contained this top-secret information as well as even more sensitive information, classified as *top secret/ sensitive compartmented information*, General Petraeus was never indicted for violating the Espionage Act. He reached a plea agreement with the U.S. Department of Justice and his sentence was very light: two years' probation and a 40,000 dollar fine.

"It demonstrates their lack of accountability," Julian Assange told[28] me in 2015, a few weeks after learning of Petraeus' plea bargain. He added: "It is part of the calculation of having power to project power, and one of the ways to project power is to show that you are unaccountable: we are untouchable, so don't try to touch us."

But despite their persecution of whistleblowers and their double standards, the Obama administration never went so far as to charge a journalist under the Espionage Act. They kept Assange and his WikiLeaks colleagues under investigation until 2010, but ultimately decided against indicting them. According to the *Washington Post*[29] in 2013, they refrained from doing so because they did not see how the U.S. Department of Justice could charge the founder of WikiLeaks without also indicting the *New York Times*, the *Washington Post* and all of us journalists who had published the same classified files in partnership with WikiLeaks. But the Trump administration decided that they could.

With the United States' extradition request and the reopening of the Swedish investigation, Assange risked never leaving prison again.

SOMETHING IS ROTTEN IN THE STATE OF SWEDEN

The handling of the rape case had been Kafkaesque ever since it was opened for the second time on September 1, 2010, then kept in the preliminary phase for a full seven years by prosecutor Marianne Ny, while never bringing charges against Julian Assange

---

28. Maurizi, "Julian Assange: 'I still enjoy crushing bastards'."
29. Sari Horwitz, "Julian Assange unlikely to face US charges over publishing classified documents," *Washington Post*, November 25, 2013.

or definitively clearing his name. And after the rape investigation had been reopened for the third time on May 13, 2019, coordinated by a new prosecutor, Eva-Marie Persson, it was closed again after six months, that time for good. It ended in the same Kafkaesque manner in which it had begun.

Scarcely two years had passed since then-prosecutor Ny dropped the investigation, blaming the lack of progress on Assange and his decision to take refuge in the embassy. Right after new prosecutor Eva-Marie Persson announced they would reopen the rape investigation for the third time, Swedish lawyer Elisabeth Massi Fritz, representing alleged victim Sofia W., declared: "My client feels great gratitude and she is very hopeful about getting restitution and we both hope that justice will win."[30] Since responsibility for the lack of progress was once again placed on Julian Assange's shoulders, I promptly contacted Massi Fritz to ask whether, in all those years of legal impasse, she had ever asked or encouraged former prosecutor Marianne Ny to question Assange in the Ecuadorian embassy. Sofia W.'s lawyer did not respond to my question.[31]

The statute of limitations on the alleged rape would expire August 17, 2020, so there was still plenty of time to charge the founder of WikiLeaks should Persson decide she had enough proof to put him on trial. Would the Swedes indict him, now that they had the chance to extradite him? At that point, Assange was in a high-security prison in London. If they had solid evidence, they could extradite him, put him on trial, and convict him for rape. Would they charge him this time? They did not; they dropped the investigation without even questioning him.

Right after the investigation was reopened, the Swedish Prosecution Authority contacted their British counterparts at the Crown Prosecution Service about possibly issuing a new European Arrest Warrant. "You will be aware of the new section 12 A of our law which makes it imperative that there is a decision to charge and

---

30. Reuters Staff, "Swedish lawyer urges prosecutor to move quickly in Assange investigation," Reuters, May 13, 2019.

31. The fact that Elisabeth Massi Fritz would not reply to my question was communicated to me by her secretary on May 14, 2019.

try a Requested Person in the Requesting state before an EAW [European Arrest Warrant] can succeed" replied[32] the Crown Prosecution Service to the Swedish Authority on May 21, 2019, adding: "If there is any suggestion that those decisions have not been made, or that JA cannot be brought to trial unless he is first interviewed, the Court will not order his surrender."

Between 2010 and 2012, when he was in British courts fighting his extradition to Sweden, Assange made every effort to contest the legitimacy of the European Arrest Warrant issued by Sweden without ever having charged him—only to question him—but lost every appeal. That his battle was well-grounded in law was demonstrated by the United Kingdom itself, when it changed its extradition regulations, introducing section 12 A. From that moment on, the UK no longer granted extradition of a suspect for questioning alone. But by then it was too late for Assange: he could not benefit from the new assurances. And the European Arrest Warrant, issued by Ny in 2010, became a sword of Damocles hanging over his head for seven long years.

Immediately after reopening the Swedish investigation, prosecutor Persson submitted an application for a detention order[33] against Julian Assange and indicated that if the court should decide to detain him, she would issue a new European Arrest Warrant for surrender of the WikiLeaks founder to Sweden. But the Uppsala Court rejected the request, noting that since Assange was already in prison in London, there was no need to request his detention.[34] The court found that the investigation could proceed with the help of a European Investigation Order, which would allow for Assange to be interviewed in London in cooperation with the British authorities. Prosecutor Persson announced that she would issue such an order and proceed with questioning. Of course this

---

32. Email from Alison Riley (Crown Prosecution Service) to Per Hedvall of the Swedish Prosecution Authority, dated May 21, 2019, 11:57. I obtained this email under FOIA from the Swedish Prosecution Authority.
33. "Request for detention of Julian Assange," Swedish Prosecution Authority, May 20, 2019: https://via.tt.se/pressmeddelande/request-for-detention-of-julian-assange?publisherId=3235540&releaseId=3257259 (accessed May 12, 2022).
34. Owen Bowcott, "Swedish court rejects request to detain Julian Assange," *Guardian*, June 3, 2019.

could have been done from the start; Assange had requested this solution ever since 2010, but Ny had refused to question him in London until November 2016. Now prosecutor Persson was expressing the intention to again question him in London. There was enough time to do so and send Assange to trial, if Persson felt she had enough evidence. Instead six months went by, and on November 19, 2019 the prosecutor dropped the investigation once and for all, without even questioning him.

After over nine years and three months, the Swedish case was definitively closed in the same absurd fashion in which it had always been handled: with justice for no one. With Assange's freedom lost in that far-off 2010 and never regained. And with his fate now hanging in the balance: he risked spending the rest of his days in a United States maximum-security prison.

Once again, the responsibility for the failed outcome of the investigation was shifted, albeit implicitly, onto him. In communicating her decision to discontinue the case, Persson took care to emphasize:[35] "the injured party has submitted a credible and reliable version of events. Her statements have been coherent, extensive and detailed; however, my overall assessment is that the evidential situation has been weakened to such an extent that that there is no longer any reason to continue the investigation." The cause was attributed to the long period of time that had elapsed since the events in question, after Assange chose to seek refuge in the embassy.

The handling of the Swedish investigation is filled with enigmas. But it is crystal clear that the case has played a decisive role in the prolonged and continuous demonization of Julian Assange, in depriving him of the empathy of global public opinion. Especially the empathy of that segment of the public which is more sensitive to revelations on war crimes and torture, often the same segment that coincides with those more mindful of women's rights.

---

35. "The investigation against Julian Assange is discontinued," Swedish Prosecution Authority, November 19, 2019: https://via.tt.se/pressmeddelande/the-investigation-against-julian-assange-is-discontinued?publisherId=3235541&releaseId=3265699 (accessed May 12, 2022).

Finally, the Swedish investigation played a crucial role in trapping Assange in London from 2010 onward, under the constant surveillance of Scotland Yard until his arrest by British authorities.

I am not the only one who finds the Swedish case replete with inconsistencies. The United Nations Special Rapporteur on Torture, Nils Melzer, whose mandate terminated in April 2022, has publicly flagged gross irregularities.[36]

A SPECIAL RAPPORTEUR

Courageous and independent, Nils Melzer took up the Julian Assange case just before the latter's arrest. At Christmas time in 2018, as the WikiLeaks founder was spending his last months in the embassy, Melzer was contacted by Assange's organization. His initial reaction, however, was to keep his distance. "When Julian Assange was still at the embassy in December 2018, his legal team actually reached out to my office. I remember it was just before Christmas, I saw this message pop up on my screen and I swiped it away immediately," he told[37] me, recalling how his perception of Julian Assange at that time was shaped by the media smear campaign: "I had this intuitive reaction: what does that guy want? He's a rapist, a narcissist, a hacker, this isn't serious, so I just discarded it," he explained.

It was when WikiLeaks sent him the medical opinion of U.S. doctor Sondra Crosby, professor of internal medicine at Boston University and a highly esteemed professional in the documentation of torture, that Melzer began to take the case seriously. He decided to visit Assange in Belmarsh prison, accompanied by two specialists: professor of forensic medicine Duarte Nuno Vieira and psychiatrist Pau Pérez-Sales. They were both experts with considerable experience in establishing the medical and psychological effects of torture and of inhumane and degrading treatment.

---

36. Melzer was UN Special Rapporteur on Torture from November 1, 2016 to March 2022.
37. Stefania Maurizi, "Assange, Nils Melzer says the treatment of Julian leaves him 'speechless'," *il Fatto Quotidiano*, April 17, 2021.

Melzer visited Julian Assange in May of 2019, just one month after his arrest. He found him in his single-occupancy 2 × 3 meter cell, 2.3 meters high, confined there "for about twenty hours a day." "Please save my life," said the founder of WikiLeaks.

The UN Special Rapporteur on Torture examined him for an hour, the forensic physician for another hour, then the psychiatrist gave him a two-hour assessment. Each of them prepared their analysis separately, to avoid influencing the others. "All three of us at the end compared our conclusions and agreed that he showed all the signs that are typical of victims of psychological torture. I must admit that I didn't expect such a clear result," Melzer told me.

Nils Melzer officially contacted[38] the four governments responsible for Julian Assange's condition: the United Kingdom, the United States, Sweden and Ecuador. "Assange," he wrote, "showed all symptoms typical for prolonged and sustained exposure to severe psychological stress, anxiety and related mental and emotional suffering in an environment highly conducive to major depressive and post-traumatic stress disorders."[39]

In his correspondence with the four governments, he expressed his "grave concern" both in relation to the fact that "starting from August 2010, Mr. Assange has been, and currently still is, exposed to progressively severe pain and suffering, inflicted through various forms and degrees of cruel, inhuman or degrading treatment or punishment, the cumulative effects of which clearly amount to psychological torture," and in relation to his risk of extradition to the United States.

Based on these assessments of Julian Assange's health, Nils Melzer set forth the responsibilities of the four countries in the persecution of the founder of WikiLeaks.

---

38.   The correspondence is available on the website of the UN OHCHR at the following link: https://spcommreports.ohchr.org/Tmsearch/TMDocuments. In particular, the letter sent to the United Kingdom authorities is available at: https://spcommreports.ohchr.org/TMResultsBase/DownLoadPublicCommunicationFile?gId=24631 (accessed May 12, 2022). Nils Melzer has also published a book on his investigation on the Assange case: *The trial of Julian Assange: A story of persecution* (London: Verso Books, 2022).
39.   Ibid.

In the case of Sweden, he contested the handling of the rape investigation point by point, specifying that he had been given access to the legal documentation. He listed fifty perceived due process violations,[40] including: "Proactive manipulation of evidence. According to evidence made available to me, once the alleged rape-case involving SW [Sofia W.] had been formally closed by the Chief prosecutor of Stockholm on 25 August 2010: On the following day, on 26 August 2010, police officer IK, who had formally questioned SW on 20 August 2010, modified and replaced the content of SW's original statement in the police database, upon instruction of her superior officer MG and without consulting SW."

After reading this and other astonishing contestations in Nils Melzer's report and book, I contacted the Swedish police to learn what had happened to SW's original statement. The Swedish police refused to provide a clear answer. I also asked Swedish prosecutor Persson why the text messages sent by the two women were not handed over to Assange's lawyers until 2019, when she opened the investigation for the third time. She replied:[41] "I don't know what considerations Marianne Ny made with regard to those text messages."

In his UN report, Melzer wrote: "Despite strong indications that the Swedish police and prosecution deliberately manipulated and pressured SW, who had come to the police station for an entirely different purpose, into making a statement which could be used to arrest Mr. Assange on the suspicion of rape, against SW's own will and her own interpretation of her experience, no investigation for abuse of function, coercion or false accusation seems to have been conducted, and no disciplinary or judicial sanctions imposed on the responsible officials."

After repeated attempts to call on the United Kingdom, the United States, Sweden and Ecuador to address his contentions

---

40. The letter to the Swedish government on the fifty alleged violations is available on the website of the UN OHCHR: https://spcommreports.ohchr.org/TMResultsBase/DownLoadPublicCommunicationFile?gId=24838 (accessed May 12, 2022).
41. Eva-Marie Persson, communication to author, April 29, 2022.

relative to their responsibilities in the Assange case, the UN Special Rapporteur on Torture was forced to acknowledge[42] that: "None of the four governments were willing to engage in a constructive dialogue. Instead, I was confronted with diplomatic platitudes or sweeping rhetorical attacks. When I insisted, the dialogue was terminated by the governments."

It was a brick wall I knew very well.

---

42.   Melzer, *The trial of Julian Assange.*

19
Only Kafka

THE TRIAL

I saw him again on February 24, 2020, shut inside a thick glass box in the Woolwich Crown Court, in London. The extradition hearing was set to begin at 10 o'clock in the morning. Judge Vanessa Baraitser, presiding over the court, was not called on to establish his innocence or guilt in relation to the United States' charges, but to decide whether to grant or deny his extradition to the U.S. for trial and, if found guilty, imprisonment. He risked 175 years in prison.

It was still dark at 5:45 when I began queuing outside for one of the seats reserved for journalists inside court 2. There were no more than thirty-four seats available in the courtroom and dozens of mainstream and independent reporters, from Australia to Germany, were covering the trial.

The darkness and freezing cold weather had not discouraged the supporters of Julian Assange and WikiLeaks. Adjacent to the massive green-painted iron fence encircling the court, along a small path lined with trees and bushes, an array of tents had been erected where supporters took shelter from the cold and the drizzle that tormented us from time to time in our queue. "Free Julian Assange! Jail the war criminals!" their banners and posters read. They were the only splashes of color in that depressing, yet threatening location.

The Woolwich Crown Court was situated in south-east London, alongside the maximum-security prison of Belmarsh where Assange was detained. The trials held in this court included trials for terrorism. There were no cabs in the area, and even finding a cup of coffee or a toilet was problematic.

At around 6 a.m., a team of Reporters Sans Frontières arrived on the scene, including Rebecca Vincent, director of international campaigns at the time, who would never thenceforth miss a hearing. At dawn, a long queue of reporters and supporters began to form. Later on Assange's father John Shipton arrived, as well as his brother Gabriel Shipton, who would soon launch an untiring campaign to free him. Then came Assange's fiancée and later wife Stella Moris, and WikiLeaks director Kristinn Hrafnsson, journalist Joseph Farrell, and Nathan Fuller, head of the Courage Foundation which Julian Assange also had helped to create to protect high-profile whistleblowers. Former British ambassador to Uzbekistan and author Craig Murray, who has always excoriated the British establishment for its treatment of Julian Assange, and American radio host and satirist Randy Credico, who broke the U.S. media's silence on the case, interviewing icons like Daniel Ellsberg and grassroots activists, were also present, as was American journalist Joe Lauria of Consortium News, who has always covered the case extensively. Then human rights activist Naomi Colvin, and hundreds of supporters. Over the years I have witnessed the dedication of activists who never missed a single court hearing, vigil, sit-in or protest: Emmy Butlin, Clara Campos and many others.[1]

After hours of waiting, we were finally admitted inside the courtroom. Assange was led into the court and made to take a seat inside a box, behind his lawyers. The thick glass walls of the box kept him isolated from everyone, especially his legal counsel, with whom he was unable to speak confidentially. Two guards sat inside the dock with him, one on each side.

I could see him quite well, because he was less than 5 meters away from me and occasionally turned in my direction. Clean-cut, but very thin, he looked stoical, his face showing no emotion. His white skin was now a greyish hue. Despite his stony expression, I could still read the look on his face. He was downcast, tense. He was definitely not doing well.

---

1.   I mention the names of some of these supporters in the Acknowledgments of this book.

In the extradition procedure from the United Kingdom, the U.S. authorities acted through the Crown Prosecution Service, as had already occurred with the extradition effort by Sweden. It was the same agency that had admitted to destroying the documents on the Swedish case and the same agency with which I have been engaged in an FOIA battle since 2015.

Representing the United States through the Crown Prosecution Service was barrister James Lewis, who most emphatically stressed that the trial of Julian Assange was not a matter of putting journalism on trial. Not at all.

The United States, Lewis argued, had not incriminated the founder of WikiLeaks for publishing files that revealed abuses by its troops or that embarrassed the government, but for disseminating classified documents that contained the names of sources and informants who had spoken with U.S. troops or diplomats, putting them at risk of being killed, tortured, or targeted for other forms of revenge. "The United States," he said[2] "is aware of sources that used unredacted names of or other identifying information that was contained in classified documents published by WikiLeaks who subsequently disappeared; although the United States cannot prove at this point that their disappearance was a result of being outed by WikiLeaks."

If they could not prove it, why bring it up in the hearing before the judge?

For ten years, U.S. authorities had been accusing WikiLeaks of "having blood on their hands." Ever since 2010 when the documents were disseminated, the authorities had never been able to name a single individual killed, wounded, tortured or incarcerated as a result of those publications. And not because they had not gone looking for one.

The revelations of Julian Assange and WikiLeaks have been examined and studied by the CIA, the Pentagon, the U.S. intelligence community and secret services of the entire world. I think it is no exaggeration to state that WikiLeaks' publications have been

2. Stefania Maurizi, "Julian Assange is the defendant, journalism is under trial," *il Fatto Quotidiano*, March 2, 2022.

pored over and scrutinized more than those of any other journalistic organization ever. In 2013, during the court martial trial of Chelsea Manning, the head of the Pentagon task force assigned to investigate the consequences of the WikiLeaks revelations, Robert Carr, testified that he had never come across a single example of an individual killed as a result of those publications. As I write, not a single such victim has ever surfaced.

How grotesque that a power whose war in Iraq alone had resulted in hundreds of thousands of innocent deaths and 9.2 million refugees was putting on trial a journalist not known to have caused a single death, and seeking to bury him in prison forever. Only Franz Kafka in *The Trial* could really express how outrageous, how mind-boggling, how absurd it was.

And if the U.S. authorities were really so concerned, why did they not help WikiLeaks keep the risk to a minimum, in 2010 and 2011, when Assange repeatedly asked for their help? They normally cooperate with journalistic organizations when they believe that publication of certain information may put someone in danger. They had done so with the *New York Times:* indeed, the powerful daily had actually held daily video conferences with U.S. diplomacy specialists while publishing the cables, according to then-director Bill Keller.[3]

The extremely few documents I have received through my FOIA litigation against the U.S. State Department showed that Julian Assange had contacted the department on at least two occasions: November 26, 2010, two days before WikiLeaks began publishing the cables, and in August 2011, when the entire database with the unredacted names was about to be published and I myself, at Ellingham Hall, was witness to the attempted phone calls.

"Dear Ambassador Susman," Julian Assange wrote[4] to the American embassy in London two days before WikiLeaks began

---

3. Bill Keller wrote about those meetings in the introduction to the book: *Open secrets: WikiLeaks, war and American diplomacy*, by New York Times Staff (New York: Grove Press, 2011).

4. Letter from Julian Assange to the U.S. Ambassador to the United Kingdom, Louis B. Susman, dated 26 November 2010. I obtained a copy through my FOIA litigation against the U.S. State Department.

releasing the U.S. diplomacy cables: "WikiLeaks would be grateful for the United States Government to privately nominate any specific instances (record numbers or names) where it considers the publication of information would put individual persons at significant risk of harm that has not already been addressed. WikiLeaks will respect the confidentiality of advice provided by the United States Government and is prepared to consider any such submissions made without delay."

The U.S. Department of State replied as follows: "We will not engage in a negotiation regarding the further release or dissemination of illegally obtained U.S. Government classified materials. If you are genuinely interested in seeking to stop the damage from your actions, you should: 1) ensure WikiLeaks ceases publishing any and all such materials; 2) ensure WikiLeaks returns any and all classified U.S. Government material in its possession; and 3) remove and destroy all records of this material from WikiLeaks' databases."

While U.S. authorities were unwilling to cooperate with Julian Assange and WikiLeaks, they kept the doors fully open for media partners like the *New York Times* and the *Guardian*. An internal U.S. State Department email[5] I have obtained through my FOIA litigation in the United States, in which I am represented by the excellent lawyers Lauren Russell and Alia Smith, chronicles a meeting between the U.S. authorities and the *Guardian*. It was a face-to-face, off-the-record conversation between U.S. diplomats and *Guardian* editors Ian Katz, David Leigh and Jan Thompson. It took place on November 24, 2010, just two days before the U.S. told WikiLeaks it would not engage in negotiation. Going by the email's content, the editors said "they will only focus on a small area of information," though "they are not prepared to tell us explicitly what they are working on."

---

5. Email from redacted Sender to Philip J. Crowley and Dana S. Smith copied to Louis Susman, Elizabeth L. Dibble, Barbara J. Stephenson and other redacted recipients, dated November 24, 2010, 18:30. I obtained it through my FOIA litigation against the U.S. State Department.

At no point during that meeting did the U.S. authorities ask the British daily not to publish the cables, cease publications, return or remove them from the *Guardian* website, as they insisted that Julian Assange should. David Leigh even told the U.S. diplomats that he believed "WikiLeaks is interested in a direct conversation with senior USG [U.S. government] officials about the data."

While the U.S. authorities' reply to Julian Assange was blunt and confrontational, their meeting with the *Guardian* appeared to have been quite relaxed. The email notes that the "editors praised the high quality of drafting and analysis and were fascinated with State channels of reporting, especially the 'dissent channel'. They joked that they were struck **not** [emphasis in original] to find evidence of coup plotting in Central America." The email describing the off-the-record meeting ends with the following comment: "They [the *Guardian* editors] came away with an admiration of what American diplomats do around the world. Of course they also noted any American diplomats who lost their jobs as a result of these WikiLeaks were welcome to apply to work as journalists for the *Guardian*."

So the Department of State had put themselves at the disposal of the *New York Times*, providing them with all kinds of instructions, and held at least one off-the-record meeting with the *Guardian* editors, but refused to cooperate in any way with Julian Assange. Why was that? Was it because from the legal standpoint cooperating with Assange and the WikiLeaks journalists would have made it more problematic to indict them for their publications later on? Or did they just want to deny him and WikiLeaks any assistance and then, if someone later wound up dead, cry that they had "blood on their hands"?

All we know for sure is that in the over one-hour phone call on August 26, 2011, one week before the cables were published unredacted, Julian Assange and WikiLeaks offered their full cooperation, showing their complete readiness to work with the Department of State to minimize the risk, while the U.S. authorities were not in the least interested.

As the extradition proceeding went forward that day, the sound of Assange's supporters chanting slogans outside grew so loud that they could easily be heard through the thick walls of the Woolwich Crown Court. It got to the point that Julian Assange, though expressing his gratitude to his supporters for coming so far, told the judge that he was unable to follow the proceedings because of the noise. There was a delegation of *gilets jaunes*, there were pacifist groups like the Stop the War Coalition, internet activists as well as activists for press freedom. Even the iconic fashion designer Vivienne Westwood had come to show her support for WikiLeaks' founder outside the Woolwich Crown Court. "It is not a crime to publish American war crimes," she declared[6] to the press outside the court, adding: "It's in the public interest, it is democracy, that he is allowed to do this. I feel really worried and frightened actually, really frightened."

After the first week of hearings, the extradition procedure was scheduled to resume in May, but then the unforeseeable happened. A pandemic changed the world.

HE REMAINED IN BELMARSH

He had no sentence to serve, because he had already served the fifty-week sentence for breaching his bail conditions, but Julian Assange remained in prison. Despite the pandemic. Thus ruled Judge Vanessa Baraitser, deeming his flight risk well-founded, should he be released under house arrest.

He remained in Belmarsh even though he was technically innocent before British law, and even though he had never committed a violent crime in his life. Even though he suffered from a chronic lung disease, severe depression and post-traumatic stress disorder. Even though the United Nations Working Group on Arbitrary Detention had repeatedly called for his release, after the UN Special Rapporteur on Torture, Nils Melzer, had observed all the symptoms of psychological torture, and 117 physicians from

---

6. Ben Quinn, "Amid the din, Julian Assange struggles to hear case against him," *Guardian*, February 24, 2020.

around the world, the "Doctors for Assange," had written a letter[7] to the medical journal *The Lancet* with a call "to end the torture of Assange and ensure his access to the best available health care before it is too late."

In an attempt to obtain his release, in April 2020 Stella Moris had revealed in an interview with the *Daily Mail* that she was Julian Assange's partner, and that they had two small children, Gabriel and Max. With the pandemic, they could not even visit him in prison any more, and Moris feared both that Assange could catch Covid, and that his isolation would have a devastating effect on his mental health.

Her statements[8] to the Woolwich Crown Court shed some light on Assange's condition. "The most difficult time in Belmarsh was in the months when in the Healthcare unit, he was in effective solitary confinement for most of the time. He finds isolation and its prospect terrifying," wrote Stella in her statement to the judge, describing how she had observed him on different occasions when he was in the embassy and "how he struggled with physical crises as well as mental." At Belmarsh, things got worse and worse: "When in the Healthcare unit," Moris stated, "he was taken from a ward into a single cell for many months in a form of isolation save for a very few hours each day. I noticed how he, as I described at the time, was visibly 'very diminished … like a withering flower'. I observed how he could no longer function coherently."

But nothing convinced Judge Baraitser to grant his release.

Similarly alarming news was coming out of the United States.

On March 11 2020, Chelsea Manning attempted suicide for the third time, following her incarceration in May of the preceding year for refusing to testify before the Grand Jury that had indicted Assange. Only the day after her third attempt did Judge Anthony

---

7.   Stephen Frost, Lissa Johnson, Jill Stein, William Frost on behalf of 117 signatories, "End torture and medical neglect of Julian Assange," *The Lancet*, February 2020, accessed May 13, 2022: www.thelancet.com/journals/lancet/article/PIIS0140-6736(20)30383-4/fulltext

8.   Stefania Maurizi, "Assange's partner and previously undisclosed documents reveal the grim conditions of the WikiLeaks founder," *il Fatto Quotidiano*, April 16, 2020.

Trenga order her release and payment of a 256,000 dollar fine levied in response to her refusal.[9]

On June 24, on the other hand, the Grand Jury issued a new indictment against Assange, which replaced the preceding indictment of May 2019. In the thick of the extradition proceedings, with the pandemic in full swing and Assange's lawyers facing tremendous difficulties in communicating with their client in Belmarsh, they changed the indictment against him.

CHANGING THE GAME

With the new superseding indictment,[10] the charges remained the same. No additional charges were added and the founder of WikiLeaks continued to risk a maximum sentence of 175 years, but the conspiracy to commit computer intrusion was expanded to include certain *conduct* that had allegedly transpired between 2010 and 2015. It was no longer conduct with regard to Chelsea Manning alone, and the accusation of agreeing to help her crack a password hash, it also included alleged conspiracy with hackers from Anonymous, Lulzsec, Antisec and Gnosis from 2010 to 2012, and political speeches given at public conferences between 2013 and 2015, interpreted by U.S. authorities as efforts to recruit hackers and whistleblowers to illegally extract documents to forward to WikiLeaks.

Between 2010 and 2012, the FBI had conducted extremely aggressive investigations into Anonymous, Lulzsec, Antisec and Gnosis. The investigations, controversial for their use of an informant, Hector Xavier Monsegur, called "Sabu," had led to the arrest, among others, of respected political activist Jeremy Hammond.

In 2013, Hammond was sentenced to ten years in prison for hacking the internal emails of the private U.S. intelligence firm

---

9. Charlie Savage, "Chelsea Manning is ordered released from jail," *New York Times*, March 12, 2020. The order by Judge Trenga is available at: https://int.nyt.com/data/documenthelper/6814-chelsea-manning-ordered-releas/3f24b02368918f605 24b/optimized/full.pdf#page=1 (accessed May 13, 2022).

10. The second superseding indictment was issued on June 24, 2020; it is available on the website of the U.S. Department of Justice: www.justice.gov/opa/pr/wikileaks-founder-charged-superseding-indictment (accessed May 13, 2022).

Stratfor. WikiLeaks had published the Stratfor files together with us media partners. These documents had revealed, among other things, that Stratfor monitored activists seeking justice from Dow Chemical, the parent company of Union Carbide. The U.S. multinational chemical corporation Union Carbide owned the pesticide plant at the center of one of the worst industrial accidents in history, that of Bhopal, in India, in 1984, which killed thousands of extremely poor Indians. Jeremy Hammond claimed that he did not even know what Stratfor was until FBI informant "Sabu" put the company on his radar. "Practically, I would never have done the Stratfor hack without Sabu's involvement," he stated.[11]

Despite having thoroughly investigated these matters, the FBI had never indicted Julian Assange and WikiLeaks in connection with them. And as early as 2012, the use of "Sabu" to entrap Hammond had immediately appeared as an attempt to implicate WikiLeaks in some sort of shady matter.

Now, almost ten years later, the investigation was being brought up again. "The allegations added in the newest indictment appear to be a gratuitous attempt to paint Mr. Assange as a 'hacker' or someone who associates with 'hackers' rather than a journalist," Barry Pollack told me a few days after U.S. authorities announced the new indictment, in the middle of the extradition proceeding and the midst of the pandemic.[12] A highly respected American lawyer who has represented Julian Assange in the United States for many years, Pollack added: "The effort amounts to nothing more than window dressing. The charges have not changed. Mr. Assange is charged as a result of newsgathering and publication of truthful, newsworthy [information]. Efforts to paint Mr. Assange as something other than a journalist cannot hide the fact that Mr. Assange is being charged for his activities as a journalist. These charges are a threat to journalists everywhere and to the public's right to know."

---

11.   Ed Pilkington, "Jailed Anonymous hacker Jeremy Hammond: 'My days of hacking are done'," *Guardian*, November 15, 2013.
12.   Stefania Maurizi, "Assange non fa più notizia e gli Usa ne approfittano," *il Fatto Quotidiano*, June 28, 2020.

In an effort to support their allegations of conspiracy to commit computer intrusion, U.S. authorities sought to force not only Chelsea Manning to testify before the Grand Jury, but Jeremy Hammond as well. Hammond refused, and in October 2019, instead of being freed within two months as he should have been, having served his sentence, he was left in jail.

The new indictment of Julian Assange was based on two known FBI informants: Sabu and Icelandic Sigurdur Thordarson, also known as "Siggi." U.S. authorities accused the founder of WikiLeaks of asking Thordarson to commit computer intrusion, based on statements made by the informant.

I did not know Thordarson: I had heard of him only marginally, as a volunteer who had carried out some minor tasks for WikiLeaks. Then in 2013 the organization announced[13] that they had reported him to the Icelandic police, accusing him of embezzling 50,000 dollars from WikiLeaks. A few months later *Wired* magazine, certainly not a fan of Assange's organization, reported[14] that Thordarson had become an FBI informant in 2011 and immediately characterized him as a person "prone to lying," who had in the past lied to the *Wired* reporter himself, the same Kevin Poulsen who had revealed the arrest of Chelsea Manning, ensnared by FBI informant Adrian Lamo. The magazine also wrote that Siggi had provided them with "a substantial subset" of the organization's internal chats and that he had given eight hard drives to the FBI.

Various press articles reported in 2015 that Sigurdur Thordarson had been found guilty of sexual abuse against nine minors aged between 15 and 17 years old, and that a psychiatrist summoned to testify on his case concluded that he was affected by a personality disorder such that "while Thordarson was capable of discerning right from wrong, he was a sociopath and incapable of genuinely expressing guilt for his actions."[15]

---

13. In 2013 WikiLeaks released a press release on the Icelandic volunteer available on the WikiLeaks website: https://wikileaks.org/Eight-FBI-agents-conduct.html (accessed May 13, 2022).

14. Kevin Poulsen, "WikiLeaks volunteer was a paid informant for the FBI," *Wired*, June 27, 2013.

15. Dell Cameron, "FBI's WikiLeaks informant sentenced to 3 years for sex with underage boys," *Daily Dot*, September 25, 2015; Sunna Karen Sigurþórsdóttir,

In order to question Thorardson, in 2011 the FBI had flown to Iceland, a country where WikiLeaks enjoyed a good reputation thanks to its revelations two years earlier regarding the Kaupthing bank, the institution at the epicenter of the scandal that had brought the country[16] to financial collapse. Officially, the FBI agents had gone there to investigate an imminent hacking attack on government facilities, but when the Icelandic authorities realized that the real purpose of the investigation was to question Thordarson and investigate WikiLeaks, they terminated their cooperation. The Minister of the Interior at the time, Ögmundur Jónasson, ordered Icelandic police not to participate in the FBI operation. The FBI continued to question Thordarson on Icelandic soil without the judicial cooperation of the country's police, per official communication from the Reykjavík authorities themselves.[17]

According to media reports, in the course of his collaboration with the FBI, Thorardson had asked for money, but apparently the bureau limited itself to compensating him 5,000 dollars for missed work. That the FBI would rely on an individual as problematic as Siggi—a key witness behind the new indictment—affords a measure of where the U.S. authorities were willing to go to put Assange in prison. These methods risk backfiring on the U.S. authorities, however; a year after the U.S. Department of Justice announced the new indictment, journalists with Icelandic magazine *Stundin* reported that Sigurdur Thordarson, in an interview[18] with them, "admitted to fabricating key accusations in the indictment against the WikiLeaks founder." *Stundin* reported that: "He also admits that he stole documents from WikiLeaks staff by copying their hard drives. Among those were documents from Renata Avila, a lawyer who worked for the organization and Mr. Assange."

"Dómurinn yfir Sigga hakkara: Bauð unglingspiltum allt að 100 milljónir, bíla og einbýlishús," *Visir*, September 25, 2015.
16. The files on Kaupthing bank are publicly available on the WikiLeaks website: https://wikileaks.org/wiki/Category:Kaupthing_Bank (accessed May 13, 2022); Simon Bowers, "Confidential Kaupthing corporate loan details leaked on the internet," *Guardian*, August 4, 2009.
17. The Icelandic authorities issued a press release: www.rikissaksoknari.is/umembaettid/frettir/nr/54 (accessed May 13, 2022).
18. Bjartmar Oddur Þeyr Alexandersson and Gunnar Hrafn Jónsson, "Key witness in Assange case admits to lies in indictment," *Stundin*, June 26, 2021.

Additionally, the superseding indictment issued in June 2020 criminalized political speeches given by Assange as well as by former WikiLeaks journalist Sarah Harrison and by American journalist and computer security expert Jake Appelbaum.

Those speeches, offered during public conferences, humorous and provocative in tone, with titles like "Sysadmins of the World, Unite!," were included by U.S. authorities in the allegation of conspiracy to commit computer intrusion, interpreted as the recruitment of sources and incitement to steal classified documents. The help given to Edward Snowden by Julian Assange, Sarah Harrison and WikiLeaks was also interpreted in this criminal conspiracy key: "To encourage leakers and hackers to provide stolen materials to WikiLeaks in the future, Assange and others at WikiLeaks openly displayed their attempts to assist Snowden in evading arrest."

The new indictment cited Sarah Harrison, Jacob Appelbaum and even Daniel Domscheit-Berg, though unlike Julian Assange, they were not indicted.

The extradition proceeding resumed September 7, 2020. The Trump administration, which had for the first time in U.S. history charged a journalist under the Espionage Act, was coming to an end. The U.S. presidential election was less than two months away. The U.S. administration changed, but Julian Assange remained in Belmarsh.

THE WITNESSES

I could not fly to London to attend the hearings in the courtroom this time, owing to the pandemic. Like all other journalists, I had to follow the trial via video-conference, amidst technical problems and incomprehensible decisions by the court. Like the decision to deny Amnesty International—which in February had sent Julia Hall, a highly experienced expert on human rights abuses during the war on terror—the opportunity to monitor the hearings.[19]

---

19. "UK: Lack of access to Julian Assange extradition hearing undermines open justice," Amnesty International, September 17, 2020: www.amnesty.org/en/documents/eur45/3076/2020/en/ (accessed May 13, 2022).

Julian Assange's defense argued that the case was politically motivated, citing the Trump administration's aggressive assertions against Assange, and its choice to charge Assange when Obama, by contrast—despite the Grand Jury's perpetual investigation— had not. This because, according to the *Washington Post*, Obama could not find a way to indict him without prosecuting the *New York Times* as well and all the other newspapers that had published the same revelations. The defense also maintained that the indictment of Assange was part of Trump's war against journalists and whistleblowers. U.S. lawyer Carey Shenkman[20] testified that while the Obama administration had indeed embarked on the path of prosecuting sources and whistleblowers under the Espionage Act, indicting eight of them during Barack Obama's two presidential terms, their prosecution on Trump's part was even more aggressive. "The US president is on track to exceed the number of Espionage Act cases brought under Barack Obama's two terms in less than four years" stated Shenkman. Among the whistleblowers charged under Trump were Reality Winner and Daniel Hale, who exposed the brutality of drone killings in which "sometimes nine out of 10 people killed are innocent."[21]

Some of the most important testimony on political interference in the case came from the protected witnesses who had been employed by UC Global and who described the spying activities allegedly performed on behalf of U.S. intelligence, and from barrister Jennifer Robinson, who has represented Assange since 2010. In her statement, Robinson reported that U.S. Congressman Dana Rohrabacher[22] had visited Assange in the Ecuadorian embassy in August 2017, and that Robinson had been asked to be present. "The proposal put forward by Congressman Rohrabacher was that Mr Assange identified the source for the 2016 Elections publications in return for some form of pardon, assurance or agreement

20.   Press Association, "US Espionage Act prosecutions jump under Trump, Assange extradition trial hears," *PressGazette*, September 17, 2020.
21.   Ryan Devereaux and Murtaza Hussain, "Daniel Hale sentenced to 45 months in prison for drone leak," *The Intercept*, July 27, 2021.
22.   Witness statement by Jennifer Robinson submitted to the Westminster Magistrates' Court in the extradition hearing of Julian Assange.

which would both benefit President Trump politically and prevent
US indictment and extradition [of Julian Assange]."

When the backstory became public,[23] the U.S. politician cate-
gorically denied that the president had had anything to do with it,
insisting that it had been his own initiative. In any event, Robinson
testified that "Mr. Assange did not provide any source of information to the Congressman." Four months after the meeting, in
December 2017, the founder of WikiLeaks was charged by the
Trump administration.

Experts like renowned journalism professor Mark Feldstein
from the University of Maryland, co-founder of the American
Freedom of the Press Foundation Trevor Timm, and prominent
New Zealand investigative journalist Nicky Hager testified that
the alleged interactions between Chelsea Manning and Julian
Assange, in which the latter, according to U.S. authorities, solicited classified documents rather than simply passively receiving
them, were normal journalistic practice. And that characterizing
such interactions as criminal conspiracy meant criminalizing journalism. "Good reporters don't sit around waiting for someone to
leak information, they actively solicit it," testified[24] Professor Feldstein, adding: "When I was a reporter, I personally solicited and
received confidential or classified information, hundreds of times.
Like Assange, I was actively 'complicit' in gathering secret records
from government employees."

While U.S. authorities accused Julian Assange and WikiLeaks
of dumping classified documents on the internet without both-
ering to protect those mentioned in the files, in our testimony
I myself and investigative journalist John Goetz, who in 2010
worked for the weekly *Der Spiegel* and who now works for German
state broadcaster NDR, went over all the work done on the mate-

23.   Peter Beaumont, "Trump 'associates' offered Assange pardon in return for emails
source, court hears", *The Guardian*, September 18, 2020.
24.   A summarized version of Professor Feldman's witness statement is available
in: *The Government of the US of America-v-Julian Paul Assange*, Consolidated Annex:
www.judiciary.uk/wp-content/uploads/2021/01/USA-v-Assange-annex-040121.pdf
(accessed May 7, 2022).

rials by WikiLeaks and its media partners. Goetz explained[25] that during publication of the diplomatic cables: "At Der Spiegel we had a conference call with a number of officials from the Department of State, including PJ Crowley.[26] They actually read numbers to us of documents they felt were sensitive, with the understanding that we would give these numbers to WikiLeaks to properly redact the documents. WikiLeaks did exactly that when requested."

Both John Goetz and I[27] testified that the cables had made it possible for us to prove that the United States intervened to ensure impunity for the CIA agents responsible for extraordinary renditions: in my case, that of Abu Omar, in Goetz's case, that of German citizen Khaled el-Masri.

Additional testimony on the shaky and contradictory foundation of the judicial case against WikiLeaks came from New York-based John Young, member of the Cypherpunks and founder of the Cryptome website whose motto is "Unauthorized disclosures of official secrets are essential for democracy."

On September 1, 2011, Young had published the entire database of unredacted cables on his website. WikiLeaks re-published the entire archive the very next day. "Since my publication on Cryptome. org of the unredacted diplomatic cables," testified[28] Young, "no US law enforcement authority has notified me that this publication of the cables is illegal, consists or contributes to a crime in any way, nor have they asked for them to be removed." So while Julian Assange and his organization had been drawn into a decade-long criminal investigation for publications like the cables, Cryptome, which disseminated exactly the same classified materials, had never been disturbed by even a phone call from U.S. authorities.

---

25. A summarized version of John Goetz's witness statement is available in: *The Government of the US of America-v-Julian Paul Assange*, Consolidated Annex: www. judiciary.uk/wp-content/uploads/2021/01/USA-v-Assange-annex-040121.pdf (accessed May 7, 2022).
26. At the time, P.J. Crowley was spokesman for the Department of State: he resigned after defining the treatment of Chelsea Manning as "counterproductive and stupid."
27. A summarized version of my witness statement is available in: *The Government of the US of America-v-Julian Paul Assange*, Consolidated Annex. www.judiciary.uk/ wp-content/uploads/2021/01/USA-v-Assange-annex-040121.pdf (accessed May 7, 2022).
28. Ibid.

Legally speaking, what justified this difference in treatment? Why did the U.S. authorities charge an Australian journalist, but not the founder, owner and administrator of Cryptome, who is a citizen of the United States, residing in New York?

During the trial, the testimony that made the strongest impression came from victims like Khaled el-Masri, who was kidnapped at the Macedonian border where he was traveling by bus. He was brutally beaten, sodomized, chained, hooded and subjected to total sensory deprivation. "Those actions were only the beginning," recalled[29] el-Masri. Though rendered in writing, his testimony conveyed the trauma which, almost twenty years later, was still consuming him. El-Masri was transferred to a prison in Afghanistan, kept in solitary confinement, interrogated continuously, beaten, held in a freezing cold cement cell. In the winter, in Afghanistan. He had just one thin, dirty blanket, and a bucket for a toilet. After thirty-four days of refusing to eat, he was taken out of his cell, strapped to a chair, and a feeding tube painfully forced through his nose. "I much later discovered that by this time," el-Masri related, "the CIA knew that my detention was the result of 'mistaken identity' and that I should be released. I was nevertheless held for several more months." He was released with the warning to never speak of what had happened with anyone. "There would be consequences if I spoke," el-Masri recalled.

The problem was finding the proof. Macedonia denied being aware of what had happened, and the United States was not willing to provide any information. "I had a long struggle to expose even the most basic facts about my case," he explained, retracing all the secrecy barriers that had hindered arriving at the truth. He added: "other incidents caused me fear, being suddenly blocked on the motorway by cars, unknown strangers approaching my children, my complaints to the police leading to their attempting to section me in a hospital for the mentally ill. I was violently restrained."

Khaled el-Masri explained that it was only thanks to the help of journalists like John Goetz, who had worked on WikiLeaks documents, as well as investigators and lawyers expert in human rights violations, that "I was able to slowly build up my credibility and gather evidence to support my story."

The cables made it possible to discover and document how the German government had yielded to U.S. pressure not to extradite the CIA team responsible for the rendition. And they revealed that the U.S. authorities interfered in the investigation in order to block it. Thanks to those documents, Khaled el-Masri was able to support his appeal to the European Court of Human Rights backed by official documentation. In his testimony, Goetz confirmed that "Without publication of information that the US Government intended to be kept secret for national security reasons, the entire truth would still be buried. Because it was only when reading the diplomatic cables that we saw the role the US Government was playing behind the scenes." Just like the pressure the United States had applied to Italian governments to make sure the CIA agents responsible for the *extraordinary rendition* of Abu Omar never had to answer for their crimes. Without the cables, this pressure would have remained buried forever.

The cases of el-Masri and Omar were only two examples of how state secrecy was used by the U.S. and its allies not to protect the safety of citizens, but to cover atrocities and ensure complete impunity for those with the institutions who commit them.

Equally powerful was the testimony from Dean Yates, head of the Reuters office in Baghdad back when a photographer and his assistant were killed by the Apache helicopter shown in *Collateral Murder*. And that of lawyer Clive Stafford Smith, founder of the human rights organization Reprieve and one of the attorneys who helped secure *habeas corpus* for detainees in Guantanamo. Stafford Smith detailed, among other things, how the cables had made it possible to acquire crucial information on a war kept completely secret: the drone war. He explained:[30] "One of my motivations for working on these cases was that the U.S. drone campaign appeared to be horribly mismanaged and was resulting in paid informants giving false information about innocent people who were then killed in strikes."

---

30.   Ibid.

During a public speech he gave in Pakistan, the attorney told the court, he told those present that in their midst there were probably one or two informants on the CIA payroll who would pass information to the CIA regarding individuals to be targeted. Stafford Smith later learned that not only was what he had said true, but that one informant at that meeting made a false statement against a teenager in the audience, who was killed by a drone together with his cousin three days later. "It is, of course, much safer for any informant to make a statement about someone who is a 'nobody', than someone who is genuinely dangerous," explained Stafford Smith, testifying how the cables had been crucial in seeking factual information to bring before Pakistan courts in pursuit of justice for innocent victims. "The result of this litigation is that the drone strikes, which were in their hundreds and causing many of innocent deaths, stopped very rapidly. There were none reported that I know of in 2019."

Professor Noam Chomsky, on the other hand, gave a brilliant analysis of secret power:[31] "Julian Assange's actions, which have been categorized as criminal, are actions that expose power to sunlight—actions that may cause power to evaporate if the population grasps the opportunity to become independent citizens of a free society rather than subjects of a master who operates in secret." Chomsky continued: "Anyone who has pored through the archives of released documents has surely come to realise pretty quickly that what is kept secret very rarely has anything at all to do with security, except for the security of the leadership from their domestic enemy, their own population."

This was markedly the case with the U.S. government documents published by WikiLeaks for which Assange had been indicted. They were not the kind of secrets that serve to protect the security of a nuclear plant or facilities which, if revealed, may put the public in danger; they were secrets that served to cover up state crimes or facts and conversations embarrassing to the U.S. government and its allies.[32]

---

31. Ibid.
32. An interesting reading on the difference between secrets protecting citizens' security and secrets protecting embarrassing or criminal revelations: Hugh Gusterson, "Not all secrets are alike," *Bulletin of the Atomic Scientists*, July 23, 2013.

The most powerful testimony of all came from Daniel Ellsberg. I was not able to hear his deposition myself, because per standard practice the U.S. authorities asked the judge to bar me from watching the extradition hearing as my own testimony was approaching. But the intellectual caliber and moral fiber of the Pentagon Papers whistleblower shone through in the media reports. Ellsberg repelled the attempts of James Lewis, representing the U.S. government, to draw a line between his revelations and those of WikiLeaks. As reported by the highly respected U.S. journalist Kevin Gosztola,[33] Lewis stated: "When you published the Pentagon Papers, you were very careful in what you provided to the media." Implying that whereas Ellsberg had carefully chosen the files to avoid putting those mentioned in the documents at risk, Assange had dumped everything on the internet indiscriminately.

The whistleblower replied that the materials he had kept for himself had nothing to do with keeping certain names from the public, and that he, like Assange, wanted the public to have access to the full documents, without alterations. Ellsberg also added that the founder of WikiLeaks had in fact taken precautions in the past, such as not publishing 15,000 classified files on the war in Afghanistan, or asking the Department of State and the Pentagon to help minimize the risks, but the U.S. authorities had refused to do so. "Is it your position there was absolutely no danger caused by publishing the unredacted names of these informants?" asked Lewis. Ellsberg responded that the U.S. government was "extremely cynical in pretending it's concerned for these people," and that in ten years he had not learned of a single such victim.

The extradition proceeding concluded on October 1, one month before the U.S. presidential elections. Judge Vanessa Baraitser would issue her ruling on January 4, 2021, after the new president of the United States, Joe Biden, had been elected. In the meantime, Julian Assange would remain in prison, in the midst of a pandemic and regardless of his poor health.

---

33. Kevin Gosztola, "Good Ellsberg, bad Assange: at extradition trial, Pentagon Papers whistleblower dismantles false narrative," *ShadowProof*, September 18, 2020.

20
A Monstrous Injustice

THE CRUELTY OF AMERICAN AND BRITISH JUSTICE

On the morning of January 4, 2021, as Judge Baraitser began reading out her decision, the situation struck everyone as desperate.

She rejected all of the defense's arguments. She rejected that the case was a political one. She dismissed the arguments of forensic expert Patrick Eller—who had cast doubt on the allegations that Assange had agreed to help Chelsea Manning crack a password hash—as "an alternative narrative to the allegations," concluding that in any case "the issues they raise are matters to be determined at a trial" in the United States, if Assange is extradited.

She rejected the press freedom arguments, affirming that "Free speech does not comprise a 'trump card' even where matters of serious public concern are disclosed," and referred to the WikiLeaks publications as "indiscriminate disclosure of all of the data." Statements by journalists and experts like Professor Mark Feldstein, Trevor Timm, and Nicky Hager highlighting the press freedom concerns posed by the incrimination of Julian Assange, and testimony by media partners like John Goetz and myself on the meticulous journalistic work behind the publication of U.S. documents by ourselves and WikiLeaks, appeared to be of no relevance to the judge.

Even the testimony from the two anonymous witnesses that UC Global had spied on Julian Assange and his lawyer on behalf of U.S. intelligence, and even discussed plans to poison or kidnap him, was dismissed by the judge, because "this allegation is currently under investigation by the Spanish High Court, the Audiencia Nacional," hence "it would be inappropriate for this court to make findings of fact on allegations still being investigated in Spain."

That morning, one by one, all the barriers to extradition fell like ninepins. Emaciated, in a dark blue suit and tie and a Covid mask covering his face, the founder of WikiLeaks listened stoically to Judge Baraitser as she read out the verdict, betrayed only by the wringing of his hands.[1]

Then came the decision that no one was expecting.[2] "I find that the mental condition of Mr. Assange is such that it would be oppressive to extradite him to the United States of America," said the judge.

Baraitser denied extradition solely and exclusively on the grounds of the dramatic deterioration in his physical and mental health. The psychiatric assessments, filed during the trial and cited in the ruling, detailed this decline in all its bleakness.

Michael Kopelman, emeritus professor of neuropsychiatry at King's College, had described Assange's condition in December 2019: "loss of sleep, loss of weight, impaired concentration, a feeling of often being on the verge of tears, and a state of acute agitation in which he was pacing his cell until exhausted, punching his head or banging it against a cell wall."[3] Julian Assange "reported suicidal ideas during this period, telling Professor Kopelman that life was not worth living, that he had been thinking about suicide 'hundreds of times a day', and had a 'constant desire' to self-harm or commit suicide."[4] He had called the Samaritans charity, which provides assistance to people with suicidal thoughts, "virtually every night and on two or three occasions, when they had not been available had made superficial cuts to his thigh and abdomen to distract him from his sense of isolation."[5]

The psychiatric assessments revealed that Julian Assange was affected by Asperger's syndrome, common in individuals gifted in mathematics, physics, computer science, and often correlated with

1.   Stefania Maurizi, "Assange, no a estradizione negli USA: 'rischia la vita'," *il Fatto Quotidiano*, January 5, 2021.
2.   The judgment issued by Judge Baraitser on January 4, 2021 is available at: www. judiciary.uk/wp-content/uploads/2021/01/USA-v-Assange-judgment-040121.pdf (accessed May 15, 2022).
3.   Ibid.
4.   Ibid.
5.   Ibid.

a high IQ. That Assange was affected by this condition had been floated as far back as 2010, but now there was a specialized, public diagnosis which also explained some puzzling behaviors noticed by many of us in our interactions with him over the years, but which as non-physicians we had struggled to decipher.

Judge Baraitser deemed it conceivable that, if extradited "there is a real risk that Mr. Assange will be designated to the ADX, Florence," the harshest prison in the United States, where drug lord El Chapo is imprisoned, and under a detention regime of ruthless isolation which goes by the name of Special Administrative Measures (SAMs). It is the very same isolation regime imposed on the alleged source of the Vault 7 CIA files, Joshua Schulte, who through his legal counsel has reported being "treated like an animal."

Judge Baraitser also took note that such a regime: "would severely restrict his contact with all other human beings, including other prisoners, staff and his family. In detention subject to SAMs, he would have absolutely no communication with other prisoners, even through the walls of his cell, and time out of his cell would be spent alone."[6]

Invoking the precedent of activist Lauri Love, whose extradition to the United States had been denied based on a diagnosis of Asperger's syndrome and risk of suicide after a complex legal battle,[7] Baraitser determined that: "Mr. Assange will not only find a way to suicide but it will be executed 'with the single-minded determination of his ASD/Asperger's'"[8] and that "He has already made suicidal plans which Professor Kopelman considered to be 'highly plausible' and taken steps to plan for his death including by preparing a Will and requesting absolution from the Catholic priest who attends the prison."[9]

---

6. Ibid.
7. Lauri Love won his case thanks in part to a campaign led by human rights activist Naomi Colvin.
8. Quote from the judgment issued by Judge Baraitser on January 4, 2021: www.judiciary.uk/wp-content/uploads/2021/01/USA-v-Assange-judgment-040121.pdf (accessed May 15, 2022).
9. Ibid.

Baraitser's judgment not to extradite Assange immediately appeared as both a victory and a defeat. "The decision to refuse Julian's extradition is welcome. It is important that the judge acknowledged his extradition would be oppressive," barrister Jennifer Robinson[10] observed to me. "However she did so on the basis of the risk of suicide, rather than on freedom of speech grounds: it is a win for Julian Assange, but it is not a win for journalism."

From Amnesty International to Reporters Sans Frontières, all human rights and press freedom organizations remarked on the threat that this ruling represented for journalism.

"We welcome this judgment as it acknowledges that Julian Assange would be at risk of ill-treatment if sent to the US and imprisoned there," Julia Hall of Amnesty International told me,[11] "But the politically motivated pursuit of Assange should never have happened in the first place. The US has put media freedom on trial and the UK was willingly complicit." And Rebecca Vincent of Reporters Sans Frontières stated:[12] "We do still believe the case was politically motivated, we do believe it is about journalism and press freedom and this judge actually dismissed all of that, so from a journalistic perspective, this judgement leaves the door open for similar cases. We would have liked to see a strong position from this court in favor of journalistic protection and press freedom, and that is not what happened in this decision."

Though professing to be "extremely disappointed in the court's ultimate decision," the U.S. Department of Justice, through spokesman Marc Raimondi, declared:[13] "we are gratified that the United States prevailed on every point of law raised. In particular, the court rejected all of Mr. Assange's arguments regarding political motivation, political offense, fair trial, and freedom of speech," and announced: "We will continue to seek Mr. Assange's extradi-

10.   Maurizi, "Assange, no a estradizione negli USA."
11.   Ibid.
12.   Ibid.
13.   Reuters Staff, "US will continue to seek Assange's extradition—US Justice Department," Reuters, January 4, 2021.

tion to the United States." After all, this was only the first instance judgment.

The U.S. authorities had every reason to be satisfied. To all appearances, the entire proceeding had unfolded in a humane, just and fair manner. Extradition had been denied on the grounds of protecting Julian Assange's life. But behind the façade of fair play, there was very little justice or humanity to be found. Both British and American justice were grotesque and cruel. The founder of a journalistic organization that had revealed war crimes and torture had been driven to severe mental illness by ten years of lawfare and arbitrary detention. And the great majority of the media, especially the British media, had helped the UK and U.S. governments keep up the façade.

KILLING JULIAN

Just eight months after Judge Baraitser's ruling, the Yahoo News website revealed that the CIA had planned to kidnap or even kill Julian Assange as well as other journalists working with the organization.

The investigation[14] was signed by three American journalists: Zach Dorfman, Sean D. Naylor and Michael Isikoff, who had collected information and confidential revelations from a good thirty former U.S. officials. What had really unleashed the CIA's fury had been the publication of the secret documents on its cyberweapons: Vault 7. "After Vault 7, Pompeo and [Deputy CIA Director Gina] Haspel wanted vengeance on Assange," wrote Yahoo News, reporting that WikiLeaks had by then become an obsession for Pompeo.

The agency had also tried to designate the organization as an agent of the Kremlin, but did not have the evidence for it. "The difficulty in proving that WikiLeaks was operating at the direct behest of the Kremlin was a major factor behind the CIA's move

---

14.   Zach Dorfman, Sean D. Naylor and Michael Isikoff, "Kidnapping, assassination and a London shoot-out: inside the CIA's secret war plans against WikiLeaks," *Yahoo News*, September 21, 2021.

to designate the group as a hostile intelligence service, according to a former senior counterintelligence official," wrote Yahoo, adding "There was a lot of legal debate on: Are they operating as a Russian agent?" said the former official. "It wasn't clear they were, so the question was, can it be reframed on them being a hostile entity."

Designating WikiLeaks as a "hostile intelligence service" rather than a journalistic organization could pave the way to all sorts of dirty war techniques against Julian Assange and WikiLeaks. Within months, "U.S. spies were monitoring the communications and movements of numerous WikiLeaks personnel, including audio and visual surveillance of Assange himself, according to former officials."[15]

But it was not just a matter of spying on Assange and the WikiLeaks journalists; "the agency executives requested and received 'sketches' of plans for killing Assange and other Europe-based WikiLeaks members who had access to Vault 7 materials."[16]

There is no indication that the more drastic measures were ever approved, according to Yahoo, but "the agency's WikiLeaks proposals so worried some administration officials that they quietly reached out to staffers and members of Congress on the House and Senate intelligence committees to alert them to what Pompeo was suggesting."[17] Moreover, there were those in the Trump administration who feared that such illegal rendition schemes could undermine U.S. authorities' attempts to criminally prosecute Assange and WikiLeaks for their publications. Some advised hastening the indictment of Assange. Indeed, he was charged on December 21, 2017, just nine months after WikiLeaks and we media partners started publishing Vault 7, and the indictment was filed under seal.

The Yahoo News investigation also confirmed some of the testimony from the two protected witnesses who had worked for UC Global, according to whom their boss, David Morales, had dis-

---

15. Ibid.
16. Ibid.
17. Ibid.

cussed plans to poison or kidnap Julian Assange. When it was published, U.S. lawyer Barry Pollack representing the WikiLeaks founder in the United States declared that he found it absolutely outrageous that his government had planned to kidnap or kill somebody simply for publishing true information in the public interest. "My hope and expectation is that the U.K. courts will consider this information and it will further bolster its decision not to extradite to the U.S.," Pollack told Yahoo.

After the ruling by Vanessa Baraitser denying extradition, Julian Assange still remained in prison in Belmarsh. The United States had filed an appeal to the United Kingdom High Court of Justice. The Biden administration, which had taken over from Trump, could have very easily dropped the charges, considering that they were a legacy of the Trump era. A coalition of civil liberties and human rights groups urged Biden to do so.[18] It included some of the most prominent human and civil rights organizations, from Amnesty International to Human Rights Watch to the American Civil Liberties Union. The Biden administration instead went ahead with the extradition request, offering diplomatic assurances to the British authorities that if they would allow Julian Assange's extradition to the United States, the United States would not imprison him in the most punitive American prison, ADX Florence, and would not subject him to the harsh regime known as "Special Administrative Measures" (SAMs). But there was a caveat. Once transferred to the United States, if the WikiLeaks founder should do anything that the U.S. authorities felt called for such measures, they would impose them.

Amnesty International promptly dismissed the diplomatic assurances as inherently unreliable and asked the United States to drop the charges against Julian Assange. Its highly respected Secretary General, Agnès Callamard declared:[19] "Assurances by the US gov-

18. Charlie Savage, "Civil-liberties groups ask Biden Justice Dept. to drop Julian Assange case," *New York Times*, February 8, 2021.
19. Amnesty International, "US/UK: Julian Assange's 'politically motivated' extradition must not go ahead," October 26, 2021; Stefania Maurizi, "Julia Hall, Amnesty International expert on national security: 'Assange should be released'," *il Fatto Quotidiano*, July 24, 2021.

ernment that they would not put Julian Assange in a maximum security prison or subject him to abusive Special Administrative Measures were discredited by their admission that they reserved the right to reverse those guarantees. Now, reports that the CIA considered kidnapping or killing Assange have cast even more doubt on the reliability of US promises and further expose the political motivation behind this case."

But the United States did not do as Amnesty International requested.

In December 2021, the United Kingdom High Court of Justice ruled[20] that Julian Assange could be extradited to the United States, because the assurances provided by the U.S. authorities were sufficient to mitigate the suicide risk concerns that had prompted Baraitser to reject the extradition. Judges Lord Burnett of Maldon and Lord Justice Holroyde ruled that the diplomatic assurances are a solemn undertaking offered by one government to another and that "there is no basis for assuming that the USA has not given the assurances in good faith."[21]

Once again, behind the façade of justice and humanity, Britain showed it had few qualms about extraditing a journalist to a country which, according to protected witnesses and reputable media, had entertained plans of killing him.

PIERCING THE WALL OF DARKNESS

In the same months when the CIA was labeling WikiLeaks a hostile entity rather than a journalistic organization, and making plans to kill or kidnap Assange and other WikiLeaks journalists, the British First-tier Tribunal in London rejected my request to access all the documentation on the Julian Assange case and established that there was "nothing untoward"[22] in the destruc-

---

20. The judgment dated December 10, 2021 is available at: www.judiciary.uk/wp-content/uploads/2021/12/USA-v-Assange-judgment101221.pdf (accessed May 15, 2022).
21. Ibid.
22. The First-tier Tribunal's judgment is available on the website of my former newspaper *la Repubblica*: https://download.repubblica.it/pdf/2017/esteri/decisione-

tion of key emails by the Crown Prosecution Service. But at the same time, the Tribunal recognized WikiLeaks as a "media organization," precisely the status the CIA wanted to deny Assange's organization. "WikiLeaks is a media organization which publishes and comments upon censored or restricted official materials involving war, surveillance or corruption, which are leaked to it in a variety of different circumstances," the Tribunal ruled.[23]

The First-tier Tribunal's decision, which dismissed my appeal to access the full documentation on Julian Assange, was only the first in a long string of defeats. My trench warfare was just beginning.

Ever since November 2017, when I first unearthed the fact that key documents had been destroyed by the Crown Prosecution Service, I have been litigating my FOIA case before the Information Commissioner, the London First-tier Tribunal and the Upper Tribunal to shed light on this highly suspicious discovery. As I write, five years have gone by and the British authorities have never provided any sensible explanation for it. They did say that the documents were destroyed in accordance with record management policies. But the Crown Prosecution Service's *Records Management Manual* states that the general correspondence relating to a criminal case file should be retained for "5 years from the date of most recent correspondence." Yet they deleted it anyway. Why is that? What exactly did they destroy, and on exactly whose instructions? When I asked the Information Commissioner to examine the Crown Prosecution Service's Manual for herself to determine if the destruction of documents was in accordance with the CPS's data retention policies set out in the manual, the Information Commissioner relied on the Crown Prosecution Service's assurances. How can a commissioner in charge of investigating a case rely on the assurances provided by the very authority she is supposed to investigate?

In the United States, Australia and Sweden, I have come up against the same pushback. Sweden, considered an excellent juris-

maurizi.pdf (accessed May 15, 2022); Ewen MacAskill, "WikiLeaks recognised as a 'media organisation' by UK tribunal," *Guardian*, December 14, 2017.
23. Ibid.

diction when it comes to government transparency, has proved no better than the United Kingdom. According to the Crown Prosecution Service, from 2010 to 2015 they exchanged between 7,200 and 9,600 pages of correspondence with the Swedish Prosecution Authority.[24] But the Swedish Prosecution Authority denies that there was ever that much documentation. How is it possible that the British had that many pages and the Swedes did not, considering that it was the correspondence between them?

The Swedish Prosecution Authority has never really clarified what they meant when they wrote: "Marianne [Ny] and I file all A-related emails in special folders, not available to or traceable for anybody but ourselves."[25]

Neither is it clear why prosecutor Ny destroyed an email she had received from the FBI at the end of March 2017. Those were the months in which the CIA was so furious at WikiLeaks for publishing Vault 7 that they would later devise plans to kill Assange. The Swedish authorities later confirmed[26] to me that the email message came "from an executive of the FBI" and that it "reached a chief prosecutor first at the end of March 2017. The message concerned a request for information. The message was answered by referring to information available at the website of the Prosecution Authority, whereupon the message was destroyed." What did the email contain?

When, together with my excellent Swedish lawyer, Percy Bratt, I appealed to the Parliamentary Ombudsmen for an investigation into these anomalies relative to the documents on the Assange case, the Parliamentary Ombudsmen refused to open an investi-

---

24. I obtained this estimate thanks to my FOIA litigation against the Crown Prosecution Service. Witness statement of Alexander Mark Smeath, July 14, 2017, Stefania Maurizi v. The Information Commissioner and the Crown Prosecution Service, case EA/2017/0041.

25. Email from an associate of Swedish Prosecutor Marianne Ny (whose name has been redacted) to Marianne Ny and to other recipients who have been redacted, dated July 12, 2012, 21:26. I obtained this email from my FOIA litigation against the Crown Prosecution Service.

26. I obtained this information on the FBI email thanks to my FOIA litigation in Sweden. Verdict by the Administrative Court of Appeal Stockholm, dated November 15, 2017, Case # 4430-17.

gation and offered no reason for this refusal. "We presented such heavy evidence that it is very remarkable," my Swedish lawyer told me, commenting on their refusal.

I have run up against this brick wall not only with my FOIA on Julian Assange but also my FOIA on Kristinn Hrafnsson, Sarah Harrison and Joseph Farrell, the three WikiLeaks journalists[27] whose Google emails were secretly handed over to U.S. authorities.

This time, the pushback came not from the Crown Prosecution Service but the Metropolitan Police, also known as Scotland Yard. I have been trying to obtain the correspondence between Scotland Yard and the U.S. Department of Justice on Hrafnsson, Harrison and Farrell since 2017. But Scotland Yard has refused to release any documents to me.

The Metropolitan Police argued that disclosing them would engage national security and prejudice their ability to fight terrorism. Two decades after 9/11, anti-terrorism laws are being applied to journalists as if we are al Qaeda operatives. Even the UK National Union of Journalists, alarmed at such an argument, filed a submission in support of my FOIA, declaring: "The Union is fundamentally opposed to the use of terror legislation as a means to clamp down on journalists working in the public interest. Journalism is not a crime; journalists report on national security, the law should not be used to curtail their reporting in the public interest."[28]

After a fabulously lengthy and expensive legal process, I did ultimately receive confirmation that the correspondence between Scotland Yard and the U.S. Department of Justice on the three WikiLeaks journalists does indeed exist, and is held by the Metropolitan Police's Counter Terrorism Command (CTC). The focus of the CTC is countering terrorism, but it also works to "combat threats posed to national security and to protect democracy, for example, from espionage, subversion, political extremism."

---

27. Sarah Harrison is no longer working with WikiLeaks.
28. Sarah Kavanagh, National Union of Journalists (NUJ) senior campaigns and communications officer, written submission dated July 20, 2020, of the NUJ to the First-tier Tribunal, Stefania Maurizi and Information Commissioner and Commissioner of Police of the Metropolis, case EA/2020/0087.

Thus through relentless FOIA litigation I was able to obtain confirmation that UK secret services were involved in the investigation of Kristinn Hrafnsson, Sarah Harrison and Joseph Farrell. After noting that "It is not in dispute that these three individuals are journalists,"[29] the London First-tier Tribunal confirmed that the only reason this correspondence is being denied to me is because it was supplied by, or "touches on," a security body, presumably the UK Security Service—also known as MI5. Based on the Metropolitan Police's evidence recorded in the judgment, it appears that the Counter Terrorism Command may have been acting as a go-between for the U.S. Department of Justice and MI5 relative to the personal information on the three journalists subject to investigation in the U.S.

Treated like terrorists, investigated as a threat to national security, singled out for drastic surveillance and targeted by the CIA for killing or kidnapping—Julian Assange and the WikiLeaks journalists have been subjected to over a decade of persecution and intimidation. Will it ever end?

---

29. Decision 049 040222, Promulgated February 4, 2022, First-tier Tribunal General Regulatory Chamber (Information Rights) Stefania Maurizi and the Information Commissioner and the Commissioner of the Police for the Metropolis, Decision Appeal number EA/2020/0087/v. The ruling is available on the website of the British and Irish Legal Information Institute: www.bailii.org/uk/cases/UKFTT/GRC/2022/2020_0087.html (accessed May 16, 2022).

21
Secret Power

He was supposed to serve a fifty-week sentence for violating his bail conditions, and be freed after twenty-five. Instead, as I write, after more than three years Julian Assange is still in Belmarsh high-security prison. The British government has already approved his extradition, which WikiLeaks is determined to fight all the way up to the European Court of Human Rights, his last chance to oppose it. Julian Assange's fate hangs in the balance.

He is now in the hands of the Biden administration, after Trump closed his presidency with two landmark decisions: he pardoned four contractors from the Blackwater military company, responsible for the Nisour Square massacre in Baghdad, and denied clemency to Julian Assange and Edward Snowden. The war criminals are free as the wind, and the journalists and whistleblowers who exposed their atrocities are in prison, on the brink of suicide or in exile. Many might say it was just the upside-down world of the Trump administration but unfortunately things were far from perfect under the Obama administration as well. None of the criminals and torturers exposed by the WikiLeaks files were ever punished. None of them have had to live under constant threat of legal action. Julian Assange on the other hand, along with his journalist colleagues, has been under permanent investigation by the Grand Jury since 2010. He went from house arrest to confinement in the embassy to Belmarsh prison.

As for the source of those revelations, Chelsea Manning, she was handed an unprecedented criminal conviction, after which she tried to kill herself twice during the Obama presidency, and once during Trump's.

Julian Assange is not the only person at risk. Other journalists with WikiLeaks may be at risk as well.

The goal of the United States military-intelligence complex and its allies is to destroy WikiLeaks, to take out a journalistic organization which has created, for the first time in history, a deep and enduring crack in that secret power which has never been accountable to anyone, and which uses state secrecy not to safeguard the security of citizens, but to ensure their own impunity and to hide crimes, incompetence and corruption.

No other journalistic organization has systematically published hundreds of thousands of classified documents, and done so for over a decade, with an impact felt throughout the world. No one else tried to help Edward Snowden.

WikiLeaks has shown that the battle against secret power can be won. So long as WikiLeaks exists and is operational, that power will perceive it as a critical threat.

Nor can authoritarian countries hostile to the United States and its allies sympathize with what WikiLeaks does. Naturally they rejoice and applaud when the organization reveals their adversaries' secrets, or embarrasses them in front of the entire world, but they also fear becoming a target themselves, and that their own dissidents could be inspired by that model. So it is not just the U.S. military-intelligence complex that hates WikiLeaks: it has many enemies.

Secret power acts with impunity in democracies just as it does in dictatorships. In authoritarian countries it uses an iron fist, and commits many of its crimes and abuses in broad daylight, in part to intimidate and bring the population to heel. In democracies, by contrast, the iron fist of secret power is often concealed inside a thick velvet glove.

A dictatorship would have sent goons and hit men to get rid of Julian Assange and the WikiLeaks journalists after the very first publications. The United States military-intelligence complex and their allies, on the other hand, have used, and will continue to use, less outwardly brutal methods. Under Mike Pompeo, the CIA did plan to kill or kidnap Assange and others, but ultimately decided against it. The U.S. authorities opted for a judicial path rather than an extra-judicial one. No doubt this is preferable. But the point is that there is no need to be physically brutal when you can bring down a journalist through psychological rather than physical torture. It is not necessary to burn Julian Assange's arms with cigarettes when you can bring him to the brink of suicide through ten years of arbitrary detention with no possible way out. It is not necessary to send goons to block the publications of a media organization when lawfare and keeping its journalists and publishers in a climate of relentless intimidation is equally effective.

The velvet glove makes the treatment of Assange seem much less vicious than the treatment that would be reserved for him by an authoritarian country, but the point is that in essence it is just as abominable. For publishing documents on war crimes, torture, extra-judicial drone killings and abuse of Guantanamo detainees, the founder of WikiLeaks has been charged with crimes that carry a 175-year sentence. The state criminals have not spent a single day in jail.

The U.S. Department of Justice under Donald Trump tried to portray Assange as a hacker and a cyber-criminal, in an effort to get around the constitutional protection of the First Amendment. The Biden administration may or may not continue along this same path; as of this writing, it is hard to make any predictions. But nothing can erase the fact that ever since 2010, when WikiLeaks revealed those files, Assange has never again known freedom, and his physical and mental health have been devastated.

Right from the start, all public discussion has focused on his personality. I have not shared every little thing he has said or done in the last ten years, but I have come to know him well enough to say that he is a profoundly different person to how he is portrayed. I am not the only one to say this. Other journalists who have come to know him over the last ten years, who can judge him on the basis of their own long-term observations, are of the same opinion.

Julian Assange is a complex human being, and the medical diagnosis concluding that he suffers from Asperger's syndrome probably helps explain some of his personality traits. Australian writer Kathy Lette, former wife of highly respected human rights lawyer Geoffrey Robertson, who represented Assange, offered a perceptive analysis.

Noting that autism spectrum disorders are common among mathematicians, scientists and artists, from Mozart to Einstein to Steve Jobs, she wrote that as far back as 2010 she realized that the founder of WikiLeaks was affected by an autism spectrum disorder. She and her former husband have a son who suffers from such a disorder, so they have developed "an astute radar for the symptoms."[1] "Autism," wrote Lette "is a lifelong neurological condition whose chief characteristics are poor communication and socialising skills, often chronic obsessive-compulsive disorder and anxiety, but also, often, a very high IQ. Assange is basically Wikipedia with a pulse—like many computer geniuses. Passionate and philosophical, Julian proved a diverting dinner guest."[2]

Lette also observed that the diagnosis of an autism spectrum disorder/Asperger's syndrome "could help explain why people so often misread Julian's single-minded absorption as 'narcissism' and why he has alienated allies so easily in the past."

The Julian Assange depicted by the media is definitely not the person I and other colleagues have come to know in over ten years of interaction. He is not the sinister, James Bond-villain type of character they describe. He is funny, affectionate and self-deprecating. He is extremely intelligent, and chose to put his intelligence to use for purposes other than founding a software firm and building up a fortune. It took his indisputable talent and bravery to unleash the WikiLeaks revolution. Of course, he did not do it all alone; the WikiLeaks journalists, staffers, lawyers, technical experts made enormous contributions.

In striving never to appear weak, he may come across as arrogant or overly self-confident. Even in his management of WikiLeaks, lest he show any chinks or vulnerability to the many who have longed for its destruction for over a decade, he has always avoided talking about its inner workings. This has projected an aura of

1. Kathy Lette, "I knew Assange was autistic—it explains why people read him unfairly," *Sydney Morning Herald*, October 15, 2020.
2. Ibid.

mystery and menace that has brought many to look upon the organization with suspicion and to consider it a shady, if not sinister phenomenon.

That he is perceived as a controversial figure has always constituted a terrific opportunity for the U.S. military-intelligence complex and, more generally, for secret power. The more the press and media portrays an individual as controversial, the more he divides the public, and the less support he receives from public opinion. And since public support is one of the very few shields from persecution by secret power, secret power has always had an easy time of it with Assange.

What I have seen in the course of my journalistic work with Julian Assange and WikiLeaks has deeply disturbed me.

I have been stunned by the state criminality documented in the files. By the impunity that war criminals and torturers enjoy in our democracies. I have been shocked that whistleblowers and journalists who reveal this criminality do not have a place to hide in our democratic societies. From 2010 on, Assange sought every possible refuge. He shut himself up in an embassy and sought protection in asylum and through international law. He knocked at the door of the United Nations Working Group. He knocked at the door of the UN Special Rapporteur on Torture. Nothing and no one was able to prevent the ruin of his physical and mental health. Nor has the Fourth Estate given him a hand; on the contrary, it bears enormous responsibility for the devastation of his freedom and health.

It is true that some journalists, like the renowned John Pilger, have always spoken out against his treatment. The legendary Daniel Ellsberg and Roger Waters, the iconic Vivienne Westwood, famous actress and activist Pamela Anderson, the celebrated writer Alice Walker, and artists from Ai Weiwei to Davide Dormino have been highly vocal in their support of Assange. It also true that the great film director Ken Loach has always fought by his side, as have others, from Nobel Peace Prize winners Adolfo Pérez Esquivel and Mairead Maguire to Noam Chomsky, from Yanis Varoufakis and Srecko Horvat to all the little-known parliamentarians who have repeatedly nominated Julian Assange for the Nobel Peace Prize. As I write, every major press freedom and human rights organization has come out in his support, and the growing empathy from the public is palpable. But it has taken so very long, and the price he has paid is so very high.

I have met many brilliant and skilled people in and around WikiLeaks. I saw Sarah Harrison, then a journalist with the organization, risk everything to help Edward Snowden. I saw other professionals toiling under the never-ending threat of the Grand Jury's permanent investigation.

And from the purely personal point of view, I have seen Stella Moris marry Julian Assange in Belmarsh prison and struggle to raise their two children under extremely difficult conditions, as he risks disappearing for good inside a maximum-security prison while the war criminals and torturers exposed by WikiLeaks continue to sleep comfortably in their own beds.

The aim of the U.S. military-intelligence complex, and of secret power in general, is clear. After the heavy blows it has been dealt by Julian Assange and his organization over more than a decade, that power wants to destroy them, to take revenge on them but also to intimidate any other journalist, whistleblower or source that might be tempted to reveal the next *Collateral Murder* or the next quarter of a million cables. It is a sinister attack on the press's power to reveal state criminality at the highest levels, and on the public's right to know about it.

That is why I have devoted more than ten years of work to this case. Years in which, unlike Julian Assange and the WikiLeaks journalists, I have not been arrested, imprisoned or intimidated. I feel an ethical duty to use my position and relative safety to report what I have seen.

I have invested so much because I want to use my journalistic work to help unmask how the iron fist in the velvet glove operates, so that the public can be aware of it and learn to recognize it.

I want to live in a society where it is possible to reveal war crimes and torture without ending up in prison and on the brink of suicide three times, as happened to Chelsea Manning. Without being forced to live in exile, like Edward Snowden. Without losing my freedom for over ten years and risking suicide, like Julian Assange. I want to live in a society where secret power is accountable to the law and the public for its atrocities. Where those who go to jail are the war criminals, not those who have the conscience and courage to expose them, and the journalists who reveal their crimes.

Today, such an authentically democratic society does not exist. And no one is going to create it for us. It is up to us to fight for it. For those who are with us, for those who are not and even for those who are against us.[3]

---

3.   This quote comes from the Italian partisan Arrigo Boldrini, who fought fascism. He said: "We fought for the freedom of all, for those who were with us, for those who were not there and even for those who were against it."

Acknowledgments

This book would not have been possible without the generosity and support of a great number of people.

I want to express my special gratitude to Ken Loach: I greatly admire his art and his values. To his assistant Emma, for her help and her kindness. To Richard Logan and the Reva and David Logan Foundation, for the investigative journalism grants that made my FOIA battle to defend the right of the press to access all the documents on the case of Julian Assange and the journalists with WikiLeaks possible.

Without Richard Logan and the Reva and David Logan Foundation, I could not have continued to seek the facts, after personally shouldering the initial costs of my FOIA battle. Thanks also go to Preeti Veerlapati with the Logan Foundation, for her assistance with the bureaucratic side.

A huge thanks to Pluto Press, which has believed in my book, especially to my editor, David Shulman, who has worked on it with great dedication and tremendous patience.

Special thanks to all the FOIA lawyers who have worked and in many cases are still working with me on my FOIA battle, and have done so for very low fees or completely free of charge. First among them an authority on the Freedom of Information Act in the United Kingdom, lawyer Philip Coppel at Cornerstone Barristers in London, who has been especially helpful. Thanks to Estelle Dehon, also at Cornerstone Barristers, an outstanding professional, and to Jennifer Robinson at Doughty Street Chambers in London, a superb and generous lawyer who made my FOIA possible. Thanks to the excellent Percy Bratt with Bratt Feinsilber Harling AB of Stockholm and Pia Janné with the Janné AB law firm in the Swedish capital. To the excellent Kristel Tupja (ex Ballard Spahr) and Lauren Russell and Alia Smith at the Ballard Spahr law firm of Philadelphia, Peter Bolam at the Broadley Rees

Hogan law firm of Brisbane, Australia, and Greg Barns at Salamanca Chambers of Battery Point, Tasmania.

I don't know how to thank Lesli Cavanaugh, the translator of this book, who over the years has helped me with translation work at all hours of the day and night. Every journalist grappling with complex investigative work spanning three continents should be able to consult with a professional like her.

Thanks to Piero DM, Alberto Ferretti, Lorenzo Pazzi, Daniele Trovato, Giuseppe Sini and Salvatore with Guerriglia Radio.

I wish to especially thank Maurizio Donati and Valentina Abaterusso at Chiarelettere: without Maurizio's interest, pressure and infinite patience, I would never have written this book. And without Valentina's help, it would definitely have been worse.

I cannot fail to mention Roberto: a whole book would not be enough to express my gratitude to him. And to Livia Polegri for her always intelligent and helpful advice.

Warm thanks to Australian journalists Mary Kostakidis and Andrew Fowler, to John Rees of the Don't Extradite Assange campaign, and to the legal observer of the Julian Assange extradition case, Deepa Driver. Huge and warm thanks also to the activists who have supported me for years with their presence in the Tribunal in London for my FOIA hearings. I would be alone without them, but the British authorities have realized that I am definitely not alone. They have always been there: the untiring Emmy Butlin, Clara Campos, David Allen, Alberto Zerda-Noriega, Guillermo Marin, Olga, Karen, Sue and Roland, Wendy Higazi, Kathy De Silva, Arcadius, Tom, Elsa Collins, Olga, Patrick, Joe Brack, Maxine Walker, Sara Chessa, Cheryl Sanchez, Katherine Porter, David Mizrachi.

I want to close this book expressing my immense gratitude to the thousands of readers who have supported my work with their interest and who fight every day for a free, inconvenient, pesky journalism and press. Unfortunately, for obvious reasons of space, I cannot name all of them. On behalf of them all I will mention the 151 who helped reach the crowdfunding initiative goal to help support my FOIA battle within just 43 hours.

The search for the truth is a collective endeavor.

Many of them donated on a completely anonymous basis, so I don't even know who to thank, while others used fictitious names like "Pinco Pallino" or "Truth Seeker." All the others provided their names, so I can at least mention them here. Naomi Pitcairn, Rajesh Panday, Hansrudolf Suter, Carlo Blengino, Richard Lahuis, Roberto Resoli, Adrian Pearl, Cinzia Mariolini, Irene M. Moreau, Stefano Caire, Dag Undseth, Rossella Selmini, Claudio Erbs, Francesca Milani, Nadir Dziri, Rory O'Bryan, Marco Gessini, Giovanni Gardoni, Giorgio Papallo, Frank Proud, Jeanie Schmidt, Dario Di Maria, Paola Morellato, Per Starbäck, Linda Jones, Paolo Cianciabella, Gabriele Zamparini, Amar Hadzihasanovic, Riccardo Signori, Dr A, Meg Vidal, Marin Medak, Alan Dow, Edward Jones, Petar Milosevic, Gian Carlo Di Leo, Claudio Coletta, Michele Arnaldi, Klaas Verhoeve, Raffaele Golfetto, Guido Cusani, David Walters, Giorgio Spiga, Brenda Bonnici, Luigi Prosperi, John Lynn, Ingo Keck, Ermanno Viola, Paolo Progetto, Gilberto Gennero, Richard Gilmour, B.E. Henriksen, Giorgio Carsetti, Giuseppe Ragno, Barbara Waschmann, Emilia La Capra, Marco Giansante, Luca Bolelli, Peter Lalvani, Georg Braun, Roberto Montanari, Leandro Notari, Andy McDowell, Alex Kross, Andrea Bovenga, Piergiovanni Cipolloni, Jose Martins, Phil Hurrle, Antonio Puliti, Alina Lilova, Ana Dimkar, Michael Wheeler, Stefania Saccinto, Daria Malaguti, Stefano Rigamonti, Davide Vismara, Alan Booker, Predrag Kolakovic, Rita Hunt, Paul Janssen, Marty Bray, Emilia Butlin, Paul Gossage, Mina Harballou, Anna Fauzy-Ackroyd, Daniela Hengst, Lydia Maniatis, Veronica Sahonero, Sergio Mauro, Monika Schallert-Marberger, Pete Butler, Denise Majocchi, Elena Andres, Giò Lodovico Baglioni, Sabrina Culanti, Timothy Smith, Dausto Cobianchi, Deborah Thomas, Adriana Cecchetto, Aaron Maté, John Joslin, Rob Juneau, George Loizou, Goran Vuckovic, Neville Reed, Grant Jarvis, Tom Marwick, Joyce Catanzariti, Louisa Allan, Meredith Hobbs, Rowan Collins, Eli Fadda, Djamila le Pair, Catherine McLean, Stefano Crosara, Alenka Sekne, Ivan Iraci, Brigitte Walz, Annie McStravick, Rosswell Gadsden, Anna Palczynska, Rob Marshall,

Gregor Liddell, Jutta Schwengsbier, Karina Prado, Christian Mair, Livia Formisani, Luca Trogni, Raymond Hill, Stefano Grandesso Silvestri, Matteo Locatelli, Laura Mussati, Anthony Coghlan, Kell Kolisnik, Roswell Gadsen, Kendra Christian, Anna-Lydia Menzel, Anna Tarbet, John Read, Esther Joly, Alison Cotterill, Terry Lustig, Elizabeth Murray, Joanne Morrison, John Edwards, Mike Barson, Janice Lumley.

Index

Thanks to our Patreon subscribers:

Andrew Perry
Ciaran Kane

Who have shown generosity and comradeship in support of our publishing.

Check out the other perks you get by subscribing to our Patreon – visit patreon.com/plutopress.

Subscriptions start from £3 a month.

The Pluto Press Newsletter

Hello friend of Pluto!

Want to stay on top of the best radical books
we publish?

Then sign up to be the first to hear about our
new books, as well as special events,
podcasts and videos.

You'll also get 50% off your first order with us
when you sign up.

Come and join us!

Go to bit.ly/PlutoNewsletter